THEOLOGY AND MODERN IRISH ART

Meinen Eltern Annemarie und Johann Hinrich Thiessen

Gesa Elsbeth Thiessen

Theology and Modern Irish Art

the columba press

First published in 1999 by
the columba press
55A Spruce Avenue, Stillorgan Industrial Park, Blackrock, Co Dublin

Cover by Bill Bolger
Cover pictures are *Christ Androgyne* by Colin Middleton (copyright the estate of Colin
Middleton and photograph reproduced with the kind permission of the Trustees of the
National Museums & Galleries of Northern Ireland), and *Goldpainting 56* by Patrick Scott
(reproduced with the kind permission of the artist).
Origination by The Columba Press
Printed in Ireland by Colour Books Ltd, Dublin

ISBN 1 85607 267 3

Acknowledgements
The publisher and author gratefully ackowledges the following permissions to
use copyright material: Michael Purser for four pictures by Mainie Jellett; Anne
Yeats for three pictures by Jack B. Yeats; Louis and Pierre le Brocquy for three
pictures by Louis le Brocquy; Gerard Dillon, nephew of the artist, for three pict-
ures by Gerard Dillon; the Estate of Colin Middleton for three pictures by Colin
Middleton; Patricia Collins for three pictures by Patrick Collins; Tony O'Malley,
Patrick Scott, Patrick Graham and Patrick Hall for three pictures each.

The photographs on pp 174 and 175 are reproduced with the kind permission of the Trustees of the National Museums & Galleries of Northern
Ireland. The photographs on pp 163, 166 and 177 are reproduced with the
kind permission of the Hugh Lane Municipal Gallery of Modern Art,
Dublin. The reproduction on pp 164 is by courtesy of the National Gallery
of Ireland.

Biblical quotations are in the New Revised Standard Version, copyright ©
1989, by the Division of Christian Education of the National Council of the
Churches of Christ in the United States of America. Used by permission.

Contents

Acknowledgements

The nature of writing and research means to work many hours on one's own. Yet, without the affection and company of family, friends and colleagues one would hardly survive the long journey toward the completion of a book.

Firstly, I thank my parents Annemarie and Johann Hinrich Thiessen, my sister Eva Maria and my brother Hans Holger for their encouragement, concrete help and support.

The book has been adapted with some modifications from my doctoral thesis completed in 1998. With profound gratitude I remember and am indebted to the late Dr John Macken SJ, theologian and former president of the Milltown Institute of Theology and Philosophy, Dublin, who first accepted my proposal and agreed to be my *Doktorvater*. I think of him with thanks for his gentleness, kindness and support. Further I am grateful to Dr Hilary Pyle (National Gallery of Ireland) for her interest in the subject from the start and for her always encouraging critique through my years of research. Dr Dermot Lane (President, Mater Dei Institute of Education) generously and kindly accompanied my thesis to its completion. For his many insightful observations, critical eye and helpful recommendations I express my sincere thanks. I consider myself privileged and lucky to have experienced the continuous support of my three readers.

I received enthusiastic interest and helpful comments throughout my voyage from Ruth Sheehy (Art History Department, Trinity College) who read the whole thesis as I wrote it. For her friendship, continuous encouragement and good spirits I am deeply grateful.

Further I owe a debt of gratitude to Dr Daniel Kletke for his recommendations, friendship and personal support. I am thankful, furthermore, to Dr Tom Dalzell SM who read the whole thesis with great diligence and care and provided a lot of valuable advice.

I am indebted to the former president of the Milltown Institute, Dr Paul Lennon O Carm, and to its present president, Dr Patrick Riordan SJ, for their kind generosity which made it possible for me to continue my study and research.

Moreover, my special thanks are due to the artists and those closely associated with them, who were willing to give of their time and hospitality for interviews and conversations. I treasure that stage of my research as a particularly exhilarating and enjoyable one; my thanks therefore to Patrick Graham, Patrick Hall, Louis le Brocquy, Jane and Tony O'Malley, Patrick Scott, Bruce Arnold, Patricia and Penelope Collins, Brian Fallon, Dr Samuel B. Kennedy, Michael Longley, Rosamund Phillips, James White and Anne Yeats.

I would like to acknowledge the friendly assistance and help of the following institutions and departments: the staff and library of the Milltown Institute, the History of Art Department and the library in Trinity College, the Arts Council of Northern Ireland, An Chomhairle Ealaíon, the National College of Art and Design, the National Library of Ireland, the library of Mater Dei Institute of Education, All Hallows College, Taylor Galleries, the Ulster Museum, private art collections and the *Institut für Kirchenbau und kirchliche Kunst der Gegenwart* at Marburg University.

I wish to thank those who, at one time or another, offered their professional help or who were supportive as fellow students, colleagues and friends through my years of research: special thanks to Dr John de Paor, Francis Dromey OMI and Tom McGrath SJ. Further my thanks go to Dr Una Agnew, the late Arthur Armstrong, Fergal Brennan SJ, Dr Peter Cherry, Dr James Corkery SJ, Dr Kieran Cronin OFM, Mary Cunningham, Caitriona Douglas, Dr Bernadette Flanagan PBVM, Pastor i.R. Paul Gerhard Fritz, Gisela Fritz, Maureen Gilheany, Aidan Higgins, Dominique Horgan OP, Patricia Howard, Phil Huston, Prof Dr Werner Jeanrond, Andrew Kadel, Michael Langston, Brigitte Martens, Prof Dr Emeritus Enda McDonagh, Dr Ciarán McGlynn, Breffni McGuinness, Andreas Mertin, Prof Dr Raymond Moloney SJ, Bríd O'Brien, Dr Fergus O'Donoghue SJ, Gearard O'Floinn, Desmond O'Grady SJ, Dr Gerard O'Hanlon SJ, Edel O'Kennedy, Dr Brian O'Leary SJ, Sarah O'Neill, Dr George Pattison, Roberta Reiners, Prof Dr Horst Schwebel, Martin Schwer, Dr David Smith MSC, Hilda van Stockum, Imogen Stuart, Pat Taylor, Rod Tuach, Sally Uí Chiardha and Brendan Woods SJ.

Dr Declan Marmion SM in Freundschaft mein Dank.

Introduction

Faith continues to seek understanding in a world flooded with and ruled by images. Ranging as they do from the wonderful and marvellous to the destructive, mediocre, exploitative or cheaply seductive, all of these images, like the written or spoken word, are expressions of the human spirit, of emotion and intellect. In recognition of the dominant role of images in contemporary society, this book is an exploration and critical appreciation of modern visual art as a source in and of theology.

In recent years the interdisciplinary dialogue of theology and twentieth century art has substantially grown. Theologians like Paul Tillich, John Dillenberger, Doug Adams, Diane Apostolos-Cappadona, George Pattison, Horst Schwebel, Friedhelm Mennekes and Günter Rombold have reflected on concrete visual works of art from a theological point of view. Others, like Rahner, Tracy, von Balthasar, or Gilkey have acknowledged the importance of the arts and the aesthetic for theological thinking from a more theoretical perspective. The basis for their theological interest in and reflection on the arts is their awareness of the intimate relationship between religion/theology and art due to the revelatory dimensions and the power of the imagination present in both.

Although the development of modern European literature is practically unthinkable without the writings of Irish poets and novelists, like Shaw, W. B. Yeats, Joyce and Beckett, outside the island of Ireland one has been largely unaware of (twentieth century) Irish visual artists, except for Yeats and le Brocquy, even if they have not been as widely acclaimed as their literary counterparts. Written in an Irish context, this book then is intended as a contribution to discourse on theology and art exemplified through the examination of the life and especially the work of ten modern Irish painters. It is the first extensive study of modern Irish art from a theological perspective.

The primary aim here is not to draw definitive conclusions on the theological aspects in Irish art as a whole. Naturally, the limited number of artists and works of art chosen would imply caution with regard to making general conclusions. Rather, the approach taken is an in-depth study of select works of art with regard to their spiritual-theological content and of the faith, spirituality and theological views of the painters.

9

Several criteria were applied in the selection of the painters: 1. Since this is the first extensive analysis of (modern) Irish art in a theological perspective, painters are chosen who have played a leading role in twentieth century Irish art. Moreover, all of them have been recognised internationally. 2. In their works, spiritual, religious and/or Christian dimensions are apparent, both explicitly or implicitly, which lend themselves and are of interest to theological discourse. 3. The painters are *not* 'church artists', i.e. those who have frequently received church commissions. The focus is precisely on art produced autonomously, i.e. the *artist's* own interest in and choice of subjects. 4. Most of the painters have given oral and/or written evidence of their spirituality, their interest in religion and their faith. 5. Their lives and the production of their works (between 1937 and 1995) span a large part of the twentieth century. 6. In order to strive for comprehensiveness, a variety of subject matter and styles is apparent in the works. 7. All painters have spent a considerable part of their working life in Ireland (except le Brocquy) and have taken an interest in Ireland and Irish culture, past and present. 8. Sufficient art historical literature and criticism on each artist had to be available in order to substantiate the discussion.

The selection includes one female and nine male artists. It should be made clear that gender considerations did not enter the choice; what mattered were simply the aforementioned criteria. The male painters were not selected for their maleness, nor Mainie Jellett for her femaleness or, worse, as a token woman. She is included because she ranks among the finest Irish painters of the century and since her ideas and her paintings are of theological interest. Indeed, as will be argued, some of these are significant from a feminist theological perspective. That Jellett and her friend Evie Hone were pivotal in the development of modern art in Ireland is a well-known fact.

The book is divided into four chapters. In order to provide the context and to lead into the field of theology and visual art, Chapter One introduces the wider discussion on this relationship. From a number of theologians, two are selected, who have played a major role in this regard: Paul Tillich's pioneering contribution and the work of Horst Schwebel (Marburg), whose theological thinking has centred on this field of study for over three decades. Not only is it of interest how theologians have engaged in the discussion so far, but their methods and findings are, of course, relevant to others involved in the field, such as this writer. My choice of Tillich and Schwebel from a number of 'image theologians' is based on the acknowledgement of Tillich's fundamental role in this sphere and on Schwebel's extensive examination of abstract art and of the image of Christ in modern art, which, as will be shown, is central to my own work.

Chapter Two deals with the artists' theological and spiritual concerns in their life, thought and painting. That this book is not limited to an examination of works of art, but also looks at the 'artist-as-theologian', i.e. what the painters themselves as well as others have said and written about the religious dimensions in their lives, is in itself of interest and relevant. Some significant parallel views and similar attitudes become apparent. It is, further, an important hermeneutical angle in trying to ascertain a comprehensive, 'round' picture: Do the ideas and concerns which are expressed orally or in writing actually reflect something of what is manifested on canvas and vice versa? Extensive interviews with those artists who are still alive, as also with relatives, critics and close friends, have been an important part in the research and writing of Chapters Two and Three. Moreover, the second chapter, as, in fact, the whole study, delves therefore into an area which art historical writing on modern art usually does not cover, at least not in detail. Twentieth century art criticism in general has paid little attention to the religious-spiritual dimensions in contemporary art and artists.

The third chapter contains the analyses of three paintings by each painter. The selection of the thirty paintings was determined by the fact that they should be representative of the artist's style and conducive to the theme of the study. Of course, the choice is ultimately a personal one in the sense that it was this writer who had to decide who and which works would and would not be included. However, I am grateful to Hilary Pyle and Ruth Sheehy for their helpful suggestions in this matter. The chapter finishes with a summary outline of the main theological currents that are evident in the works as a whole.

The final chapter raises relevant issues in the light of what has been established in the course of the book: the contemporary situation of pluralism in which the theologian and the artist find themselves, consideration of a hermeneutics for a theology through visual art, the vital importance of the imagination in theological and in artistic work, and the sensuous nature of art and its implications for a theology based on the image. It also discusses the theological aspects in the works in more detail and makes some observations as to how these compare with the theological dimensions in other European art. This concluding chapter thus hopes to make a contribution to the more theoretical and wider field of theology in and through art.

Our age is characterised essentially by fragmentation and pluralism in all spheres of life. As John Dillenberger rightly observes, there is therefore 'no discipline, theological or otherwise, accepted as the unifying discipline'.[1] Indeed, science and academia are made up by specialists or, as one might put it, by those who know more and more about less and less. However, in spite of this situation, humans increasingly long for more unifying, holistic ways

1. John Dillenberger, *A Theology of Artistic Sensibilities, The Visual Arts and the Church* (London: SCM 1986), 238.

of living and seeing reality. It is here that an interdisciplinary study, such as this one, seeks its place. And it is in this way that the interdisciplinary dimension searches for a vision, or at least glimpses, of the whole. An art theology stresses that the human being perceives and comprehends not only through using her/his intellect, but also through the senses and emotional response. It affirms that in order to glimpse the invisible, one needs to reach as deeply as possible into the visible *(Kabbala)*.

Martin Luther, in his typical colourful use of language, supposedly once said that God is present in a louse's belly, and – on a more academic note – that 'in all good arts and creatures one sees and finds imprinted an image of the Holy Trinity'.[2] Although such an imprint may not be obvious in twentieth century works of art at first glance, his statement is pertinent. What matters is the fact that the divine is felt to be present in all creation, and, more specifically, in *all good* works of art. A work well made, a great painting, a wonderful novel, a marvellous symphony, a gentle song, sensuous, sublime beauty, these are sources in which the divine is revealed.

Many of the works and banners displayed in our churches contain religious subject matter but often tend to be illustrative with little mediation of genuine spirituality. They do not capture the imagination because they themselves were created by people of perhaps sincere personal piety and intention, but who may have lacked spiritual, intellectual or artistic courage, imagination, skill or insight. Neither challenging, engaging, nor truly wonderful, these works may be seen one minute and forgotten the next. This sort of art indeed starkly contradicts the teachings of Jesus of Nazareth whose message of the kingdom was in essence challenging and wonderful. His life, death and resurrection have captivated the minds and spirits of people, including artists and theologians throughout the ages. It still does, but, as will be argued, the place to look for the spiritual and, more particularly, for the Christian message in twentieth century art is more often than not in the work of those who have never received any ecclesial commissions. That there are, however, some good and inspiring modern works of art in churches even today is, of course, not to be contested here.

Art created by poor vision will contain an equally poor theology. The artists examined in this book were and are leading painters who, at times, and some more than others, have produced outstanding works born of rich vision. It is the churches' loss if, for the most part, they neither have (had) the interest nor the courage or insight to welcome works by artists like these into their places of worship and church life.

2. Martin Luther, quoted in Gerhard Gollwitzer, *Die Kunst als Zeichen* (Munich: Chr. Kaiser, 1958), 46. 'In allen guten Künsten und Kreaturen findet und sieht man abgedruckt fein die Heilige Dreifaltigkeit.'

The terms 'theological dimension' or 'theological aspects' used in the book embrace the spiritual, religious and Christian dimensions in art. In general, the meaning and application of these terms are not clearly distinct. Usually the spiritual dimension would have connotations of grasping and coming into contact with truth, transcendence, ultimate reality, and with God, through personal experience. The human being may be taken into a realm which is unknown and which may lead to new discoveries. The religious aspect concerns the basic human search for and relationship with the Other, with the divine, and, in more specific terms, it implies the Christian religion. The Christian dimension is more particularly related to biblical stories, revelation in Christ, trinitarian faith, the church and tradition. However, a work may convey spiritual presence with or without any definite Christian content. In doing theology through art, theology and spirituality hence are not to be treated narrowly as separate disciplines. Rather an inclusive approach prevails.

The major question then which has guided this study is in what way and to what extent the modern visual work of art is a relevant *locus theologicus* and therefore can play a truly significant role in theology. Theologians, like Schwebel or Tillich, have, of course, in their own way attested to the revelatory and, more specifically, to the theological dimensions in contemporary art. By concentrating on a limited number of painters and works of art and by correlating both the artists' thought and, in particular, what is expressed in their works, with the ideas of theologians, some remarkable correspondences and mutual illumination will be disclosed. As other writers have affirmed with regard to other twentieth century art, our examination of ten Irish artists will demonstrate that modern images, often born of intense experience and sometimes without any specific Christian content, can be rich, surprising and challenging sources of and for theology. It therefore makes concretely apparent and affirms that spirit can be revealed through matter, i.e. through the material visual work of art. In this way it links in with the holistic vision advocated and stressed in contemporary theology of the essential and ultimate unity of matter and spirit, body and soul.

Finally, one must always remember that what the theologian or any interpreter does in all their writing will *fortunately never* fully reach the ground of the work itself. Painting, sculpture, films and plays must be seen, music heard, literature read as, indeed, there is no substitute. What we can hope for in interpreting is to reach some insight, to offer some reflections, to try and sincerely appreciate and explore what is presented to us. In the words of William Butler Yeats: 'Should not religion hide within the work of art as God is within ... [the] world, and how can the interpreter do more than whisper?'

List of Paintings

CHAPTER I

Theology and Art:
The Background

I. ULTIMATE REALITY IN ART – PAUL TILLICH[1]

If one wants to map the background, wider field and state of research on theology and modern visual art, Paul Tillich immediately springs to mind as one who played a decisive and leading part in the whole discussion. In his autobiography of 1967, Tillich, one of the foremost theologians of this century, described himself as a 'theologian of the boundaries'. One of these boundaries was his lifelong engagement with art in his lectures and writings, and it is he who set the agenda for the dialogue between art, especially modern art, and theology.

Today Tillich is perhaps best remembered for his theology of culture, a theology which emphasises that the religious dimension is present in all spiritual and intellectual life. Tillich maintained that 'religion is the soul (or substance) of culture' while 'culture is the form (or expression) of religion'.[2]

Born into a well-respected Lutheran pastor's family, Tillich soon began to question his bourgeois background and privileged upbringing. Consequently, and unusual for a theologian, he chose a bohemian life-style among artists, journalists and actors in Berlin after World War I. As he observed, 'the hallmarks of this group were an obvious lack of certain bourgeois conventions in thought and behaviour, an intellectual radicalism, and a remarkable capacity for ironical self-criticism ... they were anti-militaristic and influenced by Nietzsche, expressionism and psychoanalysis'.[3] Psychoanalysis, existentialism, expressionism and socialism were to influence Tillich in his own philosophical and theological journey, i.e. in his theology of culture and his theology of art.

1. This section on Tillich's theology of art is a revised and enlarged version of my article 'Religious Art is Expressionistic, A Critical Appreciation of Paul Tillich's Theology of Art', in *The Irish Theological Quarterly*, vol. 59, no. 4 (1993), 302-311. I gratefully acknowledge the critical reading and helpful comments given to me by the late John Macken S.J. in the first stage of writing the article.
2. Cf. James A. Martin Jr., *Beauty and Holiness, The Dialogue between Aesthetics and Religion* (Princeton, N.J.: Princeton University Press, 1990), 93.
3. Tillich, *On the Boundary* (London: Collins, 1967), 22-23.

The First World War was to be the decisive turning point in Tillich's life. As military chaplain he was to come face to face with immense human suffering. It was in this situation that he discovered visual art, an experience that was crucial for him as a reaction and counterbalance to the ugliness of destruction and horrors of war. The cheap reproductions in the magazines in the field bookstores would take his mind off the blood and death at the Western Front. At the end of the war he finally got the chance to see the original of one of these reproductions, 'Madonna with Singing Angels' (1477) by Sandro Botticelli in Berlin. It was to him a unique moment of ecstatic revelation, which, as he wrote, 'affected his whole life'.[4]

Tillich realised that his theology from then on should address relevant contemporary issues in an exploration of the possibilities of a new theonomy (*Gottesgesetzlichkeit*) as he termed it.[5] For Tillich theonomy meant essentially 'the state of culture under the impact of the Spiritual Presence'. Theonomy exists where life is guided by the Spirit, where creativity can flourish, where justice, truth and wholeness are sought. The church, the community of the New Being in Christ, in particular, is the place where theonomy is realised. However, Tillich was only too aware that the church is not only the community of the New Being but subject to human conflicts and thus always under threat of becoming heteronomous. With regard to art, Tillich concluded that it is expressionism, rather than naturalism or idealism, which is theonomous as it is most able of reaching into ultimate reality by breaking through 'both the realistic acceptance of the given and the idealistic anticipation of the fulfilled'.[6] I will return to Tillich's idea of expressionism in more detail below.

Concerning the relationship between religion and culture another central aspect in Tillich's theology is to be mentioned here, namely his method of correlation. Fundamentally Tillich held that systematic theology proceeds in

4. Tillich, 'One Moment of Beauty', in Tillich, *On Art and Architecture*, ed. John and Jane Dillenberger (New York: Crossroad, 1987), 234-235. 'Gazing up at it, I felt a state approaching ecstasy ... something of the divine source of all things came through to me. I turned away shaken. That moment has affected my whole life, given me the keys for the interpretation of human existence, brought vital joy and spiritual truth. I compare it with what is usually called revelation in the language of religion. I know that no artistic experience can match the moments in which prophets were grasped in the power of the Divine Presence, but I believe that there is an analogy between revelation and what I felt .... that moment of ecstasy has never been repeated.'
5. Cf. Tillich's concept of theonomy in Tillich, *Systematic Theology*, vol. 1 (Chicago: The University of Chicago Press, 1951), 83-86, 147-150, and *Systematic Theology*, vol. 3 (Chicago, 1963, here: London: SCM, 1978), 248-258.
6. Tillich, 'Art and Ultimate Reality' (lecture 1959, first publ. 1960), in Paul Tillich, *Main Works*, vol. 2, ed. Michael Palmer (Berlin, New York: De Gruyter, Evangelisches Verlagswerk, 1990), 328.

making an analysis of the human situation where existential questions arise, and then demonstrates that in the symbols of the Christian message the answers to these questions are provided. His method arose from his basic intention of relating and making relevant theological reflection to the more secular disciplines and spheres of culture, such as socialism or psychoanalysis. Tillich's theology is hence an apologetics in its attempt to make Christian faith attractive to the 'cultured among the despisers' of religion in the twentieth century.[7] He viewed the relationship between theology and art in similar correlative terms.

However, Tillich's method – or, better, his formulation of his method – has been rightly criticised by David Tracy who comments that Tillich does not, in fact, propose a method of correlation but one which 'juxtaposes questions from the 'situation' with answers from the 'message'.[8] Contemporary theology, which takes human experience and the Christian kerygma as its sources, naturally needs to look critically at both the questions and the answers given in each of these. A genuine method of correlation therefore implies, as Tracy points out, that it must be 'capable of correlating the principal questions and answers of each source'. In relationship to theology and art this means that images do not simply pose relevant questions for the theologian but rather that they also provide answers and thus challenge and further theological insight. Tracy concludes, that Tillich, *despite* his formulation, actually employed 'an interpretative correlation of the questions and answers of the message with the questions and answers of the situation'.[9]

Tillich insisted that assertions about God are always analogous or symbolic. According to him the only statement we can make about God which is not symbolic is that 'God is being-itself or the absolute'.[10] For him the analogy of being (*analogia entis*) is not only 'the form in which every knowledge of revelation must be expressed', but 'our only justification of speaking at all about God'. In other words, a 'segment of finite reality' functions as the basis for any concrete statement about the infinite. In this way it becomes symbolic, since the meaning of a symbol is 'negated by that to which it points' and at the same time it is affirmed by it as 'an adequate basis for

7. Cf. Christoph Schwöbel, 'Tillich, Paul', in Alister E. McGrath, (ed.), *The Blackwell Encyclopedia of Modern Christian Thought* (Oxford: Blackwell, 1993), 638.
8. David Tracy, *Blessed Rage for Order, The New Pluralism in Theology* (New York: The Seabury Press, 1975), 46. Tracy, 'Tillich and Contemporary Theology', in James Luther Adams, Wilhelm Pauck, Roger Lincoln Shinn, (eds.), *The Thought of Paul Tillich* (San Francisco: Harper & Row, 1985), 266.
9. Tracy, 'Tillich and Contemporary Theology', op. cit., 266. 'The fact is that Tillich does allow the answers (not only the questions) of psychoanalysis, socialist theory, existentialism ... to provide answers, not only questions, in his theology.'
10. Tillich, *Sytematic Theology,* vol. 1, 239.

pointing beyond itself'.[11] Hence for Tillich Christ on the Cross is the ultimate symbol as his self-surrendering death points towards the resurrection and thus to life and unity with God.

Symbols point to and participate in what they symbolise. Like artistic styles, they live and die, and are replaced by new ones.[12] Tillich stresses that traditional religious symbols can be validly used in modern art if they are in the artist's very being, i.e. if they are alive for him or her and are therefore used creatively to express ultimate concern. In their revelatory power symbols applied in art can point beyond the purely aesthetic to ultimate reality.[13]

On the 17th of February, 1959, six years before his death, Tillich delivered one of his most important lectures on art at the Museum of Modern Art in New York on 'Art and Ultimate Reality' where he stated that he had 'always learned more from pictures than from theological books'. In the light of this rather significant and even provocative statement, some relevant aspects of Tillich's ideas on the relationship between religion and art will now be considered.

Religious Experience and Artistic Styles

Before we look at Tillich's discussion of the relationship between religious experience and styles in art it is necessary to briefly ascertain his understanding of religion and style. Tillich defines religion fundamentally as 'being ultimately concerned' about one's self and one's world. As he sees it ultimate reality underlies all reality. According to him there are three ways by which people can relate to ultimate reality, two being indirect, philosophy (metaphysics) and art, and the direct way, which is religion. Ultimate reality 'becomes manifest through ecstatic experiences of a concrete-revelatory character and is expressed in symbols and myths'.[14]

In a more particularly Christian sense, religion implies the existence of (a) God with a set of symbols, rituals and doctrinal formulations. In the discussion of religion and art both the basic and the more particular definition of religion, need to be kept in mind.

It is to be suggested that the most valuable and influential aspect in Tillich's theology of art is his conviction that the manifestation of ultimate reality in the visual arts is not dependent on the use of traditional religious subject matter. This statement may not sound very revolutionary to us today, yet it is momentous because it really opened up modern (secular) art to the-

11. Ibid.
12. Tillich, 'Art and Society' (1952), in Tillich, *On Art and Architecture*, 37, 40.
13. Cf. ibid., 36-41. Cf. also George Pattison, *Art, Modernity and Faith, Restoring the Image* (London: Macmillan, 1991), 113.
14. Tillich, 'Art and Ultimate Reality', in op. cit., 318-319.

ological interpretation. Tillich's view that modern 'profane' works of art can convey ultimate concern – often much more so than the so-called sacred art produced for places of worship – is in line with his central idea proposed in his theology of culture that the religious is present in all spheres of spiritual (*geistigen*) life.

In 'Art and Ultimate Reality' he establishes five types of religious experience, which he correlates with five artistic styles. Tillich understands styles as pointing 'to a self-interpretation of man, thus answering the question of the meaning of life'.[15] In a work of art artists reveal through their style their own ultimate concern as well as that of their group and their period. Tillich held that the naturalistic, the idealistic and the expressionistic styles were the most important ones in the history of art.

1. The first and most fundamental type of religious experience is 'sacramental', i.e. 'ultimate reality appears as the holy which is present in all kinds of objects, in things, persons, events'.[16] Tillich relates this kind of religious experience, the most universal one, to 'numinous realism', a style which, as he perceives it, depicts 'ordinary things, ordinary persons ... but in a way that makes them strange, mysterious, laden with power'. According to Tillich, artists in whose works these tendencies are evident are de Chirico, Klee and Chagall.

2. 'Mystical religious experience', the second type, is actualised in Hinduism, Taoism, Buddhism, Neo-Platonism and, 'with some strong qualifications' in Christianity. Here religious experience seeks to reach ultimate reality without a mediation of things. This type of religious experience corresponds to abstract art, where things are merged into visual unity. Figures may be missing altogether, or are replaced by cubes, planes, colour, line 'as symbols for that which transcends all reality ...'.[17] Tillich mentions Jackson Pollock and Kandinsky as examplifiers of this style.

3. The 'prophetic-critical' type of religious experience 'goes beyond the sacramental basis of all religion'. Holiness without social justice has no room in this type of living one's religion. It corresponds to 'critical realism' in art, which reveals a critique of society, politics and/or the church. Here Tillich refers to Ensor, Daumier, Grosz, Beckmann, painters who engaged in radical, often sarcastic, social-political critique.

4. The fourth type, 'religious humanism', seeks the divine in the human and the human in the divine here and now, despite all human weakness. It

---

15. Tillich, 'Protestantism and Artistic Style' (1957), *On Art and Architecture,* 121.
16. Tillich, 'Art and Ultimate Reality', *Main Works,* vol. 2, 320.
17. Ibid., 323. Cf. Günter Rombold, *Der Streit um das Bild, Zum Verhältnis von moderner Kunst und Religion* (Stuttgart: Katholisches Bibelwerk, 1988), 91.

'expects the full realisation of this unity in history...'.[18] Idealist art, as in
Greek Classicism or in the Renaissance, for example, relates to this type of
religious experience. Works by Perugino, Piero della Francesca, Poussin and
Ingres are mentioned by Tillich in this context.

5. The last type of religious experience, that Tillich mentions, is the 'ecstatic-
spiritual' one that is anticipated in the Hebrew Scriptures, and 'is the religion
of the New Testament and of many movements in later church history'.[19]
The ecstatic-spiritual experience is characterised by its dynamic nature both
in disruption and creation. Tillich perceives it as 'realistic and at the same
time mystical'; it 'criticises and at the same time anticipates'. He pointed out
that as a Protestant theologian he was convinced that this religious element
which appears everywhere in ferment 'comes into its own within
Christianity'.[20] This type of religious experience he sees revealed in expressionist art, a style which is marked by realism and mysticism, creation and
disruption, stillness and dynamism. Tillich points out that the expressive element can be found in the art of the catacombs, in some Byzantine,
Romanesque, Gothic and Baroque art and particularly in twentieth century
Expressionism. Here it should also be mentioned that Tillich's view of the
power of modern Expressionism was much influenced by his engagement in
the politics in the inter-war years in Germany and his socialist leanings. He
regarded Expressionist art very much in political, revolutionary terms as anti-
capitalist and anti-bourgeois in an awareness of the crisis in society after
World War I and of the Russian Revolution: 'Expressionism proper arose
with a revolutionary consciousness and ... force. The individual forms of
things were dissolved, not in favour of subjective impressions but in favour
of objective metaphysical expression. The abyss of Being was to be evoked in
lines, colors and plastic forms.'[21]

It is an acknowledgement of the continuing importance of Tillich's writings on art that Günter Rombold (Austria), art historian, philosopher and
theologian, should refer positively to Tillich's article 'Art and Ultimate
Reality' in his book *Der Streit um das Bild, Zum Verhältnis von moderner
Kunst und Religion*. However, Rombold observes that Tillich postulates the

18. Ibid., 325.
19. Ibid., 326.
20. Ibid. Alexander Stock comments: 'Tillich's comprehensive definition of this type of reli-
    gion makes clear that the Protestant mode of Christianity is not understood as one form
    of religion beside others, but as the fully valid integration of all modi of religious experi-
    ence.' (Author's translation). A. Stock, *Zwischen Tempel und Museum: theologische
    Kunstkritik; Positionen der Moderne* (Paderborn: Ferdinand Schöningh, 1991), 237.
21. Cf. Tillich, 'Mass and Personality' (first publ. in German, 1922), *On Art and Architecture*,
    61-64. Tillich, *The Religious Situation*, trans. H.R. Niebuhr (Cleveland, New York:
    Meridian Books, 1956), 85-88, at 87.

correlation between religion and art to be an entirely positive one. The question for Rombold is whether 'there are not also anti- or areligious tendencies in art in which the relationship with religion seems to have broken up'.[22] This is a valid observation. In this context Rombold mentions the Surrealists, some of whom revealed anti-religious/Christian tendencies in their writings and paintings. One might suggest that Rombold's observation indirectly hints at what will be discussed in the following section, namely Tillich's somewhat problematic method of correlating artistic styles and religious experiences in broad sweeps without thorough engagement with individual works of art.

Religious Art is Expressionistic

As briefly mentioned above, Tillich maintained that the expressionist element 'has the strongest affinity to religious art. It breaks through both the realistic acceptance of the given and the idealistic anticipation of the fulfilled. And beyond both of them it reaches into the depths of ultimate reality'.[23] In this way expressionist art is, as he sees it, theonomous insight into reality as it communicates something of ultimate meaning, of the Spirit and of transcendence. Tillich believed all specifically religious art to be expressionistic throughout human history, 'expressing not the subjectivity of the artist but the ground of being itself'.[24] In 1921 he had already proposed a similar idea when he wrote that 'Expressionism wishes to reveal an objective spiritual awareness'.[25] His emphasis on the objective element was, as will be demonstrated below, another problematic aspect in Tillich's perception of expressionism, especially twentieth century Expressionism to which he referred in this context.

Certainly Tillich had a tremendous love for Expressionist art. However, his interpretation and theological conclusions of its aims have been criticised on a number of points. His understanding of this movement was, in fact, derived from his own anthropology, his political views, as outlined above, and his theology of culture. Tillich's central anthropological position holds that the human is estranged from his/her true being, that in existence he/she is not what he/she essentially is or ought to be. But this estrangement points towards salvation in which 'the division between essential goodness and actual existence is overcome'.[26] This appears in 'the manifestation of what concerns us ultimately', i.e. in revelation. Revelation and salvation are hence synony-

22. Rombold, *Der Streit um das Bild*, 94. (Author's translation).
23. Tillich, 'Art and Ultimate Reality', *Main Works*, vol. 2, 328.
24. Tillich, 'Theology and Architecture' (1955), Tillich, *Main Works*, vol. 2, 265-266.
25. Tillich, 'Religiöser Stil und Stoff in der bildenden Kunst' (1921), Tillich, *Main Works*, vol. 2, 95.
26. M. Palmer, 'Paul Tillich's Theology of Culture', Tillich, *Main Works*, vol. 2, 7.

mous. His theology of culture is therefore 'a theoretical reconciliation of the two spheres which are not alien to each other essentially but which are estranged in fact'.[27]

According to Tillich, Expressionism, more than other styles, is specifically religious as in it human estrangement as well as the hope for salvation are manifested. Tillich mentions Picasso's 'Guernica' as the 'greatest Protestant picture' since 1900 because 'such is the force of its portrayal of estrangement that the longing for reunion is inevitably raised'.[28] The work, he suggests, reflects the Protestant principle of the human as *simul justus et peccator*. In this context Tillich also refers to painters such as Nolde and Munch.

While one would certainly agree with Tillich that a considerable number of Expressionist works of art depict human estrangement, his method of arriving at such a statement as well as his assumption that these artists deliberately set out with an *objective intention* of portraying 'the ground of being itself' through distortion of natural form is too simplistic. Expressionism was not a co-ordinated movement. The artists hardly set out to reveal 'an objective spiritual awareness', as Tillich puts it.[29] Not only the different styles within Expressionism prove this but also the fact that painters like Kirchner, Schmidt-Rottluff and Marc disliked the term. Schmidt-Rottluff wrote: 'I know that I have no programme, only the unaccountable longing to grasp what I see and feel, and to find the purest means of expression for it.'[30] Lyonel Feininger, one of the few artists who explicitly acknowledged himself as an Expressionist, wrote in 1917: 'Each individual work serves as an expression of our most personal state of mind at that moment and of the inescapable, imperative need for release by means of an appropriate act of creation ...'[31]

It becomes clear that Tillich, in his focus on the objective dimension in Expressionism, did not sufficiently recognise the important aspect of subjectivity in modern artistic creation. It can be quite easily explained how Tillich's somewhat problematic hermeneutical approach came about. Through his World War I experiences he knew suffering on a very personal level, i.e. human estrangement, which would feature so strongly in his theology. He stepped on shaky ground by taking this theology as a point of departure for a theology of art. Instead of analysing works of art so as then to arrive at conclusions on the religious dimension in art, he applied his anthropological and

27. Palmer, 'Paul Tillich's Theology of Culture', in Tillich, *Main Works,* vol. 2, 7.
28. Ibid., 28. Tillich, 'Theology and Architecture' (1955), in *Main Works,* vol. 2, 266.
29. Palmer, op.cit., 23.
30. Karl Schmidt-Rottluff, quotation from the periodical *Kunst und Künstler* (1924), in Wolf-Dieter Dube, *The Expressionists* (London: Thames and Hudson, 1972), 20.
31. Dube, op.cit., 172.

theological views directly to Expressionist paintings. Dillenberger points out that because of this approach of interpretation Tillich's theory was to find little favour with art historians and philosophers of art.[32] It is thus a theology of art which is not derived from and centred in a detailed consideration of works of art but rather one which was significantly shaped by his own preconceived theological thought. One might suggest therefore that the method of correlation applied in his theology of art leaves itself open to a critique not unlike the one Tracy, amongst others, made about Tillich's formulation of the method of correlation as such.

Ideas on Modern Church Interiors

Having examined Tillich's views on the relationship between religion and art, and particularly his theories on Expressionism, I now want to look briefly at his concept of modern church architecture and interiors since here one finds his ideas concerning the actual inclusion of art into church life. Tillich's first love was, in fact, architecture; as a very young man he had even desired to become an architect.

In his article 'Contemporary Protestant Architecture' (1962) Tillich develops his ideas on the design of a Protestant church and its interior. Over thirty years later one notices that, especially in the light of Vatican II and the ecumenical movement, his emphasis on the 'Protestant' aspect of church design no longer quite applies, as modern church architecture and interiors, whether Catholic or Protestant, display very similar characteristics, i.e. simplicity and facilitation of a sense of community.[33] His views, as will be seen below, are relevant to various Christian traditions.

Tillich writes that 'it is the task of the church architects to create places of consecration where people feel able to contemplate the holy in the midst of their secular life'.[34] This point of departure corresponds to his idea that the religious is present in all secular life. Tillich proposes to include expressive, but non-figurative, art in churches instead of gaudy imitations of the old masters.

He strongly advocates modern designs for church buildings; neo-gothic or other imitations he considers inappropriate and out of context with our time. Even if many of these modern designs fail to convey something of ultimate reality to twentieth century humans he considers it important to develop

---

32. Dillenberger, *A Theology of Artistic Sensibilities, The Visual Arts and the Church*, 221.
33. Numerous articles have been written on this issue in Ireland since Vatican II. Cf. for example, Episcopal Liturgical Commission of Ireland, *The Place of Worship, Pastoral Directory on the Building and Reordering of Churches* (Dublin: Veritas, 1991).
34. Tillich, 'Honesty and Consecration in Religious Art and Architecture' (1965), *Main Works*, vol. 2, 369.

new styles because of the need for the principle of honesty in creative self-expression; he thus regards imitations as dishonest.[35] Again, as with his writing on painting, he makes hardly any references to specific places of worship.

For a Protestant church interior Tillich suggests murals, stained glass and non-figurative sculpture rather than paintings which tend to be objects of veneration. Figurative sculptures should not be used because they are 'too indicative of ancient idol worship'. These views are surprising. They reveal a rather simplistic and, one might say, 'Zwinglian' notion of the role of contemporary paintings and sculptures in church interiors which seems out of line with Tillich's extensive elaborations on the mediation of ultimate concern in visual, especially Expressionist art, which, although distorted, remains figurative.

One may quite safely suggest that after the Reformation, the Enlightenment, the Marxist critique of religion, Vatican II and with twentieth century (post)modernity we now find ourselves in an age in which idol worship is no longer part of Christian worship, if it ever was as prevalent and dangerous as some of the Reformers maintained. Expressive and sometimes provocative modern paintings or sculptures with religious content (Nolde, Rainer, Beuys, Cucchi, Ernst or, in the Irish context, for example, Jack Yeats, Middleton, or Graham) invite – if they were placed in a church – puzzled reactions, critique, even disgust, perhaps interest, admiration and maybe meditation, but certainly not idol worship.

It becomes clear that Tillich's ideas here seem somewhat self-contradictory. While he makes a very important point in stressing that the contemporary church needs contemporary art and artists, his insistence that figurative images should be excluded from church interiors might be a sign of his Protestant background and theology, i.e. the Protestant reservations with regard to figurative images in sacred spaces. This would be surprising, however, because Tillich belonged to the Lutheran tradition in which, unlike in the Reformed tradition, the fear of images and idol worship has played only a rather minor role, as Luther himself held that images, signs and sacraments were necessary for nourishing the Christian faith.[36] Should one conclude that despite Tillich's emphasis on symbol, analogy and sacramentality, his attitude here might disclose something of the tension between the 'Protestant principle', i.e. the rejection of the divinisation of anything in human or historic reality, and

35. Tillich, 'Contemporary Protestant Architecture' (1962), op.cit., 355. Cf. also Richard Egenter, a contemporary of Tillich, on this question of the untruthfulness, irreverence, and ineptitude of kitsch in churches. Egenter considers it from his viewpoint as a moral theologian. Egenter, *The Desecration of Christ* (London: Burns & Oates, 1967), 85-94.
36. Cf. Helmut A. Müller, 'Das Schöne im Gotteshaus, Zum Verhältnis von Kirche und Gegenwartskunst', *Evangelische Kommentare,* vol. 1 (Stuttgart, 1990), 46.

the 'Catholic substance', i.e. an affirmation of the divine presence in all that is?[37]

Conclusion

Tillich's greatest achievement in the area of theology and art lies in the very fact that he opened up modern art to theology. Art played an important dimension in his whole theologising; the numerous references in his works to visual art, in particular, are confirmations of this element in his thought. Among the leading systematic theologians of the twentieth century Paul Tillich stands out as the one for whom modern art was more than a marginal subject; it became a central theme in his theology. Any critique of Tillich's theology of art, as it has been made by theologians like Dillenberger, Palmer, Stock, as well as by this writer, must therefore be seen in the light of the basic appreciation and deep respect for Tillich's stature in this field.

From what has been discussed above, the main points of critique therefore are 1. that one cannot make one artistic style more or less normative for all religious art; 2. that Tillich's theory of the religious in art would thus exclude from the start many important artists and indeed works with religious content from the history of art; 3. that Tillich failed to recognise sufficiently the important aspect of subjectivity in modern art and artists; 4. that the interpretation of art demands consistent adherence to and in-depth engagement with the work of art; 5. that style, which provides a type of language and basis for communication in which religious as well as non-religious concerns are expressed, is only part – but not the whole – of the message itself; and 6. that Tillich's use of the term Expressionism (or expressionism) for the period of Expressionism in early twentieth-century European art *as well as* for expressive elements in other works from the history of art is somewhat confusing and therefore unclear. It is at times difficult to know whether he refers to the former or the latter.

These criticisms are valid and need to be taken into account when one reads Tillich's writings on art. However, his importance in this area remains unquestioned since he was the first theologian to see the theological relevance especially in modern art. Moreover, and significantly, his understanding of human estrangement and of religion as ultimate concern provided a basis for discovering religious dimensions in works of art which contain little or no religious iconography.

---

37. I thank Dermot Lane for his comment. Cf. also Ronald Modras, 'Catholic Substance and the Catholic Church Today', in Raymond F. Bulman, Frederick J. Parrella, (eds.), *Paul Tillich: A New Catholic Assessment* (Collegeville, Minnesota: The Liturgical Press, 1994), 33-42.

II. THEOLOGICAL ASPECTS IN MODERN EUROPEAN ART — HORST SCHWEBEL

Horst Schwebel[38] has been involved in research and teaching on the inter-disciplinary subject of art, theology and the church for over thirty years. His extensive writings on the subject have made him a leading scholar in the field of theology and modern art in the German-speaking world.[39]

Schwebel's doctoral thesis, *Autonome Kunst im Raum der Kirche,* which deals with abstract art, its autonomy, its reception and its interpretation from a theological point of view, as well as its location in church buildings was published in 1968. His post-doctoral work *(Habilitation) Das Christusbild in der bildenden Kunst der Gegenwart* (1980) is probably the most comprehensive theological examination of the image of Christ in twentieth century European art to date.

After a brief presentation of some main points of his doctoral thesis the focus will be on his post-doctoral work. Since the image of Christ, especially of his suffering on the Cross, of the tortured innocent human being, is central among modern artists who have worked with Christian subjects, I will look in detail at Schwebel's examination of this subject.[40]

Theological Dimensions in Non-Figurative Art
Schwebel's overall concern is a concrete mediation between the church and contemporary art. Schwebel's interests include the use of works of art in church spaces and the relationship between the work of art and the preached word. We will consider Schwebel's writings in this light.

Modern art, unlike older art, has become autonomous. No longer, as Schwebel writes, has it a servant function in the church, i.e. the visualisation of the gospels for the illiterate, the *biblia pauperum.* According to him this autonomy becomes most obvious in abstract art, as here the viewer does not

38. Horst Schwebel is professor of practical theology and director of the *Institut für Kirchenbau und kirchliche Kunst der Gegenwart* at Marburg University.
39. Cf. Horst Schwebel's post-doctoral thesis *(Habilitation), Das Christusbild in der bildenden Kunst der Gegenwart,* Textband, Schriftenreihe Bild und Raum des Instituts für Kirchenbau und kirchliche Kunst (Giessen: Wilhelm Schmitz Verlag, 1980), xii. Cf. Schwebel's doctorate, *Autonome Kunst im Raum der Kirche* (Hamburg: Furche Verlag, 1968).
40. Cf. for further, more recent, articles and books by Schwebel on topics such as art and mysticism, aesthetics, art in church life: Horst Schwebel, Andreas Mertin, (eds.), *Bilder und ihre Macht, Zum Verhältnis von Kunst und christlicher Religion* (Stuttgart: Verlag Katholisches Bibelwerk, 1989). A. Mertin, H. Schwebel, (eds.), *Kirche und moderne Kunst* (Frankfurt: Athenäum, 1988). H. Schwebel, (ed.), *Kirchen in der Stadt,* Schriften des Instituts für Kirchenbau und kirchliche Kunst, vol. 1 *Erfahrung und Perspektiven* (1994), vol. 2 *Beispiele und Modelle* (1996). Schwebel has also contributed articles to the Quarterly *Kunst und Kirche* (Darmstadt: Verlag Das Beispiel, since 1971).

receive a verbally verifiable message. She or he is only 'attuned' *(gestimmt)* in silence by the work.

Schwebel holds that in abstract art a 'realm of forms and colours has been created which withdraw from reality'.[41] For him non-figurative art is an art of 'visual ecstasy', a 'mystical emigration from reality'.[42] He stresses, however, that these works which are beyond words should not be imposed upon with biblical or other figurative meanings once they have been placed in a church interior so as to conveniently label them 'Christian' art. The way to bring the sacred space of the church and abstract art closer is not to be found in attaching Christian titles to abstract works of art but in the mystical experience of the abstract work of art. As he sees it, in visual, mystical ecstasy, the 'new creation', the 'new being', 'paradise' are anticipated; the hope of Christian faith lives essentially in this anticipation. Thus for Schwebel the experience of non-figurative art has a mystical-eschatological dimension as it is an anticipation of eternity. He points out that modern stained glass art in churches like the Sacré-Coeur in Audincourt are the greatest examples of modern abstraction since here amazing 'colour symphonies' have been achieved. He adds that wherever one encounters these works, whether in a sacred space or in a private house, i.e. the secular sphere, they provide places of anticipation. Moreover, Schwebel suggests that precisely where art ceases to be the *ancilla theologiae* it enters the realm of faith because the new being finds its greatest expression where reality is transcended, as in abstract art: 'The experience of anticipated eschatology reaches its climax in visual ecstasy.'[43]

How then does this art relate to the kerygma, the preaching of the Good News *(Verkündigung)?* Schwebel acknowledges that autonomous art cannot preach concretely or historically. Nevertheless, since the Christian proclamation of Christ is 'more than words can say', art can make us 'feel and hear' what words cannot convey. He concludes, therefore, that abstract art has a legitimate place in church life.

Stock critically points out that Schwebel's idea of mysticism is problematic since he emphasises the non-figurative light-colour sensations as the 'definiens' of mysticism rather than taking into account the wider field of Christian mysticism which is 'not without language' and includes 'visions of surreal figurativeness' just as much as non-figurative ones.[44] These observations are valid. One may suggest that Schwebel's idea of the mystical seems,

41. Schwebel, *Autonome Kunst im Raum der Kirche,* 46. 'Das Abstrakt-Bildnerische ist der gewaltige Versuch des Menschen, eine Welt zu erschaffen, die sich aus den Wirklichkeitsformen herauslöst und denoch sichtbar, konkret aufweisbar und permanent ist.'
42. Ibid., 59. '... die gegenstandsfreie Kunst, eine Kunst visueller Ekstasis, mystischen Auswanderns aus der Wirklichkeit ...'
43. Ibid., 85.
44. Stock, op.cit., 254.

in fact, a little narrow, i.e. his suggestion that 'the experience of anticipated eschatology reaches its climax in visual ecstasy' shows a bias towards the visual which would seem to diminish other sensuous experiences of eschatological anticipation, as, for example, the encounter with great works of music.[45] One needs to be aware, however, that the precise definition of what constitutes mysticism and what types of experiences can be included under this term remains problematic up to this day. The somewhat loose ideas of what mysticism means may go some way to explain Schwebel's bias towards the visual dimension in mystical experience.

Having outlined Schwebel's views on the theological and religious dimensions of abstract art, i.e. its ecstatic, mystical, eschatological aspects and its relevance in church life, I will now turn to his major work on the image of Christ in twentieth century European art.

The Image of Christ in Modern Art

In his book, *Das Christusbild in der bildenden Kunst der Gegenwart*, Schwebel divides his subject into four major sections: 1. 'The quest for the contemporary image of Christ', 2. An extensive analysis of relevant works of art, 3. The Christ image 'in the mirror of historical criticism', i.e. in the context of iconodules[46] and iconoclasts, and 4. Conclusions on the theological relevance of the modern image of Christ and its role in contemporary church life.

Schwebel begins by stating three fundamental points with regard to modern art and, more particularly, with regard to the modern image of Christ. Firstly, artistic subjectivity, rather than Christian iconography of the past centuries, is central to modern art. Secondly, in twentieth century art, unlike in older art, images of Christ often do not appear in familiar biblical surroundings. Thirdly, often Christ is not featured as the Christ of the scriptures, but as a human being without attributes which would immediately reveal his divinity.

Schwebel stresses that because art is an important source for 'understanding the self and the world in a particular epoch', we encounter in the modern image of Christ contemporary ideas on the Crucified which are important for today's theology.

Images of Christ can therefore lead to 'indirect theological knowledge'.[47] Frank Burch Brown puts this more sharply when he writes: 'Art's gift, when not given over simply to a delight that is almost sheerly aesthetic, is rather to

---

45. Schwebel, *Autonome Kunst*, 85. Cf. also Frank Burch Brown, *Religious Aesthetics, A Theological Study of Making and Meaning* (Princeton, N.J.: Princeton University Press, 1989), 37-38.
46. Those who favour icons.
47. Schwebel, *Das Christusbild in der bildenden Kunst der Gegenwart*, 3-4.

explore fictively, metaphorically, and experientially what formal theology cannot itself present or contain.'[48]

In its revelation of fundamental human concerns, art can enhance theological reflection. Thereby it is of no interest whether these works are 'theologically correct' or 'incorrect'. What matters are the 'attitudes and aspects they reveal with regard to the question of Christ *(Christusfrage)*'.[49]

Schwebel rightly points out that the 'subjective-existential moment of the [modern] artist [is] the point of departure and remains the dominating feature' in twentieth century art. The truth of artistic engagement in relation to the production of art, not the truth of the New Testament writings, constitutes the norm for the contemporary artist.

Interpretations of the 'Christ event' in art therefore need to be examined to see whether they can be defended theologically. Thus Schwebel formulates his central question: Can modern images of Christ which are 'highly subjective and often negative' still be seen at all in the context of 'God, salvation, redemption' and hence as a medium of communicating faith, or does 'the sensuous image remain in opposition to the spiritual word' and the 'biblical Christ'?[50]

Schwebel examines in detail a considerable number of works of art in order to evaluate whether and to what extent the modern image of Christ can serve theology and the church. The criterion for his choice of works is 'innovation', i.e. those depictions are of interest which show 'new approaches' *(Neuansätze)* in the treatment of the figure of Christ in the history of modern art.

Schwebel distinguishes three groups of modern images of Christ: 1. The Christ image which reveals the *'conditio humana'*, i.e. the consciousness of crisis in the modern world, 2. The image of Christ which points to salvation, and 3. The abstract image of Christ.

The *conditio humana* paintings form the largest group and are of primary interest to Schwebel. They reveal the existentialist concern, the sense of suffering and fragmentation of modernity. Common to all these paintings is the depiction of Christ as a suffering human being without glory and/or divine attributes. Christ appears as the misunderstood artist (Ensor), the suffering brother (Rouault), the dead soldier (Schmidt-Rottluff), the one who is incapable of preventing war (Barlach), the demolished flesh where any sense, reason and hope are lost, i.e. the absurd (Bacon), and he appears in the guise

---

48. Frank Burch Brown, *Religious Aesthetics,* 167.
49. Schwebel, op.cit., 3-4.
50. Ibid., 5-6.

of students who are beaten up by the police at a demonstration (Hrdlicka).[51] Depictions of and allusions to Christ such as these are typical for this group of paintings. Here 'Christ participates in alienated existence with all its threats'.[52]

The second group of works, those pointing to salvation, appears to be much smaller than the previous one. This hardly comes as a surprise if one considers the predicament of the twentieth century which is marked by the barbarity of two world wars, the invention and dropping of the nuclear bomb and the reality and awareness of large-scale human suffering.

Schwebel begins his analysis with Sutherland's famous tapestry 'Christ in Glory' in Coventry Cathedral. He rightly observes that this is untypical of Sutherland's oeuvre.[53] Sutherland's recourse to Byzantine iconography where he depicts Christ as Pantocrator is anachronistic with regard to the modern styles of Expressionism, Cubism and Sutherland's other paintings. Because this work is unconvincing as a modern image of Christian salvation, Schwebel asks whether the *conditio humana* pictures may be the only possibility for the creation of modern images of Christ or whether there are genuinely modern works, which, beyond the threshold of doubt and despair, provide us with glimpses of hope, divine power and salvation in Christ. He gives three examples of such works. In 'Christ and the Adulteress' (1918), one work in a series of woodcuts by Schmidt-Rottluff, light becomes 'the carrier of meaning in Christ's actions'. This light, which is created by the strong contrast of black and white, shows a sudden 'ray' of salvation.

Emil Nolde, an artist who produced many works of art with biblical content, also goes beyond the existentialist concerns. He created an 'ecstatic-visionary Christ ... who binds his followers into a mystical communion', as, for example, in works like 'The Eucharist', 'Pentecost' or 'Christ with the Children'. The Crucified becomes the wonderful saviour who brings light into darkness.

In Marc Chagall's work Christ is the one who reconciles what is separated.

51. Schwebel, op.cit., 24-46. Works under examination are among others: Ensor's 'Ecce Homo' and 'Christ's Entry into Brussels', Corinth's 'Red Christ', Schmidt-Rottluff's '1918 - Ist Euch nicht Christus erschienen?', Rouault's 'Miserere et Guerre', Barlach's 'Anno Domini MCMXVI post Christum natum', Bacon's triptych 'Three Figures at the Base of a Crucifixion'. Cf. also Friedhelm Mennekes' interview with Bacon in the catalogue of an exhibition of Bacon's works at the Kunst-Station St. Peter, Cologne, where Bacon states that there is no redemption: 'Was ist das, Erlösung? Es gibt keine Erlösung. Es gibt überhaupt nichts dergleichen ... Natürlich, der Tod begleitet uns immer. Er ist unser Schatten.' Interview in Johannes Röhrig, Kurt Danch, (eds.), *Bacon, Triptych '71* (Cologne: Kunst-Station St. Peter, 1993), 17-18.
52. Schwebel, *Das Christusbild*, 69. Cf. Stock, op.cit., 256.
53. Schwebel, op.cit., 48-49.

Further, Chagall, in line with the Romantics, sees Christ as the 'great poet, whose poetical teaching has been forgotten in modernity'.[54] In some works the artist identifies with Christ. It is interesting indeed to note that the Jew Chagall should have left us with such beautiful, redemptive pictures of Christ, while many modern artists, who grew up in the Christian tradition, have depicted Christ rather in 'merely' existentialist terms. These then, according to Schwebel, are examples of images which, without denying the modern 'consciousness of crisis', reveal something of the salvific power of Jesus Christ.

Finally Schwebel considers whether an abstract work of art can convey Christ. He suggests that fundamentally the modern abstract 'image' of the God-Man protects the inexpressibility and the mystery of God. Because these paintings retract from presenting Christ in figurative form and often can be recognised as religious/Christ 'images' only by their titles, i.e. the *claim* that they present something religious, Schwebel calls them 'indirect Christ images'.[55] In many of these, light and excessive coloration indicate the resurrection, salvation and redemption, as, for example, in Manessier's cycle 'Passion' (1948-49).[56]

Schwebel also looks at Leger's famous window on the Passion in the church in Audincourt where the instruments of Christ's Passion are depicted in such a way that they no longer just appear as thorns or nails but as carriers of vibrant colours.

In his analysis of abstract art Schwebel does not give a definite answer whether these paintings are images of Christ. He recognises their common characteristic which is the 'indisposability' *(Unverfügbarkeit)* of God and he makes the important observation that these works, in their *avoidance* of a figurative image of the divine, have something in common with the iconoclasts. However, he emphasises that they differ from the iconoclasts in that they express the inexpressibility of God through *the very medium* of the work of art.

54. Ibid., 62. Cf. Frank Burch Brown, *Religious Aesthetics,* 24. Brown writes on the Romantics: 'Blake, Coleridge, the Schlegels, Schelling, Ruskin ... these and other Romantics and Victorians found it easy to utter the words 'art', 'beauty', and 'religion' together in one breadth.'
    Blake wrote: "Jesus & his Apostles & Disciples were all Artists'; 'A Poet, a Painter, a Musician, an Architect: the Man or Woman who is not one of these is not a Christian'.' William Blake, 'Aphorisms on the Laocoon Group', in *Selected Poetry and Prose of Blake,* ed. Northrop Frye (New York: Random House - Modern Library, 1953), 328, 330, quoted in Burch Brown, op.cit., 24.
55. Schwebel, op.cit., 72.
56. Ibid., 77. It is interesting to note that Manessier, who created a number of modern religious works of art and at times was labelled a 'Catholic painter', once said 'I don't believe in "religious painting". It is man who should be religious.' In: Brian Fallon, 'Passing of a generation', *The Irish Times,* 5.8.1993. This article was written on the occasion of Manessier's death.

Schwebel's extensive analysis of works of art is followed by an investigation into the theological perception of the visual image of Christ in history. He expounds all the major (early) medieval iconoclast and iconodule positions, Eusebius of Caesarea, Clement of Alexandria, Epiphanius, John of Damascus, Theodore of Studios and then continues with the Reformers, Karlstadt, Zwingli and Luther. Here he stresses the different approach of the latter from the former two. Luther, who was initially against images, later considered them to be of service in spreading the word of God to the poor. Luther appreciates images only in the context of preaching *(Verkündigung)*. Schwebel points out that nobody since John of Damascus had thought as much about images as Luther did. Contrary to the spiritualistic iconoclasts, Luther was, like John Damascene, anti-spiritualistic in his approach to images. However, John's anti-spiritualistic attitude is ultimately 'naïve'. For him, the incarnation is a sort of rebirth of 'part of the lost paradise'; he does not admit, as Luther did, that the believer always remains a sinner, that one always lives in a world that should be other than it is. Schwebel concludes that from all the historical iconodule positions, Luther's is the only relevant one with regard to the modern image of Christ since this Reformer was aware of those experiences of fragmentation, contradictions and suffering which are expressed in twentieth century images of Christ.[57]

However, Schwebel observes that modern works of art with religious allusions or subject matter have nothing in common with Luther's *biblia pauperum* idea as they do not educate the poor and uneducated in the Christian faith, but, on the contrary, present highly subjective, sometimes intellectualised, concerns of individual artists which, for the most part, are only appreciated by an educated 'elite'. Indeed, it is true that the whole context of (religious) art has changed in the modern era.

In the concluding section, Schwebel discusses the theological relevance of the modern image of Christ. Here the central question is whether these images can serve in preaching the gospel. More precisely, Schwebel asks whether the *conditio humana* images can 'show Christ *in the image* as the one who under the conditions of existence has overcome the conditions of existence', i.e. does Christ appear as the 'answer to the existentialist threat'?[58]

He asserts that although there are some examples in modern art where Christ is portrayed as the one who overcomes the 'existential threat' (e.g. Schmidt-Rottluff's woodcuts, some of Chagall's works, etc.), these works can only serve in the context of preaching, but do not spread the Good News as

57. Schwebel, op. cit., 127. Here Schwebel's observation is not unlike Tillich's comment in relation to Picasso's 'Guernica' as a most 'Protestant' picture because it shows human sinfulness and therein raises the hope for salvation.
58. Ibid., 136.

such.[59] Apart from a few exceptions they do not reveal Christ as God and saviour. The 'norm and measure *(Masstab)* of Christian faith', he maintains, will not be found in these works of art.

If modern images of Christ do not function as sources of proclaiming the Good News, what theological purpose do they serve? Schwebel holds what is most important about these works is the fact that they witness to *experiences* which relate to Christ. 'What constitutes the modern image of Christ is the experience of personal suffering and of the suffering of others in connection with the suffering of the Christ-figure.'[60] Thus preaching the Good News, which takes the human person seriously, must relate to these individual experiences and their contexts. Such images therefore should be integrated into religious education and services.[61] These works of art which reveal individual religious experiences are relevant in their exposition not only of personal concerns of 'highly sensitised contemporaries', i.e. artists, but also of the deep concerns of an epoch.[62] In this way they provide directions and contexts for spreading the Good News in the contemporary world. In the modern image of Christ faith and preaching are faced with that reality in which they have to live and work.[63] In this confrontation lies the real value of the contemporary image of the crucified since here – as in other areas of the arts – the church and theology find concerns that need to be addressed if they wish to be credible and relevant to today's women, men and children in their search for the divine.

59. Ibid. Schwebel holds that one cannot speak of modern paintings as 'preaching pictures' *(Verkündigungsbilder)*.
60. Ibid., 140.
61. Ibid., 139. It is interesting to note that John and Jane Dillenberger, both of whom have worked very much in the same area as Schwebel but in a North American context and more on modern North American art, stress – like Schwebel – the educational value of the modern religious images. Cf. John Dillenberger, *A Theology of Artistic Sensibilities*, 250-256. Cf. Jane Dillenberger's reflections on her own experience of teaching art in theological faculties in 'Reflections on the Field of Religion and the Visual Arts', *Art as Religious Studies*, ed. Doug Adams, Diane Apostolos-Cappadona (New York: Crossroad, 1990), 12-25.
62. Schwebel, op.cit., 139-141. 'Man kann von solchen Erfahrungen nicht fordern, dass sie das grosse Ja Gottes zum Menschen in Christus zum Ausdruck bringen. Dies deutlich zu machen ist Aufgabe der Verkündigung. Wohl aber kann man fordern, dass die von den Künstlern aufgewiesene Erfahrung subjektiv wahrhaftig sei, dass Problemstellungen um keines Einvernehmens willen umgangen und vertuscht werden ... dass der Zweifel als Zweifel und die Anfechtungserfahrung als Anfechtungserfahrung artikuliert werden. Würde die Christuskunst 'sagen', was die Verkündigung sagt, wäre sie inbezug auf Erkenntnisvermährung belanglos.'
63. Ibid., 141. 'Da die Christuskunst aber nicht ancilla ist, da sie die Verkündigung nicht 'verdoppelt', sondern die Zweifel und Hoffnungen angesichts des Christusglaubens artikuliert, leistet sie einen doppelten Dienst. Zum einen sagt sie der Verkündigung,

Conclusion

Horst Schwebel's work on the theological and spiritual aspects in abstract art and his major study of the image of Christ in modern European art, both of which show his extensive research, systematic approach, clear language, as well as a consistent method and argumentation make his work relevant to any studies in the field of theology, the church and the visual arts.

Unlike Tillich's somewhat problematic method of theological engagement with art and his bias towards Expressionism, Schwebel adopts a practice of looking at the works first in order to draw theological conclusions afterwards. He does not apply a preconceived theology to the paintings and examines many individual works of art in detail – an element that is certainly lacking in Tillich's writings on art.

Schwebel's criterion of innovation for the choice of works under consideration, as well as his detailed examination of modern images of Christ under the headings of '*conditio humana*', 'salvation' and 'abstract images', are convincingly argued. Basically I would also agree with his conclusions, namely that twentieth century images of Christ arise from and are related to the artists' individual experiences and subjective concerns and that in this way they are significant, of epistemological value and thus should be integrated into modern church life and into religious and theological education.

However, two points in Schwebel's writing, it seems to me, might be debated. Firstly, he spends considerable time on the medieval iconodules, iconoclasts, and the Reformers, and how they would react to modern depictions of Christ. While his presentation gives a good idea of their theological views on religious images, these speculations seem a little superfluous because it is of no real relevance to us today to guess what those thinkers might have to say with regard to modern art. It is not surprising then, that the result of this speculative exercise is a little meagre. For Schwebel Luther remains the only theologian whose ideas are important for the modern visual image of Christ.

Secondly, is it true, as Schwebel suggests, that these works are to be seen only in the *context* of and as *giving directions* to the preaching of the Good News? How is proclamation of the trinitarian God to be defined, especially in the context of our (post)modern age? The Christian kerygma is traditionally understood as 'the proclamation of the crucified and risen Jesus as God's final and definitive act of salvation'.[64] The question arises whether preaching

woraufhin sie sich auszurichten habe, damit sie Antwort sei auf die aus der Existenz erwachsenen Fragen. Zum anderen tritt sie dem angefochtenen Glauben zur Seite. Anders gesagt: Verkündigung und Glauben werden angesichts der Christuskunst der Gegenwart mit der Wirklichkeit konfrontiert, in der sie zu stehen und zu wirken haben.'

64. John F. Craghan, 'Kerygma', in Joseph A. Komonchak, Mary Collins, Dermot. A Lane, (eds.), *The New Dictionary of Theology* (Dublin: Gill and Macmillan, 1987), 556.

does only happen orally and in an ecclesial, communal setting, or whether it is not also formulated indirectly, but often forcefully, in and through the image in the viewer's encounter with and reception of it, and quite likely in a non-religious setting? Given that the Spirit blows where it wills, would it not be legitimate to propose that – at least in some sense – Nolde's nine-part altarpiece or Corinth's amazing 'Red Christ' or, as we will see, Yeats' 'There is No Night' are 'sermons in paint' which in their *sensuous, authentic* and *kerygmatic* power let many bland and shallow sermons fade away miserably? Is it not perhaps – or precisely – because they did not *set out* to be sermons, at least not in the usual sense, that they actually and paradoxically 'preach' through verbal silence? Indeed, may one not suggest, as Frank Burch Brown does, that 'there is no reason why that "Word" [of God] cannot sound – and in a distinctive tone – in the prophetic, visionary, and revelatory artistic expressions'?[65] Is it not exactly this which the church, for the most part, continually fails to recognise when, instead of first-rate works, much of the commissioned 'church art' simply *reminds* the worshipper of Christian beliefs, but does little to *raise, challenge* or *inspire* the minds of the churchgoer because it often lacks vision, prophesy and imagination? If, as Schwebel holds, these images ought to be used not only in education, but also in meditation, and even in religious services, is this not, in fact, in itself a confirmation of a kerygmatic or proclamatory dimension in the works? Further, if it is true what Schwebel suggests about abstract works, for example, namely that they are anticipations of the eschatological moment, or, if there are works in modern art which point to Christ as saviour, is there not *at least* indirect proclamation of the kingdom present in these works? Or is proclamation to be understood exclusively within the traditional ecclesial boundaries of *oral* witness to Christ by the ordained?

The basic issue, then, is whether our traditional concept of proclamation itself demands rethinking. A widened perception of it may finally – and once again(!) although in a changed context, of course, – give proper recognition and appreciation to the visual arts. Burch Brown could not put it more succinctly when, in his discussion on the kerygmatic dimension of art, he concludes: 'The art that has the greatest religious significance is not necessarily the art of institutional religion but rather that art which happens to discern what religion in its institutional or personal forms needs most to see.'[66] Schwebel, one suggests, would agree. Further, some of the works which will be considered in Chapter Three will be shown as being revelatory of such kerygmatic dimensions.

65. F. Burch Brown, *Religious Aesthetics*, 111.
66. Ibid.

SUMMARY AND CONCLUSION

In this first chapter the thought of two relevant scholars from the wider field of theology and visual art were introduced. In particular, their methods and the subjects which have interested them in their doing theology through the visual image were discussed. It became apparent that while Tillich's pioneering status, especially his insistence on ultimate concern being present in modern art without religious subject matter, needs to be fundamentally recognised and appreciated, his method as well as his preference for an artistic style, i.e. the expressionist, cannot be favoured as principles for theological engagement with visual art. Schwebel's approach then – and for that matter also that of other theologians, like John Dillenberger, for example – may in some way be seen as a development from Tillich. Schwebel's method of examining works with regard to their theological import in detail, as he did with the image of Christ in modern art, without applying a preconceived theology and without preference for a certain style, is essential and a more objective, conducive and thorough approach for a theology of and through art. Thus Schwebel's method, subjects and conclusions, more so than Tillich's, will be of relevance to our examination of the theological dimensions in modern Irish works of art.

CHAPTER II

The Artist Speaks:
Theology and Spirituality
in the Life of the Painter

I. MAINIE JELLETT

Mainie Jellett was born in Dublin in 1897 into a Church of Ireland family whose forebears had been living on the island since the seventeenth century.[1] Jellett grew up in a cultured atmosphere of academic and intellectual distinction and a lifestyle that included a great interest in the arts. In fact, she became an accomplished pianist but decided that her vocation was to be painting rather than to follow a career as a musician.

In her article 'My Voyage of Discovery', Jellett states that there were 'at least three revolutions' in her work.[2] After initial studies at the Metropolitan School of Art in Dublin, her first 'revolution' was to be in London, where she and her life-long friend Evie Hone studied under Walter Sickert from 1917 to 1919. Here she became proficient in painting the human figure, in the use of colour and in drawing. After her return to Dublin she began to exhibit her work and continued studies at the Metropolitan School of Art.

In 1921 Jellett and Hone went to Paris to study under André Lhote. It was Lhote who introduced the two artists to Cubism and to the ideas and problems of modern art. This was to be the second 'revolution' in Jellett's development as a painter. However, although she appreciated Lhote as an excellent teacher, she knew that he would not lead her to the extremes of Cubism and abstract art as she desired. Thus the two women chose a new teacher, Albert Gleizes, whose influence on Jellett's development as a Cubist painter was immense.[3] Hone and Jellett took their first lessons from him in 1921 and would come back for more studies in the years to come.

1. Bruce Arnold, *Mainie Jellett and the Modern Movement in Ireland* (New Haven, London: Yale University Press, 1991), 1. Jellett was christened Mary Hariett Jellett but was always called Mainie. For an extensive biography on Jellett cf. Arnold, op.cit.
2. M. Jellett, 'My Voyage of Discovery', in Eileen MacCarvill, (ed.), *Mainie Jellett, The Artist's Vision* (Dundalk: Dundalgan Press, 1958), 47. This work is a collection of essays and lectures by Jellett.
3. Jellett and Hone kept contact with Gleizes for the rest of their lives. His admiration for Jellett was profound. In his 'Hommage a Mainie Jellett' (the preface to MacCarvill's book, Engl. trans.) he wrote: 'When I heard of her death, ... I experienced inexpressible grief.

Cubism, a parent of abstract painting, had emerged under Braque and Picasso from about 1907. Instead of the three-dimensional realistic rendering of the object, as it had been the aim of artists since the time of Giotto, the Cubists, under the influence of Cézanne, took the two-dimensional picture surface as their point of departure. The intention was to present the whole structure of an object, which meant that objects would be shown as 'dissected', i.e. several views of one object would be rendered in one picture, often super-imposed. The Cubist artists were concerned with expressing the concept of an object rather than with a particular view of it. Hone commented on the Cubist work of her friend in 1930 that Jellett had no desire to depict in a real-istic style three-dimensional forms on the two-dimensional picture plane, but rather she intended to fill the space 'with a formal composition, having a rhythm and life of its own ... The appeal is to the spirit, not to the senses'.[4] Or, as Jellett formulated it: 'We sought the inner principle and not the outer appearance.'[5]

When Jellett and Hone began to study Cubist ideas and techniques under Gleizes in the early 1920s, the movement had already entered into its late phase. However, Gleizes remained devoted to the development of Cubism throughout his life and wrote a number of influential works on the subject, notably *Du Cubisme* (1912). Despite the fact that in terms of the latest art historical advances in Europe, the two pupils from Ireland were somewhat late, apparently they were, nevertheless, the first artists in Britain and Ireland to produce abstract works of art.[6]

Although at first Jellett's work and ideas were received with ridicule and rejection in Ireland,[7] her enthusiasm, ability and single-minded attitude towards her art soon made her a leading figure of modern art in Ireland. She lectured on art and was acclaimed as a great teacher of painting, and exhib-ited in Ireland, Britain, on the continent and in New York.

Jellett, a believer throughout her life, began to paint religious works in the late 1920s. The first of these was *Hommage to Fra Angelico,* first shown in 1928. It was well received and marked something of a turning point in her

One part of myself had gone, that part which was linked up with heroic enthusiasms that demanded faith - since outside that little group of faithful that we were there had been only opposition, denial, condemnation. ... [She] was one of the first to understand all that was implied of authentic purity and true reality in the first attempts at the liberation of paint-ing through elimination of the classical subject.' MacCarvill, op.cit., 42-43.

4. Evie Hone, 'Miss Jellett's Cubist Paintings', in *St Bartholomew's Parish Magazine*, vol. 48, no. 1 (Dublin: Jan. 1930). I thank Hilary Pyle for drawing my attention to this article.
5. M. Jellett, 'My Voyage of Discovery', in E. MacCarvill, op.cit., 48.
6. B. Arnold, Interview, 30.9.1995.
7. George Russell described her work in *The Irish Statesman* (27.10.1923) as 'sub-human' and Jellett as 'a late victim to Cubism', in Arnold, *Mainie Jellett and the Modern Movement in Ireland*, 80 and 208.

career. Until her death she continued to paint religious subjects, some of which are to be counted among her finest works.

In 1943 Jellett was elected to chair the committee which had been formed to establish the Irish Exhibition of Living Art. She fell ill later in the year and was unable to attend its first exhibition. She died from cancer in Dublin in 1944.

* * *

Those who knew Jellett, describe her as a 'kind', 'considerate', 'reliable', 'sincere', 'courageous', 'highly principled', a 'naturally religious' woman with 'a great sense of humour', as an intellectual and artistic leader with 'strong ideals and ideas'.[8]

Jellett grew up in a strong Church of Ireland atmosphere. Faith was 'taken for granted' and taken seriously.[9] The family attended services every Sunday and each morning Jellett's mother would insist on reading the Bible to her children and saying prayers with them. However, it appears that matters concerning faith and theology were not discussed among family members.[10]

As an adult Jellett worshipped regularly in the beautifully ornate Church of St Bartholomew, Clyde Road, in Dublin. The fact that she preferred this church to other, more 'ascetic', Protestant places of worship indirectly hints at what was also evidenced through other events in her life, namely an interest in and openness towards, and perhaps even a fascination with, Catholicism, in particular its rituals. Her attendance at St Bartholomew's Church is evidence of this, as well as an extract from a letter to her mother about a visit to a Lutheran service while on holiday in Lithuania in 1931: 'There was a cross on the Altar and four big candlesticks and what looked like a tabernacle ... and over the altar a disastrous picture of Christ ... It was much more like the Altar in a country R.C. Church. Apparently the Lutherans can have a cross and candles when we cant *(sic)*, and Luther was the founder of Protestantism!'[11] Her words indicate her obvious surprise at the very Catholic setting in this Lutheran church and regret, even a little jealousy, that in her

---

8. James White, Interview, 14.9.1995. Rosamund Phillips, Interview, 22.9.1995. Phillips points out: 'She was a terribly sincere person about her art and her religion.' Margot Moffett, 'Young Irish Painters', in *Horizon*, vol. xi, no. 64 (April 1945). Cf. also Brian O'Doherty, 'A Tribute to Evie Hone and Mainie Jellett' (review), *The Dublin Magazine*, vol. 32, no. 2 (1957), 59.
9. Phillips, Interview, 22.9.1995.
10. Ibid.
11. Extract from a letter by Jellett, in Arnold, *Mainie Jellett and the Modern Movement in Ireland*, 126.

church, as she had experienced it, items like candles and crosses were apparently absent.

Hilda van Stockum, a painter and friend of Jellett, comments: 'Evie thought [Jellett] wanted to become a Catholic but that she wasn't encouraged.'[12] When Hone decided to join the Roman Catholic Church in 1939 Jellett was happy and even relieved by the decision.[13] Likewise, Albert Gleizes, another person close to Jellett, had announced his conversion to Christian faith in 1918 and finally joined the Roman Catholic Church in 1941. Moreover, during her final illness, Jellett found greater comfort in the spiritual guidance of her Catholic friend, the Reverend Edward Leen, than from Canon Simpson of the Church of Ireland. Leen was President of Blackrock College, a prelate and a thinker who also had a real appreciation of contemporary art and supported Jellett in her cause.

One may conclude thus, that what mattered essentially to Jellett was faith in her art, and faith in and a personal relationship with Christ[14] which she could find and live amongst friends of different denominations and beliefs in a truly ecumenical spirit, rather than through a narrow preoccupation with the Church in which she had been raised.

Further, one, if not *the* most striking aspect in the life of this artist is her sense of mission, which grew and intensified as she followed without compromise her own path as a (semi-)abstract painter in the face of opposition and misunderstanding.[15] Although art commentators in Ireland at the time were only slowly emerging and tended to be enthusiastic rather than critical, which at times could lead to a romanticisation of their subjects, there are sufficient reliable sources to suggest that this sense of mission was stronger in

12. Van Stockum relates: Jellett and Hone 'were both Anglicans – of the Anglo-Catholic variety, leaning Towards (sic) Rome.' Hilda van Stockum, Letter to the author, 16.11.95.
13. In a letter to a mutual friend, the artist Margaret Clarke, she writes: 'I do wish she could find the *peace* of Christianity and trust she will find it in your Church and I wish she had made the move sooner.' Jellett quoted by Arnold in his article 'The Turning Point for Irish Modernism', in Brian P. Kennedy, (ed.), *Art is My Life: A Tribute to James White* (Dublin: National Gallery of Ireland, 1991), 13.
14. That faith in the crucified God was central to her life is supported by the fact that she regularly attended the Three Hour Agony on Good Fridays. Cf. White, 'Mainie Jellett, A Personal Memoir', in *Mainie Jellett 1897-1944* cat. (Dublin: Irish Museum of Modern Art, 1992), 11. Another, somewhat emotional, reference to Jellett's faith in Christ is found in a letter (addressed to Dorothea Janet (Bay) Jellett, the artist's sister) by a Sister Camisias who had looked after Jellett in the nursing home run by the Irish Sisters of Charity: 'I am sure Miss Jellett is praying for us – she ... had such a personal love for our ... Lord.' in Arnold, *Mainie Jellett and the Modern Movement in Ireland*, 202.
15. Máirín Allen, 'Contemporary Irish Artists, XI. Miss M.H. Jellett', *Father Matthew Record*, vol. 36, no. 4 (1942), 4.

Jellett than in other artists.[16] There are several contributing factors. She had chosen Gleizes as her teacher, who was a radical proponent of the new style in art. Jellett, Gleizes and their friends were well aware that they formed a small minority who had to fight their convictions. Moreover, Jellett's whole lifestyle revealed what her friend, the writer Elizabeth Bowen, described as the 'religious attitude' Jellett had towards her art which was compounded by 'self-abnegation and humility'.[17]

This ascetic, religious dimension in the life of the artist has been referred to by several persons who knew and/or have written about Jellett, such as White, Arnold and her sister Rosamund Phillips. Jellett, whose sexual preference may have been for women anyhow,[18] never married and seems to have lived as a celibate throughout her life. Thus she could devote herself entirely to her mission in art and in teaching. Shortly before her death she expresses this in her own words to Hone: 'I suppose I had a desire to impart the little I had to give. I felt it was not given to me just for myself.'[19] In 'Art as a Spiritual Force', she states in even stronger terms: 'The artist, no matter what happens, dares not lose his artistic integrity. To be an artist is a vocation, it is not an easy one ...'[20]

Jellett's almost 'metaphysical' awareness of having received something which she had to transmit to others, as well as her statement on the vocation of an artist, are revelatory of a fundamental link between the life of the believer and that of the artist, namely the essential element of faith and trust – in the divine and/or in one's work – and the task of witnessing to that faith through authenticity, decision and commitment, even at the risk of being misunderstood and rejected. It is obvious that in Jellett this almost 'monastic' devotion was exceptionally strong.

A pronounced ethical dimension, namely the responsibility that an artist has towards society, is another element in the life and views of this artist. It is connected with and perhaps grew out of her sense of mission and Gleizes'

16. Amongst others: White, Interview, 14.9.95. Kathleen Brennan, 'Mainie Jellett', *The Leader*, 26.2.1944. Brian Fallon, Interview, 20.10.95.
17. Elizabeth Bowen, 'Mainie Jellett', in *The Bell*, vol. 9, no. 3 (1944), 255. Bowen adds: 'Art to her was not an ivory tower but a fortress. ... she leaves with us a spirit fortified, and fortifying, by its belief.' (256)
18. The fact that her closest friend was a woman, that, apparently, she never had been romantically involved with a male and her excellence in painting the female nude provide some indications of her sexuality. Cf. also Paula Murphy, 'Re-reading Mainie Jellett', in *Mainie Jellett 1897-1944*, p. 33-44, who argues similarly.
19. Quoted by Bowen, in Bowen, op.cit., 254.
20. Jellett, 'Art as Spiritual Force', in MacCarvill, *The Artist's Vision*, 69.

influence of thought on this matter.[21] Jellett writes: 'Artists as a whole are people with certain gifts more highly developed than the majority, but for this very reason their gifts are vitally important to the mental and spiritual life of that majority.'[22] Far from the common perception of the artist as a kind of 'exotic flower set apart', she emphasises that the 'present enforced isolation' of the artist is to be rejected.[23] Artists should be appreciated as making their contribution to society, as a nation's art is 'one of the ultimate facts by which its spiritual health is judged and appraised by posterity'. Her ideas reflect what Gleizes had written already in 1923, when he stated that the most sincere artists are occupied with finding 'new laws which will bring the work of art into harmony with the needs of modern man...'.[24] Thus both Jellett and Gleizes would hardly have approved of the notion of *l'art pour l'art* as they proposed their idea of art being a spiritual and intellectual 'gift' to society.

Jellett's conviction about the social and ethical role of art should not lead to the conclusion that she would have held that the artist as a person has to be a rather virtuous, 'good' (Christian) woman or man. She points out that the 'artistic creative faculty' is independent and therefore not to be 'confused with any moral code'. An artist may come across as an egotistic, amoral person, yet when it comes to their art their artistic sincerity and integrity are manifest.

In the interdisciplinary dialogue of faith and art this question about personal character and artistic integrity has been raised by a number of writers, for example, in more recent times, by Richard Harries and Wendy Beckett,[25] whose arguments are very close to Jellett's and, I would suggest, appropriate and relevant in this dialogue as they grant the person of the artist a necessary autonomy and privacy. Also it is significant to note that Bernhard Häring, in his capacity as a Catholic moral theologian – although more cautious and more explicitly theological than Jellett, Harries and Beckett – expresses this in similar terms when he states that 'a true artist can never be a moralist'.[26] For Häring the artist is someone who is deeply intuitive, human, open and given to the search for truth and beauty which is the 'splendour of the true

21. The fact that she was a 'highly principled' woman, which White attributes to her Protestant background, also may have been an influence here. Cf. White, Interview, 14.9.1995.
22. Jellett, 'My Voyage of Discovery', in MacCarvill, op.cit., 49.
23. Ibid. Cf. also John Turpin, 'Irish Painting in a European Context', *Eirigh* (Jan. 1968), 22. Turpin stresses how Jellett 'repudiated the romantic vision of the artist in the garrett', separated from her/his fellow people.
24. Gleizes, 'Modern Art and the New Society', in *Cubism*, (Belfast, 1984), 9.
25. Cf. Richard Harries, *Art and the Beauty of God* (London: Mowbray, 1993), 49-50. Cf. Introduction in W. Beckett, *Art and the Sacred* (London: Rider, 1992), 5-26.
26. Bernhard Häring, *Free and Faithful in Christ*, vol. 2: *The truth will set you free* (Middlegreen: St Paul Publications, 1979), 119.

and the good'. Häring and Beckett, like Jellett, emphasise that only long contemplation can reveal the work of art which often involves a genuine effort
from the onlooker. In making an analogy between faith and art, Jellett even
goes so far as to state: 'In the end, it is only the great artist who can really
appreciate great art, as a great saint can penetrate the eternal beauties of the
faith.'[27]

Although Jellett does not actually use the Platonic and later Thomist idea
of beauty as splendour of truth and goodness, we can assume that she would
have agreed with it as she does insist that the question of art and truth are
closely connected.[28] Arnold adds that Jellett 'took Platonic ideals and
absorbed them into a Christianity which had huge emphasis on the spiritual, the nature of the spirit as sublime realisation of self'.[29]

In one of her lectures Jellett expounds her understanding of the 'eternal
quality', in a great work of art. Here she quotes and agrees with Aquinas' thesis that three elements pertain to beauty, *integritas, consonantia, claritas,*
wholeness, harmony and radiance.[30] She stresses, furthermore, that the true
work of art is creative, not just description, photography or imitation. More
particularly, the modern work of art is marked by a pronounced sense of
rhythm, i.e. an '*ordered* living movement'. She concludes that the work of art
is first 'born in the mind' from 'the joys, the sufferings, the gropings towards
the infinite, the almost burning joy that may come from the contemplation
of Nature's beauty in the highest sense. It is this emotion which is the starting point and without the evidence of this emotion a work of art is dead'.

For Jellett, then, the basis for the creation of a true work of art is intellectual ('born in the mind'), emotional ('joys … sufferings'), and religious,
transcendent and spiritual ('gropings towards the infinite … contemplation').
According to her, the spiritual dimension in a work of art comes about when
it is geometric rather than realistic, while a more material dimension is
encountered in those works that are realistic rather than geometric. Not
unlike Tillich, although in a different artistic context of argumentation, she

27. Jellett, 'Art as a Spiritual Force', in MacCarvill, op. cit., 69.
28. Jellett, 'The Importance of Rhythm in Modern Painting', in MacCarvill, op.cit., 102.
Arnold, Interview, 30.9.1995. On Plato's aesthetics cf. Michael Hauskeller, (ed.), *Was das
Schöne sei, Klassische Texte von Platon bis Adorno* (München: dtv, 1994), 14.
29. Arnold, Interview, 30.9.1995. In fact, Jellett kept to the end of her life an extract from
Plato's Philebus in which Socrates discusses the beauty of form. He insists that 'straight
lines and circles, and the plane or solid figures' are 'not only relatively beautiful … but …
eternally and absolutely beautiful'. Arnold, *Mainie Jellett and the Modern Movement in
Ireland,* 82-83. It is not surprising that because of her commitment to (semi-) abstract art
these lines would have appealed to her.
30. Jellett, 'The Importance of Rhythm in Modern Painting', in MacCarvill, op.cit., 101.
Aquinas based his aesthetics on Aristotle, who had modified Plato's concept of beauty.

would conclude therefore, that a non-representational (or non-realistic) painting tends to be more spiritual than a realistic work.

Jellett finds the rhythmic, spiritual, non-materialistic and creative aspect especially revealed in Eastern art. The artist in the East paints with an 'inner vision' while Western artists, through Renaissance perspective and 'photographic materialism', work with an 'outer vision'.[31] However, she concedes that in the West also inner vision and contemplation have been revealed in art, especially in those times when art and faith were closely linked, such as in early Christian, Celtic and Byzantine times when faith in the divine found simple expression in pictorial images.

Jellett repeatedly refers to her own age as an intensely materialistic age, in which the artist, with her or his spiritual ideals fights a difficult cause.[32] Nevertheless, she encourages her fellow artists to continue to struggle, to keep the 'sacred fire' burning as art is not only part of a civilisation but reveals to future generations the spirit and culture of past epochs. She points out that both, the art forms and the religious ideas, constitute a 'species of spiritual thermometer' of a particular age.[33] Although she does not consider her own age as one in which great art emerged, she argues – much along the lines of her teacher Gleizes – that the contemporary Cubist and Expressionist painters are laying the foundations for 'a new curve upwards' from which the art of the future will be born. This is prophetic as well as romantic language, and it is modern in spirit in its belief in progress and in the future. It implies a vision of herself and of fellow artists as those who prepare the way for a great epoch in art. One hardly needs to mention that in our age of pluralism, which applies to the arts as to all other spheres of life, Jellett's almost eschatological vision of this great future epoch has not (yet) become a reality.

However, in the Irish context, Mainie Jellett's contribution as an artist, teacher, lecturer, apologist and pioneer of modern art is beyond doubt. The last word on whether she belongs to the great painters of international modern art[34] or whether she was leading only in Ireland still remains to be written.[35]

31. Jellett, ibid., 98.
32. One has to take into account that Jellett wrote her articles between c. 1930 and 1942, i.e. in very unstable pre-war and war times.
33. Jellett, 'The Dual Ideal of Form in Art', in MacCarvill, op.cit., 67.
34. Arnold, Interview, 30.9.1995. Arnold considers Jellett as greater than Gleizes, Mondrian, Calder and Robert and Sonia Delaunay. '... in terms of paint and the resolution of abstract painting she is an outstanding figure in the twentieth century internationally, but completely unrecognized and ... it may be another century before they spot it.'
35. Anthony Butler argues that neither Jellett nor Hone were 'artists of the first order', but that they significantly brought forward the development of modern art in Ireland. Cf. A. Butler, 'The Irish Art Scene', Éire-Ireland, vol. 6, no. 1 (1971), 103. Cf. also Frances Ruane, 'Mainie Jellett Retrospective at IMMA', The Irish Times, 23.12.1991. Ruane writes

Finally, it seems right to conclude from what has been established above on the religious aspect in the life of this artist, that throughout her life and in her work Jellett drew considerable strength from her Christian faith. It was not a blind faith. Bigotry and narrow dogmatist perceptions would have been anathema to this committed painter. Faith in and obedience to Christ (and to her art) might reflect something of the Protestant *sola fide* in her life as a Christian believer. On one occasion, she told the former director of the National Gallery of Ireland, James White, that although she could understand Evie Hone's conversion to Catholicism, she 'was totally happy with her own church'.[36] Despite her obvious attraction to certain aspects of the Roman Catholic Church, especially to its rituals and her friendship with Reverend Edward Leen, her faith and her own tradition, which would have allowed for greater personal freedom and a less authoritarian atmosphere, appear to have provided an important source of support to her all her life.

that with regard to being internationally significant, Jellett was chronologically a little late. Fallon argues that Jellett's exaggerated reputation is an attempt 'to build a pedigree for Irish Modernism and so bring it, by hook or crook, into European mainstream'. Fallon, *Irish Art 1830-1990* (Belfast: Appletree Press, 1994), 187. It seems to me that Butler, Fallon and Ruane are correct in their assessment of Jellett's status as an artist.

36. Cf. White, 'Mainie Jellett, A Personal Memoir', in *Mainie Jellett 1897-1944*, 11.

II. JACK BUTLER YEATS

'High solitary art uniquely self-pervaded, one with its wellhead in a hidden-most spirit, not to be clarified in any other light ... Merely bow in wonder.'[37]

Jack Yeats, the youngest child of portrait painter John Butler Yeats and his wife Susan Pollexfen was born in London in 1871. While his brother William was destined to become Ireland's national poet, Jack Yeats would be recognised as the national artist and foremost Irish painter of the twentieth century. At the age of eight he went to live in Sligo with his Pollexfen grandparents, and it was Sligo which provided much of the inspiration for his drawings, watercolours and paintings. As he stated himself: 'Sligo was my school and the sky above it.'[38]

The local travellers, sailors, characters, circus performers, acrobats and tramps feature especially in his early work. Life in all its romance and vivacity, in its psychological, physical and spiritual aspects became the subject matter of his work.[39]

In 1887 Yeats joined his family in London. He attended art classes at Chiswick School of Art, Kensington School of Art and Westminster School of Art. Until 1897 he engaged mainly in black and white work for journal and book illustration.

In 1897 Yeats and Mary Cottenham White, a fellow artist whom he married in 1894, moved to Strete in Devon. He began to concentrate on watercolours; his first one-person show took place in London in 1897. During this time he formed a lasting friendship with the poet John Masefield. However, Yeats and his wife frequently visited Ireland, where they stayed with Lady Gregory at Coole. In 1905, Yeats went on a tour of the West of Ireland with John Millington Synge and provided illustrations for his friend's book *The Aran Islands*.

His friendship with those involved in the Gaelic Revival, his growing interest in the national aspirations of Ireland, and a corresponding realisation that England was ultimately a foreign country to him, were contributing factors which made the couple move to Ireland in 1910. They first took up residence in Greystones, County Wicklow, and in 1917 they moved to Dublin.

---

37. Samuel Beckett, 'Homage to Jack B. Yeats', in J. White, *Jack B. Yeats: Drawings and Paintings* (London: Secker and Warburg, 1971), 10.
38. Brian P. Kennedy, *Jack B. Yeats 1871-1957* (Dublin: Townhouse/The National Gallery of Ireland, 1991), 9.
39. H. Pyle, *Jack B. Yeats A Catalogue Raisonne of the Oil Paintings,* vol. 1 (London: André Deutsch, 1992), xix. Also B.P. Kennedy, ibid.

In 1897 Yeats painted his first oil. In 1909 he began to devote himself exclusively to oil painting. Over the following decade his brushstroke became freer and broader; a definite painterly quality emerged; the painter became quite dramatically aware of his artistic powers.[40] Works like the enormously energetic and expressive 'The Liffey Swim' (1923), or 'Flower Girl, Dublin' (1926) show how he had been breaking away entirely from his style as illustrator and print maker.

Several works of that time contain implicit and explicit political subject matter. Yeats, to whom 'the Free Staters were middle-class, while the Republicans represented all that was noble and free', remained an ardent patriot throughout his life.[41] His patriotic ideals were not narrow or militant, however, but influenced by his interest in socialism, a 'dedication to perfect life ... where no man was subject to another'.[42]

Contemporaries and critics have described the painter as 'unassuming', 'sincere', 'quiet', 'shy', as someone who had a 'contemplative', 'strongly independent mind' and who 'hated pomposity'.[43] Further, he had a 'sense of humour', 'contempt for humbug' and 'wide tolerance'.[44]

Yeats used to claim that he was little influenced by other painters. He admitted an admiration for Goya, nevertheless, and in his early works there is, as Hilary Pyle has shown, a definite influence of his friend Walter Sickert, the leading English contemporary painter. Daumier also held an attraction for Yeats, and his work has been compared to Turner, Watteau and Mancini, among others. Later in life Yeats was acquainted with and visited by Kokoschka. However, Pyle points out that his late style, i.e. his great period, was not influenced by anybody; he was very much 'his own' painter.

In the 1930s Yeats was acclaimed as an artist of international status. He exhibited in Toronto and New York. During this time the artist painted relatively little. Yeats became interested in self-expression by means of the word.

40. Pyle, *Catalogue Raisonne*, xxiv.
41. Pyle, *A Biography Jack B. Yeats,* revised edn., (London: André Deutsch, 1989), 119. Edward Sheehy writes in 1945: '[Yeats] is the most national of Irish painters' ... 'he certainly did collaborate in that renaissance of the spirit which culminated in the Rebellion and the Anglo-Irish war; and by so doing he liberated his art from the hitherto unrelieved provinciality of painting in Ireland.' Sheehy, 'Jack B. Yeats', *The Dublin Magazine,* vol. 20 (July-Sept. 1945), 39-40.
42. Pyle, op.cit., 119.
43. Máirín Allen, 'Contemporary Irish Artists VII. Jack B. Yeats, R.H.A.', *Father Mathew Record,* vol. 35, no. 12 (Dec. 1941), 3. M. Allen, 'Jack Yeats: An Impression', *The Capuchin Annual* (1942), 586. Pyle, *A Biography Jack B. Yeats,* 170.
44. Kathleen O'Brennan, 'Jack B. Yeats, The Man and His Work', *The Leader,* 18.12.1943, 349. C.P. Curran, 'The Yeats Exhibition', *The Capuchin Annual* (1945-1946), 106.

He wrote several plays and novels during the decade, notably *Sailing, Sailing Swiftly* (1933) and *The Amaranthers* (1936).

The 1940s were to be Yeats' most prolific period when, as Pyle writes, he 'attained a masterly facility with the brush' and excels as a colourist, but he never became a technician or craftsperson. During this decade and into the 1950s, Yeats, the Irish Romantic Expressionist, paints his great works in which the transition from the local to the universal is evident. His late work is marked by an expanding vision, by intuition and emotion, by a search for the universal in the local 'much as Joyce was doing with his memories of Dublin'.[45] Many of these paintings reveal profound existentialist preoccupations. A few, like 'Tinkers' Encampment – The Blood of Abel' (1940) or 'There is no Night' (1949), contain biblical and religious references and associations.

In the last fifteen years of his life, exhibitions in Dublin, London, Washington and Paris at last confirmed the painter's international status. Yeats belongs to the great artists of the twentieth century. One suggests that had he lived in central Europe – like his compatriots Joyce and Beckett – he would have been appreciated as such more emphatically and much earlier.

* * *

Although Yeats talked about his painting at times, he was a private, even enigmatic man, and, on the whole, reticent about his life and work. Unlike Jellett, who wrote and lectured on art, Yeats held that a painting speaks for itself, that it does not require translation and that knowledge of the artist's private life and views should not matter to the spectator.[46]

Any discussion of the religious dimension in his life and work will therefore be tentative, especially since personal statements by the artist in this regard are rather scarce.

What is certain is Jack Yeats' faith in the Christian God. How he would have defined his faith, which aspects of it would have mattered to him in particular, and what significance he would have attributed to the fact that there are explicit biblical/theological allusions in a number of his works is, however, more difficult to ascertain.

---

45. B.P. Kennedy, *Jack B. Yeats*, 25. Cf. also on the universal aspect of Yeats' late work Bruce Arnold, *Irish Art* (London: Thames and Hudson, 1977), 136; and cf. Arnold, 'Noble Deeds: Jack B. Yeats', *Éire-Ireland*, vol. 6, no. 2 (1971), 40.
46. 'A picture does not need translation. A creative work happens. It does not need documentary evidence, dates, photographs of the artist, or what he says about his pictures. It doesn't matter who or what I am. People may think what they will of the pictures.' Yeats quoted in B.P. Kennedy, 'Jack B. Yeats, An Irish Romantic Expressionist', *Apollo* (March 1991), 194.

Unlike his brother, Yeats spent some formative years of his childhood with his mother's parents in Sligo. In temperament he took after her rather than his father. Arnold points out that his mother was a devoted Christian; 'faith and belief were part of the structural life' of her Protestant family background.[47] William Pollexfen, Yeats' grandfather, was 'a staunch Christian ... in the best sense because he sought to do good, to help people'.[48] Not surprisingly thus Christian faith and to some extent, at least, communal worship were to have lasting importance in the artist's life.

As an adult, and, it seems, especially in later life, Yeats attended Church of Ireland services in Dublin at his local Church, St Stephen's in Mount Street, and St Patrick's Cathedral. He was not, as Arnold stresses, a 'fervent Christian like ... Jellett', but 'he observed Christianity' and he particularly loved the music at services.[49]

An indication that his faith was not a narrow denominational one, but rather as open and non-judgemental as his views on other aspects of life,[50] is the fact that he attended the first mass of his fellow painter and Roman Catholic priest Jack Hanlon in the early 1940s. This would have been a somewhat unusual ecumenical gesture at the time, an act of friendship and solidarity in recognition of Hanlon's vocation as both painter and priest.

Pyle writes that Yeats never stated 'anything specific' about his faith.[51] Unlike other artists, he apparently did not feel the need to explore and express his spirituality and faith in any other way than through the one in which he had been brought up. His niece, Anne Yeats, relates similarly that she never discussed religious issues with her uncle, but that church and faith would have been important to him, although probably not in a most orthodox manner. Artist and critic Brian O'Doherty (Patrick Ireland) writes in an obituary in 1957 that although one can only conjecture what exactly Yeats 'formally believed in', it was 'always obvious that he believed'.[52] O'Doherty goes on to suggest that Yeats always believed in humanity: 'He had the understanding which gave belief a dimension which was not blind, but had an affectionate warmth ... Fully human, he sought his own personal truth, no matter how painfully ... Unattached to the arrogance of despair [after his wife's death in 1947], his individuality was directed inwards to belief – in the

47. Bruce Arnold, Interview, 30.9.1995.
48. Ibid.
49. Ibid.
50. Various critics and those who were close to Yeats have referred to his refraining from making judgements on other people, e.g. Anne Yeats, Interview, 13.10.95.
51. Pyle, *Catalogue Raisonne*, lxvi.
52. Brian O'Doherty, 'Obituary Jack Butler Yeats, 1871-1957', *Dublin Magazine*, vol. 32, no. 3 (1957), 55.

spirit, in man, in art – and outwards to the world seen with sympathy and understanding ...'[53]

Yeats refrained from constructing theories of art or aesthetics; he made a few statements, however, which are relevant to the present discussion. He basically conceived art to be the 'greatest' and 'freest' means of communication.[54] He exclaimed that paintings in order 'to be fine must have some of the living ginger of Life in them'.[55] This concern with the energy of life, with humanity, especially the 'common' people, is at the centre of Yeats' work and thought, arising out of the artist's affection for his fellow human beings.

'Affection' is the key term to Yeats' understanding of art, the artist and our relationship with others. He states: "The roots of true Art are in the affections, no true artist stands aloof."[56] Affection is the 'greatest tribute' an artist could feel for his/her subject. The true artist, Yeats thought, must be part of the life and land in which he or she lives, they must be given to their work without compromise. For the artist affection and beauty are one: 'The Beautiful is the Affection that one person or thing feels for another person or thing, either in life, or in the expression of the arts.'[57]

One may conclude hence, that for Yeats, love (affection), beauty and truth are deeply connected. Beauty and truth come out of love. Passionate love and emotional engagement with what he paints, the act of painting itself, are the elements which matter most to Yeats and make him the Romantic Expressionist and national artist.

It is interesting to note that there are, in fact, some parallels between Yeats and the Romantic painters, thinkers and writers. One of the most striking links is the aspect of personal and social freedom. The French Revolution with its demand for equality, fraternity and liberty, Jean Jacques Rousseau's 'Man is born free, and everywhere he is in chains' and his dream of a world where slavery is abolished and people live in harmony with nature,[58] Schleiermacher's insistence that the person can 'only perceive her/himself as freedom'[59] illustrate the Romantics' preoccupation with freedom. Moreover, Friedrich Schlegel even goes so far as to say that since the artist presents a unique vision that may be prophetic of emerging sensibilities in a culture, the

---

53. Ibid.
54. Pyle, *A Biography Jack B. Yeats,* 104.
55. Ibid., viii.
56. Ibid., 104.
57. Ibid., 103.
58. Jean Jacques Rousseau, *The Social Contract and Discourses* (London: Everyman's Library, 1973), 165, 169-172.
59. F.E.D. Schleiermacher, 'Monologen. 1800', in Heinz Bolli, (ed.), *Schleiermacher-Auswahl* (Gütersloh: Gütersloher Verlagshaus Gerd Mohn, 1983), 78.

artist has thus a religious vocation, making his or her work an offering to the divine. Here painters like William Blake, Caspar David Friedrich, who was acquainted with Schleiermacher and Philip Otto Runge come to mind.

Like the Romantics, Yeats works against the background of social and political upheaval. Throughout his life he is interested in the life of the 'common people', in social and republican affairs, in his country's right to freedom and self-determination. It therefore does not come as a surprise that he admires Goya, the most political of all the Romantic artists.

Another link with the Romantics is imagination and fantasy. Friedrich von Schelling in his extensive writing on the nature of art emphasised that art is art because it reveals the world and the Absolute in a way that only it can.[60] Imagination *(Einbildungskraft)* for him is a central prerequisite and key to the making of art. Likewise, what distinguishes Yeats is his amazing imagination that he translates onto canvas. Arnold points out that Yeats' 'spirituality and imagination are themselves the driving forces in his character as a painter' and that 'his imaginative creativity was a powerful transcending force in his life'.[61] O'Doherty describes Yeats as 'possessor of an imagination of the highest order' and as 'lover of fantasy'.[62] As Pyle has emphasised, a sense of adventure, imagination and fantasy which is not escapist but 'rooted in real life' is central to many of Yeats' paintings.

Schelling stresses the momentary aspect of a work of art; it is the moment that is captured which makes the work eternal.[63] Yeats who always held that, for him at any rate, a picture 'just happened' inexplicably, evokes Schelling's view when he states: 'The finest picture in the world will give the finest moment finest felt by the finest soul with the finest memory.'[64] A statement such as this one shows that Yeats, like Schelling, emphasised the moment which is rendered in a work of art. Moreover, as his previous statement reveals, Yeats held that no one creates, rather the artist 'assembles memories'. This focus on memory features both in his paintings and writings. In his play *In Sand,* for example, one of the characters, the old sailor, says: 'Memory is always a good garden to fall back on ... Well they've all got two sorts. The

60. Andrew Bowie, *Schelling and Modern European Philosophy,* An Introduction (London: Routledge, 1993), 52.
61. Arnold, Interview, 30.9.1995.
62. O'Doherty, 'Irish Painter, Jack B. Yeats', *The Irish Monthly,* vol. 80, no. 947 (May 1952), 203.
63. F.W.J. von Schelling, 'Über das Verhältnis der bildenden Künste zu der Natur' (1807), in Manfred Schröter, (ed.), *Schellings Werke,* 3. Ergänzungsbd. (München: C.H. Beck'sche Verlagsbuchhandlung, 1959), 403.
64. Yeats quoted in Pyle, *A Biography Jack B. Yeats,* 105.

ones they talk of and the ones they keep to themselves.'[65] In relating memory to garden, Yeats thus points to the fertile, rhythmic nature of growth and fading of memories. He differentiates between those memories one discloses to others and those which, presumably out of privacy, guilt or pain, one keeps to oneself. Yeats holds that a good artist realises thus that he or she is no more than a conduit. What is painted is a moment transmitted through memory that in its momentariness becomes eternal or 'infinite', as the Romantics put it.

Finally, what drives both Yeats and Romantic artists and thinkers like Schlegel, Friedrich or Turner is passion, vision and emotion. 'Vision' has been repeatedly used by a number of commentators especially in relation to Yeats' late works like, for example, 'Men of Destiny' (1946), in which this dimension is particularly evident.[66] However, it would be wrong to conclude that Yeats was guided by vision and feeling at the expense of reason and rational judgement. Yeats does not come across as an enthusiast, but as someone in whose personality intellectual and common sense, youthful curiosity and deep emotion are balanced. One may assume therefore that it is also rather unlikely that he would have agreed with Schleiermacher's definition of religion. The foremost Romantic theologian held that religion is primarily contemplation and feeling, rather than thinking and action.[67] Furthermore, Schleiermacher conceived religion as 'sense and taste for the infinite'. It is to be suggested that, out of his nationalist and social concern alone, Yeats would have clearly advocated the element of social action and thinking in what constitutes living faith. However, Schleiermacher's awareness that religion must relate to the human situation, and that in order to find religion one must first find humanity, which can only happen through love,[68] concurs with the prevailing aspect of affection and with the humanist concerns in Yeats' life.

A central aspect in Yeats' work is tragedy and death. Yeats' perception of death is revealed in both his paintings and writings. Pyle comments that in his works which contain political subjects, Yeats does not portray moments of sacrifice or conflict, but 'the tragic or removed emotions of those who live

65. Robin Skelton, (ed.), *The Selected Writings of Jack B. Yeats* (London: André Deutsch, 1991), 216.
66. On the visionary quality in his work cf. Elizabeth Rivers, 'Modern Painting in Ireland', *Studies*, vol. 50, no. 198 (Summer 1961), 180. Daniel Shields refers to Yeats as the 'creator of visions'. D. Shields, S.J., 'Memories of Some Recent Art Exhibitions in Dublin', *The Irish Monthly*, vol. 76 (Jan. 1948), 39.
67. Schleiermacher, 'Über die Religion. Reden an die Gebildeten unter ihren Verächtern' (1799), in *Schleiermacher-Auswahl*, 6. 'Ihr [Religion] Wesen ist weder Denken noch Handeln, sondern Anschauung und Gefühl.'
68. Ibid., 9. '... um Religion zu haben, muss der Mensch erst die Menschheit gefunden haben, und er findet sie nur in Liebe und durch Liebe.'

on'.[69] The metaphysical and the transcendent, transience and mortality are very much evident in his paintings of the 1940s and 1950s. John Berger wrote that for Yeats death is 'the condition of human consciousness and therefore for freedom – there has been no artist [since] Watteau ... who has dealt with ... [this] subject so poignantly and unsentimentally. Thus Yeats' theme is universal.'[70]

When the artist painted his late works he had witnessed the Irish War of Independence, the Civil War and two world wars as well as the death of close family members. The existentialist, tragic element in his paintings (e.g. 'Grief', 1951) is therefore one which arose out of personal experience. However, Berger is correct when he points out that Yeats' work does not reveal the sense of personal desperation which one encounters in mid-European Expressionism, but rather that it has to do with and develops out of his vision of a liberated Ireland. His great universal works are not morbid, hopeless, or depressing. The transcendent and eschatological aspect rather spring from Yeats' celebration of and belief in freedom and life. Life and death are not separated realities, but complementary ones.

Dermot Lane has stressed that the use of symbol is a primary feature in eschatological language.[71] Moreover, eschatology is not to be reduced to concern with the *eschata,* the last things, but our whole existence as followers of Christ is eschatological in that the kingdom of God is not simply a future event but is already anticipated and to some extent realised in our present existence as God is active in creation.[72] Being Christian means to live in the tension between the already and the not yet.

What and exactly how Yeats believed we do not know. He has been described, however, as a 'profoundly religious man'.[73] MacGreevy, somewhat surprisingly, even considered Yeats and Wilhelmina Geddes to be the two 'truly religious' modern Irish artists. Further, Yeats' late work contains a pronounced eschatological dimension. Not only is Yeats' language in his writings and his expression in his late paintings full of symbolism, but, moreover, one finds in his work a sense of life as journey, as well as specific references to

69. Pyle, *A Biography Jack B. Yeats,* 119.
70. John Berger, 'Jack Yeats', *Selected Essays and Articles, The Look of Things* (Harmondsworth: Pelican/Penguin, 1971), 56.
71. Dermot Lane, 'Eschatology', in J.A. Komonchak, M. Collins, D.A. Lane, (eds.), *The New Dictionary of Theology* (Dublin: Gill and Macmillan, 1987), 329.
72. Ibid., 342. Cf. also for a more extensive account on this issue D. Lane, *Keeping Hope Alive, Stirrings in Christian Eschatology* (Dublin: Gill and Macmillan, 1996), 2-4, 17.
73. Arnold, Communication, 1.9.1995.

Christ's redemptive sacrifice, to hope and the 'promised land'.[74] In his work one encounters a sense of the prophetic, of anticipation of the future in the present, of the reality of suffering and tragedy which is transcended ultimately by the promise of redemption. Immanence and transcendence, life and death, creation, i.e. the fullness of life, and salvation are closely bound up. This is evident in works like 'For the Road', painted in 1951, or in the play *The Silencer* when Hartigan, one of the main characters, says in his last speech before his death: 'All deaths are game deaths, death sees to that. It's the penultimate moment that shakes the brave.' Death is the challenge, but it is not the end. As Skelton points out, death for Yeats is not a conclusion 'but a continuance and a change of perspective and brings an understanding and recognition of the overall rhythm of the universe'.[75]

Ultimately Yeats' art and implicitly his faith are therefore about hope. It seems right to suggest that his ideas of death and redemption were essentially coloured by his Christian faith. Yeats does not preach it, he neither judges nor does he display a simplistic or dogmatist theology in his ideas and work. His late paintings reveal an eschatological faith where death is finally transcended by hope.[76] It is not an easy optimism for a life hereafter where all is well. It is hope arising from his own experience of illness and depression (1915-1916), and a real sense of the human predicament of suffering and mortality. Thus it is genuinely felt and understood. It is here that remarkable parallels between contemporary eschatological-theological concerns and Yeats are manifested. His work explicitly, and his faith thus implicitly, reflect something of the deep link between creation, redemption and consummation.

Moreover, the revelation of vision drawn from boundless imagination, of transcendence and of hope in Yeats reflect Lane's affirmation that eternal life is not simply a continuation of this life but 'something qualitatively different, new and transformative ... The logic of Christian hope is not the logic of inference but rather the logic of imagination'.[77] It is such imagination and the possibility of complete transformation that we find in Yeats.

Hope is the final message in the artist's oeuvre, and it is hope which is central to Christian eschatological faith (Rom 15:13, 1 Cor 13:13). Jürgen Moltmann, in particular, has expounded a theology of hope. Faith and hope

74. John Purser, *The Literary Works of Jack B. Yeats* (Gerrard's Cross: Colin Smythe, 1991), p. 118. Purser observes, that religious imagery is developed in a few of Yeats' novels: Christ's sacrifice and suffering are 'deliberately evoked at the end of The Careless Flower'. Love, hope and charity are 'deliberately part' of The Amaranthers. (139)

75. Skelton, *The Selected Writings of Jack B. Yeats*, 26.

76. O'Doherty comments: His paintings were always of joy, of hope, of the promise hidden in tragedy.' O'Doherty, 'Obituary', op.cit., 57.

77. Lane, 'Eschatology', in op.cit., 342.

are inseparable as through faith we find our path to true life in Christ and it is hope that keeps us on this path.[78] God in the Hebrew Scriptures and in the New Testament is the God of promise (Heb 10:23); God's faithfulness to and fulfilment of God's promise is ultimately revealed in the resurrection of God's Son, Jesus Christ. Because God is faithful to us in the sacrifice and resurrection of Jesus we can hope and trust in faith. Yet, Christian hope for eternal life does not deny the reality of life and death. On the contrary, only the one who fully lives, i.e. who is open to love and suffering, to happiness and pain, can fully die.[79] Death belongs to life and is part of it. It is unconditional love that anticipates eternal life in the present and therefore transcends death. As Moltmann points out in 'the Spirit of the resurrection, eternal life is experienced here and now, in the midst of the life that leads to death; it is experienced as unconditional love'.[80]

It is in these dimensions of life fully realised and transcendent precisely because it is loved and lived to the full, of promise hidden in tragedy and of a hope that does not deny the reality of death and temptation of despair, that one encounters the points of convergence between eschatological theology and Yeats. In the words of his friend Samuel Beckett: Yeats 'is with the great of our time ... he brings light, as only the great dare to bring light, to the issueless predicament of our existence.'[81]

78. Jürgen Moltmann, *Theology of Hope* (New York: Harper & Row, 1975), 20.
79. Moltmann, *God in Creation* (London: SCM, 1985), 268-270.
80. Ibid., 270.
81. Samuel Beckett quoted in B.P. Kennedy, *Jack B. Yeats 1871-1957*, 34.

III. LOUIS LE BROCQUY

Louis le Brocquy, who, after Jack Yeats, has become Ireland's most internationally recognised artist, was born to Irish parents in 1916. He counts amongst his forebears a Franco-Belgian grandfather; hence the name. After secondary school le Brocquy studied chemistry in Trinity College and worked simultaneously at his grandfather's oil refinery in Dublin.[82]

However, he soon realised that his vocation lay elsewhere. In 1938 the artist *in spe*, accompanied by his young wife Jean Stoney, left Ireland to study art in the great galleries of London, Paris, Venice and especially Geneva where the Prado collection of art was housed for safe-keeping during the Spanish Civil War. In 1939 le Brocquy settled in Menton, France; in 1940 he returned to Ireland. Le Brocquy's work in the 1940s and 1950s is concerned with the life of the travelling people, with children and with the isolation of the individual as, for example, in 'The Family' (1951). His semi-cubist angular and linear style at the time evokes Picasso, Braque and Nicholson. In 1945 the art dealer Charles Gimpel took note of le Brocquy; in 1947 the artist was invited to exhibit in the Gimpel Fils Gallery in London, where he had moved the previous year.[83]

During these years the painter also developed an interest in tapestry. Like Mainie Jellett, le Brocquy feels strongly that an artist should be useful to society and not merely be regarded as an eccentric outsider.[84] Woven in Aubusson, several of his highly praised tapestries contain imagery based on the biblical story of creation, such as 'Adam and Eve in the Garden' (1952).

In 1958 le Brocquy married his second wife, the Irish artist Anne Madden with whom he moved to the French Midi in the same year. During this time he began his long series of white paintings of torsos and human presences. Again there is a pervading sense of isolation, vulnerability and, at times, horror in the depiction of his subjects. The artist comments that this atmosphere of isolation arose out of his 'preoccupation with the human condition', the simple assertion that 'the final human reality is the individual'.[85]

After twenty-five years of work, le Brocquy experienced a halt in 1963, which, close to despair, led him to destroy forty-three paintings. A visit to the Musée de L'Homme in Paris was to be the turning point, where he found exhibits of Polynesian and Melanesian heads. In the following year he dis-

82. Dorothy Walker, *Louis le Brocquy* (Dublin: Ward River Press, 1981), 20.
83. Louis le Brocquy, *Images 1975-1987* (Dublin: Arts Council, 1987), 73.
84. Harriet Cooke, [Interview with] 'Louis le Brocquy', *The Irish Times*, 25.5.1973, 12.
85. Le Brocquy quoted in an Interview with H. Cooke, *The Irish Times* (1957), in Walker, *Louis le Brocquy*, 38.

covered the Celtic image as revealed in the Celto-Ligurian head cult in Provence and Clonfert in Ireland.

From then on le Brocquy began to concentrate on his major theme, the images of heads. He states in 1977 that he was fascinated with the mutability of faces and that he 'began to conceive the *head (sic)* as an image of the whole in the part'.[86] Le Brocquy's initial paintings of 'ancestral heads' in 1964 were followed by over one hundred studies of the head of William Butler Yeats as well as by series on Joyce, Lorca, Beckett, Strindberg, Shakespeare and the painter Francis Bacon. An affirmation and admiration for the great tradition of twentieth-century Irish literature and personal encounters with Yeats, Beckett and Bacon were less influential in his choice of subject matter than their existence as instances of human consciousness at its furthest reaches.

Le Brocquy's work does not fall into a particular category; he does not belong to a particular school or movement. His method has been compared to that of Joyce and Proust. Walker points out that it also seems to reflect a certain Irish character in its rejection of anything rigid and fixed; this is expressed in the artist's reliance on the accidental, on the unforeseen in the emergence of an image.[87]

Le Brocquy's work has been exhibited in museums in several European countries, in Australia, Japan and the United States. He divides his time between the South of France and Ireland, continuing his obsession with the image of the human head.

* * *

In his youth le Brocquy was, as he himself states, very religious, in fact, he secretly believed that he was to become a monk.[88] However, in his last year at primary school he experienced the painful loss of faith due to the doctrinaire Roman Catholic teachings in his school on mariology, on the question of salvation of non-Roman Catholics and on the concept of transubstant-

86. Bernard Noël, 'Commitment of the imagination', (Interview with le Brocquy, trans. from French), in *Introspect,* no. 3 (Dec. 1977), 29.
87. On the 'Irishness' in his method see Walker, op.cit., 57. In her comparison of the Joycean and Proustian methods with le Brocquy she emphasises that the similarities are to be found in the 'explication of the moment of epiphany or revelation' in a work of art in which *essence* rather than an aesthetic concern is emphasised (Joyce), as well as in the sudden, involuntary memories 'sparked off by unforeseen incidents' (Proust). Incidentally a major exhibition by le Brocquy at the Musée d'Art Moderne de la Ville de Paris was titled 'A la recherche de W.B. Yeats'. Cf. Walker, op.cit., 57-58.
88. Interview, 20.9.1995. *Note:* Unless otherwise indicated, all points of information and quotations are from this interview. Cf. also Anne Madden le Brocquy, *Louis Le Brocquy, A Painter, Seeing His Way* (Dublin: Gill and Macmillan, 1994),16.

iation which for him seemed entirely metaphysical and little related to actuality.[89]

Since then le Brocquy has, as he says, 'never been quite able to get back to the idea ... of a personal God, the idea of a [individual] God, with a consciousness analogous to if infinitely wider and deeper than human consciousness'. Although he concedes that during the course of life one might at times be 'tempted' to believe in such a God, he holds that he has 'no real indication of it', and that perhaps adherence to a revealed God may be due to the human desire 'for such a being, [for] a kind of father figure' as the critics of religion have pointed out.

Le Brocquy, however, in no way denies the realm of the spiritual and the transcendent. He has described himself as someone who does not hold definite religious views, as an 'agnostic, who tries to keep his window on to reality as widely open as possible'.[90] Central to his understanding of ultimate reality is the sense of mystery which is, as he states 'the constant lying underneath ... which cannot be explained by science'. Although he points out that he feels uncomfortable with the Christian dogma of revelation, he emphasises that throughout life he has 'perceived ... a profound mystery, which is *absolutely* unexplained by any kind of dialectical materialism or other philosophies' and which causes him above all 'wonder' and 'curiously enough, a sense of belonging'. It is this 'deep reality', this 'mysterious source' from which all life and intelligence derives which, as he sees it, one might tentatively name God. This underlying and life-giving mystery, he comments, may also explain the biblical assertion about humans being made in the image of God.

Le Brocquy has been impressed and influenced in his thought by the physicist Erwin Schrödinger and by Teilhard de Chardin. Strange as it might seem, I would argue that it is his interest in science that to a great extent lays a foundation to his perception of the transcendent in the broadest sense.[91] The artist was 'tremendously struck' when Schrödinger told him that matter could be transformed beyond all recognition but that it could never be destroyed.[92] Consciousness, Schrödinger argues, is 'never experienced in the plural, only in the singular'; a plurality of consciousness in one mind is

89. Cf. Madden le Brocquy, ibid. Also L. le Brocquy, Interview, 20.9.1995: '... I was very much disillusioned by ... the stupidities of those people who were appointed to teach us boys what we should and what we should not believe. And they were so absurd that one objected but one objected, of course, in a very banal and facile way.'
90. From an Interview with Michael Peppiatt (1977) quoted in Walker, *Louis le Brocquy*, 68.
91. Cf. Madden le Brocquy, op.cit., 57, 63, 182.
92. Cf. Interview with M. Peppiatt, in Walker, op.cit., 68.

unthinkable.[93] Moreover, the Austrian physicist-philosopher believed that consciousness, i.e. mind or spirit, likewise is indestructible. Schrödinger acknowledged that in stating such a belief he was 'talking religion, not science – a religion, however, not opposed to science', but supported by what scientific research had established.[94]

In his belief in and in his search for what lies underneath, for essence, le Brocquy's views and his art do not only have something in common with Schrödinger but also with scientist-theologians such as Teilhard de Chardin, John Polkinghorne and Thomas F. Torrance. Le Brocquy has had an interest in Teilhard's theories on the evolution of consciousness, especially in the 'noo-sphere', the 'Earth's thinking envelope', which, as Teilhard states, surrounds the biosphere like a halo.[95] Le Brocquy very much believes in the power of thought as something 'more real, more deeply real than the matter which is said to cerebrally control and project it'. Thought is a 'real force' which, metaphorically speaking, can 'move mountains'. For le Brocquy prayer is essentially a form of thought: '... I am quite certain that the prayer in the sense of thinking in a benign and care-ful (sic) way about others, possibly even those who are dead, may effect things ... I have always tended to practice that in a sense ... because I *do* think it *has* an effect and therefore I should in this limited way 'pray' more than I do ...' Although le Brocquy refers to the role of thought in the individual rather than in the totality of humankind, as Teilhard does, his emphasis on the vital force of thought reflects something of de Chardin's own idea of the power of thinking and reflection in the noo-sphere.[96]

What lies at the heart of the discourse on theology and natural science is, as Polkinghorne comments, the affirmation that both explore aspects of reality.[97] Polkinghorne stresses the necessity of a natural theology as God is not only the totally other but is revealed and known in creation, in human experience and through reason.[98] Torrance points out that it is in the dialogue between the natural sciences and theology, in the striving for a unitary rather than a dualistic outlook on the universe where 'natural theology has its nat-

93. Erwin Schrödinger, *Mind and Matter* (Cambridge: Cambridge University Press, 1958), 55-56. Also Walker, op.cit., 43.
94. Schrödinger, 62.
95. Madden le Brocquy, op.cit., 182. Teilhard de Chardin, *The Heart of Matter* (London: Collins, 1978), 31, 36.
96. Cf. de Chardin, op.cit., 35-39.
97. John Polkinghorne, *One World, The Interaction of Science and Theology* (London: SPCK, 1986), xi.
98. Cf. Chapter One on natural theology in Polkinghorne, *Science and Creation, The Search for Understanding* (London: SPCK, 1988), 1-16.

ural place'.[99] Or, as Teilhard put it in more simple terms, it was in the encounter 'with those material things' like gravel and topographical surfaces, through which he found a 'fresher contact with the roots of the spirit'.[100]

It is to be suggested that le Brocquy's painting method, the images themselves and his views to some extent are analogical to what these scholars are trying to achieve in their interdisciplinary study on science and theology. Le Brocquy describes painting as 'an archaeology of the spirit'.[101] This definition implies a merging of the scientific and the spiritual, of the immanent and the transcendent, the physical and the metaphysical. Unlike many other twentieth-century artists, he is not primarily interested in self-expression, but considers art to be a 'groping towards an image'.[102] He views the artist as a 'watcher'; who by stirring the surface waits for something to happen until, by way of accident, an image emerges. Le Brocquy points out that he strives for the *quidditas,* the 'whatness' of things. It is the attempt to discover in those heads an 'image underlying the ever-changing external appearance'.[103] In painting one tries, as he says, 'to discover, to uncover, to reveal'.[104] In all his paintings of heads he is trying to reach glimpses of the essence of the person imaged,[105] the 'interior landscape' behind the face, while being fully aware that 'one never arrives', that it is always a reaching *towards* essence.

This quest for essence in Yeats, Joyce, *et al,* or in his anonymous ancestral heads is what gives le Brocquy's work its metaphysical, spiritual and transcendent dimension. Not only are these dimensions apparent in his work, but le Brocquy has, in fact, noted that like medieval art up to c. 1300, the predominantly two-dimensional art of the twentieth century is once again conceptual, or inward-looking in its view and expression of reality.[106] The medieval artist 'gazed inwards for truth', his/her art was 'essentially spiritual'.[107] Le Brocquy stated in 1950 that the contemporary, subjective artist,

99. Cf. Thomas Forsyth Torrance, *The Ground and Grammar of Theology* (Belfast: Christian Journals Ltd., 1980), 106, 177.
100. Thomas M. King, S.J., Mary Wood Gilbert, *The Letters of Teilhard de Chardin and Lucile Swan* (Washington D.C.: Georgetown University Press, 1993), 13.
101. Le Brocquy, 'Notes on painting and awareness', in Walker, op.cit., 138.
102. Le Brocquy, 'Notes on painting and awareness', in Walker, *Louis le Brocquy,* 138.
103. B. Noël, 'Commitment of the imagination', (Interview with le Brocquy), in *Introspect,* no. 3 (Dec. 1977), 29.
104. Le Brocquy, ibid.
105. In his search for this essence, the physical appearance of his subjects provides the point of departure. Whether he has known them personally (Beckett, Heaney) or not (Joyce) thereby does not seem to make any great difference.
106. Cf. extract from an article by le Brocquy (*Arc 17,* RCA, London, 1956) in Walker, op.cit., 25-26.
107. Le Brocquy, 'The Artist Speaks', *Envoy,* vol. 4, no. 15 (1950), 38.

too, looks inward for truth, he or she is interested in 'the metaphysical reality of matter; matter seen ... from the inside out'.[108]

For le Brocquy the artist is primarily concerned with penetrating reality.[109] Polkinghorne, as stated above, holds that the same applies to the theologian and the scientist. Schrödinger even went so far as to say that it was his fundamental conviction that true art and true science of any kind are all 'essentially the same thing and aim at the same thing'.[110] Moreover, le Brocquy's view obviously has an affinity also with Tillich's central thesis of art as revelation of ultimate reality.

The spiritual strain in le Brocquy's ideas and work is enforced by the painter's actual perception of the human face or head, which, as he points out, is a 'mysterious box', 'the outer reality of the invisible interior world of consciousness'.[111] It is paradoxically 'at once a mask which hides the spirit and a revelation, an incarnation of the spirit'.

Over twenty years ago le Brocquy stated that since the advent of psychology, cinema and photography, one single, definitive image is no longer possible, hence his series of paintings on one subject. This, as Richard Kearney has observed, puts him into the postmodern perspective of ambiguity, ambivalence and plurability, from which his oeuvre must be assessed.[112]

Le Brocquy himself has repeatedly referred to the ambivalence in the head images. This sense of ambivalence is present as the human being in our postmodern age is seen as facetted and kinetic, which would deny a fixed image. He describes his work, furthermore, in terms of emergence and immergence, which are ambivalent, each implying the other.[113] The face hides and reveals; the painter tries to capture the essence, the spirit behind the mask and knows at the same time of the impossibility to paint such an 'intangible thing'.[114] These elements as well as the tension of vagueness and control,[115] of past and present, of moment and timelessness, which are central to his work, enhance this sense of ambivalence. The images thus pose more questions than

108. Le Brocquy, in Walker, op.cit., 26.
109. James White quotes le Brocquy in White, 'Contemporary Irish Artists (VI), Louis le Brocquy', *Envoy,* vol. 2, no. 6 (1950), 65.
110. Schrödinger in a letter to le Brocquy, in Madden le Brocquy, op.cit., 56.
111. Le Brocquy, 'Notes ...', in Walker, op.cit., 139.
112. R. Kearney, 'Le Brocquy and Post-Modernism', *The Irish Review,* no. 3 (Cork: Cork University Press, 1988), 61-62. Cf. also Kearney, *Transitions, Narratives in Modern Irish Culture* (Dublin: Wolfhound Press, 1988), 202-207.
113. Le Brocquy, 'Notes ...', in Walker, op.cit., 142.
114. Cf. quotation from Interview with M. Peppiatt (1979) in D. Walker, "Images, Single and Multiple' 1957-1990', *Irish Arts Review* (1991-1992), 90.
115. Cf. John Montague, 'Primal Scream, The Later Le Brocquy', *The Arts in Ireland,* vol. 2, no. 1 (1973), 6.

answers, which, as one notes, even at the risk of generalisation, is, in fact, a characteristic of much contemporary art.

However, it is not to be concluded that le Brocquy takes his point of departure in purely vague imagination. To the question whether he would ever attempt an image of Christ, he replies that he needs at least some kind of feature of physical appearance, and that therefore he cannot engage in studies of the Christian God, or Buddha for that matter.[116]

But if le Brocquy finds it impossible to depict the Jesus who suffers the most horrible death imaginable on the Cross, many of his works and his views reveal, nevertheless, a profound awareness of the human predicament. Early paintings like 'Condemned Man' (1945) reflect his concern for capital punishment and the conditions of the imprisoned.[117] His mother Sybil le Brocquy became a co-founder of the Irish branch of Amnesty International in 1963 and her son has supported the organisation throughout his life. He abhors all forms of dictatorship, and believes in the freedom of democracy and human rights. Further, his own perception of the head images is profoundly existentialist in that he sees them as essentially tragic and consciousness itself as the substance of tragedy.[118]

Yet, the very sense of tragedy, of the existential, of human suffering is ultimately transcended in both his thought and work. In his canvases it is, amongst other aspects, the colour white, which, as he himself sees it, embodies this quality of transcendence. Furthermore, his search for essence, for the meta-physical, which constitutes the basis for his painterly quest, continually points to this atmosphere where immanence paves the way to transcendence.

Finally, he refers to the eternal human search for happiness and the transcending quality of beauty. He emphasises that both beauty and happiness can never be achieved 'directly', but only by forgetting about them, turning to other concerns.[119] A direct attempt at creating beauty only leads to 'insignificant beauty',[120] or prettiness. Thus it is through 'objective' commitment as an artist, and in giving and caring for others, 'which is the old doctrine of love', that beauty and happiness, may be found.[121]

Whether for him death implies the ultimate transcending event of salva-

---

116. Interview with M. Peppiatt (1979), in Walker, *Louis le Brocquy,* 68.
117. A. Madden le Brocquy, op.cit., 65.
118. Le Brocquy, *Procession* (Kinsale, Cork: Gandon Editions and L. le Brocquy, 1994), 9.
119. Ibid. B. Nöel, 'Commitment of the imagination', *Introspect,* no. 3 (Dec. 1977), 30.
120. Letter to the author, 6.9.1996.
121. Interview, 20.9.1995. It is interesting to note that le Brocquy's existentialist concern, his emphasis on human rights and freedom and his sense of 'the doctrine of love' has certain parallels with Yeats' ideas and work.

tion and redemption in the Christian sense, le Brocquy cannot answer.
However, he stresses that 'although life can be and often is ... for most human
beings a dreadful state of affairs', nonetheless death, 'whatever it is, must be
a *natural* thing'. If, moreover, one has not been 'terribly, terribly dissatisfied
with oneself and disguised everything', death, he concedes, may conceivably
'have many of the lovely and revelatory aspects' which Christian faith believes
in and hopes for ultimately.

IV. GERARD DILLON

On April 20th, 1916, Gerard Francis Dillon was born off the Falls Road, Belfast, the youngest of eight children of Annie Dillon and her husband Joseph Henry Dillon, a postman. Dillon's childhood and youth were very much a reflection of the conditions in Belfast at the time, in which fervent adherence to Roman Catholicism and nationalist aspirations closely intertwined. His mother, in particular, was rather extreme in her religious devotions of which Dillon has left some amusing records.[122] She also had strong nationalist convictions, as well as a marvellous sense of humour and wit, which had a lasting influence on her children.

Dillon left school at the age of fourteen and first worked as a house painter. However, he soon became bored with covering huge wall spaces with one colour and rather wished to engage in drawing and composition of paintings.

He began to study art on his own, and attended the Belfast College of Art for only three months. Dillon stated in 1950 that initially it was Seán Keating's illustrations for *The Playboy of the Western World* and Marc Chagall that made him want to paint.[123] In 1934 he moved to London where he stayed until 1939. Taking on odd jobs would supply the income he needed to support himself as a painter. He said that in London he was painting 'like a mad-man'.[124]

Dillon spent the war years in Ireland. His first solo exhibition took place in Dublin in 1942. Connemara, its people and landscape, provided much of his subject matter during this time. In fact, he developed a profound love of that part of Ireland where he would spend much time, sometimes in the company of his close friends and fellow painters George Campbell and Nano Reid. He always experienced those visits to Connemara as 'heaven'. Dillon had a great romantic affection for and interest in its people, their folk traditions and culture. Ireland's only 'naïve' painter tried to get into the 'primitive consciousness' of the people,[125] depicting the life of the peasants in a dram-

122. J. White, *Gerard Dillon* (Dublin: Wolfhound Press, 1994), 19 His mother insisted on saying the Rosary each night. Dillon wrote about it: '"You'll make it quick Ma, won't you?" pleads John. "If it was at the pictures ... yous wouldn't want it cut short" ... She kneels on the hard tiles, her head high, her back straight. Some of the others grab themselves cushions and lean doubled over chairs ... "Oh yous must have your comfort, that's no way to face God, your shoulders all humped up ... ".'
123. Gerard Dillon, 'The Artist Speaks', *Envoy,* vol. 4, no. 15 (1950), 30.
124. Dillon quoted in *Gerard Dillon, A Retrospective Exhibition,* cat. (Belfast/Dublin: Arts Council of Northern Ireland/An Chomhairle Ealaíon, 1972).
125. H. Pyle, 'Modern Art in Ireland: An Introduction', *Éire-Ireland,* vol. 4, no. 4 (Winter 1969), 40.

atic, simple, child-like manner with a sense of humour and without any con-
descension.[126] Dillon was serious about his wish to paint in a child-like fashion. Nevertheless, he painted, of course, as an adult, and his work reveals
sophistication in its deliberate unsophistication, invention, subtlety and
charm.

Dillon experimented throughout his life with different materials and
styles. He did not seem to perceive any barrier between producing strongly
figurative and totally abstract compositions. His later paintings with pierrots
and clowns carry symbolist and psychological overtones, which reveal some
aspects of the subconsciousness and consciousness of the artist, in particular
his premonition of his own death.

Dillon emphasised the personal, subjective aspect of art. He commented
that 'an artist must always make his own world happen on the canvas ... The
artist paints only for himself. If he does anything else he is dishonest'.[127]
Artistic integrity and honesty was of fundamental importance to Dillon.

Dillon returned to London after the war where he stayed until 1968. He
began to exhibit regularly with the Irish Exhibition of Living Art from 1943.
He had solo exhibitions in London, Dublin and Belfast. His work was also
shown in the United States and several European countries. In 1968 the
painter returned to Ireland, where he lived in Dublin until his premature
death from a stroke in 1971.

* * *

George Campbell wrote in his obituary on his friend that Dillon had been
'the most simple complex person any one of us had known'.[128] It is this seeming sense of contradiction, or paradox, which indeed characterises Dillon's
life and work, and more particularly his religious upbringing and subsequent
attitude towards Roman Catholicism and faith in the wider sense.

In a light-hearted account, Dillon recalls how, as a boy, he had a distinct
awareness of the presence of mystery which was made up of a mixture of
Catholic-Christian and Celtic-pagan beliefs and superstition: 'My winters
were filled with saints and holy souls, ... and my father's Banshees. It made
the dark days and wild nights full of mystery and other worlds wonders ...
Though you could not hear them the Holy Souls were everywhere ... you

126. Cf. Brian O'Doherty who comments in *The Irish Imagination 1959-1971*, cat. (Dublin:
     Hugh Lane Municipal Gallery of Modern Art, 1971), 20: '*The Folk Tradition (sic)* is a
     resource that has been tapped consistently by only one painter of any stature, Gerard
     Dillon, whose early work had a wit and humour otherwise absent from Irish painting.'
127. Marion Fitzgerald, 'The Artist Talks', (Interview with Dillon), *The Irish Times*, 23.9.1964.
128. George Campbell, 'A Simple Complex Man', *The Irish Times*, 8.7.1971.

could hear them plain enough on the wind, on any wild winter's night.'[129] It was his mother who talked about saints to her children. They were always female; male ones, apart from St Francis, after whom Dillon was named and for whom he had great affection,[130] seemed non-existent: 'Any woman who did her duties and kept her dignity in spite of the hammerings her husband gave her, was a saint.'[131] Dillon wondered continually how one might be sure to reach sainthood: 'The only thing was to grow up to be a woman, get yourself a bad husband, never neglect Mass, Confession and Holy Communion, and you have to have loads of children. That was according to my mother. But how could I grow up to be a woman?'[132] These extracts from an anecdote, which Dillon titled 'Wee Women Saints and Holy Souls', illustrate the popular religious beliefs and superstition, which were so much part of the artist's childhood, as well as the brilliant sense of fun and humour which everybody who knew Dillon remembers about him.

However, his remark about how he could grow up to be a woman hints at a more serious and fundamental reality in the painter's life, namely his homosexuality. It is this aspect which not only caused him repression, loneliness and sadness, but his alienation from and break with his church. At one particular confession, a priest asked him about girls, whereupon Dillon answered that he was attracted to males rather than females. The priest told him that, if he did not change, condemnation to eternal damnation in hell would be his fate. From that time onwards Dillon tried to avoid confession and the Eucharist.

Whether the painter actually came to regard himself still as a believer in the broadest sense or as an unbeliever cannot be established for definite, as he apparently did not comment on this matter. Friends, like Michael Longley and Arthur Armstrong, who knew him for over twenty years, relate that Dillon never spoke of religion, neither scathingly nor reverentially: '[H]e appeared not to have the remotest interest in it. I think, painting was his religion & *(sic)* everything else was subjugated to that.'[133] In fact, his total commitment to his art was coupled with a pronounced disregard for material possessions. Dillon was quite prepared to live frugally and invest his money in paints. As White confirms, art indeed became a replacement for the com-

---

129. White, *Gerard Dillon,* 21-22.
130. Cf. ibid., 17, 55, 58. Dillon produced a small painting titled 'Saint Francis' (c. 1950), in which he employs his typical early style, i.e. a mixture of naïve and evocations of Celtic book illumination in a modernist manner.
131. Dillon quoted in White, op.cit., 21.
132. Ibid.
133. Arthur Armstrong, Letter to the author (not dated), Oct. 1995. Longley: 'I can't honestly remember Gerard talking about Christianity.' M. Longley, Interview, 2.11.1995.

munal religion Dillon had given up during his adolescence. Dillon himself actually gave a poignant indication of this when he stated that he started to paint out of a 'hungry inner need'.[134] It is curious and interesting to note that Wassily Kandinsky in his ground-breaking *Concerning the Spiritual in Art* applied exactly those words when he wrote that it was 'the rules of the inner need, which are of the soul', that must guide the artist, that all means which derive from this inner need are 'sacred', and all those means which 'obscure' it are 'sinful'.

As an adult Dillon refrained from attending Mass. During his adolescence and even in later years, however, it seems that he loyally accommodated his mother's Catholicism and wholly identified with her nationalist convictions. As he did not want to hurt her, he had to live with that inner contradiction of keeping up on the surface at least some of the religious praxis he no longer believed in. In order to please her, he would take part in the Rosary and the devotions at home. Moreover, despite the fact that he rejected the church in which he had been raised, he was conditioned by it, even to the point of big-otry as the following incident illustrates. When a friend of his in England wanted to get married to a non-Roman Catholic woman in an Anglican church, Dillon told him that his [friend's] mother 'would have a fit' if he had the ceremony in that particular church, and that they should rather 'go and get a proper Catholic church' instead.[135] This story – even if Dillon might possibly have made this comment jokingly – relates how he had inherited the religious prejudices which have fostered the divisions in Northern Irish cult-ure, separating, as they do, Christians from Christians and identity from identity.[136]

Later, when the civil rights marches and violence started in the North, Dillon desired to show his support by withdrawing his works from the planned Irish Exhibition of Living Art of that year, as it was due to be shown in Belfast also. He encouraged other artists to do likewise: 'I feel ... that every artist worthy of the name should make his public protest against the persec-ution of the Irish people by a planter government in the Six Counties of

---

134. M. Fitzgerald, 'The Artist Talks', (Interview with Dillon), *The Irish Times*, 23.9.1964. Dillon was not the only artist in whom this replacement of Christian communal faith by art is apparent. Vincent van Gogh, more than anybody else, serves as an example. Cf. G. Thiessen, 'Faith into Art: Religion and Vincent van Gogh', *Doctrine and Life*, vol. 43, no. 5 (May-June 1993), 267-273.
135. White, *Gerard Dillon*, 50.
136. On the whole question of sectarianism in Northern Ireland cf. Joseph Liechty, *Roots of Sectarianism in Ireland* (Belfast: J. Liechty, 1993). On the need for and problematic of the reconciliation of memories, especially in Ulster cf. Alan D. Falconer, (ed.), *Reconciling Memories* (Dublin: Columba Press, 1988), iv, 4-5.

Ulster.'[137] Dillon, a highly sensitive man, passionately felt the injustice his fellow Catholics were enduring in Ulster and strongly identified with them and their struggle.

We can thus conclude, that in political, social and cultural terms he always remained a 'Belfast Catholic',[138] due to the close connections between the position of the churches and the political, cultural and social identities of the two communities. With regard to Dillon's actual faith identity, Brian Fallon offers a rather apt, if amusingly paradoxical, description when he comments on the artist as having been '[a] Catholic agnostic'.[139] What he indicates here is the fact that Dillon, like other intellectuals, artists and writers in Ireland at the time, rejected the dogmatic, intolerant Roman Catholicism he had been brought up with, replacing it not with atheism but rather with an agnostic or simply disinterested attitude.[140] At the same time the institution of the Catholic Church, its teachings, rituals and provision of social and political identity had had such a major impact on the formative years of his life, which made it impossible for him to ever entirely transcend it, emotionally and even rationally.

Not only did Dillon retain certain elements of his mother's faith and church, despite his anti-ecclesial, anti-clerical stance, but his art reveals some distinct biblical and Christian references regarding subject matter and style.

He stated that the Book of Kells, the Italian Primitives, the carvings on the Irish medieval stone crosses and Marc Chagall had influenced his work. The subjects in all of these, whether medieval or modern, are drawn from the Christian tradition, i.e. biblical figures and scenes, and events from the life of the church, which are depicted in a simple, direct and at times childlike manner. The Jewish artist Chagall, in particular, is not only recognised as one of the finest artists of the twentieth century, but also as a leading modern

137. White, op.cit., 101.
138. White refers to Dillon in these terms. Cf. *Gerard Dillon, Early Paintings of the West*, cat. (Dublin: Dawson Gallery, 1971). Also: Interview, White, 14.9.1995. White also makes an interesting remark about Dillon in his book on the artist when he stated that for Dillon – who not only abhored any kind of violence, but 'could not bear to think about the crucifixion of Christ, which was so cardinal a part of his family's religious ceremonies' – the events in the North were a most intense experience. Yet, despite his anguish over cruelty, including the violent death of Christ on the Cross, he produced, however, several works in which the Crucifixion is hinted at or explicitly depicted (e.g. 'High Cross Panel', 'The Painter's Dilemma', 'The Crowning with Thorns').
139. Brian Fallon, Interview, 20.10.1995.
140. White, Interview, 14.9.1995. White comments: '[H]e wasn't a man who played around with religious ideas or religious thoughts or religious events after he got away from the home, as far as I know.'

painter of religious subjects.[141] Chagall produced over one hundred images of the Crucified which convey the redemptive, hopeful dimension of the Christ event rather than the more prevalent contemporary existentialist interpretations with their emphasis on the meaningless absurdity of innocent suffering.

It would be incorrect to conclude that Dillon's liking of Chagall was primarily due to the Russian artist's use of religious iconography. It is first of all Dillon's artistic *style* which has affinities with the sophisticated childlike images of Chagall as well as with the medieval Irish stone crosses. Dillon's own iconography is not predominantly religious. Nevertheless, it remains a curious fact that he painted a number of works that allude both directly and indirectly to the Bible and to the Christian tradition. His use of the symbol of the pierrot, a quasi religious emblem, is also relevant in this context. This will be discussed in more detail in the next chapter.

One can only conjecture as to why Dillon chose religious subjects, since he himself did not comment as such on this issue. Seemingly several factors played a role. Firstly, his passionate love for his country, in particular its Celtic-Christian art and culture, were of fundamental importance. Secondly, the subjects in the art he admired *were* religious, thus he naturally would have taken them at times as a source of inspiration. Thirdly, he himself had been steeped in a religious Catholic atmosphere as a child, which, as has been demonstrated, had a lasting influence on his life. Finally, his personal negative experiences with and subsequent rejection of the dogmas of the Catholic Church obviously did not in turn lead him to immaturely respond with a narrow rejection of anything related to Christianity, such as the whole tradition of Christian imagery, in particular the biblical subjects in the art of the Celtic Irish Church.

Dillon emphasised that art is a 'language' which talks directly through the senses.[142] Moreover, as stated above, he stressed that the artist must translate his or her own world onto canvas, that in order to be truthful art could not be anything but personal and subjective.[143] Dillon's work is, in fact, strongly biographical.

Perhaps one may therefore conclude that although Dillon seems to have had little interest in theological matters and possibly would have seen him-

---

141. Cf. John Tinsley, 'Art and the Bible', in Bruce M. Metzger, Michael D. Coogan, (eds.), *The Oxford Companion to the Bible* (New York, Oxford: Oxford University Press, 1993), 60.
142. M. Fitzgerald, 'The Artist Talks', (interview with Dillon), *The Irish Times*, 23.9.1964.
143. Cf. ibid. Also: Wesley Boyd's interview with Dillon, 'Dillon in Dublin', *The Irish Times*, 25.1.1968. Dillon stated then: 'What I felt was as important as what I saw.'

self as an agnostic rather than as a believer and member of the church, his most personal language, i.e. his art, with its intermittent inclusion of religious subjects, *may* indicate that he never quite abandoned his childhood faith altogether. It appears to have been a private faith that survived independently and despite the church's negative impact on his life. Is it possible that it was only in his art that Dillon could still allude to a hidden Christian faith, both by including religious iconography in his work and by the very fact, that, in a more spiritual and personal sense, art became his religion?

V. COLIN MIDDLETON

The son of a damask designer and painter, Colin Middleton was born in Belfast on January 29th, 1910. His parents, Dora Emily and Charles Collins Middleton had been brought up in England and moved to the North of Ireland in 1899. Both were members of the Church of England. In later years they gave up attending services; their son Colin, however, was baptised in Manchester Cathedral.

Due to Charles Middleton's ill health, Middleton became an apprentice in his father's firm in Belfast and worked as a designer for over two decades before he would devote himself entirely to painting. Many of his later works show hints of his familiarity with design and the rhythms of weaving.

Middleton attended evening art classes in the College of Art in Belfast for five years. A visit to London in 1928 brought him into first contact with the works of van Gogh. Later in 1931 he visited Belgium where the fifteenth century Flemish masters and the works of James Ensor made a strong impression on the young artist. These painters, as well as the surrealist dreamworld of British artists like Tristran Hillier and Paul Nash, and also of Dali, made a significant impact on his development as an artist.

The diverse influences point to the somewhat problematic aspect in Middleton, namely the incredible variety of styles in his work. A born painter, Middleton had tremendous technical facility and as a result never really had to struggle.[144] As his friend, the poet Michael Longley, points out, Middleton 'painted in almost as many styles as there are "isms"', always, however, with his own voice.[145] His amazing technical skill facilitated his incessant experimentation and eclecticism which, as could be argued, actually prevented him from becoming a truly outstanding painter, as he did not devote himself to developing his own particular style.[146] His oeuvre includes postimpressionist, expressionist, surrealist and abstract works.

Despite these diverse styles, some constancy in his painting is provided, nevertheless, by the female figure which plays an important role throughout his work, as well as the appropriation of the various styles, especially Surrealism, in his own particular manner. Middleton was familiar with the writings of Jung, who had written on the power of symbols and the female archetype.[147] The female figure appears in different guises in his canvases, especially in his surrealist works, as (earth)mother, wife, goddess and Mother of Christ.

144. Cf. Michael Longley, Interview, 2.11.1995.
145. Cf. ibid.
146. S.B. Kennedy, Interview, 2.11.1995.
147. Middleton himself described the archetype as a symbol which in turn is a 'communicating vessel', in Mike Catto, *Art in Ulster 1957-1977*, 30. John Hewitt comments on the

In 1939 Middleton had to come to terms with his first wife's untimely death. Further, the horror of World War II made him stop painting for about six months. In the 1940s his works are largely surrealist and expressionist, inspired by a deeply felt awareness of human suffering caused by the events of the war. As he stated himself: 'The whole of society became surrealist when it began dropping bombs.'[148]

In the early 1940s Middleton held his first solo exhibitions in Belfast and Dublin; he also began to exhibit with the Irish Exhibition of Living Art.

From about 1946, and, more particularly, from 1948 to 1957, a substantial number of his works have biblical or religious titles and subject matter, some of which are related to the experience of war, as, for example, 'Our Lady of Bikini' (1946). It is this period that is of particular relevance to the present study.

Middleton had socialist and humanist convictions. Longley points out that the painter and his second wife, Kate, 'believed in collectivist effort'. Middleton and his family spent 1947 and 1948 in the John Middleton Murry community in East Anglia. However, it turned out to be a disillusioning experience. They returned to live in the North of Ireland for good, where Middleton would paint and teach art in Belfast, Coleraine and Lisburn.

His paintings in the 1960s and 1970s are largely concerned with semi-abstract landscapes. Like the female archetype, the sense of place was fundamental to Middleton as person and painter.[149] He also created some further surrealist works during this time.

In 1969 Middleton was awarded an MBE, and in 1970 he became a member of the Royal Hibernian Academy. His work has been shown in Ireland, Britain, Europe and the United States. In 1976 a large retrospective was held in Dublin and Belfast. He died in 1983.

* * *

Although Colin Middleton was interviewed a few times and made comments on his art on television and radio, we only get hints rather than concrete statements about the artist's spirituality and faith. Any assessment of this

symbolist and psychological aspects in Middleton's work in 1944: 'But his most personal contribution is in the ... stupendous series of symbolist canvases in which his statement or evocation of psychological truth is paralleled and integral with a developing technical assurance.' Hewitt, 'Under Forty, Some Ulster Artists', in Arthur Campbell, George Campbell, (eds.), *Now in Ulster* (Belfast, 1944), 15. For an exposition of Jung's ideas on the female archetype, especially the mother archetype, cf. C.G. Jung, *The Archetype and the Collective Unconscious, The Collected Works of C. G. Jung*, vol. 9, part 1 (London: Routledge & Kegan Paul, 1969), 54-110.
148. Quoted in Martin Wallace, 'Moving Artist' (Profile), *Belfast Telegraph*, 4.1.1957.
149. Middleton stated this in an interview with M. Longley (*The Irish Times*, 7.4.1967).

aspect in his life will therefore remain – at least to some extent – more speculative than definitive.[150]

Hewitt writes that Middleton's parents, who had been brought up in the
Anglican tradition, stopped going to church in later years. It is to be assumed
therefore, that although baptised, Middleton grew up in Belfast in a family
atmosphere in which (Protestant) religious customs did not play a major role.
Unlike Dillon, whose childhood and adolescence were strongly shaped by the
rituals of the Roman Catholic tradition, we have good reason to suppose that
Middleton's youth would have been far less overtly 'religious' than Dillon's
early years. If his upbringing was in this sense less restricted than Dillon's, for
example, this was and is not untypical of the more 'liberal' strand in
Protestantism, which is marked by a more private, more individualistic, and
less communal faith. In fact, Longley points out that Middleton was against
any form of hierarchy. Although, as we will see later, Middleton's beliefs are
far from being confined to what might be described as conventional
Protestant Christianity, he was, as Longley states, 'definitely a Protestant' in
the sense that he was 'very much an individualist', 'a *protest*-ant'. Clichéd and
general as a statement like this may be, it is nevertheless to be taken into
account as it indicates a very fundamental aspect in the artist's character. It is
the sense of individual freedom of a liberal Protestant faith that seems to have
shaped Middleton's outlook and nature and it may possibly have enabled him
to transcend and remain 'above' any sort of religious dogmatism or bigotry.

Middleton has been described as someone who was intuitive, who pos-
sessed a vibrant energy, a quick mind, who loved jazz and was interested in
ideas and had quite decided views.[151] Moreover, the painter had an interest
in religious and philosophical issues throughout his life.[152]

Longley notes that Middleton believed in the divine aspect in all humans.
This idea would have arisen – partly at least – from his own humanist convictions which are central to his life and work. Edward Sheehy's comments
reflect Longley when he writes on the religious-spiritual aspect in Middleton's
work in 1951. He describes the painter as 'a passionate humanist, inspired and
speaking with tongues ... his best work is the result of a self-identification
with a fundamental human reality, and the transfiguration in paint of that
rare experience'.[153]

---

150. Unfortunately, his family has not been available for interview. I rely therefore to a large
    extent on Michael Longley's comments and Hewitt's writings in this respect.
151. Ibid. Here Longley remarks that a person's love of jazz 'automatically' indicates 'the
    existence of soul and spirit'.
152. Cf. *Paintings, Drawings and Watercolours from the Studio of the Late Colin Middleton,
    M.B.E., R.H.A.*, (no author's name given), cat. (London: Christie, Manson & Woods
    Ltd., 1985), no p.
153. E. Sheehy, 'Art Notes', *The Dublin Magazine*, vol. 26 (Jan.-March 1951), 51-52.

Here, let us take a leap. Irenaeus, one of the early theologians of the second century argued that in Christ God came down to humanity while humanity was raised to God through God's incarnation.[154] Later Athanasius, Gregory of Nazianzus and Gregory of Nyssa argued likewise. In the twentieth century the Orthodox theologian Vladimir Lossky takes up Irenaeus' central argument that God made Godself human that the human might become God. He outlines the fundamental Orthodox notion of redemption as deification in stating that our union with God is accomplished by the redeeming work of Christ; as God has become a human being, 'each ... person should in turn become God by grace'.[155] Or, in the words of St Peter, we 'become participants of the divine nature' (2 Pet 1:4). Although it is unlikely that Middleton would have thought in such theological terms about the divine aspect in all humans, it is interesting to note that on this point his belief does *not* reflect Augustine's *massa damnationis*,[156] and the traditional Protestant emphasis on the separation of nature and grace and the sinfulness of humanity, but rather a tradition in theology which is most closely associated with the Orthodox Church.

If Middleton believed in the divinity of all humans, the question arises as to what role he would have attributed to Christ. Longley points out that he and the artist agreed that Christ 'did exist'. Furthermore, Middleton regarded Christ as a 'genius', a 'revolutionary' and as 'extraordinary'. He thus acknowledges the special role and exceptional person of Jesus. As we do not have Middleton's own statement on Christ, it is, however, impossible to ascertain whether he believed merely in a historical, political, and perhaps even in a prophetic Jesus, who challenged the authorities, or also in the Christ of faith, the risen redeemer of humankind.

As mentioned above, in the late 1940s and 1950s biblical themes enter Middleton's work. Stories from the Hebrew Scriptures and the gospels seemingly appealed to him and perhaps even fascinated him. Longley comments that Middleton would have seen the Bible as 'a great treasure trove of images' and its stories as 'great enabling myths'.

Drawing inspiration from the Bible did not imply institutional church

---

154. Cf. Irenaeus on redemption, excerpt from: *Adversus Haereses,* in Alister E. McGrath, *The Christian Theology Reader* (Oxford: Blackwell, 1995), 176.
155. Vladimir Lossky, 'Redemption and Deification', in Lossky, *In the Image and Likeness of God* (London/Oxford: Mowbray, 1974), 97-98.
156. Cf. Johann Baptist Metz on Augustine's 'anthropological dualism' in his article: 'Die Rede von Gott angesichts der Leidensgeschichte der Welt', in Hubert Irsigler, Godehard Ruppert, (eds.), *Ein Gott, der Leiden schafft?,* Bamberger Theologische Studien, vol. 1 (Frankfurt/Main: Peter Lang, 1995), 49.

membership and regular church attendance. As Longley adds on a light-hearted note: 'If he belonged to a church it was a church who had just one person in it, and it had one member in the congregation who was also its pope and that was Colin Middleton.' Nevertheless, it should be said that Middleton, who was head of the art department at The Friends' School in Lisburn from 1961 to 1970, had, in fact, an admiration for the Quakers.[157] He did not join them, but his anti-hierarchical and anti-institutional views obviously would have concurred with the theology and *raison d'etre* of this Christian group.

Like Jellett and le Brocquy, Middleton believed that art has a social dimension. He stated: 'I don't think that one paints entirely for oneself. Unless a painting has significance to other people, it's not a painting.'[158] He believed in the wide currency of his paintings, which, presumably out of his socialist/Christian convictions, he made available at comparatively low prices.[159]

Although Middleton obviously had faith in the redemptive aspect of art, he saw the artist's role in more dialectical terms, describing her/him as 'visionary' or 'entertainer', as a 'dispenser of opiates' or 'healer'.[160] He held that as an artist one could become 'schizophrenic', as one lived on the edge 'between the devil and eternity'.[161]

One of the central aspects in Middleton's personal and artistic development was the experience of World War II and its aftermath. The Holocaust, the fate of the Jews and the incredible suffering caused by the war profoundly affected Middleton and his work. If theologians like Jürgen Moltmann and John Pawlikowski wondered where were both God and the human in Auschwitz, and how one could speak about God and continue to engage in theology after Auschwitz, Middleton faced a not dissimilar task in his painting.[162] Several works of this time, both expressionist and surrealist, show an existentialist concern with and personal response to the war and the plight of

157. John Hewitt, *Art in Ulster 1557-1957* (Belfast: Blackstaff Press/Arts Council of Northern Ireland, 1977), 174. Longley, Interview, 2.11.1995.
158. Middleton commenting in a documentary on the artist, BBC TV Northern Ireland, 1976.
159. Longley, 'Colin Middleton', *The Dublin Magazine* (Autumn/Winter 1967).
160. John Hewitt, *Colin Middleton* (Belfast/Dublin: Arts Council of Northern Ireland/An Chomhairle Ealaíon, 1976), 40.
161. Comment made by Middleton in the documentary on the artist, BBC TV, 1976.
162. Cf. 'Christology in the Light of the Auschwitz Experience', ch. 6, in John T. Pawlikowski, O.S.M., *Christ in the Light of the Jewish Christian Dialogue* (New York: Paulist Press, 1982), 136-147. Also J.B. Metz on theodicy in 'Die Rede von Gott angesichts der Leidensgeschichte der Welt', in op.cit., 57.

the Jews. Interestingly these themes are dealt with by using biblical titles and imagery. It seems that in the aftermath of the war, Middleton got particular inspiration and possibly some solace and even answers from the Bible. In 1945 Middleton exhibited a work 'Saint John: Retrospect' in which the figure of the Baptist is placed before a dilapidated building resembling the Colosseum. A critic commented at the time that the whole painting brought out the 'idea of the Triumph of the Cross'.[163] Other works like 'Give me to Drink' (1949), or 'Christ Androgyne' (1943), which will be discussed in detail in Chapter Three, point in a similar direction. The artist captures an involved God who is with God's people. As Sheehy comments, Middleton 'is a painter of life, of the immediate reality, albeit transmuted by an innate poetic vision and a warmth of human sympathy', he 'accepts and transmutes [the human condition] through faith, hope and charity'.[164]

It could be argued that what Middleton conveys through his images in the forties, Moltmann and other theologians reflect in their writings a few decades later. Moltmann concludes that if there had not been theology *in* Auschwitz, it would be impossible to engage in theology *after* Auschwitz.[165] What he means is that it is in suffering and horror that God becomes present to us as God him/herself suffered on the Cross. He points out that the 'Sch'ma Israel' and the 'Our Father' were prayed in this place of evil, i.e. in face of complete annihilation and Godlessness the victims cried out for their saviour. For Moltmann it seems to be the Auschwitz experience in which the Christ event is revealed more dramatically than in any other event since the crucifixion.[166]

It is in the basic question of theodicy, and the more particular event of the Holocaust, of 'God's pathos',[167] of God who suffers with his people, that Middleton's work and thought, i.e. his passionate humanism, and a theology of the Cross such as Moltmann's converge.[168]

Another central aspect in Middleton's life is an intense awareness of place and of nature. In his work this dimension is revealed in numerous poetic landscape paintings with their atmosphere of transcendence. In 1967 he

163. Artless (anonymous), 'Colin Middleton', (review), *The Leader*, 9.6.1945.
164. E. Sheehy, 'Art Notes', *The Dublin Magazine* (Oct.-Dec. 1953), 43.
165. J. Moltmann, *Der gekreuzigte Gott* (München: Chr. Kaiser, 1972), 266.
166. Cf. Pawlikowski on Moltmann, in Pawlikowski, op.cit., 138.
167. Moltmann, *Trinität und Reich Gottes* (Munich: Chr. Kaiser, 1980), 40-45. Here Moltmann refers to Abraham Heschel who was one of the first theologians to attack the idea of an apathetic God. Heschel referred to the theology of the Old Testament prophets as a 'theology of divine pathos'.
168. Moltmann is, of course, not the only Christian theologian who has worked on this subject. However, Moltmann has been the only one so far who has tried to develop a christology against the background of Auschwitz.

states: 'Place is everything. Place is terribly important ... I just can't go out for a day's sketching – that's meaningless ... You've got to go to a place until it does something to you ... it gets at you, it eats you. There's got to be some sort of place – particular places, holy places. Once you get there you know you are kith and kin. The stones start to talk.'[169] Middleton held that in his landscapes 'moods and qualities evoked in him by certain places; by the intimate nature of the rocks, trees and plants' are captured.[170]

Longley, in even more theological terms, refers to Middleton's profound belief in the *deus loci* and the *genius loci,* the spirit of a place. Longley emphasises that there was in Middleton a strong 'pagan' or 'pantheist' aspect: 'He would have gone along with pagan notions and God's existence in trees and stones and so forth ... He would have been interested in holy wells and shrines ... He would have felt towards Mary as he would have felt towards Sybil or one of the Gods ...'

The question which arises thus is whether Middleton was pagan-pantheist or a Christian believer. One suggests that an 'either-or' answer here would be a most simplistic, untruthful option. Hewitt and Longley have both referred to Middleton's vast imagination and endless experimentation. I would argue that Middleton's faith was complex, holistic, inclusive; this paralleled his imagination and the amazing range of styles in his work. It is difficult to imagine that an artist who repeatedly used biblical imagery, who was interested in theological questions, who admired the Quakers, and who referred to Christ as 'extraordinary', would have denied his personal faith and trust in the Christian God.

At the same time we find a dimension in Middleton which at first sight may seem pantheist. It seems that the painter actually held pan*en*theist rather than pantheist views which were deeply interwoven and in harmony with the Christian aspect in his thought and work. As the latter notion denotes that God and nature are identical and is therefore unacceptable to Christian faith, the former affirms that all is in God and God is present in all creation, but that God remains at the same time absolute, or the totally Other.[171]

One may conclude then that both humanist and social/socialist concerns played a considerable role in Middleton's life and thought as well as a panentheist-Christian aspect that had a curious affinity with the nature spirituality typical of early Irish Celtic Christianity. More particularly, his panentheist spirituality finds a resonance in a contemporary theology of creation, as

169. Middleton quoted in 'Talking to Colin Middleton' (Interview with M. Longley), *The Irish Times,* 7.4.1967.
170. Middleton quoted in Longley, 'Colin Middleton', *Introspect,* no. 1. (Dec. 1975), 21.
171. Cf. Joseph Höfer, Karl Rahner, (eds.), *Lexikon für Theologie und Kirche,* vol. 8, (Freiburg: Herder, 1963), col. 20.

expounded by Jürgen Moltmann. In his 'ecological doctrine of creation' Moltmann insists that in God 'there is no one-sided relationship of superiority and subordination', but, rather, the trinitarian concept of life is one of perichoresis.[172] Hence, he insists, 'all relationships which are analogous to God reflect the primal, reciprocal indwelling and mutual interpenetration of the trinitarian perichoresis: God *in* the world and the world *in* God; ... soul and body united in the lifegiving Spirit to a human whole ... All living things live in one another and with one another, from one another and for one another'.[173] From a theological perspective would it be too 'convenient' to claim that Middleton, whose paintings were perceived as an expression of faith, hope and charity,[174] and who himself imaged the presence of God in all humans, in the midst of human suffering, as well as in the beauty of nature, would not only have agreed with Moltmann's notion of perichoresis, but in some ways brought to expression a similar notion of divine presence in the world and of our being in God in his own ideas and work?

172. J. Moltmann, *God in Creation* (London: SCM, 1985), 16-17.
173. Ibid., 17.
174. It is interesting to note that Middleton would have agreed with the notion that the process of making art is a form of prayer. Cf. Longley, Interview, 2.11.1995.
    Note: This section on Middleton was published in a slightly altered version as 'The Theological and Spiritual in the Life and Work of Colin Middleton (1910-1983)' in *Studies,* vol. 88, no. 350 (Summer 1999), 199-207.

VI. PATRICK COLLINS

Born in Dromore West, Sligo, in 1911, Patrick Collins was the second of four children in the family of Mary Patricia and William Collins, a policeman in the Royal Irish Constabulary. During his childhood Collins was introduced to music and literature, rather than the visual arts. Joyce, in particular, was to influence his own work and ideas. He referred to the writer as a 'father' who 'shaped his thoughts'.[175] The Sligo countryside, nature in all its aspects, held a fascination for the young Collins who spent hours in the woods, living, as he said, 'absolutely wild'. It is this lifelong love and intimate encounter with the Irish countryside that determined his painting most profoundly.

In the late 1920s Collins got a job with The Irish Life Assurance Company, where he worked for about two decades. He educated himself by spending much time reading in the National Library and discovering the Hugh Lane Municipal Gallery in Dublin. Collins' initial hope was to become a writer. However, in his late twenties he took up painting and began to devote more and more time to it. He attended some art classes at the National College of Art. Although he had a great admiration for Cézanne,[176] and also appreciated the work of Pollock, Léger, Kandinsky and Paul Henry, Collins claimed that 'unfortunately' he had not been influenced by other painters.

Apart from his stay in France between 1971 and 1977, Collins lived all his life in Dublin. His dominant motif was the Irish landscape which he capt-ured mostly from memory and in an abstracted manner with his own poetic, sometimes dreamlike, vision and intense feeling. Brian O'Doherty com-mented in 1961 that Collins had 'a feeling for the Irish countryside like no other painter'.[177] His work has some affinities with Jack Yeats. His muted blue-grey, brown and sometimes almost monochrome choice of colours, nev-ertheless, differs considerably from Yeats' exuberant, brighter colouring. Along with his love for the Irish landscape Collins had a great interest in what he terms the 'celtic imagination',[178] as well as in early Irish Celtic Christian art and was influenced by it. Further, he insisted that 'the only moving thing' to come out of Ireland was the penal cross, 'they just emerged, and they were just right, startlingly right.'[179]

---

175. Frances Ruane, *Patrick Collins* (Dublin/Belfast: An Chomhairle Ealaíon/The Arts Council of Northern Ireland, 1982), 24.
176. Collins was completely struck by Cézanne's 'Blue Vase': "This thing had such an incred-ible mystery to me, a fabulous thing. It was like saying Mass, High Mass in painting'.' Ruane, op.cit., 19.
177. B. O'Doherty, 'Ambiguities: The Art of Patrick Collins', *Studies* (Spring 1961), 53.
178. Cf. Brian Lynch, 'Irish Painting? There's No Such Thing', *Hibernia*, 28.6.1979.
179. Marion Fitzgerald, 'Patrick Collins', (interview), *The Irish Times*, 27.2.1965.

After his formative period between 1950 and 1956 Collins adopts a more pronounced abstract approach in his works towards the end of that decade which was succeeded by an expressionist phase in the early 1960s. By the mid-sixties he had matured and from then on his work is consistent in style and subject matter. His paintings of the sixties and seventies also include a substantial number of works with religious themes, notably the 'Stations of the Cross' of 1964.

Between 1965 and 1970 Collins paints strongly romantic landscapes, the misty Ireland of his imagination. The paintings of his France period, where he almost suffered starvation due to lack of finances, are, as Ruane points out, 'less brooding' and more elegant and happier than those previously finished at home.[180] After his return from France his inspiration continued to come from the Irish countryside. In the 1980s his canvases are more abstract than ever before. As he said himself: 'It is the aura of an object which interests me more than the object ...'[181]

Collins' work was primarily exhibited in Ireland but has on occasion been shown abroad. He was elected HRHA in 1980, in 1981 he became a member of Aosdána. In 1987 he was the first visual artist to be elected *Saoi* by the members of Aosdána.[182] Collins died in Dublin on March 2nd, 1994.

* * *

Collins spoke about his life, his ideas and work on various occasions which provide us not with any extensive accounts but, at least, with some glimpses of his faith and spirituality.

As with the other artists discussed above, his ethical convictions on the imperative of artistic integrity and truthfulness in his work and thought were paramount. For Collins the act of painting essentially implied struggle. He insisted that the contemporary artist should go beyond his or her egotism and paint as honestly as possible.[183]

Interestingly, Collins, like Karl Rahner, perceived art to be 'in essence transcendental'. Rahner wrote that 'art is a product of ... human transcendentality ... [It] is only because we are transcendental beings that art and

---

180. Ruane, *Patrick Collins,* 77. Collins said that to get out of Ireland had been a 'mental necessity' as he got tired of the very small Irish art scene and needed to expand his horizons. Cf. Des Moore, 'Collins paints "dramatic Ireland" from Normandy", *Sunday Independent,* 13.7.1975.
181. O'Doherty, op.cit., 55.
182. Membership in the Irish artists' organisation Aosdána is open to those artists who have excelled in their work. The special honour of *Saoi* is given to only five artists amongst its members at any given time.
183. Cf. Patrick Collins, 'George Campbell - A Profile of the Artist', *Envoy,* vol. 1, no. 2 (Jan. 1950), 45. Emmanuel Kehoe, 'Horizons', *The Sunday Press,* 12.3.1978.

theology can really exist.'[184] Furthermore, Collins considered the act of painting primarily as a gift, and, like le Brocquy, as a process of finding what is already there: 'I know what I want to paint is there ... I only have to find it, to arrive ... It's like being given a gift ... afterwards you don't know where you got it ... Afterwards you wonder at it.'[185] How this gift and finding 'happens' is, as he states, a source of 'wonder', or, in more theological terms, a mysterious event of grace, which cannot be explained rationally. In fact, Collins himself was described by his friend, the writer Aidan Higgins, and by O'Doherty as a 'monk' and 'a sort of mystic'.[186] His daughter Penelope even suggested that she always felt that Collins 'was communicating with some higher person'.[187] Subjective, metaphysical and speculative as a statement like this may be, it nevertheless curiously concurs with Higgins' and O'Doherty's views and Collins' own mystical-transcendent vision which in turn is reflected in his art. It was, as he said, the aura of a subject, the search for an 'underlying order' and for truth which interested him: 'You don't believe in the thing you're painting, you believe in the thing behind it.'[188] Or, as Dermot Lane observes in his analogy of religious and artistic experience, it is not simply the surface, the actual experience, but the 'depth dimension' in it that matters and is of interest to us.[189]

It is curious to note that Collins and le Brocquy, in their emphasis on the artist as revealer rather than creator, seem to oppose a traditional notion in theological aesthetics, which was particularly held by the Romantics but apparently is already found in Renaissance thought of the late fifteenth century.[190] It is the notion of the artist as God's co-creator. While God creates *ex nihilo* in sovereign, unlimited freedom, as Augustine held, the artist, limited and constricted by the very fact of his/her humanity, is perceived, nevertheless, as a 'creator like unto God'. Nicholas Wolterstorff argues that this analogical concept has been a dominant image of the artist in Western thought. While Collins and le Brocquy might not oppose the idea of a divine creator,

184. Patrick Collins, op.cit., 44. K. Rahner, *Theological Investigations*, vol. 23 (London: Darton, Longman and Todd, 1992), 164-165.
185. O'Doherty, 'Ambiguities ...', op.cit., 54. Cf. also Collins quoted in E. Kehoe, op.cit.: 'The devastating thought in Art is that we don't create. It's all there already.'
186. Cf. Aidan Higgins, "Paddy' - An Appreciation', in Ruane, op.cit., 11. O'Doherty, op.cit., 55.
187. Penelope Collins, Interview, 29.8.1995. Interestingly Patricia Collins has commented that Collins was 'intensely sensual and intensely spiritual'; in his works he desired 'a fusion of the two'. (Interview, 29.8.1995).
188. Collins quoted in B. Lynch, 'Irish Painting? No Such Thing', *Hibernia*, 28.6.1979.
189. D. Lane, *The Experience of God* (Dublin: Veritas, 1981), 19.
190. Nicholas Wolterstorff points out that Christoforo Landino in his discussion on poets was the first to compare the artist/poet to God the creator. N. Wolterstorff, *Art in Action – Toward a Christian Aesthetic* (Grand Rapids, Michigan: W.B. Eerdmans, 1980), 51.

or, at least, an ultimate, mysterious energy through which the whole cosmos came into existence, they emphasise that the artist makes that which is already created visible. The artist uncovers, discovers, reveals but does not create as such. It may not be insignificant that this understanding of the artist has, in fact, something in common with that of the role of the theologian who, as Rahner said, discovers the God who is already there. Given le Brocquy's and Collins' view, one might pose the question whether they would concede that the act of artistic revelation could in itself be seen as an act of creation?

Linked with his understanding of the revelatory function of the artist, Collins viewed the role of the artist in terms of being a servant: The artist 'knows he hasn't made it [the work of art], that he's only a servant, an absolute servant.'[191] This is religious-devotional language, conveying an implicit sense of vocation. Like the call of a monk or committed believer who, because of his or her vocation, cannot but follow Christ's radical gospel, the vocation of the artist for Collins is one of service, or even surrender. The Dominican Pie-Raymond Régamey in his seminal *Religious Art in the Twentieth Century* compares mystical experience to the work of the artist by taking up Rouault's imperative that an artist must obey her or his 'inner voice'.[192] He echoes Collins' own ideas and those of Collins' critics when he points out that an artist will find her or his 'highest freedom in submitting to this obedience ... The work of art is something not only willed but suffered, undergone.'[193] Although this view may come across as a little idealistic in our contemporary materialistic artworld, it is true, nevertheless, for artists like Collins for whom sincerity is far more important than instant 'success'.

More than once Collins remarked: 'God is in my hand.'[194] Such a statement has a certain affinity with Irenaeus and the Orthodox belief in divinisation, as discussed already with reference to Middleton. It also alludes to the creation story in Gen 1, i.e. the human being made in the image of God, and thus the human, especially the artist's, power to create. This interpretation, the artist as creator, may seem to contradict what has been said above about Collins' idea of the artist as revealer rather than creator. Instead of weighing one statement against the other so as to arrive at a coherent answer, I suggest that both views should be acknowledged and accepted as such, since, in fact, we do not have a definitive statement by Collins on this issue. One might further argue that the notion of divine presence in the hand affirms what was

191. Collins quoted in E. Kehoe, 'The silent fight', *The Sunday Press,* 6.4.1980.
192. Pie-Raymond Régamey, *Religious Art in the Twentieth Century* (New York: Herder and Herder, 1963), 153-154.
193. Ibid., 154.
194. Patricia Collins, Interview, 29.8.1995.

concluded above, namely that the act of revealing what is already there – which is the task of the artist as Collins and le Brocquy see it – in itself can be seen in some way as an act of creation. And vice versa then, creation is also revelation. Ultimately, therefore, it asserts the intimate link between creation and revelation.

The most striking aspect in Collins' life and work, from a theological perspective, is the panentheist dimension in his faith and spirituality.[195] This element was perhaps more pronounced in him than in Middleton or any other Irish artist. It had essentially to do with his lifelong profound affection for the Irish countryside and his capturing of it on canvas. The artist's wife, Patricia Collins, has pointed out that he 'saw God in every object he looked at. He finds the spirit inside a stone, inside a tree' or in 'the dolmens'.

Collins shared the sublime vision of nature with the Romantics like Turner, Caspar David Friedrich, Schleiermacher. Collins' ideas and works, e.g. 'Abandoning Camp' (1969), Blue Landscape (1966) share something with Wordsworth and, in particular, Shelley's melancholic lyrics and longing for oneness with nature.[196] In Eliade's terminology, it is the hierophanisation of matter, the 'cosmic religiosity',[197] which was deeply ingrained in the consciousness of Collins, as also, although less radically, in Middleton and other Irish artists. It is to be suggested that this panentheistic, sublime dimension, while not being unique to Irish art – Brancusi, for example, shared similar views – is, nevertheless, in comparison to other European artists, an unusually vivid dimension.[198] Furthermore, as in Middleton, this panentheist dimension does not exist in opposition to, but mingles in holistic fashion with, Collins' Christian faith.[199]

---

195. Cf. Patricia Collins, Interview, 29.8.1995. 'I was always a great believer in the pagan.' Collins quoted in B. Lynch, 'Irish Painting? ...', *Hibernia*, 28.6.1979.
196. Julian Campbell, 'Patrick Collins and 'The Sense of Place'', *Irish Arts Review*, vol. 4, no. 3 (Autumn 1987), 49. Patricia Collins relates that a biography of Shelley (author, year?) was his 'bible'. (Interview, 29.8.1995)
197. Mircea Eliade, 'The Sacred and the Modern Artist', in D. Apostolos-Cappadona, (ed.), *Art, Creativity, and the Sacred* (New York: Crossroad, 1984) 179-183.
198. David Brett has argued that the sublime vision of nature is the most typical in Irish art. He observes that the characteristic method by which the sublime is depicted in modern art is the 'elimination of figurative references'. The artist's subjectivity in his/her depiction thereby is superior to the rendered subject. Cf. Brett, 'The Land and the Landscape', *Circa*, no. 43 (Dec.-Jan. 1989), 16.
199. This holistic view or ecological theology is evident, as has been demonstrated in the previous sections, in theologians such as Moltmann, in more recent times, and Teilhard de Chardin, who, in particular, tried to bring about a fusion of pantheist and Christian thought as he firmly believed in 'the Whole', as opposed to the separation of a supernaturally revealed God from the cosmos. Cf. de Chardin, 'Pantheism and Christianity', *Christianity and Evolution* (London: Collins, 1971), 56-75.

Also like Middleton and Dillon, Collins was anti-clerical and did not attend communal worship. For him art *was* 'worship', 'that was his church'.[200] Yet, as with the other painters, an anti-ecclesial stance did not imply a rejection of the Christian God. Not only had Collins, like Dillon, been shaped by and never fully transcended his Roman Catholic Christian upbringing,[201] but, as Penelope Collins has observed, he lived his life with a sense of the presence of and communion with the divine: 'I think there was always an underlying ... respect for God. Shrouds and veils and Mary Magdalene, all that would have interested him very much.' Other indications of his faith are to be found in his choice of subject matter that included numerous canvases with biblical themes. Indeed, would a painter like Collins, who never received church commissions, have engaged repeatedly with biblical and Christian subjects had he not had a personal relationship with the God of the Bible? In this context his 'Stations of the Cross' are particularly relevant. Brian Lynch commented at the time that they were 'humble', 'at once awkward and deeply felt'.[202] The 'Stations' certainly do not rank with the best of Collins' works, but in their sincerity they stand as a testament to his faith.

The reason why he painted these 'Stations' may partly have been his own suffering. As a boy Collins had experienced the untimely death of close family members. In later years this element of darkness would find translation on canvas as he could not talk about, and greatly feared, death.[203] In fact, the painter stated that despair 'is an ingredient of every picture'.[204] Painting the 'Stations' may therefore have been an (unconscious) act of identifying with Christ, and of catharsis.

In the face of what has been discussed above, it is to be argued that Collins' faith was a profound, inspiring, supportive reality in his life. As with Middleton, it was a faith that mirrored that of the mystics and prophets in its unconventional, anti-institutional panentheist-Christian dimension.

Collins enjoyed the company of Christians who would critically reflect on their faith. His own faith, although far from being naïve, ultimately seems to have been childlike, simple and trusting, however.

Like Middleton, Collins' nature spirituality, his deep awareness that God is present in all creation, has affinities with contemporary theologies of cre-

200. Patricia Collins, Interview, 29.8.1995.
201. Patricia and Penelope Collins, Interviews, 29.8.1995.
202. B. Lynch, 'Masculine/Feminine', *Hibernia*, 9.3.1978.
203. Patricia and Penelope Collins, Interviews, 29.8.1995. When he had a brain tumour in 1984, Collins demanded a Bible to read. (ibid).
204. Collins quoted in O'Doherty, 'Ambiguities ...', op.cit., 54.

ation, such as Jürgen Moltmann's. Deeply rooted in Ireland and inspired by his love of the Celtic Christian past, Collins at times has been categorised as an *Irish* painter. It should be said that, as with Yeats, it is precisely the local aspect that made his art, and therefore the theological dimension expressed within it, universal. What emerges is a universal vision drawn from the memory of dolmens and stones in the Sligo countryside. As theology becomes universal precisely through its contextuality and local particularity, the same may be said for art.[205]

In this context one is reminded, furthermore, that Christians must rediscover that our concept of salvation involves not only human beings but *all* creation. Enda McDonagh writes that 'trust in the earth grounds human beings' trust in one another and ultimately their trust in God'.[206] Collins' life and work was an expression of such trust and faith. As he said himself: 'God is in my hand.'

205. Cf. Gerard O'Hanlon's comment on the second Mayo Book of Theology, in G. O'Hanlon, S.J., 'Religious and National Influences on Our Vision of Humanity in Ireland', *Milltown Studies,* no. 37 (Spring 1996), 32.
206. E. McDonagh, *Survival or Salvation, A Second Mayo Book of Theology* (Dublin: Columba Press, 1994), 252.

VII. TONY O'MALLEY

The eldest child of Margaret Ryan, Callan, and Patrick O'Malley, a salesman from Clare Island, Anthony O'Malley was born on 25th September 1913 in Callan. O'Malley grew up in an atmosphere in which the arts had no role. Thus in his teenage years he kept his drawing and his interest in painting to himself. Attending art college was, as he said, 'no option for country men like myself'.[207] O'Malley joined the Munster and Leinster Bank in 1934, working in different branches in Ennis, Dublin and Monaghan. After a brief spell in the Irish Army in 1940-1941, he was to experience sickness to the point of death several times during that decade. He painted his first oil painting while convalescing from his first lung operation in 1945. After two further operations in 1947 he spent 1948-1950 recovering from TB in sanatoria, drawing and painting steadily. Later in 1961 he suffered a severe heart attack. Due to these long experiences of ill health, O'Malley has lived all his life with a heightened awareness of death and mortality.[208] What sustained him during these years was his painting.

In the 1950s O'Malley painted landscapes, portraits and still-life, which in style are close to Cézanne and van Gogh, both of whom he admired. These works reveal his great affection for the countryside and, as he said, 'simple' people. Due to ill health he finally retired from the bank in 1958.

The move to Cornwall in 1960, where he had already made contact with Peter Lanyon, Patrick Heron and Bryan Winter and other artists in 1955, was probably the most important decision in his life as an artist. St Ives meant 'a real sense of freedom' and the company and intellectual stimulation of fellow painters.

Abstraction, based on nature, dominated among the St Ives painters at the time. During the 1960s and 1970s O'Malley develops his own, very personal, imagery and (quasi) abstract style: 'I moved into abstract painting, but it was not theoretical abstract, it was very real painting to me.'[209]

His non-figurative works often take their inspiration from nature ('Winter Silence', 1965), or from other objects, such as the stone carvings in Jerpoint Abbey and other churches in County Kilkenny which he has admired since his childhood ('St. Canice's', 1971).

The early works, which tend to be sombre in colour range, convey something of the artist's introspective and contemplative character. O'Malley has

---

207. Tony O'Malley in *Works 14 - Tony O'Malley* (Dublin: Gandon Editions, 1994), 9.
208. O'Malley once commented that he had never forgotten a quotation from Michelangelo who said: 'All my life I have lived on the horizon of my death.' in 'H. Cooke talks to Tony O'Malley', *The Irish Times*, 7.12.1973.
209. Tony O'Malley quoted in *Works 14 - Tony O'Malley*, 16.

been described as humorous, emotional, but also as withdrawn, meditative and solitary. He has always kept at a distance from cities, from the artworld and has not bowed to any fashionable trends in the art scene. O'Malley is a versatile, highly imaginative artist and marvellous colourist. Respected for his sincerity, he has continually developed as an abstract painter. In the eighties and nineties, his palette has become brighter. With his wife and fellow painter Jane Harris, whom he married in 1973, he has spent prolonged periods in the Bahamas. The paintings which originate from those stays are bright, exuberant, gentle, melodic, rhythmic symphonies of colour ('Bahamian Butterfly', 1979, 'Marigot Bay, St. Lucia, West Indies', 1992). In fact, the artist has at times expressed his wish to paint music.

The most striking aspect in all his work, however, is an intense spirituality, a feeling of transcendence that reflects his own intuitive sensibility.

From 1978 O'Malley began to revisit and exhibit regularly in Ireland. At last he had found recognition as one of the finest Irish painters.[210] In 1990 he returned to his native Callan for good. In 1993 O'Malley was elected *Saoi* by the members of Aosdána. His work has been shown in Ireland, Britain, on the European continent and Canada.

* * *

O'Malley has at times spoken about his beliefs and his faith. He is, however, essentially a private person, who eschews commentators who try to find quick, convenient categories. The necessity of artistic and intellectual freedom is paramount in his views and work and therefore demands to be respected in writing about his ideas and painting.

O'Malley's sense of vocation in becoming an artist has been central to and has sustained him throughout his life: 'I suppose I had a vocation for it, although in my time a vocation was only meant for the church. My inner sense of expression was fulfilled by painting, something I could never say to anyone because it would not be understood.'[211] His experience of TB and being close to death as well as the fact that he worked in spiritual isolation, knowing his painting would be met with miscomprehension in rural Ireland of the 1950s, intensified this sense of vocation.[212]

His complete devotion to his work is in a very real sense religious, if 'religious' is perceived as submitting oneself to a 'higher call', as ultimate concern (Tillich), as a search for our 'Centre',[213] i.e. that what makes our lives whole

210. B. Fallon, 'Forty Years a-growing', *The Irish Times*, 2.8.1994.
211. O'Malley quoted in *Works 14 - Tony O'Malley*, 16. Cf. also Interview, 30.10.1995.
212. Cf. Fallon, *Tony O'Malley*, 59. Interview, 30.10.1995. 'When I was restored to health I made a vow to paint all my life ... And I carried it out.'
213. Bede Griffiths, *Return to the Centre* (London: Collins, 1978), 98-99.

and gives meaning. Art for him became a 'way of life'. His sense of vocation is linked with and arises from a deep sense of grace and redemption, which even at the darkest times of his life have made it possible for him to paint: 'I suppose it [painting] could be regarded as redemptive. It redeemed *me*. I *found* myself [in] painting.'[214]

In this context it is interesting to note that O'Malley not only admires van Gogh but has felt an affinity with the Dutch artist. Van Gogh, who in his vocation as preacher amongst the poor had been rejected by his church authorities as unsuitable, discovered his vocation as a painter and followed it despite the fact that his contemporaries completely misunderstood him. O'Malley felt similarly before he left Ireland. He sees van Gogh as a tragic figure, as a 'saint' or 'Holy Fool' in art, who found sustenance in his single-minded devotion to his work. An intense sense of vocation and awareness of the redeeming quality of art and of the process of making art is common to both painters.

As he himself has stated and as others have observed, O'Malley has a vision that is close to Collins. O'Malley, as mentioned above, has always remained a country person who has a profound love of nature: 'My intuitive side was in nature ... everything in nature is wonderful ... There is a kind of agnosticism in me because I can't fix myself, except in nature.'[215] As will be discussed in more detail, O'Malley's nature spirituality, or agnosticism, as he terms it, does, however, exist side by side with his belief in a personal God, i.e. Christ. Fallon and Lynch have referred to him as a 'believing', 'non-practising Catholic'.

Thus, as with Collins and Middleton, we find a panentheist dimension[216] in O'Malley, which is in harmony and interwoven with his Christian faith. Like Collins, his nature spirituality is enhanced by a rootedness in the Irish past, by a reverence for Early Irish Christian art with its pre-Christian influences. He has a particular love for the medieval sculptures in St Canice's Cathedral, Kilkenny and Jerpoint Abbey, which have been inspirational in his work.

I would like to suggest here that O'Malley's and, for that matter, Collins' panentheist-Christian 'theology', curiously links with that of one of their

214. Interview, 30.10.95. He points out that in provincial Ireland of his early years nobody realised that 'by engagement in art, a man could be redeemed from the triviality around him'. in Fallon, 'Appreciation – Interview with Tony O'Malley', *Éire-Ireland*, vol. 25, no. 3 (1990), 112.
215. Interview, 30.10.1995.
216. Because O'Malley allows for a personal God, it would be more correct to speak of a panentheist rather than, as Fallon suggests, pantheist element in his spirituality and work. Cf. Fallon, *Tony O'Malley*, 46.

great forebears, namely John Scottus Eriugena (810-877). This theologian, who had a wide ranging influence on subsequent theology and philosophy, was seen in his own time as challenging orthodoxy and as an advocate of independent thought.[217] In particular, he was accused of identifying the created world with God in which the absolute otherness of a transcendent God is not acknowledged, i.e. of pantheism, a term which actually did not exist until the early eighteenth century.[218] While there are statements in the *Periphyseon* which, taken out of context, could prove this charge, scholars like Dermot Moran and Willemien Otten have shown that this aspect in Eriugena was clearly misinterpreted.[219]

The fact that Eriugena makes a distinction between *creator* and *creatura* immediately disproves his accusers.[220] When Eriugena traces God's presence in nature it is a theophany whereby the divine supremacy of God is untouched. While Eriugena writes that 'both the creature, by subsisting, is in God; and God, by manifesting Himself ... creates Himself in the creature', he asserts at the same time that God 'becomes in all things all things' as God *descends* as 'Supreme Goodness, which is Unity and Trinity into the things ... So it is from Himself that God takes the occasions of His theophanies ... since all things are from Him and through Him and in Him and for Him'.[221] It is obvious that Eriugena's writing is, in fact, in line with Pauline and Johanine theology as 1 Cor 15:28 ('God may be all in all') and Jn 1:3-4 ('All things came into being through him ...') indicate.

As O'Malley, Collins and Middleton believe in the presence of God in all creation without denying a transcendent divine being, their thought thus discloses a striking parallel to the medieval theologian Eriugena.[222] Naturally, it

217. Dermot Moran, *The philosophy (sic) of John Scottus Eriugena, A Study of Idealism in the Middle Ages* (Cambridge: Cambridge Univ. Press, 1989), 84, 89-90.
218. Interestingly the word 'pantheist' apparently was first used by the deist Irish theologian John Toland (1670-1722).
219. Moran, op.cit., 84-89. Willemien Otten, *The Anthropology of Johannes Scottus Eriugena*, Brill's Studies in Intellectual History, vol. 20 (Leiden, New York: 1991), 80-81.
220. P. Sheldon-Williams, (ed.), *Johannis Scotti Eriugenae Periphyseon*, Book III (Dublin: Institute of Advanced Studies, 1981), 161, 163. Otten, op.cit., 81.
221. Sheldon-Williams, op.cit., 163. (Author's emphasis.)
222. It is interesting to note that a similar line of thinking is found in Irish poets, such as Patrick Kavanagh, for example. In her study on Kavanagh, Una Agnew has shown how Kavanagh was fascinated by and reflected his fascination with religion, both pre-Christian and Christian, in his writing. Kavanagh, like O'Malley and Collins, believed God to be present in the beauty of nature and in all human activity. He held, moreover, that the introduction of Roman Catholicism had disposed of druidic culture and established a religion that became increasingly distant from daily life. It was part of his 'genius' that he 'distilled for himself an essence of Christianity despite the local brand available'. U. Agnew, 'Religious Themes in the Work of Patrick Kavanagh: Hints of a Celtic Tradition', *Studies,* vol. 82, no. 327 (Autumn 1993), 257-264.

is not to be suggested that their thought is identical. The very different contexts and paradigms of medieval Europe and twentieth century Ireland alone prevent such a conclusion. Yet, it is remarkable that a certain continuity of thought – whether in scholastic, systematic fashion as in Eriugena, or in the more allusive, intuitive ideas and artistic expression of the painters in question – can be traced from the ninth into the twentieth century in Irish culture.

What is at the core of O'Malley's life and work is his profound spirituality which, as in the saints and mystics, is based on an acceptance and understanding of spiritual poverty and Christian humility. He has stated that for him 'all art is a spiritual activity fundamentally'.[223] The spiritual-contemplative side of painting is, as he sees it, the 'endurance' as well as the suffering of destitution that it entails. And it is precisely this poverty which makes him and his work rich.

William Johnston and other writers on mysticism argue that mysticism is 'knowledge through love' and as such the centre of authentic religious experience.[224] Johnston emphasises that mystical love and indwelling is not sterile but creative and therefore can lead to the creation of great works of art. Or, as Moltmann writes, it is the indwelling spirit who is the 'principle of creativity' in all spheres of life.[225] O'Malley's love of and unfailing devotion to his art, which is based on stillness and reflection, on inwardness, inner freedom, intuition, contemplation and on complete absorption, abundantly reveals this mystical dimension. It is this rich spiritual dimension which he shares with the mystics and prophets.

For O'Malley art is the 'manifestation of the religious instinct'.[226] Moreover, he has 'always regarded painting as a purely sacramental thing. It's a great mystery ... you work at it day after day and then suddenly something happens, a revelation'.[227] 'Sacramental', he continues, is 'not ... sacrament'; 'a thing [art] becomes sacramental because ... [it is] sacred to somebody and part of an operation'.[228] Revelation here is not to be understood in a narrow religious sense, it is revelation to and of himself, and of the 'struggle in painting and how you have elected to stay and adopt this way of life without any kind of reward'. These statements show his understanding of revelation in an artistic-immanent sense, as well as his stress on the subjective aspect in art:

223. Fallon, 'Appreciation – Interview with Tony O'Malley', op.cit., 110.
224. William Johnston, *The Inner Eye of Love* (London: Collins/Fount Paperbacks, 1978), 31.
225. Moltmann, *God in Creation*, 100.
226. O'Malley quoted in Vera Ryan, 'Transition Years', in Brian Lynch, (ed.), *Tony O'Malley* (Aldershot, Hants: Scolar Press/Kilkenny: Butler Gallery. 1996), 66.
227. H. Cooke, Interview with Tony O'Malley, *The Irish Times*, 7.12.1973.
228. Interview, 30.10.1995.

'Poetry and painting is *(sic)* a deeply subjective thing ...'[229] One may conclude that it is in this subjective, artistic-immanent revelation that the work of art reveals itself 'objectively' transcendent to the viewer. O'Malley himself seems to confirm this when he perceives art as a great mystery, which, born of the 'religious instinct', is in its sacramentality sacred. In this context it is significant to remember also, that, as mentioned earlier, he actually used the religious term of a 'vow', by which he decided to dedicate himself to his work after his recovery from TB.

O'Malley's work is both figurative and abstract. Since St. Ives abstract forms have been dominant. In metaphysical fashion he holds that abstraction allows him 'to get under the surface, to get beyond appearances, and to express the mind'.[230] He actually prefers the term 'essence' to abstraction; for him – as for le Brocquy – the search for essence lies at the heart of his work. However, he has pointed out that abstraction for its own sake holds no interest for him: '[I]n a world where there is complete and total disbelief, there is a worship of the abstract for its own sake – it's like a kind of false god – and then it's mannerism.'[231]

His choice to paint in abstraction grew out of his introspection and inwardness. For him non-figurative form instils 'power' and 'meaning' in a painting. The goal at the end of the journey of making a painting is to arrive at simplicity.

There is a pronounced musical quality of rhythm and harmonies in his works. Significantly he has remarked that music in its ability in some way to 'dissolve the differences between things' can create a 'kind of oneness'.[232] Fundamentally, it is interiority, essence, oneness, simplicity and silence that are central in his aesthetics, spirituality and work.[233]

His ideas have been influenced by Zen philosophy, to which he was first introduced by his friend, the potter Bernard Leech, who had a profound knowledge of this subject. *The Unknown Craftsman* by Soetsu Yanagi (1889-1961)[234] which deals with the beauty of pattern, in particular, had an influ-

229. Ibid.
230. O'Malley quoted in *Works 14 – Tony O'Malley*, 21.
231. Fallon, *Tony O'Malley*, 100.
232. Aidan Dunne, 'The Later Work', in Lynch, (ed.), *Tony O'Malley*, 288. Cf. also Interview, 30.10.1995: 'It sounds like an impossible thing to do ... to paint music. I just feel the music. [It is] to make a kind of equivalent to myself of the music.'
233. Another indication of the inward nature of his faith is the fact that he does not say prayers but 'wish[es] prayers': 'It's not audible, it's interior. It would be subjective in ways.' Interview, 30.10.1995.
234. Bernard Leech was a friend of Yanagi. For a more detailed account of Yanagi's aesthetics, cf. Pattison, *Art, Modernity and Faith*, 172-174. It is interesting to note that like Richard Harries, Wendy Beckett and le Brocquy, Yanagi stresses that beauty cannot be achieved by conscious pursuit. Such pursuit rather leads to contrivance.

ence on his work (e.g. 'Nassau Painting', 1977, 'Morning Painting, Bahamas', 1983). He has also admired the writings of D.T. Suzuki. The aesthetic concept of *shibui,* which is used by the Japanese in everyday language, holds special importance for O'Malley. As Lynch points out, in a larger sense *shibui* can be used for an appraisal of all spheres of human existence. In the aesthetic realm it connotes a refined taste which is neither showy nor polished but simple and elegant, yet can include an awkwardness, and a touch of coarseness and naïvety. *Shibui* beauty is not divorced from but is realised precisely in everyday life, it is not *l'art pour l'art,* beauty for its own sake, but emerges from the depth of the spirit and on the basis that art and life form a union.

This Buddhist element of Zen philosophy and *shibui* aesthetic do not exist in opposition to but, rather, are in union with O'Malley's Christian-mystical spirituality. His choice of abstraction, i.e. his iconoclasm *in* the icon, which arises from his inwardness reveals at times nothingness, empty spaces, silence, the power of darkness as well as the intensity of light. These elements are present both in Buddhist and Christian mysticism. In fact, Rudolf Otto observed that in western art darkness and silence are the two means by which the numinous, or the sublime, is expressed in art while in the East emptiness is added as a third means.[235] The sense of detachment from worldly desires, and of an infinite journey through the cloud of unknowing towards the light are central to mystics in both East and West. As mentioned above, O'Malley has spoken of the process of painting as a 'journey'.

Interiority or inwardness, as Meister Eckhart held, is fundamental to any spiritual growth; someone who does not first know her/himself cannot know God.[236] Significantly O'Malley's inwardness and subjectivity are evidenced even in some of the titles of his works which he named 'inscapes' rather than 'landscapes'. He adopted this term from the poet and Jesuit priest Gerard Manley Hopkins. O'Malley's usage of it, however, differs from Hopkins'. Inscapes are for him '[t]hings from inside my mind ... [which] become transformed ... They become in an inner way symbols to me'.[237] They are inner visions transformed onto canvas. For Hopkins 'inscape' had a more objective meaning. It is the characteristic form of a species or a thing, an 'objective reality' which exists independent of the beholder, while 'instress', another term used by Hopkins, is the artist's internal response.[238] Thus when O'Malley

235. Rudolf Otto, *The Idea of the Holy* (London: Oxford University Press, 1950), 68-69.
236. Richard Woods, O.P., *Eckhart's Way* (London: Darton, Longman and Todd, 1986), 111. Woods, like Johnston and other scholars, refers to the similarities between Zen-Buddhism and Eckhart or St John of the Cross.
237. O'Malley, Interview, 30.10.1995.
238. Philip Ballinger, 'Ruskin: Hopkins' "Silent Don"', *Studies,* vol. 85, no. 338 (Summer 1996), 116-123, at 122. A discussion on parallels and differences in the nature spirituality between the Romantics, Ruskin, Hopkins, O'Malley, Collins, and Middleton goes

refers to 'inscape' it is rather Hopkins' term of 'instress' he has in mind. Although I do not intend to further develop the parallels between Hopkins and O'Malley it should be noted, nevertheless, that on a wider level 'inscape' or 'instress' allude to something which Hopkins, O'Malley and, for that matter, Collins and Middleton have in common, namely their perception of the transcendent aspect in nature.[239]

The final point that concerns us here is O'Malley's faith in Christ which has played an important role in his life. It is a real, questioning faith that is free of any narrow dogmatism: 'I think uniquely there was a Christ and he was preceded by others.'[240] While such a statement sounds paradoxical at first, its meaning becomes a little clearer when he continues: 'What went on two thousand years ago is still going on.' Thus revelation for O'Malley is ongoing and not limited to the person of Jesus. He affirms, however, Christ's 'unique' role in salvation history: '... I think unique in all that [history] would be that there was one person crucified for holding to his own intuitive powers and energies; whether it was divine or not would be another thing.' This view might lead one to conclude that O'Malley believes in the human Jesus but that he might hesitate to emphasise that the historical Jesus is the Christ of faith, i.e. the unity and continuity of humanity and divinity in Jesus. In fact, O'Malley touches here on a, or perhaps *the* fundamental question in christology as formulated by Gerhard Ebeling, namely how did the pro-claimer become the proclaimed, how did Jesus, the 'witness of faith', become the 'ground of faith'.[241] Ebeling points out that the historical Jesus is the Christ of faith not just because the gospels are witnesses of faith, but because Jesus in his life and death was himself a person and witness of faith. O'Malley's thought actually seems to point in a similar direction when he says that Jesus was crucified 'for holding to his own intuitive powers and energies'. Jesus' intuitive power and energies were precisely his faith in God and his witness of this faith in his death and resurrection. O'Malley then acknowledges Christ as unique; for him he is the incarnate God who through his death redeems humankind: 'I believe in a Redeemer, whether he was born of a virgin doesn't matter.'[242] Not only does the artist believe in Christ, but

beyond the scope of this study, but it might be beneficial to develop this elsewhere in order to place this aspect in the three Irish painters in a wider European context.
239. Cf. Cary H. Plotkin's article on Hopkins' nature spirituality: 'Towards a Poetics of Transcendence after Darwin: The Aspect of Nature', *Studies* (Summer 1996), 136-143.
240. Interview, 30.10.1995.
241. G. Ebeling, *Wort und Glaube* (Tübingen: Mohr, 1960), 203-254.
242. O'Malley quoted in V. Ryan, 'Transition Years', in Lynch, (ed.), *Tony O'Malley*, 64.

the comment regarding the virgin birth reveals that his is a strong, mature faith in the incarnate God. He has no need of what could be interpreted as looking for 'proofs' like the virgin birth.

The death of Christ holds a special meaning for O'Malley: 'I had an inner faith in the highest, the journey up to Calvary would be a profound event always in my own mind.'[243] He adds, however, that it is 'mixed up with a lot of denial as well'. What he means here is that while Christ is 'unique', human religious sacrifice already existed in pre-Christian Jewish times, in Greek and Celtic mythology, as well as that Jesus was 'preceded by others'. O'Malley's seemingly contradictory views actually allude to and touch on the very heart of contemporary interfaith dialogue: Is Christ the unique revelation of the divine or are there, in fact, many ways to the one centre? In this context, Paul Knitter's observation is of interest, even if not conclusive. He emphasises that what is relevant in the end is not so much whether the question of Jesus' uniqueness, i.e. his normative universality, will be answered, but rather that through dialogue liberation and greater unity are brought about amongst people of all faiths.[244] Such dialogue, liberation and unity, one would suggest, can grow if one acknowledges, as O'Malley does, that all humans are truly made in the image of God: 'I think ... that all faces are figure of the divine figure.'[245] One might add that his view here is, of course, in perfect accordance with the Scriptures (Gen 1:26-27). It is this fundamental belief that makes it possible for O'Malley to affirm Jesus as redeemer and God while conceding at the same time that revelation of the ultimate is not unique to Christ.

The fact that Christ's redemptive death is a significant event for O'Malley is evidenced in his work. It is his custom to always paint on Good Friday. These 'Good Friday paintings',[246] which he has produced for over thirty years, are both abstract or figurative with religious iconography. The style and content in these paintings reveal diverse references, such as Grünewald's expressionist Isenheim Altar Crucifixion, Picasso's treatment of the same theme after Grünewald in 1932, and especially the works of the seventeenth century sculptor and craftsman O'Tunney in Callan. O'Malley's early Good Friday paintings are often sculptural or in shapes of reliefs made from driftwood ('Good Friday', 1965, and 1968). They range from a 'simple' depiction of a cross (1968) in muted colours to brighter canvases with elaborate figura-

243. Interview, 30.10.1995.
244. Cf. Paul F. Knitter, *No Other Name?* (London: SCM, 1985), 231.
245. Interview, 30.10.1995.
246. Ibid. 'I paint every day including Good Friday. And if it is Good Friday, I call it a "Good Friday Painting". But sometimes something comes into it - I'm not speaking now about magic - something happens on Good Friday ... and I call it "Good Friday Painting".'

tive incisions inspired by the O'Tunney's sculptures in St Mary's, Callan ('Calvary, Number 2', 1983). O'Malley's actual treatment of the theme will be discussed in more detail later.

One of the reasons why he has repeatedly depicted the death of Christ is his childhood memory, when his grandmother, 'a very wise woman', would take him on Good Friday to the 'Stations of the Cross' in his local church in Callan. These 'Stations', although poor in quality, moved him. When he began to paint this theme, he would transform it into his own 'subjective image' as a 'kind of commemoration' and 'also [as] a kind of reality for my own childlikeness'.[247]

Another reason for his choice of this theme was his personal experience of sickness and sense of 'resurrection'.[248] It was possibly through his own suffering by which he came to understand the meaning of Christ's death on the Cross not only intellectually but, more importantly, experientially and existentially.

From what has been said above it is clear that there are many facets in the faith and spirituality of this painter. One would suggest that the unifying thread which runs through all of these – the inward-mystical, the panentheist-Christian and the christological dimension of suffering and redemption – is O'Malley's sense of grace, of faith and his living in the Spirit. He has admired van Gogh and Cézanne precisely because spirit is, as he sees it, central to their work. He has been absorbed into his own work, as he says, in 'spirit and ... soul'. According to him, 'all art is a spiritual activity', and he holds that the Spirit must be free which, however, must be accompanied by a 'moral sense', i.e. responsibility.

The Hebrew word for Spirit, *ruach,* which is feminine in gender, means 'breath', 'wind', 'air'. Essentially therefore Spirit is life and enables life. The Holy Spirit, as Yves Congar has written, is the active presence of the divine in us.[249] The Spirit, the source and principle of creativity, is thus 'God for us and with us'.[250] Wherever the Spirit of Christ is present there is freedom (2 Cor 3:17). Those who are in Christ and liberated through Christ are truly free (Mt 17:26; Jn 8:36). The Holy Spirit and the human spirit are not opposed

---

247. Interview, 30.10.1995.
248. 'To witness a person or friend ... dying a couple of beds away was part of the Good Friday, to hear the Rosary being said for him.' Interview, 30.10.1995. In fact, his Good Friday paintings are preceded by the theme of Lazarus, which also has to do with his own survival after TB. Cf. V. Ryan, 'Transition Years', in Lynch, (ed.), *Tony O'Malley,* 66.
249. Cf. Yves Congar, Walter Kern, 'Geist und Heiliger Geist', in Franz Böckle, Franz-Xaver Kaufmann, Karl Rahner, Bernhard Welte, (eds.), in assoc. with Robert Scherer, *Christlicher Glaube in moderner Gesellschaft,* vol. 22 (Freiburg: Herder, 1982), 90.
250. Congar, *I Believe in the Holy Spirit,* vol. 1 (London: Geoffrey Chapman, 1983), 11.

to each other. The Holy Spirit dwells and works in the human spirit wherever truth is searched for and established, in the arts, in peace, in relationships, in Christian worship, etc. Or, as Paul writes, there are many gifts of the Spirit but there is only one Spirit (1 Cor 12:11).

O'Malley's life and painting are an expression of a profound awareness of the presence of the Spirit. It is his mystical inwardness, his faith in Christ and trust in the Spirit which gave him the strength to survive in the face of death and which have enabled him to paint his marvellous works. Truly spiritual and transcendent, his paintings are evidence of his open, questioning faith and spirituality. Congar wrote that he considered 'doxology the highest mode of theology'.[251] Ultimately O'Malley's whole life and oeuvre are revelatory of such a theology of praise.

251. Congar, *The Word and the Spirit* (London: Geoffrey Chapman, 1986), 5.

VIII. PATRICK SCOTT

Patrick Scott[252] was born in 1921 in Kilbrittain, County Cork into an Anglo-Irish family. According to himself, he had a happy childhood and was brought up in the Church of Ireland tradition of his parents.[253] Scott already painted while at St Columba's School and continued to do so while studying architecture at University College, Dublin. After graduation, he worked as architect with Michael Scott for fifteen years. Thereafter he devoted himself entirely to painting.

Scott is one of Ireland's foremost abstract artists. In fact, apart from the early works, like 'Birds on the Shore 2' and 'Evening Landscape' (both 1944), his paintings are almost exclusively semi-abstract or abstract. The linear emphasis, the geometrical shapes and ordered discipline in the structure of his paintings reflect his architectural interests.

1960 was an important year in the life of the artist. Not only was he acknowledged as one of Ireland's finest painters when he was chosen to represent his country at the Venice Biennale but he also won the Guggenheim National Award at the Guggenheim International Exhibition in New York. However, the most significant development was a technical discovery that would have a lasting impact on all his subsequent work. During that time, while working on the redecoration of John Huston's house in County Galway, Scott frequently had to travel to Loughrea across the midland bogs. He became interested in capturing the evening light and atmospheric, elusive colours of the bogs. He discovered that he could achieve the subtle, 'almost hallucinatory quality of the Irish twilight' by letting the colours soak into unprimed, raw and wet canvas (e.g. 'Ring device', 1964).[254]

A further major discovery was made when he began to apply squares of gold leaf onto unprimed canvas. In fact, his best known works are his gold paintings (e.g. 'Goldpainting 38', 1966; 'Gold Diptych' 5/6, both 1979) as well as his colourful tapestries ('Eroica', 1979; 'Shanagarry', c.1969). These works are represented in many public spaces and public and private collections nationally and internationally, including the Museum of Modern Art, New York and the Hirshhorn Museum, Washington.

Walker and other critics have admired the 'sure decorative sense', exquisite taste and consistent high standard which marks Scott's oeuvre. Indeed,

252. *Note:* This section on Scott was published in a slightly altered version as 'Spiritual Dimensions in Modern Art: The Painter Patrick Scott' in *Doctrine and Life,* vol. 46, no. 4 (1999), 194-201.
253. Dorothy Walker, 'Introduction', in *Patrick Scott,* cat. (Dublin: Douglas Hyde Gallery, 1981), 15.
254. Ibid., 23.

Scott is sincere about his work; what matters to him essentially is simply to concentrate on his painting.[255] He neither likes the fashionable preoccupations of the artworld, nor has he had any financial ambitions.

Walker points out that the power of Scott's paintings lies in their non-aggressive calm which is achieved through complete harmony of scale, material and colour.[256] Not only are his works of assured, simple, yet sophisticated elegance, but they have, in fact, a pronounced meditative, spiritual quality. It is this contemplative, harmonious aspect which – like O'Malley, for example, but in a very different style – makes this painter relevant to the theme of this book.

Patrick Scott has lived and worked in Dublin all his life. He has visited the Far East, i.e. China and Japan, several times. These visits and his interest in Buddhist philosophy have in turn influenced his painting.

His works have been exhibited in solo and group exhibitions, including ROSC, in Ireland, Britain, continental Europe and the United States.

* * *

Scott has been described as shy, unassuming, self-effacing and non-imperious.[257] He has always found it difficult to talk about his work.[258] He has spoken even less about his personal faith and beliefs.

Scott's parents were involved in local church life; they were, as he says, 'pillars of the church'.[259] During his childhood he regularly attended services with them. His mother read the Bible daily and also used to read to him from the Scriptures. Later she gave him a special edition of the Bible designed to be read as literature: 'I enjoyed reading a lot of it because you didn't have all these verses and numbers in it ... It was printed in the thirties sometime.'[260] As a boy he also sang in a church choir, he 'enjoyed good church hymns and bits of other things'.

However, after he finished secondary school, faith and the church ceased to play a role in his life: '[A]fter I left school I just stopped going to church. I felt that it no longer held any interest for me at all, no desire.'

Scott no longer believes in Christ or in eternal life: 'It's all gone ... I have

255. David Irwin commented in *The Guardian* on 24.4.1962, that the spiritual element in Scott as in Kandinsky is the inner need which drives their work. In Scott, however, he adds, this compulsion is evident 'but strictly controlled'.

256. Cf. Walker, 'Free Form', *Hibernia*, 6.12.1974.

257. Cf. Walker, *Hibernia*, 6.12.1974.

258. Interview, 17.10.1995. Cf. also Interview with H. Cooke: 'Harriet Cooke talks to the quiet man of Irish Painting', *The Irish Times*, 26.7.1972.

259. Interview, 17.10.1995. *Note:* Unless otherwise indicated, all points of information and quotations are from this interview.

260. Scott has kept this Bible all his life.

no belief in an afterlife at all. That's totally gone, if it ever was there. I don't think it was ever there ... I enjoy life anyhow ... So I am not looking for any rewards in the future.'

Surprisingly, he has never found it difficult to live as a non-believer in a society in which religious allegiances are fundamental. Although he does not adhere to religious faith, he, nevertheless, concedes: 'I suppose there has to be something but I can't identify with anything.' He thus holds a line between agnosticism and atheism.

It is this agnostic-atheistic element which is of special interest regarding Scott as well as in the wider discussion of the relationship between faith, theology and art. Scott's oeuvre, especially the gold paintings with their profound atmosphere of the hieratic, of contemplation, stillness, meditation and of transcendence, might seem to diametrically oppose the artist's personal views. Such a conclusion, however, would imply that an artist who is a non-believer is incapable of producing works that are perceived as spiritual, or even religious. As discussed earlier, there is wide agreement among contemporary theologians, who have written on aesthetics, that such a view is unsustainable. As Wendy Beckett rightly observes, the spiritual in a work of art is *independent* of the artist's intention.[261] For the painter, the image is her or his primary expression; it reveals what lies deepest within her or himself. In this sense art is transcendent and spiritual as it reveals something of the human spirit and imagination, and, as theologians and believers would argue, *therefore* possibly something of the divine Spirit.[262] The spiritual and transcendent in a work of art is its power to point through the material to the immaterial, i.e. to what lies beyond. It reveals the truth of the artist, which in turn can confront us with our own truth.[263] It can take the viewer further, open up new realms, unconceal and evoke something unexpected, joyful or painful in her or him. Thus it makes one reflect and react. In this way it is a spiritual and even a *religious* experience, as Rahner points out, in that it confronts the person in his or her totality since it awakens in them 'the whole question of existence'[264] which ultimately includes the search for and experience of the transcendent Other.

261. Beckett, *Art and the Sacred*, 7.
262. It is interesting to note that Daisetz Suzuki, from a Buddhist perspective, argues very much along the same lines when he writes that the great works of art 'invariably' have the quality of 'something approaching the work of God. The artist, at the moment when his creativeness is at its height, is transformed into an agent of the creator'. Daisetz T. Suzuki, *Zen and Japanese Culture* (London: Routledge and Kegan Paul, 1973), 219-220.
263. Beckett, op.cit., 7.
264. K. Rahner, 'Theology and the Arts', in *Thought*, vol. 57, no. 224 (New York: Fordham University Press, 1982), 27.

In this context it is significant that Scott sees no problem with a spiritual-theological interpretation of his works: 'I'm not in the least bit worried if anyone gets a spiritual feeling or impact from my paintings. That would please me more than anything else.' A statement like this one actually affirms that the interpretation of a work of art cannot be tied to the intentions of the artist. The image, like the text, speaks and must be allowed to speak for itself.[265] Nevertheless, the beliefs and background of the artist or writer will, naturally, always be of interest in grounding and making one's interpretation as comprehensive and truthful as possible.

If Scott does not believe in the Christian God, it is both ironic and hopeful that he has had several church commissions, in fact, probably more than any of the other artists examined in this book. It is hopeful because – being neither a believer nor a 'church artist' – his works have found recognition with the institutional churches as conveying what is in accordance with the Christian kerygma. As Gabriel Daly observes, it is the power of great art 'to touch our religious sensibilities even when the artist ... rejects religious faith in its conventional sense'.[266]

Scott made an 'enormous' reredos for St Paul's School in London and also for the Church of Reconciliation at Knock.[267] He made a screen for a church in Texas and he has also painted a couple of canvases which show crosses, as well as several diptychs.[268] However, he has emphasised that no religious inspiration or intentions were involved in their making.

If Scott does not believe in the Christian God, he, nevertheless, stresses the importance of love: 'Love is very important. The unfortunate thing is religion creates so much hate ... [and] a lot of *Angst*.' Although Scott denies that social concern has played a great role in his life, he has, in fact, revealed his humanitarian interests in both his works and in social involvement. He was one of the founder members of the Irish Anti-Apartheid movement and supports a number of aid organisations. In the early sixties he painted a series of works which he titled 'device[s]' (e.g. 'Yellow device', 1962, 'Purple device', 1963).

265. Cf. Jeanrond on the interdisciplinary aspect of hermeneutics in his book *Theological Hermeneutics, Development and Significance* (London: Macmillan, 1991), 3-5.
266. Gabriel Daly, 'Faith and Imagination', *Doctrine and Life,* vol. 32, no. 2 (1982), 75.
267. In 1984 D. Walker commented that the religious dimension is almost absent in contemporary Irish art. Two works which she found convincing, however, were Scott's altarpiece for the school in London as well as a painting of the 'Last Supper' by Michael Mulcahy: 'Both these works embody the necessary qualities of art: an energy that immediately makes itself known, and a pure spirit of faithfulness to the art itself.' (Walker, 'Searching for the Heart of Saturday Night', *Circa,* no. 14 (Jan.-Feb. 1984), 13.
268. One of his gold paintings was included in the *Art and Transcendence* exhibition in Maynooth College. Cf. *Maynooth College Bicentenary Art Exhibitions, Ecclesiastical Art of the Penal Era & Art and Transcendence,* cat. (Maynooth: St. Patrick's College, 1995), 58.

These paintings explore the sphere, which is a dominant motif in many of his works. 'Device' was a euphemism for the bombs that were tested at that time. He painted his works in protest at those tests: 'I painted them in sort of anger. They were all very explosive kind of paintings.' These canvases, like Picasso's 'Guernica', are indirectly revelatory of the beautiful as the glory of the true and the good. They are particularly vibrant examples of the fact that in art ethical and aesthetic aspects may be strongly linked, that the aesthetic can become a force and expression of some deep moral concerns. Indeed art, as Cyril Barrett and Patrick Sherry point out, has moral value.[269] Such a view opposes the notion of *l'art pour l'art*. Rather, as art, especially great art, is a product of and conveys what is deeply felt and reflected, it can widen our aesthetic and ethical sensibility. Fundamentally then, it is the search for and revelation of beauty, truth and goodness (in art) which forms the central link between aesthetics and ethics.[270]

Scott, like several of the previously examined painters, has always had an interest in the (pre-)Celtic past. As Walker has noted his 'geometric abstraction of the circle ... combined with rectilinear interlaced white bands of white ... relates directly to ancient Irish gold objects of the pre-Celtic era'.[271] The sphere, especially the sun, is a recurrent symbol in his work. The painter has an obsession with the sun, which, as Barrett has commented, is an echo of the ancient Celtic sun worship.[272] Scott himself has spoken about his interest in the (pre-)Celtic artefacts, archaeology, the Irish countryside and the sun: 'The sun gives everyone life, it's a very important thing ... I have always been a sun worshipper'. His acknowledgement of being a sun worshipper, even if light-hearted, hints at what has been discussed in detail in relation to

269. Cf. Cyril Barrett, S.J., 'The Painter's World, An Introduction', *Capuchin Annual* (1961), 317. Cf. also Patrick Sherry, *Spirit and Beauty, An Introduction to Theological Aesthetics* (Oxford: Clarendon Press, 1992), 4.
270. Cf. Sherry, op.cit., 4. For further discussion of the relationship between ethics and aesthetics cf. Eric Fuchs, 'The Mutual Questioning of Ethics and Aesthetics', *Crosscurrents, The Journal of the Association for Religious and Intellectual Life*, vol. 43, no. 1 (New York: College of New Rochelle, 1993), 26-37. Fuchs, like Beckett, points out that engaging with a work of art involves a confrontation with truth. In this way an encounter with it can be a decisive experience in one's life.
271. Walker, 'Introduction', in *Patrick Scott*, 26. Cf. also Walker, 'Indigenous Culture and Irish Art', in M.P. Hederman, R. Kearney, (eds.), *The Crane Bag Book of Irish Studies (1977-1981)* (Dublin: Blackwater Press, 1982), 135. 'Patrick Scott in his personal preoccupation with geometric abstraction and his sensual appreciation of gold leaf on raw canvas, has effected the fusion of abstract mathematics and physical aesthetic beauty which is a criterion of powerful art; and in particular of the early Bronze Age gold ornaments of Ireland, uniquely elegant and fine among objects of archaic art anywhere.' Ibid.
272. Barrett, quoted in *Patrick Scott*, 42.

Collins, Middleton and O'Malley, namely the panentheistic dimension, which is rooted in Ireland's past and still holds a fascination and presence in Irish literature and visual art. It therefore does not come as a surprise that although he lives and works in Dublin, he spends much time in the countryside which for him is a contemplative, transcendent experience.[273]

Scott's travels to China and Japan brought him into contact with Eastern philosophies, in particular (Zen-)Buddhism, which for him is the most meditative religion he has encountered: 'I've always found religions a bit disturbing because they seem to generate hate so often. But I have found Zen the most ... meditative religion that I've come across.' What particularly appeals to him is the notion of 'sorting ... [one]self out by meditating' which he finds 'more realistic' than other religious practices. His canvases directly reflect this meditative quality. He himself perceives his works as 'contemplative', 'restful', producing a 'sort of calm'.

In conclusion, one would suggest that it is his positive, life-affirming vision, expressed in his art through the symbol of the sun, bright colours, especially his choice of pale white tempera and gold, which convey a sense of the sacred, of ultimate reality, of redemption and eternity. Indeed, it is radiance, wholeness and harmony (Aquinas) which essentially characterise his oeuvre. His works are not existentialist, they do not express the human predicament of war or suffering in contemporary society, except for the 'Devices' which he painted in protest to the testing of nuclear bombs. Scott's works provide glimpses of transcendent beauty, of anticipated salvation.

As Patrick Sherry rightly points out, the Spirit – 'the source of all real beauty ... because of his work in creation and because of his freedom to inspire whomever he wills' – blows where the Spirit wills, and 'often, it seems, without much regard to the recipient's ... religious orthodoxy'.[274]

273. 'I go out and sit on rocks for long periods.'
274. Sherry, *Spirit and Beauty*, 182.

IX. PATRICK GRAHAM

One of Ireland's leading contemporary artists, Patrick Graham was born in Mullingar in 1943. In his childhood Graham already showed a remarkable facility for drawing. He attended the National College of Art and Design from 1960 to 1964, a time when academic art was still the dominant style. Graham was recognised as brilliant by teachers and fellow students. He, however, had doubts and felt dissatisfaction since academic painting presented no challenge to him. He taught art for a few years, but felt a constant sense of failure. By the late 1960s Graham drank heavily and stopped painting for several years. In times of deep despair he would return to his art, producing expressive pieces that derived, as he said, from seeing with his 'heart and soul' rather than his eyes, and functioned as a form of catharsis.[275] In 1974, Graham resumed exhibiting. Through his personal experiences of being close to death through alcoholism and his introduction to German expressionist art – Emil Nolde,[276] in particular, whose work has been inspirational to him – he discovered art as a means of self expression. What impressed him most was the humanity and attitude of painters like Munch, Nolde, or Beckmann.

Graham, like Patrick Hall and Brian Maguire, has been labelled Neo-Expressionist. He himself resents this tag as unhelpful as he feels that his art comes from within and is his own. While he holds that the work of the New Expressionists is 'all about sensation', he insists that 'above all else' a painting 'has to be still'.[277] It is in such works as 'The Gift' (1984), 'The Ark of Dreaming' (1990), 'The Lark in the Morning I' (1991-93) and in several works from the series of 'The Blackbird Suite' (1992-93) that this sense of expressionism and stillness is especially achieved.

Apart from Nolde, he admires and has drawn inspiration from Renaissance artists. In fact, he stated once that he desired to return to the Old Masters, 'the purity and silence of a della Francesca', the sacredness of a van

275. Graham quoted in Henry J. Sharp, 'Patrick Graham', in *Patrick Graham, Brian Maguire, Paintings 1984,* cat. (Belfast: Octagon Gallery, 1984), (no p.).
276. His [Nolde's] painting had a wisdom that shattered by facilitative posturing. Having seen it, heard it, I set about defending myself from it. I denounced Nolde to all who would listen ... In my heart I loved and dreaded this stranger. I knew he was the stranger I wanted to walk with in those times when I allowed truth to come from secret places.' Graham, 'A Letter from the Artist', in *Patrick Graham,* cat. (Los Angeles: Jack Rutberg Fine Arts, Inc., 1989), 5.
277. John Hutchinson, 'Interview with Patrick Graham', in *Irish Arts Review,* vol. 4, no. 4 (Winter 1987), 16. Cf. also Graham in *Works 5 - Patrick Graham* (Dublin: Gandon, 1992), 26: '[G]reat art is stillness personified ... it is to be contemplated.'

Eyck altarpiece, the 'putrid force of a Grünewald crucifixion, and the human-ity of a Goya".[278]

Graham's predominant subject matter centres on religion, sexuality, poli-tics and social issues, often drawn from the Irish context, and sometimes alluding to its traditional poetry and music (e.g. 'Ire/land III' (1982), 'The Life & Death of Hopalong Cassidy' (1988), 'Song of the Yellow Bittern' (1988), 'The Lark in the Morning' (1991-1993). For him art 'in the real sense is creation out of nothing but one's own experience'.[279] Certainly, personal expression lies at the heart of his work and paradoxically, as in Collins, it is precisely this subjective, particular element which gives his art a universal, objective dimension. Moreover, his Catholic upbringing and background, his enquiring faith, his interest in religion and search for truth, are central to his life and work.

Graham lives and works in Dublin. He has taught art and has had an influence on Irish painters like Maguire and Hall. Graham has exhibited in Ireland, Britain, continental Europe and the United States, where his work has been especially acclaimed.

* * *

Religion, the Catholic Church, its ethos, its repression, especially of sexuality, played a formative role in Graham's youth. In fact, he developed an extreme, 'unhealthy' obsession with religion: 'I wanted to be a priest. I wanted to be a martyr[280] ... My first notoriety as an artist was drawing popes.'[281]

Later Graham developed friendships with some priests. On the other hand, however, he felt 'this kind of hatred for it all'. In the sixties he admired John XXIII: 'I thought there is possibility, this could be something to return to ... [a]nd you felt they [priests] were actually in a living church.' Graham shared their enthusiasm for a renewed church, and was saddened when 'it all kind of disappeared'.

Graham rejects much of traditional Catholicism, but emphasises that reli-gion, 'whatever it is', is 'absolutely essential to the whole of the human self,

278. Graham quoted in Donald Kuspit, 'Patrick Graham: Painting as Dirge', in *The Lark in the Morning, Patrick Graham,* cat. (Dublin/Cork: Douglas Hyde Gallery/Crawford Gallery, 1994), 7.
279. John Carson, P. Graham, 'Two Points of View', *Circa,* no. 14 (Jan.-Feb. 1984), 33.
280. Interview, 28.9.1995. 'It had to do with my life. The men were gone, they were not send-ing money back, the poverty was extreme ... The hopes that women had were the church.' *Note:* In this section on Graham many of his personal statements from two inter-views (28.9.1995 and 10.10.1995) with the author are used. Unless otherwise stated all quotations are from these interviews.
281. 'I drew popes everywhere ... especially Pope Pius XII ... right wing fascism which he brought to the church.'

[to] the sense of being', 'to completeness'. He insists that the 'whatever' is 'very important' and 'must always remain'. In *that* sense' he feels it is 'practically the same' as art as it is 'related entirely to human process of thought, logic conclusion, and disbelief and then curiosity'. He understands religion as 'looking up out of myself in otherness for the completeness of me'. Graham's personal need for religious faith today is simple and basically the same as it was during his childhood: 'I need it [religion] as a child, I do not need it as an arrogant, complete knowing human being ... There is a child in me which needs this child's reality and needs to actually depend on it ...' Like O'Malley, Graham stresses the element of childlike innocence through which he wants to find and live his faith. For him this includes a sense of 'mystery and magic'. He thus takes to heart Jesus' command of the need to receive the kingdom of God like a child (Mk 10:14-16). For him prayer, especially praying for others, as an expression of that faith is the demand for 'less self-centredness'.

Graham's search for innocent faith goes hand in hand with a critical, enquiring mind. His desire for authentic faith has involved a lot of struggle. Unable to accept much of what the church taught, he nevertheless felt that he had to believe in order to survive. He compares himself to doubting Thomas but points out: 'At least what I *have* is something to stick my finger in. Before I hadn't and that's why I nearly died.' In this context of faith coupled with doubt he also concedes that he 'cannot but' believe in redemption. His belief here is partly based on some moments when he actually experienced 'a reality of otherness', of 'transcendence'.

Graham stresses the centrality of human experience out of which and by which our faith is shaped. Rules and irrelevant, static religious dogmas deny this sense of experience, process and creative journey. For him, as for a theologian like Sölle, religion is to be lived as question rather than as dogma.[282] Moreover, he echoes Gerd Theissen, who has pointed out that modern, critical faith is essentially based on an acceptance of the human condition as a pre-requisite of religious experience, on ongoing search for truth and for meaning.[283] Graham's thought and theological awareness reveals therefore parallels with Sölle, Theissen and, for that matter, with contemporary theology in general in his emphasising of empirical human reality as the starting point for authentic, contemporary faith.

Graham is primarily concerned with search for truth, both in his art and life. Significantly he has remarked about his wish to always try to live as if five minutes before death. Not only does it provide a sense of urgency about his work, but it makes life 'very simple' as only that what is essential, i.e.

---

282. Cf. D. Sölle, *The Truth Is Concrete* (London: Burns & Oates, 1969), 12-13, 91.
283. Gerd Theissen, *On Having Critical Faith* (London: SCM, 1979), 15, 25, 98.

truth, matters.[284] For him the locus of truth as of faith is essentially in experience. If truth is perceived as unchanging rather than as an open process, it becomes a 'power-concept' which always implies the danger of corruption: 'For me the notion of power is simply basically corrupt. Once people hold on to it as a need to control, manipulate, [there is] the inevitability of corruption.' It is the human desire for power, as manifest in politics, sexuality and religion, which makes humans 'deviate from truth. Yet we are all essentially moral, and like all living things, we naturally turn towards the light'.[285] Graham, through his painting as well as through his own background of alcoholism and hospitalisation is under no illusion about the arduous journey involved in this search for light and truth. In his work he tries to 'avoid judgement and propaganda' as this could lead precisely to dogma and power. He rather prefers to wait 'until things reveal themselves'.[286] In fact, it has been said about Graham's work that it is 'Augustinian', as it is 'an art of musing rather than declaring'.[287]

For him truth is more exciting than anything else precisely because it is not static. Truth can be experienced as revelation and can give wisdom if one believes in it. As he points out, his 'reference' in art is always the humanity of the artist that finds expression in his or her work.[288] 'Humanist art', as he terms it, challenges collective, 'rationalised' truth and 'seeks the individual spiritual truth of ourselves as individual and unique'.[289]

Graham rarely attends Mass. Like most of the other artists examined – except for Yeats and Jellett – he believes without taking part in communal worship.[290] In fact, he suggests that if he did go he would prefer to spend time in a Protestant church because it has a 'stillness' that one does not experience in a Catholic place of worship. The Catholic Church is 'too fond of its ... own grandeur to allow a moment of silence ... Protestant churches ... are there for contemplation'.[291]

284. Graham is, of course, aware that such a sense of urgency cannot always be maintained.
285. Graham quoted in Hutchinson, op.cit., 17.
286. Ibid. '[I] believe that I'm after truth, and that the journey is a very murky one - you're always having to turn the light on things you don't understand or like.'
287. Peter Frank, 'Patrick Graham: between inner and outer vision', in *Patrick Graham, Plain nude drawings, studies for the blackbird suite,* cat. (Galway: Arts Festival Ltd., 1994).
288. Graham, 'On Irish Expressionist Painting', in *The Irish Review,* no. 3 (Cork: Cork University Press, 1988), 31.
289. Ibid.
290. In this context Schillebeeckx – as, of course, other theologians and writers – has observed that the 'institutionalisation of belief in God' is the fundamental problem and the reason why many people believe in God but no longer take part in church ceremonies or cease to be members of the institutional church altogether. Cf. E. Schillebeeckx, *Church, The Human Story of God* (London: SCM, 1990), 59-62.
291. Here one might suggest that Graham's view may be slightly stereotyped. While it is true

On the question of church art he significantly remarks that while the encounter with a great work of art can be a 'living experience', church art does not provide the worshipper with such experiences.[292] Graham is actually uncertain whether he would like to see works of art in churches. However, he loves both Rothko's and Matisse's Chapels (Houston, Texas and Vence, France) because of their atmosphere of silence. Also, he would like to locate a work like Grünewald's Isenheim altarpiece or his own 'Life and Death of Hopalong Cassidy' in a place of worship because rather than providing pleasant, non-challenging religious images, they relate to the human predicament, pose questions and make people react.[293]

Graham reads the Bible every now and then and has frequently used biblical references in his work, as, for example, in 'The Life and Death of Hopalong Cassidy', 'The Life of Christ' (1983-84) and in 'The Blackbird Suite'. For him the scriptures provide 'affirmation' and a real sense of something original: 'There is nothing so beautiful as "I am the word"'.

Stillness and silence are central to his understanding of his work as an artist: '[A]ll I am going to know is going to come from silence, and from silence the painting and so on.'[294] This silence implies for him abandoning certainties of truths, of ideologies or aesthetics. He asserts that genuinely real painting comes from not knowing. Painting from silence happens when it is 'no longer an act of doing or making but of receiving'.[295] In this way it is an experience of grace and becomes redemptive: '[T]he silence I speak of is redemptive of my life as an artist in and of itself.'[296] This awareness of the necessity of abandoning all certainties for the redeeming silence from which the painting emerges as gift reflects not only the views of Gadamer[297] or

that Roman Catholic places of worship display more grandeur and pomp than Protestant churches (especially of the Calvinist tradition), and thus could distract from contemplation, some Protestant churches or prayerhalls, on the other hand, display such a deliberate lack of aesthetic awareness and interest that they do not invite to meditation either. What Graham seems to have in mind are churches in which neither extreme applies and which exude a quiet and real atmosphere of the sacred.

292. 'I mean I am so sick of all these granite blocks, although it's nice, but it's about taste. What I would love to see is a kind of raw rock with moss on it and maybe some candles ... A living kind of experience.'

293. 'It's ... whether you see religion as dogma or ... as question. Or painting as question or painting ... as artistic linear dogma.'

294. *Works 5 - Patrick Graham*, 21.

295. Ibid., 17.

296. Ibid.

297. Gadamer, in an essay on visual art, pointed out that the modern artist 'is less a creator than a discoverer of the as yet unseen ...'. Hans Georg Gadamer, 'The speechless image', in *The Relevance of the Beautiful and Other Essays* (Cambridge: Cambridge University Press, 1986), 91.

artists like le Brocquy and Collins – who emphasised that art is not so much creation as uncovering what is already there – but something that is common to mystics from all traditions. As Tracy points out, in the last instance it is silence which may well be the most adequate mode of communication for religion.[298] Yet silence is possible only because of speech about the divine. Silence is the pre-condition for a Meister Eckhart or a Thomas Merton to write and contemplate, and for artists like O'Malley or Graham to paint. Both the artist and the mystic share the sense of silence, of void, of empti-ness, as well as the experience of mystery, mystery precisely because it cannot be clearly defined yet desires expression. This expression is not systematic, logical or necessarily rational as in theological discourse, but immediate, experiential, symbolic and indeterminate.[299]

For Graham silence is essentially 'emptiness' or 'lostness' and as such 'the best ... form of prayer' because it is the 'potential for discovery', the state where one searches for 'light': 'The light for humanity is completeness, which is otherness ... Otherness can be God, godness, we can call it whatever we like. It is holy nature.' He holds that the 'spiritual truth' which the artist needs to know is a 'realised unity of self to world and self to 'godness', or the 'it' of God'.[300] What Graham basically seems to have in mind is somewhat akin to Rahner's anthropological-transcendental theology. When Graham speaks of a 'realised unity' of self to both the world and to God, he, like Rahner, is aware of the necessity of the human being to live fully and con-cretely in this world while longing at the same time for transcendence. This view compares with what Rahner describes as the 'supernatural existential', i.e. the human natural order which is oriented towards the supernatural order, the human being who, in her awareness of herself as the subject of transcendence, becomes 'the event of God's absolute self-communication'.[301] It is interesting to note that Graham equates completeness with otherness, God, and 'holy nature'. In more theological terms, his view indicates a belief in a continuity between nature and grace, immanence and transcendence. Again one is reminded of Rahner when he writes: 'God in his innermost real-ity makes himself the innermost constituent in the human being' while, at the same time God remains mystery or the totally other.[302] When Graham

298. David Tracy, 'The Religious Classic and the Classic of Art', in D. Apostolos-Cappadona, (ed.), Art, Creativity, and the Sacred, 245.
299. Cf. Burch Brown, Religious Aesthetics, 111, 166-167. Cf. also George H. Tavard on the 'Openness of Images' in George Tavard, The Church, Community of Salvation, An Ecumenical Ecclesiology (Collegeville, Minnesota: The Liturgical Press, 1992), 88, 92-93.
300. Patrick Graham, 'On Irish Expressionist Painting', op.cit., 31.
301. K. Rahner, Grundkurs des Glaubens (Freiburg: Herder, 1976), 132.
302. Cf. ibid., 66, 122-126.

talks about 'holy nature' or 'Godness' it reflects, in fact, Rahner's idea of the human as being oriented to the divine in the here and now as he or she shares in the divine being and in the *pneuma* through the direct experience of God's self-communication.

What Graham seeks to achieve in his work – at times out of despair – is an 'absolute surrender' and 'loss of self-will combined with an awesome sense of ... some sort of "God experience"'.[303] Painting is thus fundamentally an act of self-giving, i.e. of love and in that way prayer and the locus of experiencing the presence of the divine: 'Great art is a true prayer. I have no hesitation saying that.'

A central aspect in his art, as critics and Graham himself have observed, is demythologisation.[304] This element is particularly evident in his works that contain religious subject matter. Demythologising is 'an effort to make life human ... The only way I can return religion to any kind of integrity, at least for myself, is to try to bring about some understanding of what love is'.[305] His demythologisation of political, social and religious issues springs from his profound search for love and truth. He uses formats like literary quotations, collage, parody, scribbled texts in his, at times frighteningly frontal, attacks on traditional religious and social myths. Graham's aim here is not to eliminate myths as such but rather to find new ones, to re-appraise, to make new sense. Grünewald's Isenheim altarpiece appeals to him precisely as it shows the reality of Christ's death in all its horror. He emphasises that other crucifixion images do not 'allow that Jesus became a human being ... and I don't know whether the church allows it'. Graham observes that in this painting Grünewald posed a 'serious question' which those who simply repeat representations of the mythological Christ, i.e. sanitised, idealised or sentimentalised images of the God-man hanging on the Cross in Golgatha, do not tackle.[306]

Interestingly, Graham's concern with demythologising reveals some striking parallels to the thought of Rudolf Bultmann. Both their starting point is the human condition. Graham's insistence on experience and truthful living as being formative for authentic faith concurs with Bultmann's view that general statements about God and ourselves are impossible since one can speak only in and from the concrete situation of one's life both about oneself and

---

303. Hutchinson, op.cit., 16.
304. Hutchinson, 'Myth and Mystification', in *A New Tradition, Irish Art of the Eighties* (Dublin: Douglas Hyde Gallery, 1990), 83.
305. Hutchinson, 'Interview with Patrick Graham', op.cit., 17.
306. Graham points out that this image confronts the viewer in 'asking the question: You have looked at something all your life. Here it is again. What ... really is it?'

about God's action in one's life.[307] Bultmann insisted on the necessity of eliminating the mythological view of the world in the New Testament as the condition to preserve the truth of the kerygma.[308] Like Graham he is not interested in abandoning all myths but rather he holds that myths express a person's understanding of her/himself and thus should be interpreted existentially. The real crux is Jesus, whose life and death in the New Testament are presented in mythical fashion. In him we have the 'unique combination' of the historical and the mythical. Jesus' life is historical; at the same time we believe him to be the pre-existent Son of God. The Jesus of history is the Christ of faith. As 'an ever-present reality', the Cross, Bultmann ascertains, is both an historical and an eschatological event which has 'revolutionary significance'. He stresses that to believe in the Cross means to 'undergo crucifixion' with Christ, to 'make it our own'. Redemption, Bultmann holds, therefore is not a supernatural miraculous event but a real, historical one. Graham remarkably echoes Bultmann when he states: 'Nobody relates to ... [the crucifixion] as a personal experience. People relate to it as a mythic experience.' Like Bultmann's insistence on our need to be crucified with Christ, Graham points out that instead of it being a real experience it 'is removed in the sense that the Cross is not something you are going to carry'. As someone who through his illness once stood on the threshold of death and who has genuinely struggled with his faith, Graham speaks with authority from his own experience.

For Graham, God 'ultimately ... has to be love ... only love'.[309] In relation to Christ's death on the Cross and its portrayal in art, he points out that a 'living sense of Godness comes in the eye to eye contact with the reality of goodness, not the mythology of goodness'. Jesus Christ in his sacrifice on the Cross is this *reality* of goodness, or, as Bultmann notes, faith in the love of God is not abstract or wishful thinking because in Christ God's love is concretely revealed.

From what has been said above it is clear that Graham's faith, based on personal experience and much struggle, is authentic, critical as well as childlike. In his life and in his art he strives for wholeness, i.e. for an integration of the spiritual and the physical. He has dealt with religious subjects through demythologisation which pose some radical, fundamental and sometimes uncomfortable questions. In his work and thought he radically affirms that God became flesh. At the same time, in his emphasis on contemplation, still-

---

307. R. Bultmann, *Jesus Christ and Mythology* (New York: Charles Scribner's Sons, 1958), 63-66.
308. Bultmann, 'New Testament and Mythology', in Hans Werner Bartsch, (ed.), *Kerygma and Myth,* vol. 1 (London: SPCK, 1964), 10.
309. 'But what ... do we understand about love? We know nothing about it.'

ness and otherness, Graham affirms God as eternal mystery, as transcendent, as Spirit.

The art critic Donald Kuspit has described Graham's work as portraying what is hopeless, 'morbid' and nihilist.[310] Although some of his works might lead one to that conclusion, his whole oeuvre is not simply about destruction, death and suffering. Here and there it provides glimpses of hope, at times hard-won and seemingly hidden but for that matter real. Graham does not regard himself as a nihilist. As someone who still manages to believe in a God who is love, he does not just see blackness and a world of estrangement, but rather he has longed for and has found a sense of 'spiritual hope': 'For me ... all things are a coming to believe.'[311]

310. Kuspit, 'Patrick Graham: Painting as Dirge', in *The Lark in the Morning, Patrick Graham,* 10-11.
311. *Works 5 - Patrick Graham,* 18.

X. PATRICK HALL

One of seven children, Patrick Hall was born in County Offaly in 1935. His parents were farmers and business people of both Protestant and Catholic backgrounds. Hall has commented that he grew up with a sense of 'dissociation from the material world', of isolation and vulnerability.[312] He enjoyed solitary pursuits like gardening and developed interests 'in mysticism and other hermetic areas'.[313] As a young man he spent two years in a religious order. Finally, however, he decided to become a painter. It was solitary work, but, as he has pointed out, it was *material* and gave him meaning.

Hall studied in the Chelsea School of Art in London from 1958 to 1960. His early works, still-lives and portraits of friends, reflect his daily life. In 1966 he went to Spain where he stayed and worked until 1973, leading basically a solitary life. In Dublin he had already exhibited with an innovative group, the Independent Artists, from 1961 and resumed exhibiting with them on his return from the continent.

Hall admires Titian and Spanish art, especially Velázquez and Goya. His series of male nudes in the late 1970s and early 1980s (e.g. 'It was Ever Thus' (1983), 'Limited, already Spanned' (1983)) reveals the influence of Spanish painting, as well as the artist's personal experience.[314]

Hall spent three years in New York from 1984 to 1986, where he continued to paint. In the 1980s and 1990s his subject matter contains increasingly mythological themes and symbolism. He paints in an Expressionist style and has drawn inspiration from artists like Munch, Nolde, Bacon, Auerbach and Graham. Another major series, 'The Flaying of Marsyas' in the 1980s lays bare an intense sense of incoherence, violation of form, pain, suffering, death, masochism, aspects which have been fundamental to his work.

Hall is a deeply introspective and private person. For him painting is search for meaning, self-discovery, journey and a kind of ritual. It is thus in some ways cathartic. As he has commented, his experience of life has been one of difficulties and complications. In recent years, however, he has striven to make painting more simple, joyful, and he has achieved for himself a greater sense of optimism. Partly this may be due to the fact that for the last decade Hall has been a practising Buddhist. This aspect is of particular relevance in the context of this book and will be discussed later, especially as it adds an inter-religious dimension to our discussion.

312. P. Hall cited in 'Patrick Hall in conversation with John Hutchinson', in *Works 12 - Patrick Hall* (Gandon Editions: 1993), 13.
313. Ibid.
314. Aidan Dunne, 'Life Lines: The Paintings of Patrick Hall', in *Patrick Hall, "Heart" and other recent paintings*, cat. (London: The Pentonville Gallery, 1987), (no p.).

Hall's strongly symbolic series of paintings, 'mountain' (1992-1995), shows his aiming for greater simplicity. Again his theme here has to do with death, but also with childhood memories of burning mountains as well as with the sacred aspect of mountains. In their mysterious beauty these works are revelatory of contemplation and stillness. In fact, his works of the late eighties and nineties convey a pronounced atmosphere of the mystical-transcendent and sacred (e.g. 'Orange Hill' (1991), 'The Tale is Told that Shall be Told' (1989), 'Ancestors' (1990-91), 'Painting' (1994)). These are hard-earned works which portray the painter's faithfulness to his own, rather personal, vision.

Hall has also concentrated on drawings and smaller works on paper, which, as Fallon has observed, show his 'genuine, inventive and highly personal vein of visual wit'.[315]

Hall is entirely sincere about his work. His oeuvre is difficult, rigorous, uncompromising. His images tend to articulate issues rather than providing answers or solving problems. An artist who developed relatively late, he now ranks among Ireland's foremost painters. Hall is a member of Aosdána. His paintings have been exhibited in his home country, in Britain and in the United States.

* * *

For Hall inwardness is 'essential' to the spirit of an artist.[316] For him the creative process of making art is a 'meditational' rather than a 'logical' journey.[317] He reflects the mystics' theology of knowing the divine through darkness and *un*knowing when he speaks about his 'reverence [for] what is truly incomprehensible' and his drawing energy from 'wells of feeling', from 'darkness', from the 'inner desert'.[318]

Hall stresses the importance of the 'capacity for contemplation', simplicity, stillness and harmony: 'Maybe it is necessary to have lived a lifetime to discover that harmony with the world is more important than truth, indeed, maybe it is truth.'[319] He holds that living in harmony with oneself contributes to universal harmony. Here, his emphasis that in his painting he aims 'for something that is totally still, … a kind of innocence' fits in with his notion of striving for harmony.

This awareness of the need for meditation and harmonious living hints at what has become central in the life of this artist, i.e. his commitment to the

315. B. Fallon, 'Playful pieces come off best', *The Irish Times*, 7.7.1995.
316. Hall, 'On Irish Expressionist Painting', *The Irish Review*, no. 3 (Cork: Cork University Press, 1988), 29.
317. Hall, (undated) Letter to the author, Sept. 1993.
318. Hall, 'Presentation to the 8th General Assembly of Aosdana', unpubl. paper, 25.5.1988.
319. Hall, Letter to the author, 12.12.1993.

Buddhist path. His interest in Tibetan Buddhism did not develop in opposition to the Roman Catholic faith in which he was raised. He had given up adherence to his church long before he discovered this religion.[320] What appeals to him especially is the concept of emptiness, which is, as he points out, the realisation that 'all phenomena depend for their existence on one another and have no intrinsic reality'.[321] He finds this idea of emptiness relevant to his life since 'it seems to absorb fear and the loss of immortality'. Buddhism in its belief in rebirth unburdens one 'of this awful responsibility of immortality'. Emptiness is not nihilism, but rather, it is somewhat akin to the old Christian idea of humility, of compassion, of letting go.

The essence of Siddhartha Gautama's teaching, i.e. the Four Noble Truths, recognises the existence of suffering as well as the possibility and the way of liberation from suffering, i.e. the remedy of the Eightfold Path, which ultimately leads to Nirvana.[322] In Nirvana, the state of perfect bliss and enlightenment, there is 'only emptiness', one is relieved of everything, including oneself, i.e. passions, hate, greed, unknowing. Emptiness, Hall points out, 'can only be apprehended through "realisation"'. It is this element of ethical-spiritual *praxis* in Buddhism, i.e. living the Eightfold Path – that is, morally right views, right aspirations, right speech, right conduct, right livelihood, right effort, right mindfulness, right concentration[323] – which is of great importance to Hall.

The concept of emptiness mattered greatly to him when he first discovered it. In 1987 Hall felt he had 'exhausted the possibility of further painting and living' as the painting seemed to draw him more and more into an abyss: 'I called this 'death', and the great thing for me was that ... in Buddhism ... I was able to turn this around and call it emptiness.' In this way he desired to both detach himself from and retain motivation for painting. He comments that the 'process of letting go is crucial to the freedom on which painting is founded'.[324]

320. Interview, 1.12.1995. *Note:* Unless stated otherwise, quotations are from this interview. Whether Buddhism is to be considered a religion or rather a philosophy is debatable. Unlike Christianity, with its set of doctrines and creeds, Buddhists concentrate on the practice of the Dharma (teaching) rather than on stating truths. Cf. George Chryssides, *The Path of Buddhism* (Edinburgh: The Saint Andrew Press, 1988), 36.
321. Hall, Letter to the author, 30.8.1994.
322. Cf. Chryssides, op.cit., 20-22. Cf. Arindam Chakrabarti, 'Buddhist philosophy', in Ted Honderich, (ed.), *The Oxford Companion to Philosophy* (Oxford: Oxford University Press, 1995), 107.
323. Chakrabarti concludes that these virtues 'promote the overarching moral qualities of clarity, desirelessness, universal friendliness, and compassion. Suffering ceases through *self-lessness (sic)*, metaphysical and moral'. Cf. Chakrabarti, op.cit., 107.
324. *Works 12 - Patrick Hall*, 24.

Hall engages in meditation on a daily basis, which he finds very beneficial to both his life and work. In particular, he notes that it has lessened his
pre-occupation with death. For him death, as sex, is the longing for continuity. Like the sexual act it is 'a way of entering into wholeness'.[325] He points
out, however, that it is important to achieve a 'fruitful balance' between life
and death as 'too much death is not good ... It's easy to go for death'.

Ultimately he finds what matters in the Buddhist way of life is to be present, to be aware. Meditation, concentration, or 'mindfulness' make the person aware of what is going on in oneself and with others. Like the Buddhist
monk, scholar and teacher Thich Nhat Hanh, Hall sees striking parallels
between Christianity and Buddhism:[326] 'I believe that, at bottom Christianity
in its full realisation is no different from Buddhism.'[327] What he means by
'full realisation' is the Christian idea of God as love and of loving one's neigh-
bour. Indeed, it is in their stress on compassion and love that both religions
concur fundamentally.

Another aspect that attracts Hall to Buddhism is its monasticism, which,
at any rate, plays a major and far more significant role in the contemporary
Buddhist context than in twentieth century Christianity. Although he is not
quite able to say what exactly draws him to the monastic way of life, it is, nevertheless, a dimension that has been with him for a long time. He suggests that
it might have something to do with the relationship between asceticism and
masochism. As stated above, he is a solitary, private person, which may go
some way to account for this interest.

For Hall God is essentially 'energy'. The divine is 'universal energy as
expressed in all living form'. God is 'life', 'being': 'I see God in every person,
in every creator, in all energy.' At the same time he allows for the transcen-
dent·otherness of God, 'a kind of energy out there which is a kind of sum of
all energies, ... energy ... of material, of the wind, of the universe, of memory,
... of voices since the beginning of time ... It's something we haven't got words
to cover'. The divine is present in all spheres of life, yet God is incomprehensible mystery. His perception of God makes obvious that Hall considers
nature and grace not to be separate but to be in continuity. He uses terms
like 'energy' and 'life' in reference to the divine and, in doing so, thus parallels McFague's central and important statement that talk of God is always

325. Cf. also Hall, 'Presentation to the 8th General Assembly of Aosdana', op.cit.: 'It is the
presence of death that you see in all great art, the demanding silence.'
326. Cf. for an extensive and convincing discussion on the parallels between the two religions
Thich Nhat Hanh, *Living Buddha, Living Christ* (New York: Riverhead Books, 1995).
327. Letter to the author, 30.8.1994.

indirect, i.e. metaphorical.[328] In this context, Hall, also agrees that the transcendentals truth, goodness and beauty are appropriate in speaking of God.

Moreover, he echoes the apophatic theology of the mystics – of whom he has read a great deal – in his assertion that God is beyond words and definition. Scholars like Suzuki and Johnston have written on the connections between Eastern religious thought and the theology of the Christian mystics. Unknowing, darkness, emptiness, religious-mystical experience, self-knowledge and contemplation are key terms in this context. It therefore does not come as a surprise that Hall reflects these parallels in his religious adherence and in his thinking, which, while being firmly Buddhist now, have nevertheless been shaped by his Catholic-Christian background. In fact, he curiously anticipates Rahner's significant observation that the Christianity of the future will be either mystical or will cease altogether.[329]

What matters to Rahner or Schillebeeckx matters to artists like Graham, Hall, O'Malley *et al;* that is an authentic faith which pertains to and grows through the immanent-transcendent experience of each individual. As Schillebeeckx, amongst others, reminds us, our thinking remains empty if it does not draw on living experience.[330] In the human search for goodness and truth, experiences (of faith) have a liberating, critical, and productive power and thereby attain authority as a means to gaining knowledge.[331]

Hall's idea of the eschaton, of eternal life, is that of wholeness and completion. The more a person advances towards completeness, the more divine she or he becomes. He notes that the idea of wholeness, holiness and completion is both Christian and Buddhist. Instead of aiming at perfection, he is hoping to finally achieve a sense of completion. For him, perfection here refers to career and artistic achievement, while completion is the desire for becoming fully human and whole.

Indeed, Hall strongly rejects the idea of perfection, especially in artistic creation, as it does not allow for weakness: 'Art is about human weakness, in fact increasingly so today when man is weakened by social and personal alienation.'[332] Acknowledging weakness basically affirms the truth about one's self, the 'raw material' of one's life, the situation in which one finds oneself and with which one has to work. He holds that neither the great prophets, nor the mystics and not even Jesus were perfect, but rather 'they worked with

---

328. Cf. Sallie McFague, *Models of God, Theology for an Ecological Nuclear Age* (Philadelphia: Fortress Press/London: SCM, 1987), 32-34.
329. Cf. Rahner, *Theological Investigations,* vol. 7 (1971), 15.
330. Schillebeeckx, *The Schillebeeckx Reader* (Edinburgh: T. & T. Clark, 1984), 44.
331. Ibid., 40-44.
332. Michael O'Brien, 'A Talk with the Painter Patrick Hall', *The Beau,* no. 3 (1983-84), 32. Cf. also Interview, 1.12.1995.

what they had'. Interestingly, his thought on weakness echoes St Paul in 2 Cor 12:9-10: '[B]ut he [Christ] said to me, "My grace is sufficient for you, for power is made perfect in weakness." ... Therefore I am content with weaknesses, insults, hardships ... for the sake of Christ; for whenever I am weak, then I am strong.'

In his assertion that Jesus was not perfect he curiously hints at something Christians at times fail to fully believe, namely that Jesus was truly human. Like Graham, he admires Grünewald's Isenheim Crucifixion which so radically images Jesus' suffering, or his 'weakness', as Hall might put it: 'Grünewald's syphilitic Christ fills one with wonder and admiration, not disgust.'[333] He comments that it is precisely because of this element of weakness or deformation that the crucifixion continues to be a fascinating subject in western art.

Hall believes in the historical Jesus, but not as the Son of God: 'I don't believe in Christ as God. It doesn't fit in with my perception of things and my apprehension of my own experience.' Yet, he believes in Jesus as a 'great prophet' ... 'a very important person, a very enlightened being, as a Buddha, or a Boddhisatva'. For him, Christ, like Buddha, mediates the divine 'more than others because he was enlightened ... But everyone has that potential.' Here one might suggest that if enlightenment could be seen in some sense as a parallel concept to the Christian (Orthodox) idea of divinisation, Hall's idea may actually be a little closer to Christian theology than it might first appear. However, while enlightenment and divinisation both have to do with human salvation, the difference between them lies in the fact that enlightenment in the Buddhist sense is reached by following the Eightfold Path, while divinisation essentially implies revelation of and faith in the personal God Jesus Christ, who effects it through the Spirit.[334]

Although Hall does not believe in Christ as the only Son of God, he nevertheless finds the Trinity, i.e. '[t]hree in one ... a kind of attractive idea'. Moreover, he has drawn inspiration from the Bible. He sees the biblical stories as 'archetypal', as touching 'something primitive': 'They are very beautiful stories and have an eternal ... immortal meaning.' For him the Bible fundamentally speaks about 'the simplest things, it's about feeling, it's about saying the truth about something ... It's so simple that they are, of course, universal.'

---

333. Hall quoted in M. O'Brien, op.cit., 39.
334. Cf. Simeon the New Theologian who, as one of the most eminent early Byzantine theologians, emphasised the divinisation of humanity through Christ: 'So uniting with your body, I share in your nature, ... uniting with your divinity, ... and that you have made me a god, a mortal by my nature, a god by your grace, by the power of your Spirit ...' in A.E. McGrath, *The Christian Theology Reader*, 181.

As with the other painters examined, Hall regards the church primarily as an institution in which power dominates over imagination, feeling and love: 'They are about power and that's why people in crises and artists are no longer fed by the churches. The church now only gives stones and people want bread.' His use of metaphors succinctly expresses his point; stones are dead matter, while bread is basic, life-giving nourishment. 'Stones' here symbolise not only what artists but many people feel, namely that the institutional churches – especially the hierarchy in the Roman Catholic Church – have lost all relevance in their lives as they are unaware, ignore or are afraid to recognise and respond imaginatively to what goes on in contemporary culture. Increasingly people therefore turn to other sources of inspiration, like the arts. In this sense it is true that, at least for the educated, the gallery or the concert hall has become the modern temple as it is in these environments, rather than at Mass, that people find contemplation, truth and meaning.[335] However, Hall, like Graham or Scott, would be happy to see his works displayed in churches. To him it does not matter where the paintings are located as long as people benefit from them.

Hall reflects Tillich in asserting that all art is an 'intimation of ultimate reality'. Moreover, he points out that while there 'is an element of self-expression in all art', there is, paradoxically, at the same time a desire for eliminating oneself out of the painting so that it becomes 'almost anonymous'. Tillich, in his pronounced emphasis on the objective element in art, wrote in similar fashion that a work of art that merely expresses the subjectivity of an artist 'remains arbitrary and does not penetrate into reality itself'.[336]

Hall points out that the artist, in being 'more aware than others', has a special responsibility towards his or her fellow humans: 'It's taking on a responsibility to question humanness, meaning, meaninglessness.' Over thirty years ago he already noted that art 'must go beyond the self'.[337] Not only is it essential for the painter to 'fully devote' himself or herself to the work, but 'painting must serve the interest of human beings ... It must contribute to the harmony and the peace of the universe and to the energy of the universe'. For Hall art therefore has a profoundly ethical dimension. He emphasises, furthermore, the link between the aesthetic, ethical and religious realm when he compares the subjective and objective dimension in the artist to Buber's concept of the dialogical character of human and religious life, i.e. the I-Thou

335. Cf. Hall in *Patrick Hall, 'Heart' and other paintings*, op.cit., no p.: 'Unfortunately the artist in the twentieth century is caught in the role like the priest's.' Cf. also A. Mertin, H. Schwebel, 'Hinführung', in *Bilder und ihre Macht* (Stuttgart: Verlag Katholisches Bibelwerk, 1989), 8.
336. Tillich, 'Art and Ultimate Reality', *Main Works*, 327.
337. Cf. Hall, 'Notes on Painting', *Arena*, no. 1 (Spring 1963), 4.

principle: 'It's in relationship that you become a human being.' According to Hall, the same applies to the artist as he or she makes works for, and exposes them to, fellow human beings. In this context it is not surprising that he agrees, like most of the artists examined, with the notion of art being a form of prayer.

As a young painter Hall wrote in 1963: '[Art] must reach out in adoration and pain to the mysterious source of life, the God of love.'[338] Over thirty-five years later, it seems right to argue that Hall's artistic integrity and compassion and his work in all its pain and darkness, mystery and introspection, contemplation and sublime beauty, have proven his claim.

338. Ibid.

CONCLUSION: DIVERSITY, PARALLELS, COMMON ASPECTS

In this chapter I examined what the painters have said about their faith and spirituality, both personally and in relation to their work. The writings of critics and commentators were included, especially when primary documentation was scarce, i.e. particularly in those cases where the painters are no longer alive.

Moreover, it was my concern to try and correlate theological thought with the ideas and, to some extent, the work of the painters. This method of correlation and analogy, which is, of course, central in theological discourse,[339] made it possible to show – at times remarkable – correspondences between the artists in question and theological conceptions, and so to throw more mutually-illuminating light on, and concretely affirm the connections between, theology, faith and art.

From what has been written in this extensive chapter it is clear that a unified theology of art does not emerge from these artists as a whole. The biographies, interests, spiritualities and ways of living and expressing faith are to be recognised and respected in their individuality. Their ideas and, as has been shown to some extent already, their works reveal a wide variety of religious, theological and spiritual aspects and insights. At the same time, however, it is obvious also that numerous and striking parallels are to be found among several of the artists. Moreover, there are certain elements that all painters share. In the following three sections I want to briefly summarise and outline these various dimensions.

Diversity

With regard to the variety of concerns it was possible to ascertain:

– Jellett's open, ecumenical, church-going Christian faith, her prophetic-missionary approach to her art, her choice of biblical themes in her paintings.

– Yeats' 'hidden', perhaps somewhat unorthodox, non-judgemental, but definitely Christian faith and attitude, the eschatological and social dimension in his thought and work.

– Le Brocquy's search for essence, i.e. for what lies 'beyond' the surface, his agnosticism which, however, includes a metaphysical sense of the presence of an inexplicable profound mystery and of the transcendent.

– Dillon's deep political-religious embeddedness in a nationalist Catholic Belfast environment which – despite the fact that he gave up communal wor-

339. Cf. Tracy's examination of analogy as primary language in theology. David Tracy, *The Analogical Imagination, Christian Theology and the Culture of Pluralism* (London: SCM, 1981), 405-21.

ship and apparently dealt with religious subjects only in his art and hardly in personal discussions – never let him 'overcome' his Catholic background.

– Middleton's passionate humanism and social concern, his 'protest-ant', non-conformative character, his non-churchgoing, panentheist Christian faith which seemingly was free of bigotry and manifested itself perhaps more in his works than in his words.

– Collins' mysticism, his stated conviction that all art is in essence transcendent, his intense panentheist vision and his childlike, yet enquiring Christian faith.

– O'Malley's profound 'religious' sense of vocation, his belief in the revelatory aspect of art, his faith in Christ and the importance of Good Friday in his life and work, as well as an agnostic strain alongside his Christian faith, his inwardness and mystical contemplation, aspects that are revealed both in his ideas and paintings.

– Scott's agnostic-atheist convictions and his highly spiritual-transcendent works of art, some of which have been included in places of worship, which proves an important point in the whole dialogue of art and theology, namely that the spiritual or even the religious-Christian content in a work of art does not depend on an artist's religiosity.

– Graham's continuous search for truth rooted in personal experience, his articulate theological insights, his sense of 'Godness', his emphasis of silence and stillness, his questioning of ecclesial hierarchy and power, his demythologising in the quest of what is true, radical and real, his hard kept/won faith in Christ, in God who is love, in redemption through suffering.

– Finally, Hall's deep inwardness, his eschatological preoccupation with death, his perception of God as universal energy and mystery, his idea of art as an 'intimation of ultimate reality', his stress on the ethical dimension in art and his practice of the Buddhist path which has played a major and positive role in his life.

Parallels

A significant number of parallels of perceptions are apparent. The names of the artists in brackets indicate that this has been ascertained particularly in relation to them. It still may also apply to some of the other painters mentioned, even if it has not been explicitly expressed:

– An existentialist and/or social concern in their life and work (Jellett, Yeats, le Brocquy, Dillon, Middleton, Graham, Hall, Scott).

– Panentheist faith and spirituality which is interwoven with faith in Christ and allows for a transcendent God (Collins, O'Malley, Middleton).

– A mystical-apophatic dimension which is linked to the panentheistic dimension as stated above (Middleton, Collins, O'Malley, Hall).

   – An emphasis on contemplation, meditation and silence in their works and/or in their artistic lives (Collins, O'Malley, Scott, Graham, Hall).

   – A quasi religious understanding of the artist as servant (Jellett, Collins, Hall).

   – Questioning and criticism of the institutional church, its hierarchy and power, and, as a result, personal distance from the church and its rituals (le Brocquy, Dillon, Middleton, Collins, Scott, Graham, Hall).

   – Faith in a personal God as revealed in Jesus Christ, which seems to be evidenced more openly through their works of art than through personal statements (Yeats, Jellett, probably Dillon, Middleton, Collins).

   – Christian faith generally without taking part in communal worship (O'Malley, Graham, Collins, Middleton, and almost certainly Dillon).

   – A longing for a childlike, simple, living faith which at the same time is critical and reflective (Collins, O'Malley, Graham and there seems sufficient ground to suggest also Middleton, Yeats, Hall).

   – An (initial) desire for religious/monastic life (le Brocquy, Graham, Hall).

   – A fascination with the Irish Celtic pre-Christian past and/or art (Dillon, Collins, O'Malley, Scott, and to a lesser extent, Jellett, Yeats, Middleton, le Brocquy and Graham).

   – An interest in eastern philosophies and/or aesthetics, in Buddhism/Zen (Jellett, Scott, O'Malley, Hall).

Common Aspects
Several spiritual, theological and ethical dimensions that all ten artists have in common are evident. These aspects have been either stated explicitly or are implied in each one of these painters:

   – A thoroughly authentic commitment to their art, i.e. artistic sincerity.

   – A sense of vocation.

   – Search for truth and meaning in their lives and works of art, a fact which is linked with their sincerity and vocation.

   – A basic humanist concern and attitude.

   – A sense of personal, intellectual and spiritual freedom (maintained despite and against a background of authoritarian Catholicism and insularity until the 1970s).

   – A general perception that basically all art is spiritual and that the making of art can be considered as a form of prayer and/or contemplation (even le Brocquy and Scott would agree with these views).

   – If the artists hold that art, i.e. the material work, essentially has a spiritual transcendent or metaphysical dimension, it therefore implies that for them nature and grace are not to be regarded as entirely separate spheres and that hence divine revelation is not – as Barth and neo-orthodox theology held – restricted to the Word, the life and death of Christ.

– An affirmation of the traditional notion of beauty as the splendour of the true and the good and, moreover, of the concept of the divine as supreme beauty, truth and goodness.

– All artists have at one time or another included Christian/biblical imagery into their paintings.

– Apart from very few exceptions none of these painters has ever been invited to work on church commissions which is, in fact, one more proof that in twentieth-century Ireland, as elsewhere, the leading artists generally have no connections with the church.

– Although not everyone of the painters has explicitly referred to the issue of the relationship between modern art and the church, it appears that all would (have) welcome(d) an openness to, and interest and trust in, modern art from the institutional churches, i.e. the desire for genuine dialogue and collaboration which respects the artist's autonomy.

– There are sufficient grounds to suggest that none of the ten painters would object, but rather would be delighted and feel honoured, to have their works displayed in places of worship.

* * *

From what has been said above it becomes obvious that not only are there quite a number of convergences among the individual painters, but further that these feature in and are relevant to the wider interdisciplinary dialogue between theology and art. Theologians, like Tillich, Schwebel, Dillenberger, Pattison and Rombold, discuss issues in their writings on art which also came up in relation to the selected Irish artists during the course of this chapter and its conclusion. Aspects like artistic commitment and vocation, search for truth and meaning, humanist and existential concerns, art as a form of prayer and revelation of the transcendent, the spiritual-sacramental aspect of art, faith in Christ lived without adherence to institutional religion, the divine described as ultimate truth, beauty and goodness, the separation of the modern artist from the church, etc., recur in many of the writings on art by theologians. Despite the fact that only ten painters are examined in this book, it seems right therefore to conclude that, with regard to the dialogue between theology, church, and twentieth century visual art, the concerns of the artists on this island are not to be seen in any way in isolation from other modern European and North American art but rather as corresponding to and reflecting the same or similar issues. What seems to be more pronounced in the spirituality of some Irish artists, however, in comparison to others, is the panentheist dimension. This, as discussed earlier, is grounded in a particular affinity with nature, i.e. the Irish countryside, and in an awareness and romantic love of the Celtic-Christian past in which pre-Christian rituals and beliefs, including nature spirituality, were integrated with Christian faith.

We will now turn to the interpretation of individual works of art from a theological perspective, which, as will be shown, corresponds to and expands in more detail what has been established thus far.

CHAPTER III

Images of Transcendence:
A Theological Interpretation
of Selected Paintings

In this chapter three works of each artist will be interpreted from a theological point of view. This is to show that even among this comparatively small, but relevant, group of artists and works, one encounters a plurality of styles and subjects which ranges from the explicitly Christian to 'mere' glimpses of 'something' transcendent. It thus reflects the diverse faith and spirituality found among the artists as established in the previous chapter. It should also be made clear from the outset that these interpretations, of course, do not claim an exclusive way of looking at these works. Rather from a concrete, detailed engagement with each work, the aim here is to uncover and draw out something of their meaning, i.e. especially their theological aspects. They are intended as an invitation to see a range of works of art particularly with regard to their theological aspects, but not as definitive, once-for-all theological statements – which in any case are impossible to make or claim.

The question of a hermeneutics for a theology of and through art will be discussed in more detail in the final chapter.

I. MAINIE JELLETT

1.1. Man and Woman (See page 161)

Mainie Jellett began to paint works with religious themes in the late 1920s. This diptych of 1937, painted only seven years before her premature death in 1944, can therefore be regarded as a mature work not only in her career but more particularly in her approach to biblical and Christian themes.

What strikes one at once is the title, which as such has no religious connotations. However, after one glance of the diptych, those who are familiar with Christian iconography and, more particularly, with Jellett's engagement with religious themes, may easily associate the figures with Adam and Eve – even if Eve appears unusually submissive. Jellett's choice of the form of a diptych has itself, of course, a religious association as the medieval altarpieces often consisted of diptychs or triptychs.

Adam and Eve in Genesis have been interpreted in the Pauline writings and subsequent Christian theology and church history as prefiguring Christ (Rom 5:14, 1 Cor 15:21-23, 45) and Mary, or even the church. This work – partly due to its ingeniously open title – allows for an interpretation that takes account of this link between the Hebrew Scriptures and the New Testament, Christ, the new Adam, and Mary, the new Eve.

The two depictions, both semi-cubist in style, show two clearly recognisable figures, one male, one female. We are reminded of the Priestly account of creation: 'So God created humankind in his image ... male and female he created them.' (Gen 1:27) Moreover, since one associates the diptych with Adam and Eve, the Jahwist story of creation comes to mind in which the first humans are named, 'the (hu)man', or 'earthling', Adam (who stands, of course, for all humankind), and Eve, the 'mother of all living' (Gen 3:20). The posture of each figure is remarkably traditional, the almost aggressive red colour dominates in the painting of the man, the lines are angular, he stands upright and emphatically frontal. By contrast, green, which alludes to nature and fertility, and flowing, gently curved shapes prevail in the depiction of the woman. Unlike the man, her inclined head and her left arm raised protectively before her chest convey submission. Both are enclosed in a womb-like mandorla shape. This shape is far more pronounced, however, in the female than in the male figure.

The Aristotelian-Thomist aesthetic criteria of harmony, wholeness and radiance[1] were important to Jellett. These elements pervade the diptych. If one interprets the two figures as Adam and Eve, it shows the two first humans in the paradisiacal state before the Fall. This is especially emphasised through their halos which affirm the human being made in the image of God, i.e. the goodness and sacredness of creation and of the human being.[2]

The presence of the halos is a relevant feature also in allowing us to make the link with the New Testament. The male figure's halo is elaborate and signifies the divine aspect, thus pointing us to interpret the figure as the new Adam, i.e. Christ. Furthermore, the red colour, reminiscent of blood, and the vaguely outstretched arms evoke Christ's redemptive sacrifice on the Cross. Apart from the halo, it is the posture of the female figure that alludes to Mary. Her inclined head and protective arm are somewhat reminiscent of traditional depictions of the Virgin, such as Fra Angelico's frescos of the Annunciation, for example.

Jellett's presentation of Mary (Woman, Eve) in her submissive position and that of Christ (Man, Adam) in his upright frontality is indeed traditional. If

---

1. Cf. for an elaboration of Aristotle's and Aquinas' aesthetics J.A. Martin, *Beauty and Holiness, The Dialogue between Aesthetics and Religion*, 15-18, 23-28.
2. Cf. on the theology of creation Walther Zimmerli, *Grundriss der alttestamentlichen Theologie* (Stuttgart, Berlin, Cologne, Mainz: Kohlhammer, 1982), 24-29.

one thinks of Jellett's own emancipated life it is almost surprising that she would render the figures in such postures. On the other hand, Jellett, never-theless, emphasises through the womb-shape mandorla, which encloses the female figure, the life-giving aspect of the Mother of Christ, her sexuality and womanhood. The halo then is symbolic of Mary's special place in the history of salvation while, at the same time, the mandorla affirms her as woman amongst women, who 'forms of her own flesh and blood, the flesh and blood that will be recognised as the person of God's very self walking on the path of history'.[3]

Jellett through the choice of the title and in her depiction affirms the beauty of creation and the divine aspect not only of Christ and Mary, but ultimately of all humankind. Moreover, the openness of the title makes it possible to suggest a creation-theological, christological and mariological interpretation of the work, i.e. a rich, diverse, yet coherent theology.

1.2. Madonna and Child (See page 162)

In this work Jellett treats of one of the oldest themes in Christian art, the Virgin and Child. It is a subject with an extensive iconography that is based only to a small extent on the Bible and developed through the centuries due to the need in the church for a mother figure as an 'object' of worship.[4] Mary came to be seen and referred to as *theotokos,* i.e. 'bearer of God', as glorified mediatrix and intercessor. In recent times her liberating role as the one who because of her own poverty and through her affirmation that God 'casts down the powerful from their thrones' speaks especially for and with the poor has been emphasised, especially by feminist and liberation theologians. Leonardo Boff has even gone so far as to see her as 'enthroned into the mys-tery of the Holy Trinity'.[5]

Jellett renders the 'Madonna and Child' in a semi-abstract cubist style. The colours red, brown, yellow, green and blue are radiant and warm. As in the previous work, the whole canvas exudes harmony, wholeness and clarity. It ranks among the most beautiful works by this artist. The two figures, although rendered in a more angular, abstract fashion than in the work exam-ined above, are clearly recognisable. What surprises a little perhaps is Jellett's choice of pointillist spaces that serve like a frame around the circles and semi-

---

3. Cf. Maria Clara Bingemer, Ivone Gebara, *Mother of God, Mother of the Poor* (Tunbridge Wells: Burns and Oates, 1989), 56, 100-108 as an example of a feminist-liberation theo-logical approach to mariology. The writers attempt to reconcile Mary's virginity with a positive view of womanhood and sexuality.
4. James Hall, *Dictionary of Subjects and Symbols in Art* (London: James Murray, 1974), 323.
5. L. Boff, *Ave Maria, Das Weibliche und der Heilige Geist* (Düsseldorf: Patmos Verlag, 1985), 126. (Author's translation)

circles that enclose the figures. These spaces contribute to the sense of the sacred as they remind the viewer of the incisions used in icons and Early Renaissance altarpieces, or the dotting technique which was applied in Irish illuminated manuscripts, such as the Book of Durrow, i.e. of Celtic-Christian art which Jellett regarded as a 'treasure house' that could make one 'conscious of a reality that would give ... [Irish] art a national character'.[6]

The Virgin's halo is particularly elaborate, pointing, as it does, to her role as *theotokos*. The (semi-)circles which enclose the figures stress their belonging to one another, i.e. the close relationship of mother and child. In fact, there are basically three (semi-)circles which encapsulate the figures; this could be read as an allusion to Celtic art with its iconographic detail of interlocked spirals, as well as to the Trinity. Interestingly the figures are attached to one another by their clothes which seem to flow into one another. The figure of Jesus is particularly striking. He is not (semi-)naked as in conventional depictions, but rather his body is covered by a long garment, not unlike an ancient tunic or even a female dress. His head, notably his hair, also appears emphatically female. It is impossible to know whether and/or why Jellett consciously or unconsciously chose to portray Jesus in such fashion. Apart from the fact that the long garment is used in Celtic painting of the evangelists, for example, and in the present work possibly anticipates the priest's robe, a sense of the 'female' in this depiction of the child Jesus can hardly be denied. The painting thus points in a special way to the God incarnate, i.e. God's true humanity in Jesus Christ, born of a woman. It reveals that what ultimately matters is not that Jesus is male, but that God becomes a human being in Christ. Jellett, with or without intention, thus manages to express and anticipates in pictorial form what is relevant to contemporary (feminist) theological concerns, namely the humanity, wholeness and liberating aspect in Jesus, rather than his sex which served as the justification for the perception of God as male and for a patriarchal church throughout church history.[7]

Apart from giving such unusual expression to God's humanity, Jellett captures equally the otherness and transcendent aspect of the divine in this work. The elaborate halo crowning Mary's head, the pointillist spaces and the figures, which seem to float enclosed in auratic crescents in space above the ground, convey a hieratic, otherworldly atmosphere of the sacred. Further, the warm colours signify the sense of joy and anticipate the hope and salvation that is brought about in the God incarnate. Thus one might view the whole composition as a somewhat unconventional modern icon.

6. Jellett, quoted in Arnold, *Mainie Jellett and the Modern Movement in Ireland*, 181.
7. Cf. Catharina J.M. Halkes, *Gott hat nicht nur starke Söhne, Grundzüge einer feministischen Theologie*, trans. Ursula Krattiger-van Grinsven (Gütersloh: Mohn, 1980), 40-42.

1.3. The Ninth Hour (See page 163)

Painted in 1941, this is probably the finest of Jellett's numerous depictions of the crucifixion. Indeed, in time to come it would not surprise if it came to be counted among the most beautiful paintings of the crucifixion in twentieth-century art. It is above all Jellett's marvellous choice and subtle application of colour, purple, deep greens, blue and reds of fire, as well as its pervading sense of harmony which give this work its mysterious beauty.

At first glimpse, the structured, proportionate, almost symmetrical setting of the figures seems to suggest a canonical, traditional rendering of this theme.[8] Christ in the centre, the two thieves – one on either side, one penitent who looks towards Christ, the other bent and impenitent in darkness – and the mourners John, Mary, as well as Mary Magdalene and possibly Mary, mother of James the younger and Joses, and Salome (Mk 15:40) are present. It is my contention that there are theological aspects in Jellett's interpretation, however, which are, in fact, rather *un*canonical and have hitherto not been discussed by other commentators on this painter's work.

My first point curiously links in with the interpretation of the 'Madonna and Child', in which the child Jesus appears somewhat female. The figure of Christ on the Cross in the 'Ninth Hour' is not male but rather androgynous. The lower part of the body especially is strikingly female. Moreover, in contrast to conventional portrayals of this theme, the bodies of Christ and of the thieves are entirely naked. Again, it cannot be ascertained why Jellett depicts the Crucified in this manner, and whether there may even be a (non)deliberate continuation between the rendering of the child Jesus and the Christ on the cross. One could suggest that her accomplishment in painting the female nude and possibly her own sexual orientation may have been an unconscious influence. On the other hand, one might speculate that her rendering of a rather female Christ was quite deliberate. One might even wonder whether Jellett, due to her aesthetic and Christian awareness, would have considered a Christ in androgynous form to be more beautiful and more truthful to the meaning of the incarnation than a purely male one.

Whatever about such speculative efforts, Jellett's work emphatically shows, in fact, what Boff and other – especially feminist – theologians would write several decades later, namely that Jesus never made a principle of his maleness.[9] What matters is that God so much loved the world that God became *human* and redeemed humankind through Christ's death on Golgatha.

8. Cf. Elizabeth Mayes, Paula Murphy, (eds.), *Images and Insights* (Dublin: MGMA, 1993), 110.
9. Cf. L. Boff, *Church: Charism and Power, Liberation Theology and the Institutional Church* (London: SCM, 1985), 35-36. Cf. also Rosemary Radford Ruether who argues similarly.

The yellow-red colour, which rises like a fire from the bottom of the painting, presents another interesting element in Jellett's depiction. In this context it is important to remember the title of the painting, 'The Ninth Hour', which refers to Christ's cry on the Cross: 'When it was noon, darkness came over the whole land until three in the afternoon. At three o'clock Jesus cried out with a loud voice, "Eloi, Eloi, lema sabachthani?"' (Mk 15:33-34). The impression of fire thus alludes to Christ's experience of Godforsakenness, his descent into hell, as affirmed in the Apostles' Creed. Hell here does not, as one might assume, imply a place of punishment, but rather it connotes the *Sheol*, the traditional place of rest of all the dead (e.g. Is 38:18, Ezek 31:14-18).[10] What makes this place hell is the fact that in *Sheol* the dead are separated from God, that they can no longer see the divine face and worship and praise God.[11] The idea of Christ descending into hell vividly acknowledges the reality of his death, and it is this reality which is depicted, or at least evoked, in 'The Ninth Hour'.

In Christ, however, death is not the end. In fact, if the descent into hell so forcefully expresses the reality of Jesus' separation from his God in his sacrificial death, his ascent from hell into heaven, as affirmed in the same Creed, powerfully reveals Christ's triumph over death. In his death and resurrection then humankind's last enemy, death, is finally destroyed (1 Cor 15:26). It could be argued that the warm yellow-red not only refers to Christ's descent into hell but that, at the same time, it furthermore anticipates the new life and the light which Christ brings into the world through his resurrection from the dead, his rising to heaven and thus our own resurrection in him and with him. Seen in this way, Jellett's work becomes a powerful expression that there can be no *theologia crucis* without a *theologia gloriae,* no Good Friday without Easter and vice versa.

It is the fact that, despite its theme, the work actually conveys not only darkness, death and Godforsakenness, but life and light as expressed through the warm colours, especially the yellow and reds, which allows for such a rich theological interpretation of the work. This and the wonderful harmony and transcendent, mysterious beauty in the painting convey something of what von Balthasar stressed in his theological aesthetics: Christ, the form and revelation of love, a love so great that it must be perceived as the 'Wholly Other'.[12] It is in Christ's death on the Cross that the beauty of God shone most radiantly.

Radford Ruether, 'Catholicism, Women, Body and Sexuality', in Jeanne Becher, (ed.), *Women, Religion and Sexuality, Studies on the Impact of Religious Teachings on Women* (Geneva: WCC, 1990), 221-232.

10. Lionel Swain, 'Descent of Christ into Hell', *The New Dictionary of Theology,* 280.
11. Cf. K. Barth, *Dogmatik im Grundriss* (Zürich: Theologischer Verlag, 1947), 139.
12. Cf. Hans Urs von Balthasar, *Love Alone: the Way of Revelation* (London: Sheed & Ward, 1968), 8, 102-105. Von Balthasar emphasises that his aesthetics must be seen in a 'purely theological sense: the perception in faith of the self-authenticating glory of God's utterly

2. JACK YEATS

2.1. *Grief* (See page 164)

Although the bulk of Yeats' work may not seem immediately conducive to theological reflection, there are a number of paintings among his mature oeuvre which reveal humanist-existentialist as well as explicitly Christian concerns. Yeats painted his great works in the 1940s and 1950s. They are marked by an expanding vision, by emotion, intuition and by a transition from the local to the universal. Bruce Arnold has pointed out that Yeats' painting was essentially driven by his artistic imagination and spirituality.[13] Pyle has referred to Yeats' imagination and fantasy which were not escapist but 'rooted in real life'.[14] In his works human experience forms the basis of his artistic and religious imagination. Likewise, it is our human experience which inspires and enables theological imagination and thinking.[15] Indeed, the reality of human existence lies at the heart of art and theology, of artistic and religious imagination. It is in some of Yeats' late works, then, that his artistic-religious imagination powerfully transpires.

Painted in 1951, 'Grief' is a relatively late work in the artist's life. In 1947 Yeats' wife had died, in 1949 his sister Lily, the last member of his immediate family, also died. His pictures during this period reveal that he was coming to terms with deep emotions of sadness, loneliness and despair. Not only had the painter experienced these personal losses, but he had lived through the Irish War of Independence, the Civil War and two world wars, thus he knew about the horrors of evil and violence.

'Grief' deals with and warns us about war. Against a background of two rows of houses – typical of an Irish town – that are facing one another, one detects a group of fighting men, probably soldiers, rendered in indigo blue.[16] Their leader on a white horse is placed almost exactly in the centre of the

free gift of love.' His insistence that church authority can ultimately only be credible through manifesting the glory of God's love is pertinent.

13. Arnold, Interview, 30.9.1995.
14. Pyle, 'About to Write a Letter', *Irish Arts Review* (Spring 1985), 43.
15. Cf. William V. Dych, 'Theology and Imagination', in *Thought*, vol. lvii, no. 224 (New York: Fordham University Press, 1982), 120-122. Interestingly, Dych affirms – as I have done in the previous chapter – that images precisely in being subjective are also objective. In this way they constitute 'our most concrete, most real and most "objective" knowledge' of the world. Cf. also Langdon Gilkey, 'Can Art Fill the Vacuum?', in Apostolos-Cappadona, *Art, Creativity, and the Sacred*, 188-190, who argues similarly in his emphasis that the role and significance of art is to enhance and re-create ordinary experience into value and hence into meaning.
16. Cf. Pyle, *Jack B. Yeats in the National Gallery of Ireland* (Dublin: National Gallery of Ireland, 1986), 82.

work. His aggressive posture is emphasised by the flame-like red that sur-rounds him. In the foreground one notices a crouched figure, apparently an old white-haired man, and to the right a mother who, with an archetypal ges-ture, protectively holds her small child whose lower body is stained with blood. These three figures symbolise the innocent victims of war. The whole scene presents an image of destruction, chaos and suffering. The flames that burn the houses and the empty, desolate courtyard on the right enhance the atmosphere of evil destruction.

This work is, not in style but in content and meaning, reminiscent of Picasso's 'Guernica' of 1937.[17] It is possible that Yeats may have seen a reproduct-ion of this great work. Neither Picasso nor Yeats were artists who set out to use art as propaganda. In these works, however, the message is strong and clear as they both express their abhorrence of war and the inhumanity of suffering.

'Grief' thus is a painting inspired by a profound humanist and social con-cern. An existentialist work, it deals with the troubled human condition in the twentieth century. Yeats in his art and life was, as mentioned before, guided by great affection, by a love especially of the 'common' people of Ireland, as well as by the love of freedom, particularly of Ireland liberated from the bonds of colonialism. What he reveals in this work pertains to this love and to a strong desire for a world free of war and destruction.

If tragedy and death play a significant part in his oeuvre, they are not the final word, however. The eschatological dimension in Yeats is one that ulti-mately speaks of hope, hope that transcends death. In showing us what the world *should be* precisely through showing it as *it is*, Yeats conveys in paint what Dermot Lane has stressed in his eschatological theology when he writes that hope 'arises out of the experience of the negative. The reality of evil in the world therefore evokes hope and so we are thrown back once again on hope against hope in the face of evil'.[18] But, one might ask, does Yeats actu-ally present us with a merely humanist vision and compassion; is the sense of hope, which arises out of his portrayal of evil, a religious-Christian hope, a hope that reaches to the transcendent divine?

In this context also Langdon Gilkey's comments are pertinent. He affirms the transformative power of art, i.e. its ability to make us see in new ways in its revelation of truth 'hidden behind and within the ordinary'.[19] Art, as it

17. Pyle makes the same observation in her interpretation of 'Grief'. She comments that the head of the soldier on horse 'bears a resemblance, in its distortion, to some of Picasso's heads deriving from African carvings'. She has pointed out, moreover, that 'Grief' seems to have originated from a sketch by Yeats, entitled 'Let there be no more war'. Pyle, ibid.

18. Dermot A. Lane, *Keeping Hope Alive, Stirrings in Christian Theology* (Dublin: Gill and Macmillan, 1996), 165.

19. L. Gilkey, 'Can Art Fill the Vacuum?', in D. Apostolos-Cappadona, *Art, Creativity, and the Sacred*, 189.

leads us away from a conventional way of viewing, discloses reality. This he claims is no more obvious than when outrage at dehumanisation is expressed in a work of art; in doing so art hence attains a political and moral role. He concludes: 'When art thus condemns present reality in the name of humanity and justice and seeks for its transformation, it becomes itself the vehicle of the transcendent and approaches the religious.'[20]

Interpreted in such fashion, 'Grief', in its condemnation of a distorted, crucified humanity, indeed points us to the God who *is* love. The work achieves this not directly by supplying us with a Christian theme – such as Jesus healing or performing miracles, for example – but indirectly *and* forcefully through a humanist rather than an explicitly religious subject, in confronting the viewer with the opposite of love, namely violence, hate, suffering and war. One might also add that his application of surprisingly bright hues, especially the blue sky, despite the bleak subject, contribute somewhat to the sense that ultimately goodness and life will overcome the darkness of war.

2.2. Tinkers' Encampment: The Blood of Abel (See page 165)

This work, painted eleven years prior to 'Grief', also deals with the subject of war. The setting, however, is a different, more specific one. Unlike with 'Grief', we find in the title both a definite allusion to Ireland, i.e. its indigenous 'Tinkers', or travelling people, as well as a biblical reference (Gen 4:2-16).

The painting shows a travellers' camp in which someone has been murdered during the night. Like a magnet the gruesome event draws everyone near; the travellers are streaming down the mountains towards the camp, crossing the river. A police inspector has come for investigation. The primarily dark, sombre colours interspersed with blood red convey the sense of evil and death. In the foreground on the left someone holds a lit torch to the ground which shows up a patch of bloodstained earth. In the far background the sky over the mountains is almost surprisingly bright.

What, one might ask, is the significance of the travellers' camp? Yeats, who loved Ireland and the people who lead 'simple' lives, frequently depicts those in his works. With his strong sense of and desire for both personal and political freedom and his social awareness, the nomadic travellers, a social and underprivileged minority, would be representative of and symbolise exactly this dimension. Moreover, in contrast with other minorities, many of the travelling people are related by blood. Therefore we are not witnessing a simple murder but one which takes place amongst relations, i.e. within a family. It is this aspect which plays a role in explaining the second part of the title.

20. Ibid, 190.

Cain murders his brother Abel out of jealousy (Gen 4:2-16). Unlike Cain, Abel had found favour with God for his offering. God then tells Cain that the earth will no longer yield crops for him and that he will be a 'fugitive and wanderer' on the earth. Thus the earth which drank his brother's blood becomes the very instrument of punishment.[21] Cain answers that his punishment is more than he can bear and pleads with God: '... I shall be hidden from your face ... and anyone who meets me may kill me' (Gen 4:14). Finally, God shows Godself not as a God of justice but rather as the God of mercy and compassion in assuring Cain that whoever will kill him will 'suffer a sevenfold vengeance' (Gen 4:15). God then puts an unspecified mark on Cain so that no one would practise blood vengeance on him.

Why does Yeats allude to this biblical, mythological story in his title? The answer here naturally must be a speculative one, but it seems to me that it encourages a very strong theological interpretation that would concur with what has already been established about the artist, i.e. the existentialist, eschatological dimension in his work.

Thomas MacGreevy, in his analysis of the composition, points out that the travellers' encampment is to be seen as a metaphor for the 'human odyssey', 'the world being in effect a human encampment, a transient place', while the biblical reference in the title is metaphorical of the innocents who lost their lives in the Second World War.[22] His interpretation is significant and relevant to my own reading of the painting.[23]

One would suggest that Yeats' choice of his title in the war year of 1940 was a very deliberate one. In relating the murder in a travellers' camp – a symbol for innocent suffering and death in war – to Cain and Abel, he actually links the present with the past, contemporary humankind with the beginning of humankind.[24] The murder of Abel stands as a symbol for the first murder ever. It is not just the killing of anyone but of a relation. The same happens in the travellers' camp. If the violent death in the encampment symbolises all innocent deaths in the World Wars, the whole composition thus expresses a vision of humanity not simply as an assembly of persons, but as a family. In a sense all humans are related and thus should have love and responsibility for one another. It is this love, this relationship which is violated to the core in innocent death through the sin of murder, be it of one

---

21. Richard J. Clifford, S.J., Roland E. Murphy, O.Carm., 'Genesis', in *New Jerome Biblical Commentary*, 13.
22. Thomas MacGreevy, *Jack B. Yeats* (1945), 35-37 quoted in S.B. Kennedy, *Irish Art and Modernism*, 302.
23. In this context it is important to remember that MacGreevy and Yeats knew one another, thus it may be possible that MacGreevy's interpretation alludes to Yeats' own ideas on the work.
24. Whether this was intentioned, of course, cannot be established.

person or whole nations.[25] In making the link between the murder in the original human family and in the contemporary family of travellers, and thus in the family of humankind, Yeats' work becomes a powerful expression and moral condemnation of all innocent death in all time. In theological-biblical terms, the painting states the universality of sin in the history of the whole human family.

But is it sin without any hope for redemption? Is it death without hope? Does Yeats capture humankind from Cain to our century as one in which barbarism wins over civilisation, i.e. whose face is irredeemably hidden from God (Gen 4:14) forever?[26] As stated before, Yeats' late works are often concerned with tragedy and death, but death ultimately transcended by eschatological hope. This aspect is, in fact, conveyed in this work, both in the biblical allusion in the title and in the actual composition, although this may not be immediately apparent. Abel, through his death, becomes a symbol of all innocent death and martyrdom. Cain, symbol of all evil, on the other hand, when he pleads with God - which seems to imply some degree of repentance – is not condemned to be murdered in return but saved by God. Lane points out that within Judaism 'the object of hope was largely a this-worldly one'.[27] The ending of this story, the fact that even someone like Cain who has sinned gravely is not beyond redemption, is indicative of such hope. He is not given the promise of redemption in an afterlife, but is saved in this world from those who might lay their hands on him.

If, moreover, this work is to be seen in the wider context of the Second World War, Cain's redemption would imply that those who are involved as war leaders will still be redeemed despite their sin. Hence one may conclude that for Yeats sin and death are finally transcended by God's boundless mercy, by the hope of and for salvation.

Apart from his reference to the story in Genesis, this is expressed in the canvas by his application of colour. While the foreground is dark, signifying as it does the sinful event, gradually the colours become somewhat brighter; the wild sky on the horizon is striking in its bright white. Although the impact of evil in the world is an ever-present reality, this white light may indicate that life and goodness will finally overcome all turning away from God, i.e. sin. It is divine love that forgives Cain and therefore all who murder.

25. In this context one might mention Tillich who pointed out that it is love which is fundamental to all ethics when he writes that '[t]he forms and structures in which love embodies itself are the forms and structures in which life is possible, in which life overcomes its self-destructive forces. And this is the meaning of ethics: the expression of the ways in which love embodies itself, and life is maintained'. Tillich, *Morality and Beyond* (London/Glasgow: The Fontana Library, 1963), 95.

26. Cf. Ronald S. Hendel, 'Cain and Abel', in Metzger, Coogan, (eds.), *The Oxford Companion to the Bible*, 97.

27. Lane, *Keeping Hope Alive*, 66.

'Tinkers' Encampment: The Blood of Abel', like 'Grief', is a deeply existentialist work. However, the biblical allusion in the title gives way to a distinct theological interpretation whereby it is legitimate to apply central Judaeo-Christian concepts such as sin and salvation. If, despite and because of the very real presence of evil in this canvas and its title, salvation is the final message, then it is indeed a work which is ultimately – if *in*directly – revelatory of eschatological hope. If in Cain's salvation this hope is a this-worldly one, the light on the horizon in the canvas may be indicative of a more transcendent, ultimate hope. Yeats does not present this hope as an 'opium' for the people, salvation which may be attained only in a life thereafter which justifies human suffering on earth. His portrayal and condemnation of evil in this canvas is far too radical for such a conclusion. The sense of hope in the work is glimpsed rather than obvious. What is revealed is what Jonathan Sachs affirms when he writes that whatever freedom we have to reject God, 'it is not strong enough to prevent God from being truly present in unbreakable love to the sinner'.[28]

Finally, the eschatological aspect in its transcendent dimension which confirms Yeats' sense of the continuity between life and death is asserted in MacGreevy's comment that this work is a metaphor for the human odyssey, the world as a human encampment and therefore a transient place.[29] For Yeats this odyssey ultimately ends not in hell but in salvific hope.

28. J.R. Sachs, S.J., *The Christian Vision of Humanity*, 100.
29. Pyle, *A Biography Jack Yeats*, 145. MacGreevy quoted in S.B. Kennedy, *Irish Art and Modernism*, 302.

2.3. *There is No Night* (See page 166)

Hilary Pyle has drawn attention to the usage of words which play a particular role in Yeats' oeuvre. They are relevant to his sense of creativity and cannot be separated from the actual canvases for which they form the titles.[30] His late visionary paintings, such as this one, attain, in fact, enhanced significance from the metaphorical language in their titles. The caption Yeats has chosen here is taken from the last chapter in the Book of Revelation 22:5: 'And there will be no more night; they need no light of lamp or sun, for the Lord God will be their light, and they will reign forever and ever.' Yeats adapts the wording and makes it into the more concise 'There is No Night'.

In the foreground the figure of a man is rising from a recumbent position. Like John, Christ's servant, apostle and, as has been traditionally held, author[31] of the Apocalypse, he appears like a visionary. Like John he sees a white horse: 'Then I saw the heaven opened, and there was a white horse! Its rider is called Faithful and True, and in righteousness he judges ... and his name is called The Word of God ... and he will rule them with a rod of iron ... he has a name inscribed, "king of kings and Lord of lords"' (Rev 19:11-16). Unlike in the Apocalypse, Yeats' horse is riderless and heaven is not opened. Instead the man and the horse blend and almost seem to be one with the very expressionist landscape, with its predominantly purple colour and the wild sky in indigo blue, one of Yeats' preferred colours. Despite the almost abstract landscape, one would easily associate it with the wild scenery, bogs, heather etc. common to the West of Ireland. This sense is underlined by the water, probably the sea, to the middle right of the canvas. The whole work conveys a sense of the metaphysical, of dream, of transcendence, even if the turbulent movement of the sky and the galloping horse seem at the same time almost palpably real.

Yeats has obviously transformed the references from Revelation into his own painterly expression. Pyle comments that the work may be interpreted on three levels: Firstly, as an image of a man resting from a journey and waking up who sees his horse galloping in the moonlight; secondly, the title adds meaning in that it affirms that the artist's sense of grief (after his wife's death), of fear and darkness which one equates with the night, are overcome by hope,

---

30. Pyle, 'There is No Night', *Irish Arts Review*, vo. 3, no. 2 (Summer 1986), 36.

31. Cf. Adela Yarbro Collins, 'The Apocalypse (Revelation)', in *NJBC*, 998. Cf. also Metzger, Coogan, op.cit., 653-654. A discussion of the authorship of Revelation goes beyond the scope of and is not directly relevant to our discussion. However, it should be mentioned that the widely held assumption that St John the Evangelist was the writer of the Apocalypse is no longer supported by New Testament scholars such as Collins, Brown, Fitzmyer, Murphy. Rather, they conclude that the author, by the name of John, was an early Christian prophet.

light and life; and thirdly, the deliberate choice of the title with its Christian meaning pointing, as it does, to the 'promised land' for all humans.[32] Indeed, Yeats here confirms, perhaps more explicitly than in other paintings, that death is not the final answer, but life both in the here and now as well as in the eschaton. Interestingly, by his adaptation of the future promise 'And there will be no more night' into the absolute, timeless 'There is No Night', his faith in salvation in our present life as in eternal life is powerfully professed and seemingly free of doubt. Painted four years after the war, and two years after his wife's death, it is a true and real testimony of hope. Here again, his title concurs emphatically with the eschatological theology of Lane or Sachs, since Yeats' hope, as expressed in this work, is one that pertains both to this world and the next. Lane stresses that Christian hope embraces the presence of the divine in history and eternity and that it must 'assume an incarnational presence in this life if it is to be more than a wishful projection'.[33] Yeats could not express this immanent-transcendent aspect of Christian faith and hope more forcefully than by his ingenious title adapted from the apocalyptic vision of Christ's Second Coming and of the new Jerusalem. While the author in Rev 19:11-22:5 puts forward his vision of the last things, Yeats affirms that, at least to some extent, the last things, redemption and salvation of all, are already reality in the present. The blue sky, the man, i.e. humanity awakening, the running horse reveal that the morning has already come, no lamp is needed because God will not only be but *is* our light already now (Rev 22:5).

Even if Yeats provides a personal rather than a literal rendering of the theme, the actual canvas and its title do, in fact, evoke the Apocalypse's vision of the Second Coming of Christ (Rev 19:11-16). Yeats' interpretation of this passage is a sign and, one may assume, an affirmation of his faith, yet indirectly rather than directly. The horse,[34] the animal that normally carries the victor, is riderless in Yeats' composition. Furthermore, the heavens are not opened, but closed. Christ, the 'Faithful and True', 'The Word of God', the 'King of kings and Lord of lords' is absent. Yet his presence seems *implied* by the very fact that Yeats took inspiration for his work from this very passage of Rev 19:11-16. Why he chose to render the horse *without* rider[35] is, of course, a matter for speculation. Possibly he may have felt that it would be inappro-

32. Pyle, op.cit., 37, 40.
33. Cf. Lane, *Keeping Hope Alive*, 129.
34. The theme of horse and rider is one which can be traced back into Yeats' early career when he painted circus posters. Later it appears again in works like 'Homage to Bret Harte' (1943), 'For the Road' (1951), 'My Beautiful, My Beautiful' (1953). Cf. Mayes, Murphy, op.cit., 86.
35. It should be mentioned that Yeats painted a few works where Christ *is* actually depicted, such as 'Simon the Cyrenian' both in watercolour (1901) and oil (1902) and 'The Crucifixion' (watercolour, 1901). He also designed sodality banners depicting the Sacred

priate or impossible for him to image Christ, especially since it would be an image not of the Son of God on the Cross but of the return of the Saviour in glory, i.e. something too grandiose to capture in paint.

The True and Faithful One in his Second Coming will reveal Godself in many ways; ultimately, however, Yeats' depiction declares that it passes his (and our?) imagination. What he does affirm, nevertheless, in his canvas and in his title is his faith that what is now and what will be is hope, life and light. In Christ, death and darkness are overcome. He is the way, the truth and the life (Jn 14:6), he is the light of the world (Jn 8:12), he is the Faithful One because of his love which conquers all strife.[36] It is this hope and a vision of a resurrected humanity that Yeats conveys in one of his greatest works.

What is so remarkable is the fact that this painting, not unlike the previous one, can be interpreted in such an eschatological and christological fashion *without* the presence of any overt Christian iconography in the work. It is above all the title in each work that makes this interpretation possible. In fact, the application of religious/biblical captions to works, which contain no overt traditional religious iconography, is a recurrent feature in modern Irish art as in other Western twentieth-century works of art, such as in Bacon, Klee or Newman, for example.

Moreover, the hints of Irish settings in the three paintings do not pose limitations on the interpretations but rather serve as transcending realities whereby the images attain universal significance.

Heart and male saints for Loughrea Cathedral, and made several cartoons of saints. Cf. Pyle, *Jack B. Yeats, His Watercolours, Drawings and Pastels* (Dublin: Irish Academic Press, 1993), 101-102 (cat. number 326, 327), 121-125 (cat. number 447-459).

36. I am grateful to Hilary Pyle for drawing my attention to an article by William Ebor 'The Sealed Book' in *Theology* (February 1941), 65-71, which belongs to the Yeats archive and may have been read by him and hence may have influenced his interpretation of the theme. Ebor stresses especially the sacrifice of Christ's love for humankind. He states that the Book of Revelation provides us with hints for interpreting history and gives us a 'criterion for progress. The inner meaning of history is the conflict between the Lamb and the Wild Beast – love and pride ... Only the increase of love is real progress'. One might suggest that in Yeats' 'There is no Night', as also – but in an indirect manner – in the two previous works examined, this dimension of salvific love is affirmed.

3. LOUIS LE BROCQUY

3.1. *Lazarus* (See page 167)

One of le Brocquy's small number of works with Christian content, 'Lazarus', painted in the mid-fifties, is one which marks the artist's transition from his grey period (c.1951-1954) to the white 'Presences', i.e. presences of the human figure, usually single, which emerge from a white background. After he had moved to London in 1946, le Brocquy produced works which convey a sense of human isolation, of melancholy and vulnerability. The grey hues dominate and emphasise the existentialist preoccupations in these canvases. Both, 'A Sickness' (1951) and 'A Family' (1951) show, in semi-cubist style, family members co-existing in rooms reminiscent of operating theatres or prison cells. They are key examples of his concerns at the time. Towards the end of this period the figures become increasingly isolated (e.g. 'Child in a Yard', 1954).

The depiction of 'Lazarus', a single figure against a grey-white background, then is, as Alistair Smith has pointed out, the 'most obvious prefiguration of the 'Presences'. The Presences, which differ considerably from these earlier works, emerged when le Brocquy's own life and art underwent 'radical revision' as he met and married Anne Madden and moved to France.[37] It is in these works and later in the 'Head' paintings that his interest and continuous search for 'essence', for the 'invisible interior world of consciousness',[38] for spirit in and 'behind' matter,[39] and thus the metaphysical, transcendent, mysterious quality in his work become emphatically apparent. I will discuss this in more detail with regard to his painting 'Ecce Homo'.

The large canvas 'Lazarus' confronts the viewer with an image of the risen friend of Jesus (Jn 11:1-44), who in height is almost life size. The body is depicted in angular, simple outlines. Unlike in John's story, which relates that Lazarus' hands and feet were 'bound with strips of cloth, and his face [was] wrapped in a cloth' (Jn 11:44), here the figure's *torso* is tightly wrapped with dark bands. These show some small blood-like red stains. His lower body down to the knees is wrapped with a grey-white, transparent cloth.[40] The

37. Alistair Smith, 'Louis Le Brocquy: On the Spiritual in Art', in *Louis Le Brocquy Paintings 1939-1996* (Dublin: Irish Museum of Modern Art, 1996), 36.
38. Le Brocquy, 'Notes on painting and awareness', in Walker, *Louis le Brocquy*, 139.
39. In this context it is interesting to note Brendan P. Devlin's analogy of the task of an artist and that of a saint. He holds that both are our teachers. Although they work at 'different levels' both have been granted with 'the gift of divining the spiritual behind and beyond the material'. B.P. Devlin, 'The Christian and the Arts', *The Furrow*, vol. 13, no. 6 (June 1962), 340.
40. John Russell points out that for 'Lazarus' le Brocquy used sketches made from Egyptian mummies. J. Russell, 'Introduction', in Walker, *Louis le Brocquy* (1981), 9-10. I also thank Brian O'Leary S.J. for his comments.

head, bent forward, makes the face invisible. The background with grey-black horizontal and vertical lines alludes to the open tomb, in which, according to ancient Jewish funeral rites and confirmed by John, Lazarus had been buried upright.[41] A square on the bottom right stands out due to its green-blue colouring. Apart from its torso, the figure and the background are painted in grey-white.

In the history of art the 'Raising of Lazarus' features from earliest times as a 'type' of resurrection. The present painting is unusual as Jesus and Lazarus' sisters Mary and Martha are absent. Since the figure is presented in frontal position, it might imply that Christ, who 'cried with a loud voice "Lazarus, come out!"' (Jn 11:43), actually occupies the space of the viewer. In fact, it is the title which clarifies the theme since the figure as such associates Christ rather than – or at least as much as – Lazarus. In this way le Brocquy's treatment, in accordance with John, reveals Lazarus' raising as an anticipation of Christ's resurrection and the resurrection of his followers: 'I am the resurrection and the life. Those who believe in me, even though they die, will live, and everyone who lives and believes in me will never die' (Jn 11:25-26).

What is particularly striking in the work is the fact that it does not only deal with the theme of Lazarus but that it suggests, moreover, the Christ event, i.e. both Christ on the Cross *and* the risen Christ. While the bent face and the outstretched arms are a clear reference to Jesus crucified, his lower left arm raised with the hand opened as if to receive God's grace of life, as also the slightly parted legs which show the figure in a standing position, are indicative of Christ's resurrection. The blue-green square in the foreground on the lower right emphasises the soteriological aspect as it could be interpreted as the green grass, the new life, on which Christ/Lazarus steps.[42] This depiction and its title, which at first seems rather simple, thus leaves itself open to a complex interpretation.

Alistair Smith observes that the painter's use of overt religious subject matter during that time – the time of the Cold War – 'confront[s] us with le Brocquy's questioning of life and death, time and timelessness'. Given that this figure is Lazarus but also evokes Christ on the Cross and the risen Christ, the work, in more theological terms, therefore discloses the continuity and relationship between the historical Jesus and the Christ of faith, between his/our existence on earth and his/our life in the eschaton, between immanence and transcendence. Lazarus'/Christ's strangely drooping head and

41. Byzantine art and some Renaissance works show Lazarus in this position. Perhaps le Brocquy's painting alludes to this through the upright position of Lazarus.

42. Here one might even think of Piero della Francesca's 'Resurrection' in which the leaves on the trees in the background on the right, as opposed to those bare trees on the left, symbolise the resurrection to new life.

hence his hidden face evoke the reality of suffering, resignation and desola-
tion, of God becoming sin for our sake. At the same time, the rendering of
an 'anonymous' face, rather than a more clearly defined one, adds to the sense
that resurrection is promised to *every* human who believes in, and wholly
entrusts her or himself (Lazarus) to, the God of Jesus Christ. This painting
with its biblical theme thus conveys what is central to Christian faith, namely
that those who believe will be raised from the dead.[43]

Lazarus then, symbol of the ones who trust in Christ, is resurrected so as
to make manifest the glory of God. It is this sign which perhaps more radically than any other of the miracles led those around Jesus to faith in him.[44]
Indeed it does not come as a surprise that after this sign the Pharisees and
chief priests finally decided that Jesus should die (Jn 11:53, 57).

Le Brocquy's austere 'Lazarus' – or, 'The Risen Christ', as one might easily perceive it – points us to the 'essence' of the divine, to the God who is
faithful to God's Son and to humankind in sustaining, redeeming and raising it to new life.

3.2. Ecce Homo (See page 168)

In the fifties, le Brocquy became increasingly concerned with 'essence'; or as
John Montague writes, it is the numinous aspect,[45] the spiritual-transcendent, metaphysical dimension, that becomes more and more transparent in
the rendering of his subjects. In this context le Brocquy's comment that for
him painting is 'an entirely different form of awareness' since 'an essential
quality of art is its alienation, its otherness' is pertinent.[46] Actuality, i.e. 'exter-
ior reality', as he sees it, is 'relevant, parallel, but remote or curiously dis-
located'. It is this element of tension between actuality and otherness that will
be of interest in the discussion of this work.

'Ecce Homo' is a typical example of the style of his White Paintings in the
late 1950s.[47] It is unusual in two respects, however, as here le Brocquy chooses
a male rather than a female figure, and, furthermore, he deals with a religious
subject, i.e. Jn 19:4-6, when Jesus, wearing the crown of thorns and a purple

43. Cf. Richard Bauckham, 'God Who Raises the Dead: The Resurrection of Jesus and Early
    Christian Faith in God', in Paul Avis, (ed.), *The Resurrection of Jesus Christ* (London:
    Darton, Longman & Todd, 1993), 150.
44. Pheme Perkins, 'The Gospel According to John', *NJBC,* 970. Cf. John Fenton, 'The Four
    Gospels: Four Perspectives on the Resurrection', in Avis, op.cit., 47.
45. John Montague, 'Primal Scream – The Later le Brocquy', *The Arts in Ireland,* vol. 2, no. 1
    (1973), 6.
46. Le Brocquy, 'Notes on painting and awareness', in Walker, *Louis le Brocquy* (1981), 135.
47. 'Nude in Movement' (1957) and 'Young Woman (Anne)' (1957), for example, are very
    similar in style.

robe, is brought before the people who demand his crucifixion. Pilate responds that he does not find any case against him, and exclaims: 'Here is the man!'

Le Brocquy's approach is a rather individual one. The theme 'Ecce Homo', which was hardly depicted before the Renaissance, was normally treated in two distinct ways. Either Christ in half-figure or only his head with thorn crown is shown; or, as narrative, it includes the many persons involved in the event in the setting of Pilate's praetorium or in a town square. Christ is always garbed with the crown of thorns and with the kingly garments which the mocking soldiers put on him. Sometimes he has his wrists crossed and holds a reed or sceptre. His expression is normally one of resignation.

In the present work the only pictorial allusion to the theme is the fact that the figure's wrists are crossed. Otherwise none of the traditional elements feature. Christ, whose head is barely indicated through a shadow, is one of le Brocquy's typical isolated figures; the title and crossed wrists are therefore the only references to the religious subject. One should add also that despite the fact that white was, of course, le Brocquy's preoccupation, here in the canvas, especially in the figure, it enhances the meaning of Christ as the innocent victim.

This work then is one more example of le Brocquy's few depictions of a Christian theme. It is to be seen in the context of the painter's questioning of life and death against the background of the Cold War years. His treatment, in particular the absence of any outlines of a head, is in line with his statement that the reason why he would not attempt to paint an image of the head of Christ was due to the fact that he had no idea of Jesus' physical appearance. Thus the concrete historical event of Christ flagellated and presented to the people by Pilate becomes in le Brocquy's approach to the theme, one in which reality and transcendence merge in the sense that the figure seems, at least in part, evanescent, otherworldly. In this way it curiously provides a glimpse of the central doctrine of the hypostatic union of the human and the divine nature in Christ, God's incarnation and his life in glory, immanence and transcendence, actuality and otherness. This is not achieved through the use of a symbol like the halo as in the art of the past but through le Brocquy's particular painterly technique and style, its sense of ambivalence that is central in his work. In fact, it even has been suggested that there might be an element of irony or paradox in the title, as 'Ecce Homo' emphasises the human nature of Jesus while the actual painting is quite evocative of the divine mystery of Christ.[48]

Further, le Brocquy's approach provides a rather striking example of

48. I thank Hilary Pyle for her comment.

Heidegger's dialectical notion of truth in art as disclosure and concealment.[49] Le Brocquy's 'Presences', the suggested-actual human figures which emerge out of space and immerge into space, unconceal as much as they conceal, lending them their mysterious, metaphysical character. In this context of disclosure and concealment it is important to remember once more that critics and le Brocquy himself have repeatedly spoken about his art in terms of ambivalence, immergence and emergence and about the human head as the box which hides and reveals the spirit. What is shown is not simply concrete fact but rather reality perceived as 'that which is possible, conceivable and not merely ... actual, phenomenal'.[50]

It is this notion and manifestation of reality as possibility rather than as mere actuality in the 'Ecce Homo', as in many of his other works, which has affinity with and evokes diverse, yet not mutually exclusive, theological concerns. These include the eschatological notion of the already and not yet, the apophatic theology of the mystics which refrains from definitive statements on God, the *deus absconditus* and *deus revelatus,* and lastly David Tracy's propounding of a 'mystical-prophetic model' for contemporary (inter-religious) theology, which corresponds to and is based on the 'religious dialectic of manifestation and proclamation'.[51] If Barth held that the *proclamation* of the incarnate Logos is what constitutes theology and faith, i.e. a word-centred Christianity,[52] Tracy rightly points out that in Christian ecumenical theology today it is essential to recognise both, the proclamatory word and the power of mystical, aesthetic manifestation of the sacred in the cosmos, in nature and in art. This is so because it is the Christ event itself, 'Jesus Christ as true word and decisive manifestation', which is the paradigm for theology. As he states: '[T]he Christian ethos [is] rooted in the dialectics of an enveloping always-already manifestation constantly transformed by a defamiliarising, often shattering, not-yet proclamation.'[53] It is this tension-relationship of proclamation and manifestation which is central to Christian life and faith, and revelatory of God as immanent *and* as the radical Other. Here it is significant to note that Tracy, with reference to Heidegger, Gadamer and Ricoeur, defends the notion of 'truth-as-manifestation'. In particular, he points out

49. Cf. M. Heidegger, 'The Origin of the Work of Art', in Heidegger, *Basic Writings* (London/Henley: Routledge & Kegan Paul, 1978), 175-184.
50. Le Brocquy, 'Notes on painting and awareness', in Walker, *Louis le Brocquy* (1981), 146. Le Brocquy has spoken of his notion of reality in relation to his painting of heads. It seems to me to apply equally to the Presences.
51. Tracy, *Dialogue with the Other: The Inter-Religious Dialogue* (Louvain: Peters Press/Grands Rapids, Michigan: Eerdmans, 1990), 7.
52. Cf. Karl Barth, *Einführung in die evangelische Theologie* (Gütersloh: Mohn, 1980), 44, 72. Tracy, *The Analogical Imagination*, 213.
53. Tracy, ibid., 214, 218.

that the truth of religion as the truth of its closest cousin, art, is essentially the truth of manifestation.[54]

One might argue that le Brocquy's rendering of 'Ecce Homo' expresses in paint something of Tracy's description of religion. The sense of the prophetic-mystical is conveyed in the title and in the depiction of the flagellated Christ. His physical presence is captured as 'figured' *and* 'transfigured', which thus emphasises the material-transcendent dimension, i.e. God incarnate and God as Other, the already-not-yet, indeed the dimension of possibility, which le Brocquy himself has referred to in his writing on his perception of art. In fact, this sense of possibility again curiously reflects Tracy, who has stressed – in relation to his notion of 'truth-as-manifestation' (disclosure-concealment) in both religion and art – that the category of possibility has a 'fundamentally aesthetic' dimension.

Alistair Smith concludes in his essay on the artist that it is 'in some strange area between spirit and appearance that le Brocquy' work makes its mark'.[55] Although one may not go so far as to entirely substitute spirit with prophesy-proclamation-word and appearance with mysticism-manifestation-sacrament, they point, however, in a remarkably similar direction. It is here that Tracy's wider theological perspective converges with Smith's particular interpretation of le Brocquy and thus broadens and enhances our understanding of the artist's works, such as 'Ecce Homo', which expresses immanence *and* transcendence, 'epiphany *and* historical event',[56] the revealed and hidden God in and of Jesus Christ.

Le Brocquy and commentators on his work have repeatedly spoken of his interest in 'the metaphysical reality of matter', of his 'search for essence'. One hardly assumes that le Brocquy had theological concepts like the hypostatic union in mind when he approached his subject. However, in his continuous striving for a glimpse of the essence of his subjects, in this case Jesus Christ before his death, he has, in fact, succeeded in pointing to the 'essence' of the God-Man, God wholly incarnate and wholly mystery.

54. Tracy, *Dialogue with the Other*, 43.
55. A. Smith, 'Louis Le *(sic)* Brocquy: On The Spiritual In Art', op.cit., 52.
56. Tracy, *The Analogical Imagination*, 218. Tracy speaks of the dialectical sense that is present in the whole Christian symbol system, such as epiphany and historical event, sacrament and word etc.

3.3. Procession with Lilies IV (See page 169)

The series of 'Procession' paintings from the 1980s and 1990s were inspired by a photograph in the *Evening Herald,* 16th June 1939, of schoolgirls return-ing along the Liffey quays from an annual religious ceremony and ritual of the Blessing of the Lilies in the Franciscan Church of Adam and Eve, Merchants' Quay, Dublin. In the same year Joyce published *Finnegan's Wake,* in which appears the line 'riverrun, past Eve and Adams ...', from where the subsequent title of the series, 'Riverrun. Procession with Lilies', derives.[57] In the 1980s and '90s le Brocquy painted a parallel series 'Children in a Wood', a theme which was originally inspired by the work 'Boys Playing with a Goat' by the Dutch artist Nicolaes Maes (1634-1693) which le Brocquy had seen in London in 1953. In 1954 he produced the painting 'Children in a Wood (after Nicolaes Maes)' in semi-cubist style. Forty years later he returned to the theme in serial form.

The 'Procession' and 'Children in a Wood' paintings show several simil-arities in style. Instead of isolated figures or heads, the canvases display a multiplicity of figures, 'blending and overlapping in flickering friezes'.[58] They are, as Alistair Smith has pointed out, reminiscent of the Renaissance and ancient classicism in their relief-like composition and shape. Le Brocquy himself stated that what struck him about the photo of the schoolgirls was that to him it resembled 'Renaissance imagery on a Dublin street-corner'.[59]

A most significant aspect in both series is the way in which le Brocquy has been able to convey the sense of time as passing, ever-present and eternal, i.e. his contracting of time into one image as action follows action 'in a succes-sion of movements across the canvas'.[60] In the 'Procession' series this aspect is even more pronounced than in 'Children in a Wood'. With regard to the former series, le Brocquy has stated that he has returned again and again to render 'this past event arrested within a succession of present moments'. Another relevant element, from a theological perspective, is the colour white that dominates in the 'Procession' series. With regard to this series the artist has commented that for him white 'embodied the quality of transcendence' and of mystery. Like the girls in their white dresses and veils in the photo-graph, the girls in the canvas are painted in white.

In both series then, innocence of childhood as well as time and ritual in form of youthful processions are captured.[61] While 'Children in a Wood' is a

57. A. Madden le Brocquy, *Louis le Brocquy, A Painter, Seeing His Way,* 228.
58. A. Smith, op.cit., 49.
59. Le Brocquy, *Procession* (Kinsale: Gandon Editions, 1994), 7.
60. Smith, op.cit., 49.
61. Cf. le Brocquy quoted in A. Madden le Brocquy, op.cit., 228: 'For many years I have been fascinated by both themes, but it was not until quite recently that I recognised a relation

more secular theme, the 'Procession' series is based on a specific annual religious ceremony in the Roman Catholic Church. Dressed in white and carrying lilies, symbols of purity, the girls in the photograph evoke associations with Mary and her traditional portrayal in art, as well as with the idea of the vocation of a nun as bride of Christ. Le Brocquy's treatment of the theme conveys a similar sense of youthfulness, purity and innocence. What differs, obviously, is the fact that one is a painting, the other a photograph. The semi-cubist, linear, partly angular shapes, i.e. the figures, which are separate, yet blend, reveal the sense of time as both transient and eternal. Thus it is through his painterly technique that he manages to reveal something of the essence of what constitutes time and ritual. Further, the sculptural relief-like aspect of the work enhances the impression of permanence and continuity that is intrinsic to the meaning of ritual and time. Also, in comparison to his Head images and the Presences, these paintings are more joyous which pertains to the celebratory aspect in ritual.

Despite the fact that Ireland has become increasingly secular within the last twenty years, with church attendance falling, especially among the working class unemployed, and less trust in the institutional church, rituals, either Christian, as this one, or those in which Celtic-pagan and Christian elements merge, continue to play an important role in Irish culture. Michael Drumm has rightly observed that while many of the traditional religious practices, pilgrimages, holy wells, wakes etc., have provided rich material for artists, playwrights and poets, such as Heaney or Friel, they have been largely ignored in the work of Irish theologians.[62] Le Brocquy's 'Procession' series serves as an example of where a religious custom has inspired the work of a painter. In fact, the Blessing of the Lilies still takes place annually on the Feast of St Antony of Padua (1195-1231) on 13th June in the Church of Adam and Eve, as in other Franciscan churches in Ireland.[63] In this work le Brocquy has thus

ship between these two youthful processions, 'sacred and profane', one a Joycean charade, a fleeting actuality in a continuous progression of present moments; the other, as I see it, a constant condition of being, a return in the mind to the sensuous magic of childhood, when meaning lay within each hollow tree and time was a measure of eternity.'

62. Michael Drumm, 'Irish Catholics: A People Formed by Ritual', in Eoin G. Cassidy, (ed.), *Faith and Culture in the Irish Context* (Dublin: Veritas, 1996), 84-85. In this context le Brocquy's observation that the Celtic *fili* (poets) were regarded as 'seers' is pertinent. 'I have long been moved by ... the Celtic vision and by the prolonged tragedy of its inevitable suppression since Roman times.' Le Brocquy, quoted in *Procession*, 11.

63. It is the second most important feast in the Franciscan order. Antony, a Franciscan, who was declared doctor of the Church in 1946, is popularly invoked as finder of lost articles and his cult has always included the memory of his miracle cures and his devotion to the poor. In art he is often represented with a book and a lily, with the infant Jesus sitting on the book. Cf. David Hugh Farmer, *The Oxford Dictionary of Saints* (Oxford, New York: Oxford University Press, 1987), 23.

depicted a moment of a Christian ritual which has played and continues to play a role in contemporary popular devotion in – predominantly working class – inner city Dublin life. The painter's joyous composition calls up diverse associations of innocence and goodness, of a return to the Garden of Eden and of Christ's command that one needs to become like a child to enter the kingdom of God. Furthermore, le Brocquy's remarkable way of revealing the transient, yet unending aspect of time suggests in some sense the continuity of communal celebration of Christian customs, especially by those who are called the 'simple people of God'. The work thus assumes a soteriological and doxological dimension.

4. GERARD DILLON

4.1. Fish Eaters (See page 170)

Gerard Dillon was Ireland's only 'Naïve' painter. However, his style was, of course, far from naïve, as commonly understood. In fact, his art often reveals a high level of sophistication, which underlines George Campbell's view that Dillon was the 'most simple complex person' he and his friends had known.[64] The three works under consideration here, 'Fish Eaters' (1946), 'The Brothers' (c. 1966) and 'Entertaining Friends' (c. 1968) reveal something of the breadth of his style, subject matter and use of symbol. While 'Fish Eaters' is set in the West of Ireland, from where Dillon drew much of his inspiration, the latter works with the pierrots are strongly personal as they pertain to himself as painter, to his family, and especially to the experience and premonition of death. Again, as with some of the other painters, it is, seemingly paradoxically, this very subjective aspect which gives them a more universal dimension.

Christian subjects or at least allusions to it appear in several of his canvases in the 1940s and 50s when he was painting in Connemara and the Aran Islands,[65] such as 'Forgive Us Our Trespasses' (exh. 1942), 'Dust to Dust' (exh. 1946), 'Fish Eaters', 'High Cross Panel' (c. 1949), 'St Francis' (exh. 1950), and 'Fast Day' (exh. 1950).

'Fish Eaters' is an example of his maturing as a painter. Emphasis on narrative, as well as a curiously distorted perspective which heightens the two-dimensionality of the picture plane and which thereby enhances the symbolism in the work, are characteristics in many of his canvases. The work shows four figures at a meal, which consists of fish, potatoes and wine. The figures, plates, cups and a bottle of red wine are presented in clear, simplified, expressionist-naïve style. In the background on the left, a 'Madonna and Child', not unlike those painted by Jellett or Hone, hangs on the wall. In the middle background one sees a window through which one looks 'out' onto a West-of-Ireland scene of mountains and cottages, and on the right one perceives another window which is not square but strangely presented as an arch. The whole work exudes a certain intensity, frontality and directness as the figures and the table occupy almost the entire picture space.

---

64. G. Campbell, 'A Simple Complex Man', *The Irish Times*, 8.7.1971.
65. Both Samuel B. Kennedy and Brian Fallon have noted that Dillon's works from around 1950 in Connemara remain his best due to their 'formal strength', their 'directness' and fresh handling of colour and paint. B. Fallon, 'Gerard Dillon retrospective at the Municipal Gallery', *The Irish Times*, 5.1.1973. S.B. Kennedy, *Irish Art and Modernism 1880-1940*, 140-141.

Although at first glance one might simply think of Connemara peasants at a meal, this work invites a more complex interpretation. Samuel Kennedy has rightly pointed out that the Hone/Jellett type of 'Madonna and Child', as well as the bottle of Chianti wine, reveal an unexpected sense of sophistication, as neither such a painting nor wine would have been found in a 1940s peasant household in the West of Ireland. Dillon's art was intensely personal and it is here that his own subjectivity, i.e. his knowledge of modern art and his acquaintance with a more cosmopolitan (Italian) culture, is evidenced in his subject matter.

Further, Kennedy has referred to these figures as a 'quasi-monastic group of peasants'.[66] This interpretation hints in the direction of my own view, namely that the whole work exudes what might be described as a religious atmosphere; in particular it alludes to the theme and depictions of the Last Supper. Despite the fact that this scene is inspired by life in the West of Ireland and that instead of Christ and his twelve disciples there are only four figures, Dillon's style and his use of symbolism evoke an *agape* meal and/or even the Eucharist. The fish is a very old and widely used symbol in Christian art, connoting, as it does, Christ, Christian baptism, resurrection in the story of Jonah, in the gospels the feeding of the five thousand and the miraculous catch of fish in the post-resurrection account of John. Not only do the title as well as the fish on the plates indirectly and symbolically refer to Christ and the Eucharist, but also the red wine, i.e. the blood, alludes to the sacramental communion. The size and central position of the table ('altar'), the white table cloth,[67] as well as the bottle which is placed almost exactly in the centre of the canvas, also points to this eucharistic dimension. The sacramental, christological aspect is further enhanced by the figure on the right who not only appears slightly bigger than the others but who is clad in a long, dress-like garment, which could be read as alluding to traditional depictions of Christ in art. The figure with the moustache and the long garment is reminiscent of figures from Irish High Crosses. Moreover, the arched window slightly to the side of this figure appears both like a halo and a Romanesque church window. In fact, on closer inspection, all four figures are depicted with a thin, bright, halo-like line on their heads. The picture of the 'Madonna and Child' on the left also points to the Christian aspect in the work, i.e. to the faith and Catholic culture of the 'simple people' in the West of Ireland who are depicted here.[68]

66. S.B. Kennedy, op.cit., 140.
67. I thank Ruth Sheehy for her observation.
68. Dillon's depiction may also *vaguely* hint at a possible influence of van Gogh's 'The Potato-Eaters' (1885). Like Dillon's painting it exudes a religious atmosphere in its communal sharing of a simple, 'agape-like', meal. As in Dillon's work, a small picture with an apparently religious theme (Mother and Child?) hangs on the wall on the top left corner.

The whole composition – the peasants at their meal with its symbolic ingredients, the 'Madonna and Child', the window with the Connemara scene and the Romanesque arch or halo-like window - alludes thus to the link between Christ's birth and his last meal with his friends, his life, death and resurrection, his time and our time, his sacramental presence, his reality and contemporary Irish reality. It conveys therefore the dimension of *anamnesis* and the sense of community or *koinonia,* both of which are central to the meaning of the Eucharist.[69] Lane's interpretation of the Last Supper as sacrament of the eschaton refers especially to these two aspects, as he stresses the 'liberating', 'redemptive' and 'creative power' of memory, the 'memory that makes the past operative in the present and in doing so holds out promises for the future'. It is this power of *anamnesis* which is central to the celebration of the Last Supper; as a memorial of Christ it makes present the divine, the kingdom of God in the here and now. Dillon's 'Fish Eaters' in its revelation of the link between present and past, the secular (Connemara peasants and landscape) and the sacred (wine, fish/Christ, 'Madonna and Child') hence curiously captures something of Lane's insistence that eschatological theology is 'false' if it separates the sacred from the secular and time from eternity.

The kingdom is essentially a kingdom of community; it is the communion of Christ and his disciples and our own communion and community with him and with one another which we celebrate in the Last Supper, i.e. the meal which anticipates the messianic banquet and the final coming of Christ. Dillon – whether intentionally or unintentionally – evokes the sense of the Eucharist, of *koinonia* in table fellowship, in depicting a group of peasants in a West-of-Ireland-cottage who are united not by conversation but rather by their common meal, a meal which due to its symbolic content alludes to the Last Supper and which they share as Irish peasants and as the *sanctorum communio.*[70]

---

69. Cf. D. Lane, *Keeping Hope Alive,* 194-210. Lane develops the eschatological dimensions of the Eucharist whereby he emphasises the memorial aspect of the celebration of the Last Supper which in its power to link past, present and future keeps Christian hope alive.

70. Cf. D. Bonhoeffer's 'sociological examination' of the church as *sanctorum communio,* in particular his stress on the communitarian aspect in the celebration of the Eucharist in *Bonhoeffer Auswahl, Anfänge 1927-1933,* vol. 1 (Gütersloh: Mohn, 1982), 19-38.

4.2. The Brothers (See page 171)

Dillon began to paint his works with pierrots in the 1960s. The pierrot, a type of comical figure who often represents the betrayed lover, appeared first in theatre in the seventeenth century and has been used by painters such as Goya, Watteau and in our century notably by Picasso and Rouault. As White has pointed out, one may assume that it was Picasso's example that encouraged Dillon to use this masked figure so as to project himself into his works.[71] The clown or pierrot, symbol of fun, humour and laughter on the one hand, also incorporates an underlying sense of tragedy, sadness, even despair. It is this dimension which is apparent in several of Dillon's pierrot works, in particular in the painting under consideration.

The title refers to his own three brothers, all of whom died as a result of heart defects within a five year period between 1962 and 1966. In 1961, ten years prior to his death, Dillon himself got ill with heart pains. In fact, he correctly predicted that he would not live beyond the age of 55. All of his works are deeply subjective, but the paintings of this last decade in his life are perhaps even more emphatically so as, in their symbolism and psychological overtones, they are revelatory of the conscious and subconscious state of the artist.[72] 'The Brothers', in particular, deals with and shows his awareness of death, i.e. his brothers' death and the anticipation of his own.

The canvas shows three skeletons buried in coffins in the ground. Above the grave the pierrot/painter in typical white garments and black mask is depicted in kneeling posture on a yellow-blue striped field, his head close to the ground and arms crossed. In the background to the left we see bare trees, on the right a West-of-Ireland stone wall and cottage. The sky behind is painted in dark blue tones. On the very right top three tiny, sketchily depicted figures in yellow before a golden-yellow background appear to be walking towards or alongside what seems to be the entrance to a church.[73]

Dillon referred to this work in a letter in 1967 to White as 'an important pic *(sic)* in my life of painting'. In fact, he wrote: 'I ... did a big one of three skeletons in a grave. I think it's the best in the show – tho' I wouldn't say this ... The whole show is cheerful in colour, has a humour with underlying sad-

---

71. White, *Gerard Dillon*, 90.
72. 'Clowns, pierrots and mask-faced figures explore a world of gentle humour which has a hinterland of pathos, and reaches towards the universality of the human condition.' M. Longley, *Causeway: The Arts in Ulster* (Belfast: Arts Council of Northern Ireland in connection with Gill and Macmillan, 1971), 47.
73. Whether this building with golden entrance and brown roof, was, in fact, intended as a church is not clear. From its appearance, one would have grounds to interpret it as such.

ness about it – is poetic (I think) Is very subconscious indeed – they all came from the side of me that's "over there".'[74]

His comment indirectly, yet clearly, points to the meaning (of the pierrot) in the exhibited works, namely his awareness of an 'underlying sadness', and especially the anticipation and treatment of death, i.e. 'the side of me that's "over there"'. The posture of the pierrot/painter is of particular interest here. Against the foreboding dark blue sky which almost appears to be a night scene with its connotation of sleep, the state closest to death, the pierrot/painter does not stand but kneels crouched, seemingly mourning, watching, listening to and perhaps even praying for his dead brothers whom he knows he will follow before too long.[75]

It is this anticipatory aspect, this connection and relation between the one who is still alive and those who have already gone before him, that gives the work its deeply eschatological dimension. It is the reality of his own – and hence of everyone's – death which is the theme of this work. It is the factual irreversibility and unavoidability of death, the finality of earthly life, an intense awareness of our 'being towards death' (Heidegger) which Dillon confronts in, as he says, a poetic yet concrete and definite manner.[76] The fact that he uses the impersonal pierrot in order to paint a profoundly personal painting curiously enhances his direct, unsentimental treatment of the theme which thus lends the work both a strongly subjective *and* objective dimension. Indeed his approach shows remarkable intellectual sophistication and his complexity of thought at the time.

If, as Dillon held, these late works with pierrots such as 'The Brothers', 'Cut Out, Drop Out' (exh. 1968), or 'Entertaining Friends' (c. 1968), a painting which again refers to his dead brothers, came from the side of him that was already 'over there', they evidence thus something of our fundamental attitude and 'knowledge' of death, namely that, as Jüngel puts it, which is totally alien to and at the same time innermost part of us.[77] *Incerta omnia,*

---

74. Quoted from Dillon's letter to White, reproduced in White, op.cit., 91.

75. An Irish song/poem Dillon would have known and which might have provided some inspiration for this work was related to the author by Patrick Taylor: 'Táim sínte ar do thuama, is gheobhair ann go síor mé, Dá mbeadh barra do dhá lámh agam, ní scarfainn leat choíche.' ('I am stretched on your tombstone, you will find me there always. If I had the tips of your fingers, I would never let you go.')

76. In 1967 Dillon suffered a coronary. He wrote to his nephew Gerard from hospital: 'I feel like I've walked the path of life on to the lane that leads to the tomb. There's no doubt about that. Looking around me here I can see that death has put his hand on each one of us.' Dillon quoted in White, op.cit., 93.

77. Eberhard Jüngel, *Tod* (Gütersloh: Mohn, 1983), 16. '[D]er Tod ist nämlich nicht nur das dem menschlichen Dasein gegenüber schlechthin Fremde, sondern er ist zugleich *unser Eigenstes*.'

sola mors certa (Augustine); the fact and the facing of this certainty is expressed in Dillon's work.

Death, the radical break with and end to our earthly existence, and that which follows, i.e. physical decay in the grave, is captured in the painting. The fact that he contrasts the realm of death, the bleak brown ground and skeletons, which occupies almost three quarters of the picture space, with the realm of earthly life, the light green-blue striped ground with pierrot, enhances this sense that death means *the* radical, undeniable, permanent break. In Rahner's words, death is 'the absolute end of the temporal dimension of a being of the kind to which man belongs'.[78] And, moreover, it is that ultimate dimension over which we have no power but rather which rules us throughout our whole life.

Today we live in a culture that increasingly denies death; it is an epoch which is more and more incapable of dealing with death as belonging to life and hence keeps it as far away as possible from our social and personal consciousness.[79] Paradoxically and unsurprisingly the human being in the twentieth century who is – partly through experience and partly through the media – only too aware of (mass) death through world wars, hunger, accidents and illness is fed by the same media with the cult of the healthy 'ever-young' which tries hard to avoid facing the reality of death. Dillon's work, the pierrot/painter looking 'into' death, is a reminder that such cults, of course, are nothing but illusions. The painting states the simple and most difficult fact, namely, as Jüngel writes, '*that* death is'.[80] Life cannot be thought of without death and vice versa. Hence it is the affirmation of the reality of and confrontation with death which enables us to appreciate and affirm life, life as wonderful and pure gift. The tiny yellow figures beside the church-like building on the top right, who may be a reference to his brothers either in their youth or resurrected into the house of God, i.e. eternal life in the kingdom, point to this sense of appreciation of life in the face of death. This painting, which arose out of Dillon's love and mourning for his three brothers and the premonition of his own death, thus conveys something of the radical break between, and ultimate unity of, life and death.

78. Rahner, 'A Theology of Death', *Theological Investigations*, vol. 13 (London: DLT, 1975), 174.
79. Küng, *Eternal Life?* (London: Collins, 1984), 199-203. Cf. Jüngel, op.cit., 46-50.
80. Jüngel, op.cit., 24.

4.3. Entertaining Friends (See page 172)

This work, also with pierrots, dates from about the same time as and them-atically relates to 'The Brothers'. In the previous chapter I concluded that it was perhaps through his remarkable artistic sincerity and perhaps only in his art, rather than anywhere else, that Dillon – who apparently did not talk about religion and who certainly distanced himself from the church – could still reveal his faith.

I now want to demonstrate that 'Entertaining Friends' may indeed indic-ate something of the artist's personal faith, and that in its subjective allusions, strange and bizarre as they may be, it points to some more objective central Christian themes and beliefs.[81]

The canvas shows three pierrots draped in green with yellow-green foliage covering their bodies and black masks, while the host pierrot in white with green mask, but visible eyes, kneels on the right with a rose in his hand. In the yellow-green foreground, on what seems to be a striped carpet or table-cloth, is placed a teapot, four cups, plates and saucers. The figures' space, sur-rounded by a green fence, appears like a garden or terrace in front of the sea or lake with mountains in the background. The sky is 'lit' with warm orange and clearly visible yellow sunrays, which shine above and onto the scene. A bird, apparently a duck, is depicted on the left before the mountain range.[82]

Again the viewer is confronted with a symbolist work. As White has remarked, the three figures, i.e. the three friends, can be assumed to be the painter's brothers. Their relationship is expressed in that all four are shown as pierrots. Their different garments, three in green, one in white, and postures signify that there is a difference between them, namely three are dead, one is alive. Unlike in the previous painting 'The Brothers', the figures, i.e. the brothers, are no longer depicted as skeletons in the grave but rather they appear as a dreamlike apparition to their brother/white pierrot. No longer are they lying dead in the ground, but they are sitting up 'alive', invited to a meal. The yellow-green colour which dominates the foreground adds to the strange, transcendent atmosphere or dreamlike event. The fact that the fig-ures are green, with leaves all over their bodies, is an emphatic sign of new

81. I have at various times referred to the subjective-objective dimension in the interpretation and revelatory meaning of the work of art. Interestingly Tillich in his treatment of revela-tion emphasises this subjective-objective dimension: 'Revelation always is a subjective and an objective event in strict interdependence ... If nothing happens objectively, nothing is revealed. If no one receives what happens subjectively, the event fails to reveal anything. The objective occurrence and the subjective reception belong to the whole event of reve-lation.' Tillich, *Systematic Theology*, vol. 1 (Chicago: The University of Chicago Press, 1951), 111.

82. Whether the bird is 'merely' decorative or has a deeper meaning is unclear.

life, indeed, of a strong sense of hope, of resurrection. They are still rendered in physical human form, yet their colour and drapery is utterly strange. Dillon, with or without intention, therefore curiously alludes to something important in the Christian idea of creation and eternal life: The material and spiritual spheres are not to be seen as separate but as forming a unity. Yet, the apparition of these figures in all their strangeness and otherness provides a hint that life after death must not be seen as somehow a continuation of this life, of time, but rather as atemporal, as the mystery of the fulfilment of creation.[83] At the same time, because the figures appear in human form, they disclose the connection and relationship between present and future, creation and redemption, this world and the other. They reveal, moreover, that it can only be through our limited human language and understanding that we can imagine analogically, metaphorically or symbolically something of eternal life,[84] i.e. that sphere which is ultimately beyond all human conception.

Another aspect that links in with the overall implication of resurrection of the dead and eternal life in the work is its eucharistic and trinitarian dimension. Whether Dillon had this in mind will never be known, of course. The painting, however, strangely reminds one of Rublev's famous icon of 'The Trinity' with the three angels who appear to and are entertained by Abraham and Sarah at their dwelling at Mamre (Gen 18:1-15). From early times this theme has been seen as an anticipation of the Trinity. In Rublev's icon the three angels (Father, Son and Holy Spirit) are placed around a table on which is placed a cup, a symbol of the Eucharist. The present work shows some striking parallels. Like the angels with their very similar, yet slightly different appearance in the colour of their garments, the three brothers also look very similar, yet the shape and colouring vary slightly in each figure. God, Father, Son and Holy Spirit are different, yet related; analogically the same applies to the brothers. God is eternal; the brothers likewise have entered eternity. The trinitarian divine aspect is enhanced in Dillon's work by the fact that the white pierrot/brother kneels before them which implies a sense of reverence, even worship. The red rose, which symbolises the blood of martyrdom as well as love, here links in with the allusion to the eucharistic theme of Christ's sacrificial death, as also with the death which the painter/pierrot anticipates for himself and which his brothers already have endured.

Rublev's cup on the table is replaced by a tea set. Thus, as in 'Fish Eaters', the painting points to the sense of *koinonia* in the eucharistic meal, and to the messianic banquet in the eschaton, the final reign of God, which the dead brothers have already entered.[85] In depicting those who are already there and

83. Cf. Rahner, *Grundkurs des Glaubens* (Freiburg: Herder, 1976), 417.
84. Cf. ibid., 415-416.
85. Cf. Lane, op.cit., 196-199.

the one who still finds himself in the 'here' in the same (fenced) space, Dillon therefore merges the next life with this life, immanence with transcendence. The whole work then becomes an intensely eschatological vision of what happens when future and present merge, the dead and the living commune. It is remarkable in the way the painting says something about brotherly love, anticipation of death, faith in the resurrection and eternal life, the Trinity and eucharistic communion/messianic banquet not only without the use of Christian iconography, but in a most unusual, personal, imaginative painterly 'language'.

In the history of art the sun or bright (yellow-golden) light signifies salvation, hope, life and, more specifically, the divinity of and redemption in Christ, often through the halo. According to Luke 'the dawn from on high will break upon us, to give light to those who sit in darkness and in the shadow of death ...' (Lk 1:78-79). In modern art the sun or bright light likewise has a salvific quality, or, at least, it indicates hope.[86] In the present work the sun, which shines from the distance and above the whole scene, finally affirms and enhances the sense of eschatological hope, of community, of faith in the resurrection, salvation and eternal life. The painting thus may not only provide solace and theological insight for the recipient, but possibly *may* be a rather individual, indirect, enigmatic, unconscious, yet rich and complex expression of the artist's faith.

86. This is obvious, for example, in works by van Gogh, Rouault, Corinth, Kandinsky, Natkin, Patrick Scott.

5. COLIN MIDDLETON

5.1. Jacob Wrestling with the Angel (See page 173)

Middleton turned to religious subjects especially in the forties and fifties. As stated before, the nature of his faith seems to have 'paralleled' his expansive artistic imagination in its holistic, panentheist, humanist and christological dimensions. Throughout his life Middleton had an interest in religion, evidence of which are his many canvases with biblical-Christian themes, treated in his personal eclectic manner. The three works under consideration here, all of which are biblically inspired, are only a few of a considerable number of works with religious content. These paintings not only show Middleton's theologically rather interesting, fascinating and individual treatment of these themes, but, it is to be suggested, they reveal that the painter believed in the God of Jesus Christ who is love, a questioning and unconventional faith lived without adherence to the institutional church.

The present painting is based on the story in Gen 32:24-32 of Jacob struggling with a 'man', i.e. God, at Peniel at the Jabbok.[87] It is an enigmatic story that marks a turning point in Jacob's life as after that episode he meets and reconciles with his brother Esau from whom he had taken his birthright and Isaac's blessing. Jacob survives the struggle with a limp; God blesses him and lets him go: 'You shall no longer be called Jacob, but Israel, for you have striven with God and with humans, and have prevailed' (Gen 32:28). Jacob, or Israel, the third of the patriarchs, is thus shown in an ambiguous light as a trickster on the one hand, and on the other as one to whom God reveals Godself at the Jabbok and at Bethel (Gen 35:9-15) and who is revered as the ancestor of the people of Israel.[88] The aim of this mysterious pericope apparently was to honour the patriarch, whose history so far had been one of betrayal and cheating.[89] In contrast to his cheating Esau for Isaac's blessing, here he struggles for and receives it from God. The man, i.e. God, who refuses to reveal his name, says to Jacob that he has 'prevailed'. Jacob, however, claims much less than a victory for himself: 'For I have seen God face to face, and yet my life has been preserved.' He holds he has simply survived, although he had seen God. The common Hebrew Scripture understanding was that one could not see God without incurrence of death. At the heart of the Esau/Jacob conflict

---

87. Peniel means 'face of God'.
88. John Barton, 'Jacob', in Metzger, Coogan, (eds.), *The Oxford Companion to the Bible,* 338. In folklore etymology Jacob means 'he betrays', while Israel means 'Jacob's struggle with El'. Cf. Klaus Koch, Eckhart Otto, Jürgen Roloff, Hans Schmoldt, (eds.), *Reclams Bibellexikon* (Stuttgart: Reclam, 1978), 229, 234.
89. Richard J. Clifford, S.J., Roland E. Murphy, O.Carm., 'Genesis', *NJBC,* 33.

then is the theme of blessing *(beraka)*, of divine grace and favour, which is as mysterious as it is gratuitous.[90] Jacob, unlike Esau, is neither the firstborn nor the beloved of his father and of very questionable character. It is he who, nevertheless, receives the blessing in the end.

Middleton's treatment of the theme is symbolic and expressionist. Jacob, against a noticeably high sky, appears in monumental size in the centre of the canvas. His face, with its pronounced nose and dark hair and beard, hints at the Semitic type. His sloped shoulders and body are wrapped by a blanket garment, which on the right side is striped and cheerfully polychrome, while the left, as if in shadow, is painted in dark black and blue colours. His raised right hand draws the viewer's attention since it is clenched, big and strong, symbolising, as it does, Jacob's struggle with God. The delicate, fragile butterfly on his thumb, which signifies the angel/God, makes a pronounced contrast with the strong hand.

Middleton's iconographic choice of a butterfly is interesting. In the history of art it is a symbol of the resurrected human soul. It is shown either in the hand of the infant Jesus or in Still Life painting. Caterpillar, chrysalis and butterfly connote life, death and resurrection. Given that Middleton was probably aware of the meaning of these symbols, he therefore links Jacob with Christ, i.e. Old and New Testament, which, in fact, concurs with the commonly held notion of the three Hebrew patriarchs as 'types' of Christ. Further, the story of Jacob at the Jabbok came to be seen as a symbol for the spiritual struggle of the Christian in this life.

Aware of the plight of the Jewish refugees and the Holocaust, Middleton's work, painted three years after the war, can be interpreted as a complex, symbolic expression of the human predicament, of struggle, of God's redeeming activity even for those who by human reasoning should be condemned (Jacob, and the ones who – like the Nazis – commit evil). On the one hand, Jacob's strong hand, in comparison to the fragile butterfly, is a reminder that the human, including those who call themselves followers of Christ, are, in fact, able to 'kill' God, the God who is love, as in the concentration camps or wherever evil reigns. On the other hand, his face, anguished, sad, accepting, shows him also as repenting, or even suffering which, in the context of Middleton's concern with the Holocaust, associates him as the Jewish victim. These aspects in Jacob, the one who incurs suffering, the penitent, and the one who suffers and is redeemed, is, moreover, enhanced by the two 'sides' of his garment, one in dark colours, i.e. evil, suffering, the other bright, pointing towards salvation.

90. Ibid., 28. In the Esau/Jacob stories the 'event' and 'effects' of blessing form a particularly central theme. Moreover, divine blessing is gratuitous, it cannot be simply earned by good works. Cf. Claus Westermann, *Der Segen in der Bibel und im Handeln der Kirche* (Gütersloh: Mohn, 1981), 57-58, 65.

It is finally the struggle of conscience, Jacob's and ours, and the unde-served, mysterious experience of God's grace that forms theological meaning in the story and is effectively captured in Middleton's work. Conscience is the voice of God; it is this voice, the 'direct manifestation of God's presence'[91] which Jacob experiences at the Jabbok. Hermann Gunkel once remarked that this enigmatic story was worthy of a Rembrandt.[92] This is not Rembrandt but Middleton, and his sensitive, imaginative and emotive portrayal of the event and the story itself are an expression and 'proof' that, as Gabriel Daly has pointed out, conscience understood properly is not a 'merely' moral or eth-ical but also a mystical and religious experience.[93] It is mystical and religious precisely because of the possibility, reality, free gift and unmerited experience of God's grace.

(Interpretations continue on page 191)

91. G. Daly, 'Conscience, Guilt and Sin', in Seán Freyne, (ed.), *Ethics and the Christian* (Dublin: Columba Press, 1991), 73.
92. Hermann Gunkel, *Genesis* (Göttingen: Vandenhoeck und Ruprecht, 1902), 323.
93. Daly, op.cit., 73-74.

1.1. Mainie Jellett: *Man and Woman*
         (1937, diptych, oil on canvas, 115.5:45.5cm each, private collection)

1.2.   Mainie Jellet: *Madonna and Child*
          (c. 1936, oil on canvas, 61:46cm, private collection)

1.3. Mainie Jellet: *The Ninth Hour* (1941, oil on canvas, 86:64cm,
       Hugh Lane Municipal Gallery of Modern Art, Dublin)

2.1. Jack B. Yeats: *Grief* (1951, oil on canvas, 102:153cm,
       National Gallery of Ireland)

2.2.   Jack B. Yeats: *Tinkers' Encampment: The Blood of Abel*
       (1940, oil on canvas, 91.4:121.9cm, private collection)

2.3. Jack B. Yeats: *There is No Night* (1949, oil on canvas, 102:153cm,
       Hugh Lane Municipal Gallery of Modern Art)

3.1. Louis le Brocquy: *Lazarus* (1954, oil on canvas, 175:120cm,
      Gimpel Fils, London)

3.2. Louis le Brocquy: *Ecce Homo* (1958, oil and sand on canvas,
116:81cm, private collection)

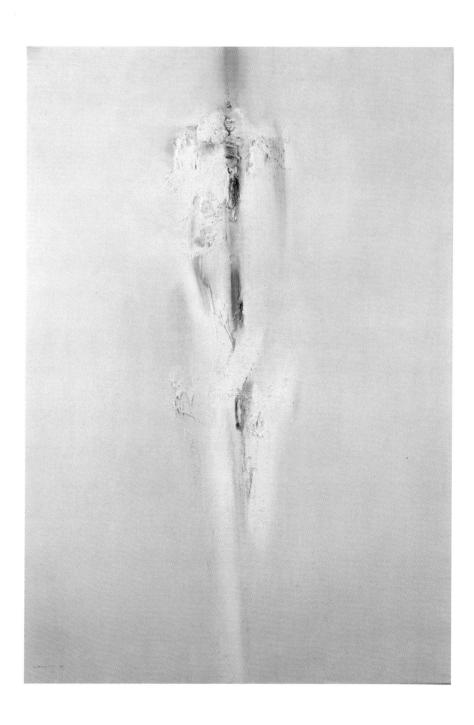

3.3.   Louis le Brocquy: *Procession with Lilies IV* (1992, oil on canvas, 129.5:165.7cm, private collection)

4.1. Gerard Dillon: *Fish Eaters* (1946, oil, Arts Council of Northern
Ireland, Belfast. The measurements of this painting were unobtainable.)

4.2.   Gerard Dillon: *The Brothers* (c. 1966, oil on canvas, 48":36",
       Taylor Galleries, Dublin)

4.3. Gerard Dillon: *Entertaining Friends* (c. 1968, oil on canvas, 30":25",
Institute of Public Administration, Dublin)

5.1.   Colin Middleton: *Jacob Wrestling with the Angel* (1948, oil on canvas, 81:66cm, private collection)

5.2. Colin Middleton: *Give Me to Drink* (1949, oil on canvas, 66:76cm, Ulster Museum, Belfast)

5.3.   Colin Middleton:*Christ Androgyne* (1943, oil on canvas, 38.1:27.8cm,
       Ulster Museum, Belfast)

6.1.   Patrick Collins: *Stations of the Cross* (1964, oil on board, 60:45cm each, private collection)

6.2. Patrick Collins: *Hy Brazil* (1963, oil on board, 75:90cm,
      Hugh Lane Municipal Gallery of Modern Art, Dublin)

6.3. Patrick Collins: *A Place with Stones* (1979, oil on canvas, 104:94cm, Allied Irish Banks Art Collection)

7.1. Tony O'Malley: *Good Friday* (1966, oil on board, 48":48",
      private collection)

7.2. Tony O'Malley: *Shadowy Carvings of an Ancient Execution, Good Friday* (1992, oil on board, 48":36", private collection)

7.3. Tony O'Malley: *Earth Lyre* (1990-91, oil on board, 48":36",
       private collection)

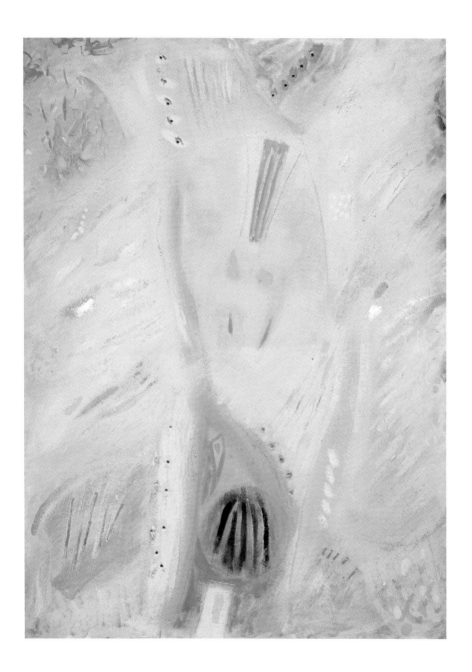

8.1. Patrick Scott: *Goldpainting 48* (1968, gold leaf and tempera on
unprimed canvas, 122:122cm, private collection)

8.2. Patrick Scott: *Goldpainting 56* (1968, gold leaf and tempera on
      unprimed canvas, 61:61cm, private collection)

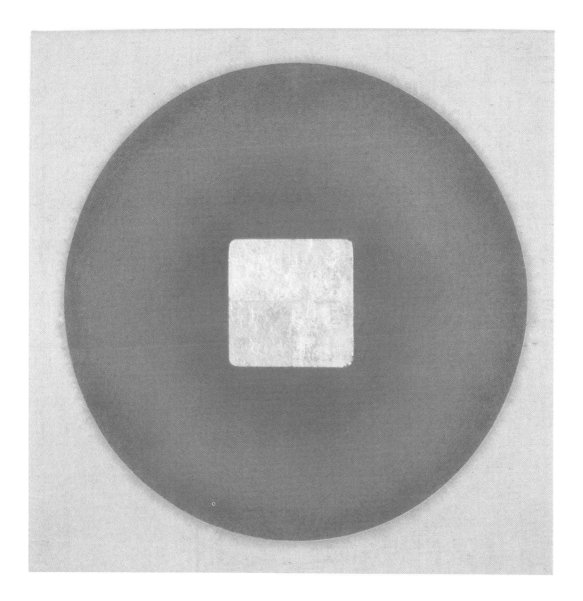

8.3. Patrick Scott: *Chinese Landscape* (1989, gold leaf and tempera on canvas, 122:122cm, private collection)

9.1. Patrick Graham: *Scenes from the Life of Christ* (1983-84, oil on canvas, 167.5:518.5cm, private collection)

9.2. Patrick Graham: *The Lark in the Morning I* (1991-93, oil, mixed
media on canvas, 214:366cm, courtesy of Jack Rutberg Fine Arts Inc.,
Los Angeles, USA)

9.3.   Patrick Graham: *The Blackbird Suite* (1992-93, mixed media on board, one of a series of nineteen works, each 81:112cm, courtesy of Jack Rutberg Fine Arts Inc., Los Angeles, USA)

10.1. Patrick Hall: *The Tale is Told that Shall be Told* (1989, ink and acrylic on paper, 81:112cm, private collection)

10.2. Patrick Hall: *Mountain* (1994, oil on canvas, 183:198cm,
       collection of the artist)

10.3. Patrick Hall: *Burning Mountain III* (1995, oil on canvas, 183:198cm,
        IBEC collection, Dublin)

5.2. *Give Me to Drink* (See page 174)

Close in its expressionist style and colouring to the previous work, the present canvas has another biblical theme as its subject, this time from the New Testament. It is the story of Christ and the woman of Samaria in John 4:4-42.

Given the socio-historical context, it is certainly astonishing that the writer of the fourth gospel gives such prominence to women in his narrative.[94] In fact, Jesus' public ministry begins and ends with events in which women – Mary, his mother, in the wedding feast in Cana and Mary of Bethany who anoints him – are involved. This pericope is a significant example of the discipleship and apostolate of women in this gospel and in the New Testament on the whole.

On the way back from Judea to Galilee Jesus had to go through Samaria, where, near the town of Sychar, he rests at Jacob's well. A Samaritan woman, who passes by, he addresses with the words: 'Give me a drink.' Due to the strained relations between the Samaritans and Jews, his demand presents a challenge. The woman shows her surprise: 'How is it that you, a Jew, ask a drink of me, a woman of Samaria?' He replies that if she knew who was asking her for a drink, *she* would have asked *him,* and he would have given her 'living water'. Jesus gradually reveals himself to her; she, however, first challenges him further: '... Are you greater than our ancestor Jacob ...?' She finally comes to believe and becomes the first missionary: 'Come and see a man who told me everything I have done! He cannot be the Messiah, can he?' The climax is reached when the Samaritans finally confess Jesus as universal Saviour: 'It is no longer because of what you said that we believe, for we have heard for ourselves, and we know that this is truly the Savior of the World.'

The narrative has as its central themes revelation, faith and mission. Living water here serves as a symbol for the fullness of life that the revealer provides. Moreover, no longer will those who believe worship in the temples in Jerusalem or at Gerizim, but in the temple of the 'body' of the risen Christ. They will 'worship in spirit and truth' because 'God is spirit' (Jn 4:24). As Schüssler Fiorenza observes, it is 'the worship of those who are made holy through the word and for whom social-religious distinctions between Jews and Samaritans, women and men, no longer have any validity.'[95]

In his treatment of the theme Middleton has captured the first part of the story, the actual meeting of Jesus and the woman. The people from the town of Sychar, who are converted to Christ through her mission, as also the disciples, who are 'astonished that he was speaking with a woman' but refrain from making any comments, are absent. There is a possible hint, however, of

94. Elisabeth Schüssler Fiorenza, *In Memory of Her* (London: SCM, 1983), 326.
95. Ibid., 329.

her missionary activity in that houses and roof tops are placed in the background which might function as a symbol that '[m]any Samaritans from that city believed in him because of the woman's testimony'.

Middleton emphasises the theme of the encounter by the figures' monumental size. The coming face to face with an *other* is expressed in their different facial features and colour of hair; Christ the Jew, as Jacob in the previous work, has a Semitic face, while hers, especially the mouth, appears somewhat negroid. Moreover, her face could hardly be described as particularly beautiful. Middleton said that what gave his work unity was the female archetype. In many of his canvases, including those with religious subjects, the female subject, sensuous and frequently with bared breasts, plays a significant role.[96] However, his (female) figures are often distorted, even ugly. Despite their sensuality, there is a curious absence of the feeling of the male gaze merely delighting in the female as an *object* of desire. It is rather, as Edward Sheehy observed, that many of his figures are 'ugly, distorted, clumsy, gross; but that very fact adds to their final significance; for Middleton has that *agape* which transmutes the [figures] ... into living symbols, frequently tragic in the true sense that they evoke in us, not merely pity and compassion, but exaltation'.[97] It is this sense of compassionate love, his profound humanism and, I would argue, indeed his faith that comes to expression in his rendering of these figures. This is greatly enhanced by the 'empty' space between them. Whereas the direction of the brushstrokes behind the back of each figure is more or less vertical, between them they run in curves from one figure to the other. This space therefore strongly underlines their dialogue, Christ's self-revelation to the woman and her subsequent faith in and unity with him. This 'wavy' light blue space alludes, moreover, to the main symbol used in the story, namely the living water that leads to eternal life, the Spirit and grace of God, which Jesus reveals to humankind. The shape of her neck and head leaning forward further emphasise her being drawn towards Christ. One might suggest that Middleton's rendering of the woman even implies her need for Christ as her bent head toward Jesus and her strange 'hanging' arm also convey an air of misery.[98] Jesus is shown with his hands folded reminiscent of prayer and with a facial expression of solemnity and concentration.

Apart from the fact that many of Middleton's female figures are semi-nude, in this painting Middleton may be referring to the woman's sexual past.[99] Her eye-catching earring may be a further indication in this respect.

96. For example, 'The Coming of St. George', 'I - Thou', 'Metro: St. George Day', 'Fortune Teller'.
97. E. Sheehy, 'Art Notes', *The Dublin Magazine,* vol. 28 (July-Sept. 1953), 37.
98. I thank Breffni McGuinness for his comment.

Jesus points out to her that the husband she 'has now is not [her] ... husband'. Yet, in a certain sense he replaces the previous ones as in him the God who is true love is revealed; she responds by believing and following him.

In feminist theology the metaphor of God as friend has become relevant in the perception of divine-human relationship as it emphasises reciprocity and mutuality rather than a dualistic, hierarchical notion of God. It is a holistic notion which, moreover, points to the interdependence and relatedness of everything in creation. One might suggest that the theme itself, and Middleton's portrayal of it, captures something of this God-friend idea. Not only are the two figures of equal height,[100] rather than, as in older art, a Christ who often appears taller than any other figure depicted in a canvas, but also the colour of their clothes and, more importantly, the space between them shows a sense of mutuality in their encounter. Jesus is not rendered as a heavenly ruler but very much as the incarnate Son, as the one who is with and among his people. In fact, Christ *needs* his people, his friends, women and men, Jews and Non-Jews, to proclaim his message. It is his composed, gentle posture and serious, sincere face that hints at his divine authority, an authority of compassionate love, rather than of patriarchal dominance and rule. He has revealed himself to the most unlikely person, a woman and 'enemy' Samaritan. It is this choice which indicates the universality of revelation and faith, a kingdom of equality, community, diversity and respect between all believers. Painted only four years after the end of World War II and the Holocaust, the work and its theme – i.e. the faith in and proclamation of the kingdom of God through Christ's self-revelation where all social, sexual, racial, national and political distinctions become irrelevant[101] – attains urgency as it captures something of the possibility of a theology after Auschwitz. Moreover and in particular, the story itself and Middleton's treatment of it, i.e. his stress on the mutuality between the Samaritan woman and Christ, pertain to and anticipate current (feminist) theological concerns.[102]

99. Cf. Pheme Perkins, 'The Gospel According to St John', *NJBC*, 957. It should be noted that, as Sandra Schneiders has observed, the five husbands, in fact, refer to the five gods the Samaritans had worshipped and that this passage therefore has to do with idolatry rather than with female promiscuity as it has been traditionally interpreted. Cf. Sandra M. Schneiders, *The Revelatory Text: Interpreting the New Testament as Sacred Scripture* (San Francisco: Harper and Row, 1991), 180-199. I am indebted to Tom Dalzell for bringing my attention to this matter.

100 The fact that Christ is seated, even enthroned perhaps, is irrelevant in this regard.

101. Cf. McFague, *Models of God, Theology for an Ecological, Nuclear Age* (London: SCM, 1987), 224-225.

102. Whether Middleton consciously intended to bring out this aspect, of course, cannot be ascertained.

5.3. Christ Androgyne (See page 175)

In a note on his work Middleton once commented: 'The significance of any symbol is infinite, depending entirely upon degree of perception and awareness ... [it] remains constant; its significance is relative and infinite. We cannot expect more than we bring.'[103]

In this work the painter makes use of *the* symbol in Christianity and in Christian art, Jesus Christ on the Cross. His suggestion that the significance of a symbol depends on what we make of it due to our experience is pertinent. Middleton painted 'Christ Androgyne' during the war year of 1943. He saw and placed himself within the context of survival both as an individual and as 'a member of the human race'. Many of his canvases are deeply existentialist in the light of his war experience and are frequently imbued with what one might describe as a metaphysical,[104] spiritual, and/or explicitly Christian-religious quality.

This small exquisitely painted work must rank as one of the most imaginative, fascinating and finest depictions of the crucifixion in modern art. The large Dutch-style frame, both unusual and appropriate, enhances the awe-inspiring feeling that this painting exudes. Around the time of his first wife's death, Middleton began to paint in a Surrealist style. In 1939 he became a committed Surrealist since in the dropping of bombs, according to him, the whole of society had turned surrealist.[105] 'Christ Androgyne', even more than the previous two canvases, relates to the experience of the Second World War and the fate of the Jews. It needs to be interpreted in this context; and, furthermore, it is also of special interest from a contemporary theological perspective.

Painted in sombre, predominantly dark blue and grey-brown hues, the canvas shows an overtly androgynous Christ. In fact, Christ's left breast, the lower part of the body from the hip down, the thin right arm, as well as the face with wavy, veil-like hair (hair-like veil?) and red veil/halo, are female rather than male. Indeed there are some rather unusual, enigmatic features in this crucifixion. The female breast, above all, is, of course, striking. In 1943 one imagines the traditional believer might have been amazed, if not simply shocked, by such a pronounced female, sexual, reference to the incarnate God. The right breast is not exposed, but has a strange plant-like shape.[106] The arms of the Crucified are stranger still. Christ's left arm is implied rather

103. Middleton quoted in John Hewitt, *Colin Middleton*, 41.
104. Elgy Gillespie, "What's the point of painting?", *The Irish Times*, 11.5.1972. This article is an interview with Colin Middleton.
105. Martin Wallace, 'Moving Artist', *Belfast Telegraph*, 4.1.1957.
106. I describe it as 'plant-like' since in other canvases, such as in 'The Coming of St George' he uses similar shapes in the depiction of an image that suggests both a female and a flower.

than depicted as a cut-out in timber with what appears to be a nail at the far end; his right arm with a gentle, elegant hand is not outstretched and nailed onto the Cross but carries its, proportionately-too-short, bar. In the place where the hand should be nailed, one discovers a small white square like a piece of paper on which appear four red hearts, somewhat reminiscent of the Maltese Cross. There is a downward movement in the left arm of the Cross, as it is placed slightly non-rectangularly to the vertical and slightly lower than the right arm. The head, emphatically bent and invisible in shadow except for the mouth, nose and hair, seems to suggest Semitic features. The colours red and white in the little square emblem are taken up again in the red, veil-like halo that contrasts with the white rectangular plane behind Christ's head.

Why did Middleton render Christ in this fashion? It is a work that arose out of deeply felt compassion and humanist concern for the innocent victims of the war and the unbelievable suffering of the Jews. Further, his use of symbols and his unusual depiction is of great theological interest in its christological-soteriological and feminist dimension. What distinguishes faith in the God of the New Testament from any other faith is God's becoming weak and powerless for our sake. Christ, free of any sin, takes on the sin of the world, suffers for all on the Cross; he is powerful precisely in his powerlessness.[107] Middleton captures this emphatically through the cut-out arm, as if blown off by a bomb, the blood red of the veil, perhaps reminiscent also of the crown of thorns, the blood on the breasts, and the square behind Christ's head in white, the colour of innocence.[108]

However, unlike traditional western depictions of the crucifixion with a 'European' Christ, Middleton's canvas stresses Jesus' Jewishness. In the context of the Second World War when the Nazis would have 'justified' their atrocities with an argument such as that the Jews crucified Jesus and hence deserved their fate, his painting is a stark reminder of what the Auschwitz survivor Elie Wiesel wrote in his book *Night*. When Wiesel and his camp witnessed the hanging of two men and a boy someone standing behind him asked where was God in all this, upon which Wiesel heard 'a voice' saying within him that it was there on the gallows that God was present.[109] Moltmann rightly remarks that, indeed, there would have been no other answer possible in this unspeakable suffering.[110]

In this context Middleton's work then can be read on two related levels. On the universal level, he states in pictorial form what theologians like

107. Cf. D. Sölle, *Stellvertretung, Ein Kapitel Theologie nach dem 'Tode Gottes'* (Stuttgart: Kreuz Verlag, 1982), 171-184.
108. I thank Ruth Sheehy for her observations.
109. Cf. E. Wiesel, *Night* (1969), 75-76, quoted in Moltmann, *Der gekreuzigte Gott*, 262.
110. Moltmann, ibid.

Moltmann or Sölle would write a few decades later, namely that God dies wherever humans die innocent, violent deaths. This universal aspect is strongly pronounced by the androgynous aspect in the crucified. It is the male-female yet-always-greater God who delivers Godself for women and men, for all humankind. God is all, thus God 'dies' wherever women, children and men die through murder, torture or the concentration camps. The hint of blood on both the female and male breast particularly points to this aspect. On a more particular, historical, level, Middleton shows us a Christ not crucified by the Jews, but Christ, the Jew – and here symbol of all Jewish victims – crucified by Christians, i.e. his followers. Enda McDonagh's question, in his writing on the Holocaust, about how Christians 'can survive as credible witnesses to the God of love, to the God of history, to the God of creation and power' when we 'allowed this horrifying episode to happen', is pertinent.[111] What appears to be, or at least hints at, the Maltese Cross on the left arm of the Cross, seems to curiously concur with and enhance this interpretation, as this cross became the emblem of the first religious military order, the Hospitallers, which developed out of the Crusades. The Crusaders had set out in 1095 to recover the Holy Land from Islam and to keep it in Christian hands thereafter. Thus, in a similar way, they too, as Christians, sacrificed the God incarnate by causing suffering and violent deaths.

Christians believe that because Christ through his sacrifice is raised from the dead we also will be redeemed. Middleton's crucifixion conveys something of that eschatological-soteriological hope despite its bleakness and emphasis on suffering. The meaning of the little emblem is ambiguous. While on the one hand it is reminiscent of the Maltese Cross, on the other it has similarities with the flag which symbolises the victory of life over death; it is held by Christ particularly in resurrection images. The banner is white with an imprinted red cross. Hence, if first this emblem was interpreted in the context of suffering, war and death, it also might imply exactly the opposite, i.e. resurrection and eternal life. Moreover, the red heart is a symbol of love, while white connotes innocence. In the work, Christ's thin arm and gentle hand carries the left arm of the Cross with the emblem. Is this perhaps a special reference to the idea of Christ being our substitute, who carries the sin of the world and thereby redeems the world? This perception has been particularly stressed by Protestant theologians and believers. For Luther, Jesus has really taken on the place of the guilty, he is the one who is cursed and suffers for all. Middleton indeed conveys – unconsciously rather than consciously, one imagines – something of this notion. The fact that the Jews,

111. E. McDonagh, *Between Chaos and New Creation* (Dublin: Gill and Macmillan, 1986) 66-75. Like Moltmann or Sölle, McDonagh stresses that it is 'somewhere there in the heart of darkness that we discover the God of Israel and the God of Jesus'.

whom he represents here through Christ, became the *Sündenbock* in Nazi Germany (and elsewhere), underscores such an interpretation. Apart from the flag, the glimpse and hope for salvation in and through Jesus Christ is enhanced by the fact that the red and white appear again in the halo, the sign of his divinity, and in the white rectangle behind Christ's head which points to his innocence, to the resurrection, redemption and eternal life. This is enhanced by the fact that his feet and the lower end of the Cross are not shown which conveys the impression that in some sense Christ has already risen beyond earthly life.

Finally, the work evokes traditional depictions of the crucifixion by the fact that Christ's left cut-out arm symbolises death, while the right arm points towards the resurrection. In crucifixion scenes, or even in a work like Michelangelo's 'Last Judgement', those who are condemned are to his left, such as the impenitent thief, the ones who are to be redeemed on the right. However, Middleton does not put any other figures into his work and his overall message seems to be that salvation and eternal life is what God intends for all, that hope can be glimpsed in the midst of human suffering and death, precisely because God himself has already suffered and died for us.

Longley has pointed out that Middleton believed in the divinity of all humans. In this context I referred in the section on Middleton in the previous chapter to the idea of divinisation as held especially in the Orthodox tradition. If God became incarnate so that we might become divine (Irenaeus), this work – in its portrayal of the suffering of the innocent Jesus/the Jews and all innocent victims and their final redemption – as also the previous two canvases – the struggle and blessing of the trickster Jacob, the conversion of the rather unlikely person of a Samaritan woman – perhaps provide us with some insight into how we may understand, and how Middleton might have understood, the divinity and divinisation of all humans. Certainly the three themes and the artist's treatment of these seem to imply that it is through God's infinite grace, through God's lowliness in Jesus on the Cross/in the Jews in their suffering, through God's forgiveness and compassionate love, that we are made divine. Furthermore, in his striking depiction of human suffering and struggle, he indirectly, yet unequivocally, calls us to be what we are meant to be, i.e. responsible human beings.

Moreover, his remarkable rendering of Christ in androgynous form presents – not unlike the previous work examined, even if with a different subject – a radical, poignant and surprising anticipation of contemporary feminist theological issues.

6. PATRICK COLLINS

6.1. Stations of the Cross (See page 176)

One can hardly think of any other painter whose profound love for the Irish landscape has inspired his or her work as consistently as Patrick Collins. His landscapes are romantic, dreamlike visions, abstracted, still, contemplative, painted from memory. As he said it was the 'aura' of a subject which interested him. Collins, as I concluded in the previous chapter, had an essentially panentheist vision, an awareness that the divine is present and manifested in all things. In his perception of art being essentially transcendental he looked for the metaphysical aspect in his subjects, for an 'underlying order',[112] for 'the thing behind it'. His fascination for the 'Celtic imagination' and 'the pagans'[113] lived side by side with a Christian faith to which he did not adhere as a conventional 'practising' churchgoer; rather it was very much private, anti-institutional and witnessed in his art probably more than anywhere else. The artist produced several works with biblical, often christological, themes, such as 'Crucifixion (After a Child's Drawing)', 'The Nativity', 'The Flight into Egypt', 'Head of Christ after the Shroud of Turin', 'The Dead Christ', 'God's Candles', and the 'Stations of the Cross', the set of paintings to be examined here.

The devotion of the Stations of the Cross, also named 'Via Dolorosa' or 'Way of the Cross', was introduced into the West under the influence of the Franciscans in the late Middle Ages as a series of stopping places in a church nave. The stops, initially seven, later fourteen, in front of which the faithful pray, present each an image from the various incidents of Christ's journey through Jerusalem to Golgatha. Even still in the twentieth century some artists have approached this theme, notably the American Jewish Abstract Expressionist painter Barnett Newman, whose series 'Lema Sabachthani, The Stations of the Cross' (1958-66), with black and white spaces and lines, are truly awe-inspiring.[114] While in Ireland artists like Evie Hone or Patrick Pye received commissions for Stations for new churches, Collins' series was neither commissioned nor was it ever hung in a place of worship.

---

112. M. FitzGerald, 'Patrick Collins, The Artist Talks to Marion FitzGerald', *The Irish Times,* 27.2.65.
113. B. Lynch, 'Irish Painting? There's No Such Thing', *Hibernia,* 28.6.1979.
114. For theological interpretations of Newman's Stations cf. the following writers: Schwebel, 'Bildverweigerung im Bild, Mystik - eine vergessene Kategorie in der Kunst der Gegenwart', in Andreas Mertin, Horst Schwebel, (eds.), *Kirche und moderne Kunst* (Frankfurt: Athenäum Verlag, 1988), 117-119. Dillenberger, *A Theology of Artistic Sensibilities,* 162. G. Thiessen, 'Imaging God: Spiritual Dimensions in Modern Art', in Anne M. Murphy, Eoin G. Cassidy, (eds.), *Neglected Wells: Spirituality and the Arts* (Dublin: Four Courts Press, 1997), 102-104.

Human figures are unusual in Collins' work. When they do appear, they seem clumsy, awkward; yet and curiously because of their awkwardness, they come across with a remarkable sense of honesty, feeling and simplicity. Such is the case in Collins' 'Stations of the Cross'. It tells of Christ's journey to Calvary in very simple, childlike fashion. If the religious subject matter and the depiction of the human figure are unusual, his choice of colour, predominantly grey, blue, and purple-blue, as well as the painted frame-within-a-frame are, however, characteristic features. The painted frame within the actual frame intensifies the sense of isolation of the subject 'from the reality of its surroundings, reinforcing its timeless nature'.[115] It also heightens the actual aloneness/loneliness that Christ must have experienced on his way to Golgatha.

Four works, Station I, II, VI, and XII, from the series provide a sufficient idea of Collins' treatment of this old Christian subject. The painter prepared himself for his task by a journey to Donegal, studying sets of Stations in small parish churches on the way. Finally he decided that he would use the sun as a motif throughout his series. This, one would suggest, might have been influenced by his knowledge of the typical Irish High Crosses with circles, often interpreted as symbolising the sun. The artist commented that he had used the sun *'to help create design and mood – hot and violent during a fall, remote and sad at the entombment. Each incident is enclosed in a large outer shape, all separately different for the same reason.'*[116] These shapes and the sun were intended to *'give something of significance to each picture without destroying the continuity'.* For him the sun was important as *'it identifies the Passion with the present day or any ordinary day in time. It is externally contemporary.'* From a theological perspective this is, in fact, a rather significant statement. Deeply eschatological, he uses the sun to signify the link between past, present and future, the historical Christ on the Cross and the memory and experience of the passion and resurrection, i.e. God's presence in the daily life of each believer.[117] Collins' panentheist idea, his awareness of God being present in all things, is therefore revealed once more in this essentially eschatological understanding of the Passion. Moreover, one could almost imagine that the artist had read Augustine, who invoked the image of the sun as being 'co-present in the human act of seeing ... symbolising the permanent co-presence of

115. Ruane, *Patrick Collins*, 28.
116. Collins quoted (in italics) in Ruane, op.cit., 40.
117. Cf. Lane, *Keeping Hope Alive*, 21-22. It is interesting to note that Lane's emphasis on the idea of God's presence in our daily lives and experiences, a notion of the divine which, as he says, is described in contemporary language as 'pan-en-theist', remarkably parallels Collins' perception. Moltmann who has dealt with this concept in his theology of creation would argue similarly.

God' in everyone's life.[118] Collins concluded that in his work *from the remote hint of light in Christ receiving the cross, it [the sun] travels in blazing indifference and varying moods to the final, remote and lonely night at the crucifixion. The result is something which I can only describe as country Irish in a contemporary manner.*'[119] 'Blazing' and 'indifference', as well as 'blazing indifference' and 'varying moods', seem somewhat contradictory; one wonders why he would comment in such fashion.

Station I shows Christ before Herod. The separation between them, Christ's isolation, aloneness and loneliness is particularly emphasised by the spacial distance between the two figures, which is underscored by the line in the foreground. In fact, the scene curiously conveys the idea of the sinner before God through the elevated position of Herod on the throne and his white garment, sign of innocence, in comparison to Christ dressed in dark purple-blue who stands humbly, humbled in the foreground. It is an ironic scene: the sinless Son of God before the sinner Herod. In Station II Christ, with strong hands, takes up the Cross. His face, as the faces in the other figures, is indicated rather than clearly depicted throughout the series. The light of the sun is barely visible in the distance behind the vertical arm of the Cross. In Station VI Veronica approaches Christ to wipe the sweat from his face with a linen cloth on which, according to legend, was imprinted the image of his face thereafter. In devotional representations she is shown holding the cloth with an image of Christ, sometimes with a crown of thorns. The fact that here the blood is pouring from his head may be a reference to this traditional treatment of the subject. The sun is clearly visible in this Station. Station XII shows Christ on the Cross, his body is pale with blood pouring from his nailed hands, feet and face. The blue colour of the background is more brilliant than in the other canvases, pointing, as it does, to the suffering, solemn, sad aspect which in turn evokes an emotional, meditative, compassionate response in the viewer. The receding sun is blurred and seems to go down; Christ, the light of the world, dies on the cross and enters into darkness. The fading sun is symbolic of his experience of Godforsakenness, his descent into hell. At the same time, the very fact that the sun still radiates a glimpse of light could be interpreted as a sign of hope, as an anticipation of the resurrection. In this context it should be remembered that the sun – already for Plato a symbol of contemplating the true and the divine – became a symbol for Christ; in modern art the sun often indicates hope for and belief in redemption.

Indeed, the sun, the background colour and the frame-within-a-frame lend harmony to and provide a sense of unity in the set of the 'Stations of the

118. Ibid., 22.
119. Collins quoted in Ruane, op.cit., 41.

Cross'. Moreover, the sun together with the Cross is revelatory of Collins' interest in the Irish Celtic pre-Christian and Christian past, i.e. his panentheist, holistic vision.

Unlike Middleton's crucifixion with its complex meaning or Jellett's sophisticated semi-cubist 'Ninth Hour', Collins' 'Stations', especially the crucifixion, move the viewer by the unselfconscious, childlike, humble, compassionate rendering of Jesus' way to the Cross. The series is interesting not so much with regard to complex theological interpretations but rather as a personal statement of faith. The work seems to confirm what I concluded earlier, namely that Collins believed in Christ and that this faith was ultimately simple and childlike. It almost comes across like a pictorial rendering of a child's or a 'simple' person's prayer. In this way his work becomes a prayer, a very personal, surprising and moving expression of his belief in the Crucified. It is a special example of what Patricia Collins pointed out, namely that his art was his worship and prayer,[120] whether with or without religious content. It is even more remarkable if one considers that Collins was anything but an unquestioning person or believer. If Christ said that we should become like children in order to enter the kingdom of God (Mt 18:2-5), this work certainly witnesses his command.

In 1978 Desmond MacAvock observed that it was only then, over ten years after their completion, that the 'Stations' had been shown as a set for the first time in an exhibition of Collins' works. He wrote: 'While ... maintaining the traditional narrative, they are still and contemplative; more hymns than icons, they distil compassion in a kind of nimbus and are altogether remarkable.'[121] Brian Lynch, who also reviewed that exhibition, likewise admired the 'deeply felt' 'Stations'. Significantly he added: 'I hope some day they will find a church to match them.'[122] Indeed, Collins – quite unintentionally, I suggest – ultimately presents us with nothing less than a personal testament of faith, a gentle sermon in paint, neither polished nor intellectualised but of sincerity and simple goodness, truth and beauty.

In this context, what comes to mind are the words of one of the finest artists of this century. Rouault, devout believer and painter of many Christian subjects, stated once that he hoped that some day he would be able to paint a Christ so moving that people would come to believe in him. In his 'Stations of the Cross', does Collins in his own way not capture – even if not consciously intended – something of Rouault's profound wish?

120. Patricia Collins, Interview, 29.8.1995.
121. Desmond MacAvock, 'Patrick Collins at the Tom Caldwell Gallery', *The Irish Times*, 7.3.1978.
122. B. Lynch, 'Masculine/Feminine', *Hibernia*, 9.3.1978.

6.2. *Hy Brazil* (See page 177)

Painted a year prior to the 'Stations of the Cross', this work shows a similar colour tonality in blue and grey typical of Collins' work in the 1960s as well as the frame-within-a-frame. In the 1950s the artist had already used themes from Irish mythology. In 'Hy Brazil' this happens in a more generalised manner since the canvas does not employ any of the narrative as in the earlier paintings.[123] In fact, the work is almost abstract with its large 'empty' space. Hy Brazil, the physical counterpart to *Tír na-nÓg* in Irish mythology, is an imaginary island of feasting, pleasure and eternal youth, somewhere in the Atlantic off the West coast of Ireland. Indeed, in Collins' work the island, apparently with other tiny islands before it, is indicated simply by a small irregular band of colour. It can only be glimpsed in the far distance through the grey mist.

The painting, romantic and expressionist, fascinates and captures the viewer's attention and admiration through its atmosphere, its sense of mystery, of otherworldliness, evanescence and transcendence. It is revelatory of Collins' imagination, of his subjective painterly interpretation of landscape, of his deep feeling for the Irish past, its myths, its legends, its dreams and hopes as symbolised by the land of eternal happiness and youth.

Schwebel, as discussed in the first chapter, has written on the theological meaning of abstract works of art. According to him, abstract art, or 'pure' painting, is autonomous since it refrains from being a visual means of rendering and repeating theological doctrines.[124] He argues that what makes abstract art theologically relevant is precisely the fact that it no longer serves as the *ancilla theologiae*. Rather than simply confirming what we already know, abstraction confronts and invites the recipient through 'visual ecstasy' into 'the New Being', into anticipation of the world to come.[125] For Schwebel, abstract art is therefore essentially eschatological. It can make us 'feel' what is beyond words, beyond given reality, it reveals something of the paradisiacal future glory in the now. Although not every recipient might describe his or her experience of abstract art in such a manner, it is, I would suggest, an apt perception from a theological perspective.

Further, mystical, apophatic theology, which affirms that ultimately we cannot make any statements about God and that God is known primarily through personal, (ecstatic) experiences and also through experiences of

123. Ruane, op.cit., 45.
124. Schwebel, *Autonome Kunst im Raum der Kirche*, 85.
125. Ibid. 'Sie ist in der Lage, mehr zu erhellen als eine Kunst, die sich damit abfand, Interpretin der biblischen Geschichte zu sein. In ihrem Überschwang wird sie Bild des Neuen Seins, dessen Geheimnis uns immer verborgen bleibt.'

nature, is a view which is evidenced in artists like Collins or O'Malley. Schwebel points out that pure painting often has a pronounced mystical dimension due to the silence, the being-beyond-words, the iconoclasm *in* the image, which these works express.[126]

'Hy Brazil' contains an atmosphere of the mystical and the eschatological. In fact, these dimensions are 'doubly' revealed. The canvas as such exudes a mysterious, transcendent, spiritual atmosphere through the misty colours, the open, 'silent' space along with the sense of isolation achieved through the frame-within-a-frame.[127] The thin band of land exists yet seems almost out of reach. The title 'Hy Brazil' significantly adds to the mystical and eschato-logical aspect as it implies that the painter does not capture an actual island, but one that exists only in the mind, in the mythological imagination of the Irish people. It is not the 'here' but the 'not yet' which Collins images in this work. It is the land we long for; in theological terms it is thus the 'land' of heaven, the totally other reality of eternity. Collins, in giving his work this title, provides us with a glimpse of hope, an anticipation of a world where all is well. For him this land is obviously far away, yet it *is,* it does exist and will ultimately be seen and reached.

Leon Ó Mórcháin has commented that the 'Irish trait of other-worldli-ness ... was a Celtic gift of gliding easily between two worlds ... And the Celts and their descendants believed in their own version of Utopia ... of never-never-Hy brazil ... It is almost too easy to see the Christian parallels ...'[128] Certainly, the 'pagan' Celtic utopia of Hy Brazil and the Christian idea of heaven where time ceases to exist have something in common. It therefore seems appropriate to interpret Collins' work both in terms of Celtic mythol-ogy and Christian theology. Hence Collins' canvas speaks of, fuses and affirms Celtic-Christian hope and faith through and in a mysterious, vision-ary, beautiful, quietly doxological depiction of the distant reality of Hy Brazil/heaven.

126. Schwebel, 'Bildverweigerung im Bild ...', in Mertin, Schwebel, (eds.), *Kirche und mod-erne Kunst,* 113-123. 'Die Deutung der sogenannten 'radikalen Malerei' als Mystik scheint mir nach wie vor angemessen.' (120)
127. It appears that Collins felt that the eye does not see through a rectangular aperture, but rather that vision happens through an oval with a blurred edge. The frame would there-fore signify the limits of the eye's vision. I thank Hilary Pyle for this information.
128. L. Ó Mórcháin, 'A Lost Tradition?', in E. McDonagh, (ed.), *Faith and the Hungry Grass, A Mayo Book of Theology* (Dublin: Columba Press, 1990), 55-56.

6.3. A Place with Stones (See page 178)

In an interview Collins said that 'Field of Old Stones' (1978), a work similar to the one under consideration, reminded him of his childhood in Sligo: 'I knew it; it looked eerie in certain lights, somehow I suppose the field of old stones is common to everyone's experience in this country ... rocks are things out of time, ancient.'[129] For Collins the bogs, earth and stones in Ireland thus present the physical link with the past, the link between contemporary and ancient Ireland, as also the personal connection with his boyhood in Sligo.[130]

Again the canvas contains the frame-within-a-frame, this time, however, there is a change in the palette. The work was executed after his return from France. Although Collins continued to paint predominantly Irish subjects during his stay on the continent, France, nevertheless, had an influence on his choice of colour. A warm light yellow radiates from the centre, a few rocks are lying in a field, amongst them what appears to be a dolmen, a prehistoric burial site. The whole scene exudes something archaic, ancient, yet it is an image based on contemporary experience of the Irish landscape. In this way it attains a quality of timelessness, ever-presence. Only the atmosphere changes, the canvas seems to evoke the moment when the grey mist and rain are superseded by the warm light of the sun – if only temporarily.

Although Collins' work here takes its point of departure in objective reality, he depicts it, however, in a highly individual, abstracted style. In fact, as in the previous work, it is the title that indicates the subject, as the shapes in the canvas itself, except for the dolmen perhaps, are indefinite rather than obvious. What the artist captures is thus revelatory of his felt experience of and reaction to the atmosphere of the place. It is this that gives the whole work its numinous, spiritual, transcendent dimension.

Not only Schwebel, but other writers, like Tillich or Günter Rombold, or even artists themselves like Newman, Rothko and indeed Collins, have referred to the sense of transcendence, ultimate reality and the sublime which is experienced through and seen in abstract works of art.[131] These are terms, which if not narrowly Christian nevertheless express the element of otherworldliness, of the metaphysical, of the beyond that the works convey. Collins admired the American Abstract Expressionists, and his works show, in fact, some similarities with Rothko's canvases of squares with blurred edges. The religious experience of the Romantics, the stress on subjectivity,

129. Collins quoted by Frances Ruane in her article 'Patrick Collins' in *Six Artists from Ireland, An Aspect of Irish Painting* (Dublin: An Chomhairle Ealaíon/Cultural Relations Committee Department of Foreign Affairs, 1983), 85.
130. Ruane, ibid.
131. Cf., for example, in reference to the Abstract Expressionists, Rombold, *Der Streit um das Bild*, 129-140, and Newman, 'The Sublime is Now', (1948).

on the notion of religion as 'contemplation and feeling', as 'the sense and taste of the infinite'[132] (Schleiermacher), the awe-inspiring sublime, the *mysterium tremendum et fascinans* (Otto), can be traced from Caspar David Friedrich, Philip Otto Runge to van Gogh, Kandinsky, Rothko and Newman.[133] Due to the Enlightenment and its questioning of religion, Romantic artists like Friedrich – who was acquainted with Schleiermacher – searched for religious experiences outside traditional, organised religion. Transcendence in nature, the panentheist idea of divine revelation in all creation, was part of their religiosity and expressed in their canvases. Friedrich's Tetschen altarpiece 'The Cross in the Mountain' (1807/8) and his 'Monk by the Seashore' (1809) are important examples of this new religious expression in art.

Collins' works convey – in his own painterly style, of course – something of the wonder-and-awe-inspiring in nature. The present canvas serves as an example. Further, the fact that he himself repeatedly stressed his holistic, panentheist beliefs, his nature spirituality and the importance of feeling, aligns him to the ideas of the Romantics.

Collins' allusive, indirect landscapes with their 'haunting emotional intensity', as Ruane describes them, hence are more expressive of a poetic imagination than of reality. It is this poetic sense, which commentators have repeatedly observed in relation to Collins, which again concurs with the Romantic strain in his work. As Joachim Rieder has observed, it was 'the poeticisation of the world and of life',[134] 'a progressive universal poetry' (Friedrich Schlegel) which was the main concern in early Romanticism around 1800. It is the poetic imagination that drives Collins' paintings and lends them their subtlety, their visionary, mystical quality and fascination.

Finally, 'A Place with Stones', as many of his other works, is a celebration of creation, ancient and new, light and dark, mysterious and sublime. It is an expression of his faith in the divine who is present in every stone, bog and field, the God who is encountered in creation in the here and now. In its allusive, poetic, rather than realistic, depiction of nature, it speaks both of God's eternal immanence and transcendence. In this way, his works are in a very real and fundamental sense religious. Patrick O'Brien, priest and poet,

---

132. Schleiermacher, 'Über die Religion. Reden an die Gebildeten unter ihren Verächtern' (1799), in *Schleiermacher Auswahl*, 6.

133. Cf. Rombold, *Der Streit um das Bild*, 71-84. Cf. also Albert C. Moore's article 'Religion und Landschaft, Die spirituellen Landschaften von Caspar David Friedrich und Colin McCahon', in Schwebel, Mertin, (eds.), *Bilder und ihre Macht*, 80-95. Moore compares the twentieth century New Zealand painter McCahon with Friedrich and concludes that the numinous is expressed in both artists' works.

134. Joachim Rieder, 'Kunst und Religion in der Frühromantik', in Schwebel, Mertin, (eds.), *Bilder und ihre Macht*, 68-69.

similarly puts forward a holistic, ecological vision of God when he writes: 'From the hermit monks we must learn that love of God must be one with love of humanity and the created universe. We cannot bow down before the creator while we destroy his creation.'[135] Collins, not an ancient hermit monk from the seashore of the West of Ireland, but a 'sort of' worldly mystic, monk and seer in twentieth-century Dublin, 'bows down' before his creator by revealing in his works the sublime grandeur and transcendent beauty of creation inspired by the memory of particular places which in turn embraces the universality of God in creation.

The 'Stations of the Cross', 'Hy Brazil' and 'A Place with Stones' thus clearly affirm what was ascertained about Collins in Chapter Two, i.e. his ultimately simple, childlike faith in Christ, which lived in harmony with an emphatically panentheist vision and consciousness typical of a romantic Irish Celtic nature spirituality.[136]

135. Patrick O'Brien, 'Cassandra Island in Mayo', in McDonagh, (ed.), *Faith and the Hungry Grass,* 154.
136. Cf. Seán McDonagh, *The Greening of the Church* (London: Geoffrey Chapman, 1990), 168-170. McDonagh, with reference to Eriugena a.o., comments on the panentheist dimension as being 'so central' to Celtic (pre-)Christian spirituality.

7. TONY O'MALLEY

7.1. *Good Friday* (See page 179)

Commentators and O'Malley himself have stated that his vision has much in common with Collins. Profound reverence for nature, the panentheist dimension, the conviction that art is fundamentally a spiritual activity, an interest in the Celtic past, contemplation, a mystical quality and faith in the Crucified are shared by both painters. What is even more openly confessed in O'Malley than in Collins is his faith in Christ which he has witnessed throughout his life by painting a work of art each Good Friday – which in itself is a kind of prayer – as well as through personal statements. Moreover, his canvases reveal a wide range of subjects and sources of inspiration, mostly depicted in and transformed by his (quasi) abstract style. Since the 1970s a joyous sense and atmosphere pervades many of his works, and, as Ruane has rightly pointed out, even his darkest paintings exude 'no angst or despair, only solitude'.[137]

   The present abstract work evokes, or at least hints at the Cross, even without the title. Enclosed by cubist, slightly geometrical shapes, predominantly in sombre, dark colours, the near white and pale green-white areas outline the form of a cross, even if the 'arms' are not rectangular but rather somewhat elliptic with a pinnacle end.[138] His typical incisions, here predominantly vertical, and some wide-spaced horizontal ones, enhance the allusion to the cross. His choice of colour is rather interesting. The reality of Good Friday is acknowledged in the dark shapes as well as in the red areas, symbolic of the blood shed in Christ's sacrificial death. In fact, the dark surrounding of the Cross might indicate the hours from noon when 'darkness came over the whole land' and Jesus finally cried 'Eloi, Eloi, lema sabachthani?' (Mk 15:33-34). The hint of earth colour rising from the bottom of the Cross could be seen as alluding to God's immanence, God's incarnation in the man Jesus. The pale green/white in the Cross as well as the other areas where a similar hue appears, particularly to the left of the Cross, could be interpreted as signifying Christ's innocence as well as an anticipation of new and eternal life with Christ in the kingdom. Easter Sunday, resurrection hope, is glimpsed in Christ's darkest hour, redemption is promised. The continuity between Good

137. Ruane, 'Personal Inscapes', in B. Lynch, (ed.), *Tony O'Malley*, 240.
138. The style of this work, as much of his oeuvre, has some affinities with artists like Manessier or American Abstract Expressionists like Newman, Still, de Kooning, or Rothko. O'Malley has expressed his admiration for painters like de Kooning and Guston. Yet he has always been his own painter.

Friday and Easter Sunday, suffering and salvation, is indicated by the soft merging of the contrasting dark and light spaces in the Cross.

Without taking any recourse to traditional crucifixion iconography, O'Malley thus gives expression to the drama of the Christ event. It is worth noting that Schwebel, in his discussion of whether it is possible at all to use the term 'abstract' images of Christ, concludes that 'indirect' Christ images would be more appropriate then 'abstract' images of the Crucified since, in fact, these works really are abstract paintings which make the claim, through their titles, that they are concerned with the theme of Christ.[139] What this indirect image of Good Friday captures, or at least alludes to so remarkably – simply through the abstract shapes and the various colours – is the solemnity, the atmosphere associated with Good Friday. It points to the mystery of Christ, to the unfathomable divine, to the God whose awe-inspiring presence and transcendence leaves us in and reduces us ultimately to silence,[140] or, as the mystic St John of the Cross apophatically wrote, 'without understanding, Transcending all knowledge'.[141] The work hence mediates the meaning of Good Friday despite and because of its imagelessness, its silence. Meditative, profound and mysterious, it invites the viewer to contemplation. One needs to be aware, of course, that the title, i.e. the artist's intention, clarifies the theme. Without the caption those who look with the eyes of Christian faith might still interpret the work in terms of the event at Golgatha while others may not relate to it at all in this fashion.

O'Malley painted 'Good Friday' not as a commission but purely from his own desire. As with Collins' 'Stations' or Middleton's 'Christ Androgyne', it is precisely the subjective approach, through which the work becomes a confession of faith and thereby curiously assumes an indirect, unintended kerygmatic dimension. Unlike in the works by Collins or Middleton just mentioned, the aspect of proclamation in the present painting paradoxically arises from O'Malley's imageless, 'wordless' rendering of the cross. It hence 'doubly'

139. Schwebel, *Das Christusbild in der bildenden Kunst der Gegenwart*, 72.
140. Cf. Otto, *The Idea of the Holy*, 68-69. Otto observes that the 'spontaneous reaction to the feeling of the actual numen praesens' is silence. Gerhard Tersteegen (1697-1769) likewise speaks of the sense of silence in the presence of God in verse one of his hymn 'Wunderbarer König', engl. 'God Himself is Present': 'God him-self is pre-sent; Let us now a-dore him And with awe appear be-fore him! God is in his tem-ple; All with-in keep si-lence, Pro-strate lie with deep-est rev-'rence.' *Lutheran Book of Worship* (Minneapolis: Augsburg Publishing House/Philadelphia: Board of Publication, Lutheran Church in America, 1978), Hymn 249. Both Otto and Tersteegen refer to Hab 2:20: 'But the LORD is in his holy temple; let all the earth keep silence before him!'
141. St John of the Cross, 'Stanzas Concerning an Ecstasy Experienced in High Contemplation', in *The Collected Works of St. John of the Cross*, trans. Kieran Kavanagh, O.C.D., Otilio Rodriguez, O.C.D. (Washington, D.C.: Institute of Carmelite Studies, 1979), 718-719.

expresses the death of the Logos, i.e. the fact that the death of the proclaimer entailed the death of his proclamation.[142] However, the pale green-white spaces point beyond death to the resurrection, and thus to the God in whom is hope and life. 'Good Friday' reveals, therefore, something of the eternal mystery of the crucified God.

7.2. Shadowy Carvings of an Ancient Execution, Good Friday (See page 180)

Painted almost three decades after the Good Friday painting just examined, this work was inspired by the O'Tunney Calvary sculptures in St Mary's Church in Callan. As mentioned in Chapter Two, O'Malley admires the work of the seventeenth century artist O'Tunney, probably an itinerant craftsman, who worked locally in Callan, County Kilkenny. What strikes the recipient immediately are the pervading bright colours, the light pale yellow, turquoise, and hints of pink, which one hardly associates with the day of the crucifixion. Painted in sketchy outlines or incised into the canvas are two figures and the instruments of the Passion. Both or one of them are/is possibly intended to signify Christ, although their long garments do not correspond to traditional paintings of the Crucified. They are reminiscent rather of figures on the High Crosses or in the Celtic manuscripts. Several instruments and symbols are shown: nails, two pincers, two small 'T' shapes to the left and right of the larger figure which allude to the cross, possibly two feet with nail marks left of the small figure, and a hand with nail mark on the far right of the work in reference to the crucified, a cross with circle on the far right towards the top of the work, possibly an allusion to the crown of thorns in the blue short curved outlines left of and below the small figure, and, finally, the cup and superimposed on the lower end of it seemingly the four gospels/the Bible in form of a rectangular shape with a cross and decoration of dots typical of the Book of Kells or the Book of Durrow. What appears to be the cup also resembles a pot on top of which appears the vague image of the cock. The cock has various meanings in the Christian tradition; it often connotes Peter's betrayal of Christ, and also it became a symbol of the resurrection. The cock crowing out of the pot is a common feature on the Irish Penal Crosses of the 18th century which O'Malley would know and which might also have been inspirational in this work. There are also some other shapes, especially the small lozenges and triangular incisions characteristic in many of O'Malley's works. Within the canvas there are, furthermore, long vertical and horizontal lines that give the impression of a large rectangle within the painting. This feature, as also some of the vaguely depicted symbols, cor-

142. Moltmann, *Der gekreuzigte Gott,* 115-116.

respond to the title of the work, i.e. the 'shadowy' aspect of the carvings. However, the crucifixion was a real historical event and the instruments of the Passion, sketchy as they may be, refer to this fact.

Paintings or plates which show the instruments, the *arma Christi,* are present in the Orthodox tradition especially and also in Western churches, particularly from the thirteenth century onwards[143] in the context of growing devotion and personal contemplation of the Passion. Seemingly they were intended to remind the believer that these were the items with which Christ had been tortured.

The whole composition, the fading, shadowy carvings and the colours, convey an enigmatic atmosphere, a sense of transcendence, of evanescence, of the otherworldly. The artist's preference and reliance on intuition and free imagination rather than clear concepts may be one reason for his unusual rendering of the subject. Moreover, the unexpected, even cheerful, luminosity may be due to the Bahamian influence, which has made his palette on the whole much brighter. The seventeenth century carvings by O'Tunney probably have faded, which also may have influenced his vague depiction. The fact that in the title the word 'ancient' is used underlines this aspect.

Theologically this Good Friday painting, compared with the previous one, emphasises that the solemn darkness of Christ on the Cross will finally be superseded by the hope for the resurrection. The death of Christ is still glimpsed, not forgotten, but will definitely be overcome by the light of salvation. Further, compared with two other works, i.e. 'Calvary Number One' and 'Calvary Number Two' (both 1983), which were also inspired by the O'Tunney carvings, the present painting is brighter than both and the least clear in the outlines of its subjects. It therefore exudes a more pronounced sense that life in the eschaton is to be believed in as a beautiful, mysterious, yet still hidden reality. However, the beauty of that other world does not deny the shadow of the Cross. One is reminded of von Balthasar when he writes: 'The 'glory' of Christian transfiguration is in no way less resplendent than the transfiguring glory of worldly beauty, but the fact is that the glory of Christ unites splendour and radiance with solid reality, as we see pre-eminently in the resurrection and its anticipation through faith in Christian life.'[144]

143. Edouard Urech, *Lexikon christlicher Symbole* (Konstanz: Christliche Verlagsanstalt, 1992), 141. Friedhelm Mennekes, Johannes Röhrig, *Crucifixus, Das Kreuz in der Kunst unserer Zeit* (Freiburg: Herder, 1994), 6.
144. H.U. v. Balthasar, *The Glory of the Lord, A Theological Aesthetics,* vol. 1: *Seeing the Form* (Edinburgh: T. & T. Clark, 1982), 124.

7.3. Earth Lyre (See page 181)

The third work to be considered is one without any Christian iconographical detail in the painting itself or in its title. As mentioned before, the
Bahamian influence, the bright palette of the recent decades, is apparent in
many of O'Malley's later works, as in the present one with its delightful symphony of predominantly light yellow, green, blue and purple colours and
some sparks of red, ochre and black interspersed. Several commentators have
remarked on the musical quality that pervades much of the artist's oeuvre,
and it is this rhythmic, melodious and harmonious aspect, which strikes the
viewer here. O'Malley himself has referred to his wish to 'paint' music since,
as he sees it, music can create 'oneness' in its dissolving of 'differences
between things'.[145] Not surprisingly he has even stated that he wishes to paint
silence, which, of course, stands in corresponding relationship to music, i.e.
silence as the prerequirement for listening to and the 'end' to sound. As
Pieper puts it in more metaphysical terms, 'music opens up a great ... space
of silence within which, when things come about happily, a reality can dawn
which ranks higher than music'.[146] A number of his picture titles, like
'Birdsong' (1987), 'Sea Requiem' (1987), or 'Sea Harp' (1989), 'invoke Orpheus,
the mythic poet who produced music of such beauty with his ninestringed
lyre', that it charmed rivers, trees and wild beasts.[147] In the present work this
musical, Orphean aspect is stressed by the title. An abstract work with
O'Malley's typical little details, short strokes, dots, all merging within a sea
of luminous colours, it seems like a hymn by and to the earth and creation.

Despite the absence of any Christian references, it is possible to interpret
this work in rather theological terms. The lyre, probably the most ancient of
all string instruments, was used from the beginning to accompany singing,
and hence became a metaphor for poetry as well as music. An attribute of
Apollo and Orpheus, it later became an attribute of David, who traditionally
was thought to have written most of the Psalms.[148] For a while the lyre even

145. In this context also the words of the Irish musician Brian Boydell come to mind when
     he writes: 'There are the saints, the mystics, and those really great creative artists who
     have revealed to lesser mortals who have ears to hear, or eyes to see, a vision of portion
     of that Truth after which we all search ... Music in my opinion, is especially endowed
     with the ability to express mystical ideas; or revelations of Truth which can only vague-
     ly, if at all, be conveyed in words alone.' B. Boydell, 'The Virgin Mary in Music',
     Milltown Studies, no. 22 (Autumn 1988), 88.
146. Cf. Josef Pieper's reflection on 'Music and Silence' in J. Pieper, *Only the Lover Sings: Art
     and Contemplation*, trans. Lothar Krauth (San Francisco: Ignatius Press, 1988), 55-56.
147. A. Dunne, 'The Later Work', in Lynch, (ed.), *Tony O'Malley*, 286. Ovid, *Metamorphoses*,
     trans. Mary M. Innes (London: Penguin, 1955), 227-228.
148. In fact, the Greek *psalmos* means 'the song played with the stringed instrument', i.e. the
     lyre. *Reclams Bibellexikon*, 405.

connoted Christian worship as the hymn and music of Christian faith, hence
it assumed a doxological function.

It is this sense of praise, poetic and sensuous, that the title and the painting
itself convey. It is praise of the beauty of the earth; thus it is praise of creation.
In Teilhard de Chardin's words, it is the hymn of and to the universe, the
spiritual power of matter, i.e. the affirmation of the goodness of creation and
the fact that through matter the spiritual can be experienced, which this, as
many other of O'Malley's works, abundantly express. It confirms thus what
had been ascertained in Chapter Two, namely the panentheist dimension in
O'Malley's life and painting, his belief that the divine is manifested in and
can be experienced through nature. I suggest that even without the title and
familiarity with his work, the painting purely by way of its tiny details, hues
and rhythm evokes the sense of praise of nature, nature especially in its joyous, non-threatening aspect. Teilhard de Chardin speaks of holy matter,
which 'attracts, renews, unites and flowers' and that it is by such matter that
we are 'nourished, lifted up, linked to everything else, invaded by life'.[149]
O'Malley's exuberant composition corresponds to and evokes something of
de Chardin's perception through its revelation of the sacredness and glory of
creation.[150]

Finally, it is to be argued that in its doxological dimension the work does
not only praise the beauty and holiness of creation, but that through its wonderful colours and transcendent atmosphere, it becomes a 'beatific' vision and
anticipation of redemption. Even more strongly than the two previous works
examined, it suggests and might even make one believe that when we come
face to face with the divine we will see God who is light (Jn 1:8-9) and who
wills salvation for all creation. 'Earth Lyre' achieves this vision precisely in its
'figurelessness', its splendour of light. In this way the painting as an ecstatic,
yet peaceful, hymn of creation is a hymn of faith; the 'here' and 'not yet' have
truly become one.[151] Thus O'Malley's, like Collins', works become – unintended – homilies in paint, which sing of the beauty of heaven and earth.

O'Malley's artistic output – rich in imagination, colour and form – has
progressed through the decades from a darker to a brighter palette as well as

149. T. de Chardin, *Le Milieu Divin* (London: Collins, 1960), 106. Cf. also *Hymn to the Universe* (London: Collins, 1961), 68-70.
150. Here it is also interesting to note that Gabriel Daly, in an essay on the relationship between religion and art, comments with regard to the role of the artist, that 'the won-der' lies perhaps not so much in the fact 'that there is so much beauty in the world which God has created' but 'that within God's creation a creature has evolved who is capable of seeing it and responding to it with appropriate depth of experience'. G. Daly, O.S.A., 'Art and Religion', *Doctrine and Life*, vol. 46, no. 10 (December 1996), 590-591.
151. Schwebel's observation on the eschatological dimension in abstract art is affirmed in this and similar works by O'Malley.

towards increasing abstraction. Theologically one might speak of this development in terms of an ever-growing sense of eschatological anticipation of
and hope for salvation, of God whose glory is revealed on the Cross and
eventually perceived in totality in the eschaton, in which death and darkness
are overcome by eternal life and light. Produced by an artist whose life and
work are marked by contemplation and inwardness, O'Malley's paintings are
truly spiritual, revealing, as they do, the Spirit who 'ensure[s] the reflection
of divine beauty in the world'.[152]

152. P. Sherry, *Spirit and Beauty,* 109.

8. PATRICK SCOTT

8.1. Goldpainting 48 (See page 182)

Scott's work, through its simple, sophisticated elegance, calm serenity, balance and great sense of harmony, has been perceived by most critics as exuding a pronounced spiritual, meditative and contemplative quality. It is this dimension which makes his painting interesting for the present study, even more and particularly so, in the light of the fact that Scott regards himself as an agnostic/atheist. As shown in the previous chapter, this element in the artist affirms that the spiritual in a work of art is – for the most part at least – independent of an artist's religiosity. In Scott's case this seems abundantly, even ironically, confirmed by the commissions he received from the church on several occasions.

The stillness in his works 'reduces' the recipient to silence. It is, as Michael Dibb pointed out in 1962, 'visual fascination allied to verbal inarticulation with which one responds to his paintings'.[153] For Dibb, this likely reaction to Scott's oeuvre was an affirmation that 'paintings are to be looked at, not talked about'. Dibb here concurs with Schwebel's emphasis that abstract art is essentially 'beyond words'. Hence an attempt at 'articulating' the inexpressible, as is the task here, can only take place in that light. The rather tentative nature of interpreting abstract works has already been noted in relation to Collins and O'Malley, and in Scott it needs to be stressed once more before embarking on 'reading' his works.

Scott's Goldpaintings, i.e. the numerous works which show his technique of applying gold leaf and tempera onto unprimed canvas, have been especially appreciated for their spiritual quality.

'Goldpainting 48', a square canvas, shows two colourfields of equal size, one light grey-white, the other light yellow-beige, which divide the work horizontally into two parts. A band, half in white and half in gold leaf, forms a vertical axis. Two curved lines branch out from the lower end of the vertical axis in the upper plane. The lower ones of these lines each describe a half circle within the painting.

The whole composition exudes balance and harmony, even radiance, through its hues, size, gold leaf and geometrical arrangement. As with others of Scott's works, one is reminded of Aquinas' idea of beauty. According to Thomas, 'three qualities' are necessary for something to be beautiful: 'integrity or completeness (*integritas/perfectio*) ... right proportion or harmony (*debita*

---

153. M. Dibb, 'Art, Six of One', *The Dubliner*, no. 4 (July-Aug. 1962), 62.

proportio/consonantia); and brightness (*claritas*)'.[154] Right proportion is essential as 'the senses delight in rightly proportioned things'.[155] For Aquinas, beauty and goodness both have the same basis in reality ... [i.e. in their] possession of form, thus – as Augustine and Plato had already ascertained – they are ultimately one.[156]

Scott's paintings are not concerned with existentialist pain, suffering and expressionist distortion. Rather, they reflect and body forth a sense of salvation, of quiet splendour, of the light and beauty of creation in their harmony of abstract forms and colour. For Thomas the beautiful 'refers to that which gives pleasure when it is perceived or contemplated'.[157] Few people, one imagines, would dispute that Scott's works not only please the senses and the mind, but, moreover, that in their calm elegance and hieratic quality, evoked especially by the gold leaf, they have a decidedly meditative and even healing effect on the beholder.

It is likely that the bands of gold leaf and white in the work associate different shapes for different interpreters. For this writer they suggest, first of all, a tree and possibly also a fountain. Already in pre-Christian cultures trees were worshipped as sacred objects inhabited by gods. In a more biblical-theological sense, the tree would be symbolic of the tree of life (Gen 3:22-24), of the tree 'pleasant to the sight and good for food' (Gen 2:9), of the 'good tree [that] cannot bear bad fruit' (Mt 7:18), of the tree on which Christ was hanged (Acts 5:30; 10:39), i.e. the Cross. Finally, it hints at the tree of life in eternity producing 'twelve kinds of fruit ... and the leaves of the tree are for the healing of the nations. Nothing accursed will be found there any more' (Rev 22:2-3).

Gold leaf was used in icons and altarpieces referring to the sacred aspect in the Christian subject matter. In this way the tree's stem in gold could be seen as pointing to the sense of goodness, beauty and sacredness of the tree; in a wider sense then it symbolises that creation is essentially – 'from the root', so to speak – sacred. The stem, which extends from the lower into the upper plane, thus connects two spheres: earth and heaven, this world and the other, creation and salvation, salvation through the one who died on a tree. Indeed, the pervading atmosphere in this brightly coloured work is one of redemptive beauty and the beauty of redemption. Further, the association of

154. Thomas Aquinas, S.T., Ia, q. 39, a. 8 in T.C. O'Brien, (ed.), *St Thomas Aquinas Summa Theologiae* [henceforth S.T.], *Father, Son and Holy Ghost* (Ia. 33-43), vol. 7 (London: Blackfriars, 1976).
155. S.T., Ia, q. 5, a. 4 ad 1 in Timothy McDermott, O.P., (ed.), S.T., *Existence and Nature of God* (Ia. 2-11), vol. 2 (London: Blackfriars, 1964).
156. S.T., ibid. Cf. J.A. Martin, Jr., *Beauty and Holiness*, 20.
157. S.T., I-IIae, q. 27, a. 1, ad 3 in Eric D'Arcy, (ed.), *S.T., The Emotions* (Ia2ae. 22-30), vol. 19 (London: Blackfriars, 1967).

the fountain of life underlines this interpretation, as, like the tree, water is symbolical of life, spirit and salvation. Indeed it is 'the throne of God and of the Lamb' from which the rivers of Paradise, 'bright as crystal', flow (Rev 22:1).

Towards the end of what has emerged as a rather pronounced theological interpretation, one could ask once more whether such a particular perspective is legitimate? I conclude that for several reasons it seems appropriate. Firstly, as stated at the very beginning of this chapter, the interpretations do not and cannot claim exclusivity. Secondly, the 'reading' I have put forward here is substantiated by arguments that find their basis in iconographical details in the canvas instead of being imposed so as to 'suit' a theological agenda. Finally, it is Scott himself who welcomes such an interpretation when he states that he would 'not be the least bit worried' if anyone perceived his works in spiritual or theological terms. On the contrary, as he says, it would please him 'more than anything else'.[158]

8.2. *Goldpainting 56* (See page 183)

Painted in the same year as the previous work, this canvas shows a typical motif in Scott's oeuvre, the sphere or, more specifically, the sun. This meaning, i.e. the sun, is not only apparent through the actual depiction but has been facilitated by Scott's own comments as he has acknowledged his helio obsession, describing himself as a 'sun worshipper'. Sun worship was part of the pre-Christian Celtic Irish past, which holds a fascination for the artist.

This relatively small painting is dominated by the glowing orange-red of the sphere set off against the near-white canvas. The whole composition is geometrically arranged, and thereby – as in 'Goldpainting 48' – achieves a great sense of harmony, proportion, balance and radiance. The radiant aspect is enhanced by the square of gold leaf, which shines in the centre of the sphere. The contrast of colours is pronounced even more by the thin green blurred line, which, like an aura, encompasses the sphere. Curiously this line, although green and not red, conveys – due to its blurred outer edge – the sense of the sun burning. Further, the orange-red of the sun is not entirely even but varies in intensity, the red is stronger both towards the margin and especially towards the centre of the sphere while orange is more pronounced as a subtle wide circular 'band' between the deeper-red areas. This application of colour is especially revelatory of the sun since it brings out her glowing, burning, energetic, life-and-light-giving aspect.

Again, as in the previous work, the aesthetic qualities of harmony, proportion and brightness are apparent in the canvas. The sun here symbolises

---

158. Scott, Interview, 17.10.1995. Cf. also Chapter Two, section on Scott.

life; this aspect is emphasised by the green rim as green indicates (new) life, growth, nature and hope. Again, the gold lends the whole composition a pronounced hieratic dimension. It seems as if universal creation, signified here through the sun and the green thin band, is not only acknowledged as good and beautiful in itself, but as originating in and from the divine. The golden square in the work points like a window out of, into and beyond the sun to the transcendent God who, at the same time, reveals Godself in creation. Or, as the Neothomist philosopher Jacques Maritain wrote, God is beautiful in Godself because God 'gives beauty to all created beings, according to the particular nature of each, and because he is the cause of all consonance and brightness'.[159] This wonderfully radiant painting certainly could make one believe that natural beauty is a reflection of and created by the supreme creator who is the 'fountain of all beauty'.[160] Like in an icon or in an early Renaissance altarpiece, the application of gold evokes the sacred aspect of the subject. The sun is sacred, not only in pre-Christian and Celtic times, but always and for everyone as, without her, life, which is in itself sacred, could not exist. A glimpse of God, who is light and the source of light, is revealed in this canvas, not through religious iconography but through abstract form. Maritain observed that in touching a transcendental, 'one touches being itself, a likeness of God, an absolute'; and that it is through this touch that 'one enters into the domain of the spirit'.[161] Scott's works, in their unassuming splendour, harmony and light, are revelatory of this touch. Indeed it is the sense of contemplation and awe, that these gold paintings evoke in those who are confronted with them, which 'affirms' that in the work of art matter and spirit meet. The beauty of the material pigments, canvas and forms can disclose the depths of beauty of the human and of the divine spirit. Through reality we are lead to ultimate reality, even if we must remember at the same time, that God always remains the unfathomable Other.

Finally, I would argue that the application of gold in this work greatly contributes to the meaning of what is depicted. Unlike the Impressionists, who were interested in depicting *en plein air* the fleeting moment of sun light and atmosphere in landscape, Scott's painting, in particular his rendering of light and his application of gold in this work, gives the sun - as one of the most powerful symbols of life-giving light – a remarkably sacred, consistent and thereby eternal dimension. It is not the momentary, but the everpresent

159. Jacques Maritain, *Art and Scholasticism and the Frontiers of Poetry*, trans. Joseph W. Evans (New York: Charles Scribner's Sons, 1962), 31.
160. Ibid.
161. Ibid., 32.

light, symbolising the eternal light of the Creator,[162] which matters here, reminding one of Schelling when he wrote that 'the universe is formed in God as an absolute work of art, and as eternal beauty'.[163]

8.3. *Chinese Landscape* (See page 184)

The last work of Scott's for examination is more figurative than the previous two canvases and influenced by his travels to the Far East. The representational aspect is indicated through the title and apparent in the canvas which shows a stylised, linear landscape of rocks and mountains. What is so remarkable, even amazing, about these rocks is the fact that they seem hollow or caved inside. While the outer shapes evoke mountainous rocks, the ovals, the pointed and round arches, plants, decorations and window-like openings inside suggest facades of Gothic and Romanesque churches and cathedrals. Above the landscape/churches towers the sharply defined sun entirely in gold leaf which contrasts with the rest of the almost ephemeral atmosphere created through the use of pale, light hues.

Scott's series of Chinese Landscapes[164] were inspired by his experience of a particular landscape in China. His aim was not to present a realistic depiction of their appearance but rather 'to give the feeling of the fact that they are like cathedrals ... It was really a kind of trick to try to give the feeling of the inside and the outside of them ...'.[165]

As with the other two works, this one through its meditative quality conveys a pronounced sense of the spiritual and of contemplation. It is again a striking example of the fact that often a work of art attains a universal dimension through its particularity. The particular is the landscape which the painter encountered. In his attempt to reveal something of his felt experience of the mountains, he depicts them as both mountains and cathedrals. It is

162. Cf. Gabriel Daly, O.S.A., *Creation and Redemption* (Dublin: Gill and Macmillan, 1988), 97.

163. F.W.J. Schelling, *Philosophie der Kunst*, cf. paragraphs 16, 21, 33, in Hauskeller, *Was das Schöne sei, Klassische Texte von Platon bis Adorno*, 296-298. (Author's translation) 'Die Schönheit ... ist überall gesetzt, wo Licht und Materie, Ideales und Reales sich berühren ... Das Universum ist in Gott als absolutes Kunstwerk und in ewiger Schönheit gebildet ... Schönheit ist das real angeschaute Absolute.'

164. Scott painted a number of works titled 'Chinese Landscape', such as 'Chinese Landscape J/'86' (1986), Hugh Lane Municipal Gallery of Modern Art, Dublin, which is very similar in appearance to the painting under consideration. Cf. my article 'Imaging God: Spiritual Dimensions in Modern Art', in Murphy, Cassidy, (eds.), *Neglected Wells, Spirituality and the Arts*, 108-109.

165. Interview, 17.10.95. 'I was in China where there are these extraordinary mountains and they are really all hollow inside and they are exactly like cathedrals and they are really most fantastic ... I was totally bowled over.'

this meaning and interpretation given by the painter through the style and content of his depiction, and which in turn is - or, at least, may be – experienced as such by the viewer, that lends the work its universal aspect. The painting connects East (Chinese landscape) and West (cathedrals). Cathedrals, especially the great Gothic cathedrals, were intended to give the faithful an impression and foretaste of heaven, of the New Jerusalem, of the glorious and most beautiful city of the transcendent God. Mountains likewise have always had a sacred dimension in non-Christian and Christian cultures. In this way, it could be said, the depiction of the landscape/cathedrals attains a wider ecumenical, inter-faith dimension as it merges Eastern and Western religiosity. This is enhanced by the sun, symbol of truth, which shines over the Chinese landscape and over every house of God, every faith and every land. Thus it parallels in pictorial form what an ecumenist like Panikkar points out, namely that the 'ultimate religious fact does not lie in the realm of doctrine' but 'may well ... be present everywhere and in every religion'.[166]

This painting then, through its light, harmony and sacred aspect – evoked through the use of gold and through the shapes resembling cathedrals – exudes a sense of the hope for and promise of universal salvation, of the belief that truth is to be found in all cultures, of mystery, transcendence and eternity glimpsed through the awe-inspiring grandeur of nature and through the beauty of human creation. It is a promise not only for the followers of Christ but for all creation, East and West.[167]

Probably the most important aspect, as mentioned earlier with regard to Scott and in the context of this book, is the fact that the spiritual in a work of art is not dependent on the religiosity of the artist. Scott considers himself an agnostic/atheist. Yet he has produced works which are experienced by those who have seen and commented on them as spiritual and contemplative, a fact which brought him a few church commissions. My interpretations of three of his works show that not only are his paintings spiritual and meditative, but that they can even be perceived in more specifically theological terms. Scott's paintings remind one of John F. Haught when he observes that as long as one is drawn towards beauty one is drawn towards God who is 'the horizon of ultimate beauty'.[168] Haught, I suggest, rightly points out that it would be artificial and untruthful thus to make a sharp segregation between

---

166. Raimundo Panikkar, *The Intrareligious Dialogue* (New York/Mahwah: Paulist Press, 1978), 57.
167. It seems to me that Scott's interest in Buddhism would encourage such a reading.
168. John F. Haught, *What Is God, How To Think About the Divine* (Dublin: Gill and Macmillan, 1986), 71.

religious and aesthetic experience. Rather it is through the encounter of concrete beauty, as in a work of art, that one may be lead into another dimension, i.e. to ultimate reality. Beauty as the 'supreme exemplification of the
"transcendentals"'[169] provides us with and is a glimpse of the divine.
Something of God who is ultimate beauty may be discovered in Scott's work,
not because of the painter's adherence to religion but because of his subject
matter and style as well as artistic authenticity, skill and imagination, qualities which in themselves could be seen as attained through grace.

169. Ibid., 73.

9. PATRICK GRAHAM

9.1. Scenes from the Life of Christ (See page 185)

Graham's preoccupation with religion from childhood, his radical questioning of it as an adult both in his art and in what he has said, and his assertion
that faith and religion are and have been 'absolutely essential' to him as an
existential reality, as a need and longing for 'completeness' and 'Godness',
were discussed in the previous chapter. For Graham the act of painting is an
act of self-expression essentially based on and driven by experience, by a
desire for self-loss and self-transcendence, born of silence, of not-knowing
and of emptiness, a view which, as with some of the other artists, places him
in the company of the mystics. In his works religious and sexual allusions and
imagery, as also political issues, are central, in particular the demythologising
of these in his continuous search for truth.

   Graham has especially emphasised the radical humanity of God in Jesus
Christ, as also the mysterious otherness in his perception of the divine. An
explicitly christological work is his 'Scenes from the Life of Christ' (1983-84).
A large triptych, it depicts Christ's 'Agony in the Garden' on the left panel,
'The Nativity' in the centre, and 'The Resurrection' on the right. On the far
left of the left panel the title and the themes are clearly written in capital letters of varying colours. One could suggest that the blue in the main title
alludes to the kingly role of Christ. The red in 'The Agony in the Garden'
possibly pertains to Christ's tormented state of mind and to the anticipation
of suffering and shedding of blood. The hint of white in the 'The Nativity'
could imply the purity and innocence of the Christ child. The mixture of the
red and beige-white in 'The Resurrection' finally conveys a sense of the entire
Christ event, i.e. the innocent God-man who in giving his blood for all is resurrected and effects salvation. The contrast and merging of the almost flame-
like colours in the letters of the subtitles give a feeling of the drama, of the
light and darkness of the whole life of Christ.

   A sense of unity and continuity between the three events in Jesus' life are
achieved and evoked primarily through the pervading light to dark mostly
brown colour, as also through the expressive brushwork and the rough,
sketchy and partly distorted figures. The figures blend in with the background as each is coloured in rather similar hues to the rest of the canvas. The
sombre background itself, with the nervous, light-coloured zigzag lines in
each panel and perhaps a hint of a mountainside on the left, is a little enigmatic due to the obvious absence of figures and subjects.

   On the left, Christ is shown on his own kneeling in prayer in
Gethsemane: 'Abba, Father, for you all things are possible; remove this cup

from me; yet, not what I want, but what you want.' (Mk 14:36) Again the dashes of red in the Christ figure heighten the sense of agitation and distress Jesus experienced in the garden (Mk 14:33), as also the anticipation of suffering.

In the centre panel Joseph appears on the left; on the right one discovers an unconventional portrayal of Mary seated with her upper body bare, and with a radiant halo-like and otherwise non-descriptive 'face'. Joseph's face, in comparison, is more clearly outlined with a striking spot of red on his eye. Between the two figures the new-born Jesus is lying in the cradle, with an ample halo, his left arm firmly placed on his mother's lap. There is a reference to the wounds of the crucifixion in the red colour on his hand. Perhaps the most striking feature is the shape of a Cross over the child, the thin, vertical arm of which is held by Mary, the thicker, horizontal one by Joseph.[170] The two arms cross almost exactly over Christ's face. Strokes of red, especially on Mary, again enliven the scene.

On the right the risen Christ in frontal position emerges from the tomb on the lower right. His face, set off clearly against the background, shows remarkable eyes in red with white eyebrows. On his head one detects the shape of a Cross. His arms are outstretched, one with the lower arm and hand cut off, the other leaning on the tomb and angularly adjusted with the left hand on his heart. The rest of the body is hidden behind the tomb.

The question arises why Graham would paint the theme of Christ in this fashion. In particular, one wonders why the crucifixion as *the* central event in Jesus' life, without which the resurrection is, of course, unthinkable, is only hinted at in 'The Nativity' and has been 'replaced' rather by 'The Agony in the Garden'. Graham has commented on his choice of the latter theme that for him 'one of the beautiful things' in the Christ story 'was not the crucifixion itself', but rather Christ's asking that the chalice be taken away from him. 'It was in that fall and resurrection ... The courage all comes in making the decision will I take the chalice'.[171] The painter has conceded, moreover, that 'in a limited way' there is a personal identification with the choice of the three themes, an element that is enhanced by the face of the risen Christ, which shows a vague similarity with that of the artist.[172] Further the face recalls – also vaguely – Piero della Francesca's 'Resurrection', i.e. the frontally

170. Graham, as was noted previously, has a particular reverence for the Old Masters, such as Piero and Grünewald. The fact that he includes the cross in this scene serves as an example of his knowledge of Christian iconography, since such references were common in traditional nativity depictions.
171. Interview, 28.9.1995.
172. Cf. also, for example, his work 'The Gift' (1984) in which the artist has also put himself into the painting, however, in a different context.

depicted Christ with the remarkably sad, 'knowing' eyes stepping out of the tomb, the resurrected Son of Man who has experienced the horror of an utmost violent death. Graham's own 'rising' from the depths of despair might possibly pertain to his choice and manner of the depiction of 'The Resurrection'.

Theologically Graham's approach is rather interesting. The soteriological-christological question about Christ's free will in choosing his sacrificial death has been a recurrent issue in theology. Anselm, in his classic *Cur Deus Homo* affirms that Jesus drank the cup because 'the world could not otherwise be saved; and it was his fixed choice to suffer death rather than that the world should not be saved'.[173] Anselm's theory of redemption thus stresses the voluntary aspect in Christ's dying, a view which is foundational to modern soteriology. Graham alludes to this when he notes and brings to expression that the crucial point in the Gethsemane experience was Christ's decision, his free acceptance, to give himself up to divine will. However, the decision was not a light-hearted one, hence the Agony in the Garden, an event, which, as Alistair Kee has observed, has been little discussed in theology. It is and has been omitted precisely because it shows the man Jesus discouraged, doubting, bewildered, weak, afraid of the unknown[174] as any human would be in the face of death. It is this aspect which has been glossed over, since it shows Christ as truly human, which indeed Christians often have found difficult to really believe. In this way Graham's 'Agony in the Garden' demythologises any assumption that for the God-Man to undergo suffering and death on the Cross would have been any easier than for 'mere' mortals.

This demythologisational approach continues in the Nativity panel. Mary is not shown as an otherworldly pure Madonna, but rather as a female, sexual, partly distorted, human being with exposed breasts. The red line along her right leg seems to flow into the Christ Child which could be an allusion to their blood relationship, i.e. God made flesh from human flesh. However, while his carnate human nature is thus emphasised, the halo over the child and the Cross refer to the soteriological, divine aspect in Christ. Here the Cross, held by Mary and Joseph over the body of the Child, is rather enigmatic. Does it indicate that they knew what had been ordained for their Son? Does it refer to the fact that Jesus was not even accepted amongst and crucified by his own people, as Simeon foretells Mary when the baby Jesus was

---

173. St Anselm, *Cur Deus Homo,* I, x, in *St. Anselm Basic Writings,* trans. S.N. Deane (Peru, Illinois: Open Court Publishing Company, 1962), 213.
174. Alistair Kee, *From Bad Faith to Good News* (London: SCM, 1991), 50. Kee writes: 'No, the agony arose from the unknown, from an experience which has nothing to do with sin, or guilt, judgement or punishment.'

brought to be circumcised in the temple in Jerusalem: 'This child is destined for the falling and the rising of many in Israel, and to be a sign that will be opposed so that the inner thoughts of many will be revealed – and a sword will pierce your own soul too' (Lk 2:34-35)? A clear answer seems impossible. However, the Cross over the child reveals the link between Jesus' birth and life and his redemptive death on Golgatha, i.e. the kingdom of God begun and fulfilled in Christ.

If Graham's 'Nativity' anticipates the Cross, his 'Resurrection' makes a link back to the Cross in the depiction of Christ's body emerging from and rising behind the tomb, a real and yet again a partly distorted body with outstretched arms and the image of the Cross on his head. The redeemer is the one who has suffered, the lowly, despised and mutilated one is the one who is raised in glory and who is Saviour of the world. Graham thus affirms in his triptych, like Bultmann in his writing, that the resurrection of and redemption in Christ is not supernatural and mythological but rather real and historical.[175] The whole work then relates to Graham's view that 'faith has to come from a realised notion of resurrection or salvation ... It has to be realised, otherwise it is just a word'.[176] In this way his emphasis on and pictorial allusion to the historical actuality of the Christ event further connects him to the concerns of liberation theologians, who stress the humanity of Jesus, especially as the liberator involved in the struggle of the oppressed.[177] Graham not only reveals this in his work but has spoken about his interest in liberation theology, particularly in Ernesto Cardenal whom he has read. He points out that 'we made it [Jesus' life and death] a religious experience, rather than the political experience [that] perhaps it was'.[178] Might this view imply that Graham's Christ becomes a mere human, political, radical revolutionary? This is not the case. Not only has he explicitly mentioned his sense and longing for 'Godness', for transcendence, but the fact that he includes the resurrection, the Christ of faith, in his triptych – a subject which is rare in the history of art precisely because of a likely shyness on the part of the painter to image the eschatological event which is ultimately beyond human imagination – suggests the opposite. What Graham therefore expresses both

175. Cf. Bultmann, 'New Testament and Mythology', in H.W. Bartsch, (ed.), *Kerygma and Myth*, vol. 1 (London: SPCK, 1964), 43.
176. Interview, 28.9.1995.
177. Cf. Phillip Berryman, *The Religious Roots of Rebellion, Christians in Central American Revolutions* (London: SCM, 1984), 390. 'Latin American theologians have sought to carry the paschal mystery further by insisting on "historicising" the life, death, and resurrection of Jesus in two senses: (1) taking seriously the specific history of Jesus of Nazareth; (2) seeing it as Jesus' purpose to stimulate further history.' Cf. also L. Boff, *Jesus Christ Liberator* (London: SPCK, 1980), 11.
178. Interview, 10.10.1995.

in his words and in his work is that authentic faith in the divine, in resurrection and redemption is rooted in and can only arise from reality and
experience.

Finally, a detail which easily could be overlooked is the horizontal border
in blue-green with small triangles at the top of the triptych. This slim rim is
significant as it conveys a sense of decoration, simple beauty and continuity
in the three scenes from the birth, life and resurrection of Christ.

9.2. The Lark in the Morning I (See page 186)

Painted in the early 1990s, 'The Lark in the Morning'[179] takes its title from
an old Irish song, the first lines of which are written on the frame at the top
right: 'The lark in the morning she rises off her nest and she comes home in
the evening with the dew all on her breast.' Graham has mentioned his love
of traditional Irish culture, especially 'that Irish trickery of language' which
often, instead of speaking straight, conveys its message indirectly, as here with
the lark and the blackbird (3.9.3.), 'the language of love-making'.[180] It is this
aspect of erotic love that is central to the painting.

The work consists of two large parts, with two smaller sections in the centre left which form a transition between the two. In comparison to the previous work, this one employs less narrative and instead symbols, which invite
a more complex interpretation. On the left side, which immediately strikes
the recipient due to its bright colours, the white square areas suggest a bed,
or bedlinen. Within this shape there is a triangular shape pointing downwards which may be the front part of a boat, a symbol which, like other 'vessels', i.e. the heart, or the womb, recurs in a number of Graham's paintings
of the early 1990s. Within the square, stylised flowers decoratively surround
another, slightly darker, small square which contains the central iconographic
detail: Here the canvas is cut, a slit emerges with two lashes hanging off on
each side; the whole suggests the form of a Cross with an embedded vagina.
Within the slit another slit is inserted with a little pearl, the clitoris, at the
top end. Directly above, the widened opening is rendered in gold, and further above one detects a little golden heart. Graham's signature and the words
'in the morning' as well as '91-92-93' are written in a vaguely outlined top
square. Stylised floral decorations appear at the top of the square and zigzag
lines decorate the frame and the bottom of this section.

Two small rectangular parts are contained in the centre-left of the work,

179. 'The Lark in the Morning' is the title of a series of three works of about equal size. Each
    of them, however, can be seen and interpreted as a self-contained unit.
180. Interview, 28.9.1995.

which - in contrast to the large section on the left – are painted in darker shades of beige, brown, and grey, blue. In both appear what seem to be bits of torn sails / (bed)-sheets / or even veils. These cloth materials make the link with the two other main parts of the work, in which these sails / cloths also appear.

The right section is made up of an upper and a lower part which, however, merge through their colouring and theme. The upper part, predominantly in grey, blue and beige-white, shows two details that again are not quite clear in their meaning. The most likely reading would imply torn sails flying above and onto water. This interpretation is supported by what seems to be a grey boat with many short rudders in the background. Towards the right one sees a bar with zigzag decoration and with an inscription which reads: 'CANTO'. On the frame on the left appear some more decorative details in light to dark blue.

The lower part, in shades of grey-blue, has a large section cut out and partly replaced with light golden-beige paper, possibly suggesting a table cloth, on which appear three vessels, this time in form of three, partly distorted, chalices. The words 'CANTIO-CANTUS' and Graham's signature are written on the bottom. The grey square directly above the chalices suggests the top of an altar that on the left is supported by two elegantly curved legs. Several strikingly blue 'strokes' of water float from above onto the altar and thus connect the upper and lower part.

The description of the work reveals the complexity of symbolism and thus of meaning. Typical for Graham, the painting suggests rather than declares.[181] An interpretation of this painting will be equally one of suggestion and the artist's comments on this work are, in fact, most helpful in trying to grasp it, especially from a theological angle.

'The Lark in the Morning I', as several other of Graham's works in the late 1980s and early 1990s, was inspired by his mother's death. Graham points out that although this event was the key, the use of symbols, however, was to provide a wider, more universal aspect and reading of the work.[182] In this context he mentions especially the recurrent symbol of the boat which struck him as marking the sense of passage, life, time and death. If this aspect of death and passage is disclosed in the right section of the work in the boat, the torn sails, the flowing water and the chalice, the left with its symbols of the

181. Cf. Chapter Two, section on Graham. Graham has also pointed out that what his 'paintings reveal, if anything, in a religious sense is far from certain ... For me, painting is not the solution, it is the question. The paintings are a journey, and you and I both are tourists, and I like you do not know what there is to admire about them because nothing is resolved ... there are no great highways to revelation'. *Works 5 - Patrick Graham*, 21.
182. Interview, 28.9.1995.

female genitals, bed linen, and boat centres on eros and sexuality. Graham remarks that in his mother's generation when many women had lost their husbands in war, they became celibates at a very young age. This in con-junction with the all-pervasive Catholic ethos of condemnation of sexuality produced 'the terror of the body', the total sense of shame and guilt with regard to anything sexual. 'The Lark in the Morning I' thus emerged as a reaction to this destructive view of the body. It was Graham's intention to show his growing sense that 'things are gift innately', that to 'love our heart and souls and hate our genitals' was not appreciative of the wholeness of the human being, of the body as glorious gift.[183]

Kuspit has described Graham's works in nihilist terms as morbid, 'obsessed with the body', concerned ultimately 'with the tragically flawed fig-ure', the 'body in decay'.[184] For him, as we saw earlier, Graham's art is 'about death, defeat, and raw madness', and without any sense of hope. While the artist's oeuvre often deals with *eros* and *thanatos,* Kuspit's view is too simplis-tic. Not only are there glimpses of hope, of the sacred even, in the darkest of Graham's works, through little details like stylised flowers, decorations, bright and golden dabs of colour, but the artist himself has written and com-mented on his hard won hope and faith.[185] This applies in particular to 'The Lark in the Morning I' as an affirmation of his repeatedly stated belief in the beauty and, especially, the wholeness of the human being and of creation: 'All I am saying it's all about wholeness. That's the only thing I consciously bring to painting – wholeness.'[186] In this way, the work attains a soteriological dimension, an awareness not simply of death and passing but, as Graham points out, also of resurrection 'in a very human way'. Against a background of repression and denial of the physical-sexual, Graham's 'Lark' sings its song of the wholeness of life, of the gift of erotic, sexual love, of beauty, always combined with the knowledge that suffering, transience, death (chalice, altar, cross) are part of and determine all being. The shape of the cross with the inserted vagina is perhaps the most striking symbol of Graham's pronounced sense of wholeness as it alludes to the ultimate oneness of agape and eros, of highest sexual ecstasy and deepest suffering, hence of the emotional pain, dif-ficulties and transcendence involved in all genuine human (sexual) love. Far from providing us with a morbid vision of reality, Graham's desire for whole-ness reflects and shares much with the holistic sexual ethics of a theologian like James Nelson. Nelson affirms the necessity to be positively aware of our-

183. Ibid.
184. Kuspit, 'Patrick Graham: Painting as Dirge', in *Patrick Graham – The Lark in the Morning,* 7-11.
185. Interview, 28.9.1995. *Works 5 - Patrick Graham,* 18. Cf. Chapter Two, section on Graham.
186. Interview, 28.9.1995.

selves as 'embodied selves', and, moreover, to acknowledge that our sexuality 'is intrinsic to our relationship with God'.[187] He reminds us that sexuality, far more than genital sexual involvement, 'is who we are as body-selves who experience the emotional, cognitive, physical, and spiritual need for intimate communion – human and divine'.[188] It is such a holistic understanding of sexuality, and of the human being as such, that transpires both in Graham's art and words. He concurs with Nelson's stress of the sense of sexuality as divine gift, i.e. the sacramental nature of sexuality, as the 'fundamental dimension of our created and our intended humanness'.[189] Like Graham, Nelson draws attention to the central Christian belief in the incarnation, the 'embodied Word', which empowers a vision of the person reconciled to and appreciative of her/his body and of love as the union of eros, philia and agape.

Graham places the celebration and affirmation of human, especially female, sexuality alongside suffering and the passage of life towards death. It is a holistic and realistic expression therefore of what is fundamental to human existence, the joy of love and the ever-present awareness of suffering and of the finality of life. Further, the symbol of the Cross, the altar and the chalice lend the work a christological and eucharistic dimension. God becomes incarnate and dies for our sake, and we in turn live and die as embodied human beings, as those who long for communion. Graham thus presents us with an encompassing, reflective, complex, at times melancholic, but not morbid view of what constitutes human reality. It is a reality in which hope for – even if derived from deep darkness – and faith in the God who is love still has a place.

187. Cf. James B. Nelson, *Embodiment, An Approach to Sexuality and Christian Theology* (Minneapolis, Minnesota: Augsburg Publishing House, 1978), 16-18.
188. Ibid., 18.
189. Ibid., 272.

9.3. *The Blackbird Suite* (See page 187)

A series of nineteen works, 'The Blackbird Suite' contains many of the symbols that appear in 'The Lark in the Morning', like the altar, chalice, stylised flowers and, most frequently, the boat. Again Graham has chosen a lyrical title, the blackbird, famous for its beautiful song, and celebrated in Gaelic literature and music. Also, as with 'The Lark in the Morning', the paintings in this series can be seen and examined individually. A single continuous narrative is not apparent, rather the connection between the works is established through the recurrent symbols and the distorted human figures.

The work for discussion from the series bears the words 'Poured out like' at the bottom, and – since none of the nineteen works has its own title – I will, for convenience sake, refer to it as such below. Above these words, which indeed appear like a title at the lower end, a dividing line, like a margin or frame, is inserted, partly enhanced by decorations. An image of a boat, the bottom of which touches the line, is placed in the centre of the work. On the belly of the ship a frame with legs out of which leaves are growing is placed, seemingly an altar without a tabletop. Some of the leaves and the top ends of the legs are decorated with tiny blobs of gold. Above one detects the barely visible outlines of a sail in which a shape, reminiscent of a window, appears with words from Psalm 22:12-15 against a blue background. The words read: 'me / they open wide their mouths a[t me][190] / like a ravening and roaring li[on] / I am poured out like water, / and all my bones are out of j[oint] / my heart is like wax; / it is melted within my breast / my strength is dried up like a / [pot]sherd, / and my tongue cleaves to my j[aws] / thou dost lay me [in] the du[st of death].'

Above the sail and window another horizontal line again functions like a frame. Several iconographic details in light grey can be detected, the upper part of a male nude from the back, the lower part of a reclined female nude with exposed genitals, floating sperms, a bird, and a chalice are clearly visible. The whole painting is striking not only because of its sexual and religious symbols and biblical reference, but also due to the dominant white colour.

Graham has commented that the painting, with the included words 'I am poured out like ... you lay me in the dust of death' from Psalm 22, emerged out of a sense of 'mourning and loss' – loss and mourning of certainties which the church might have once provided for him, but which did not hold.[191] The only way to cope thus was to live with the 'notion of journey'.[192] The boat signifies the journey, the passage; also, as in the previous

190. Letters/words in brackets do not appear on the canvas.
191. Interview, 28.9.1995.
192. Ibid.

work, the boat as vessel connotes for him a sexual symbol of the female. The Psalm's words are revelatory of mourning, despair, resignation and even being close to death. It is an individual lament in which the author, David,[193] sees himself as 'despised by others' and calls for God to hear and rescue him. At the same time he praises God for having come to his rescue in the past, and he calls all Israel and finally all humankind (vs. 27-31) to join him in his praise. Although Graham's extract is purely lament, there is, as will be shown, something of the whole psalm in the work, i.e. suffering, death, despair is not the entire picture, either for the artist or for the recipient.

If the boat is journey and passage it is so for both the female and male; both are figuratively depicted in the painting. In between them floats the enigmatic altar-boat, the female vessel combined with the sacrificial Christian symbol of the altar. However, the tabletop, the locus of the Last Supper, the memory of Christ's death for the redemption of humankind, is removed. The space is open, and from and around the legs, graceful leaves are growing, i.e. the promise of life is given. The dabs of gold enhance the sense not only of life, but that life is sacred, eternal. The reality of godforsakenness and death (chalice, lament) giving way ultimately to eternal life and hope (leaves in the altar, gold, the colour white) is strangely enhanced by what one might experience as rather unorthodox, provocative symbols, namely the sperm and vagina, i.e. the potential for the conception of new human life. Thus in the work suffering, pain, loss *and* the life-giving potential of sexual union and love merge with union in Christ through his godforsakenness, sacrifice, death *and* his resurrection into eternal life. This then may be the little blackbird's song, who – towards the top left – hovers over the scene. No doubt, it is loss, sadness and mourning that feature here; it is the Psalmist's cry from the bottom of his heart for his God. But the leaves elegant and beautiful, the sperms plentiful and the pervasive white hue cannot be overlooked. As the artist himself has commented on the work: In the midst, despite and in conclusion to suffering there is redemption.[194] In the midst of David's anguish and cry 'My God, my God, why have you forsaken me?' (Psalm 22:1), he praises his God. In the midst of Jesus' same cry of forsakenness on the Cross, his God is with him. In the midst of graced sexual ecstasy, death and rising is experienced in the 'temporary sense of loss of self-conscious individuality, ... the self's death in surrender to the other. Then the self is received back with new life, joyful and replenished from the divine plenitude itself'.[195] Graham's work manages to point to the God of love whom we experience not just in what is to come but in the here and now through human (sexual) love and in the moments of greatest despair.

Interestingly, Graham's allusion to the Eucharist and to sexual union in one image finds an echo in Nelson when he draws 'sacramental parallels' between the celebration of the Eucharist and 'acts of true sexual love'. As Nelson writes, in both events the body, 'joyful gratitude to God' and 'an eschatological dimension' of 'an earthly experience of the ultimate unity promised to all in the kingdom' can be experienced.[196]

If, at first glance, Graham's paintings predominantly seem to centre on suffering, dehumanisation and death, as a critic like Kuspit maintains, a second, more detailed look reveals and confirms what has been already concluded on Graham in Chapter Two. What one discovers both in his words and in his art is a faith and a theology which – partly through personal experience – in the face of the reality of abandonment, absurdity, human estrangement, destruction and the inevitability of suffering and death, affirms, through demythologising and mostly in hidden rather than open fashion, the ultimate presence of the incarnate, crucified and transcendent God who, through God's own suffering love, wills our salvation.

195. Nelson, op.cit., 255. On the life-giving aspect and the analogy between human sexual love and God's love for humankind cf. also Jack Dominian, *Proposals for a New Sexual Ethic* (London: Darton, Longman and Todd, 1977), 82-84.
196. Nelson, ibid.

IO. PATRICK HALL

10.1. The Tale is Told that Shall be Told (See page 188)

Introspection, inwardness, solitariness have been characteristic of Hall's life as a painter. As someone who has been drawn towards monasticism and who over the last decade has actively followed the Buddhist path, Hall views art as a journey and agrees that it can be seen as a form of prayer. In the 1980s and 1990s mythological, mystical, symbolical and implicit and explicit religious aspects have played a role in his painting. Hall's often awkward and difficult works gain their vitality through their tension and ambivalence, their sense of turmoil at the edge of disaster, at times touching the forbidden.[197] Painting for him is a kind of ritual, a ritual of self-discovery, a search for meaning, a possibility of personal transformation.[198]

Not only is the act of painting a type of ritual for the artist, but the subject matter and style of a work like 'The Tale is Told That Shall be Told' itself strongly suggests the atmosphere of ritual. An open book, which is also reminiscent of a rib cage, in striking pink-red dominates the painting. It is set off against a mostly grey-black background and is partly surrounded by a trace resembling a halo. A candelabra is placed on either side of the book with lit candles. Little red strokes resembling blood or fire emerge from the book. The bottom of the painting is decorated by a nervous zigzag line that creates a somewhat unsettling effect.

The whole composition exudes a rather mysterious atmosphere. The colours, the striking sensuous pink-red and the almost morbid black greatly enhance this feeling. The book, the 'shawl', the candelabra, although not with seven arms but with two, point to what the artist had in mind at the time, namely the 'consciously Jewish' aspect in the work.[199] Hall's interest in Jewish culture has been already mentioned; this work is an example of this interest. The painter was thinking of the shawl with which the Torah is held in synagogue worship. At the same time, its 'fringe' of red dabs, as Hall notes, can also be interpreted as conveying the idea of blood, which is meant as an allusion to the blood sacrifices of animals, like sheep, cattle, goats, pigeons and doves, carried out by the Israelites to effect atonement for the offerer (Lev 1-7).[200] For Hall the blood, moreover, refers to 'all the people who died

197. John Hutchinson, 'Foreword', in *Patrick Hall, Mountain,* cat. (Dublin: The Douglas Hyde Gallery/Belfast: The Ormeau Baths Gallery, 1995), 7.
198. Michèle C. Cone, 'Patrick Hall', in op.cit., 8-9.
199. Interview, 1.12.1995. 'Judaism has always been a religion that has interested me. Its absolutism interests me. And I think it's very beautiful.'
200. Christopher T. Begg, 'Sacrifice', in Metzger, Coogan, *The Oxford Companion to the Bible,* 666-667.

of the law', the Torah, as symbolised in the work through the book.[201] Hall may have had in mind all those who suffer death through capital punishment according to the laws of their country, and, in particular, the capital punishment in the Hebrew Scriptures for offences like murder, kidnapping, the striking or cursing of parents (Ex 21:12-14, Num 35:29-34).[202]

Further, in the context of the red strokes resembling flames of fire, the painter has pointed out that he was thinking also of the burning of books 'all through the ages', whether under 'Hitler, ... Clement of Alexandria or the censors in Ireland under de Valera.'[203] Finally the title of the work is the slightly altered first line of Bartok's opera *Bluebird's Castle:* 'The tale is old that shall be told'. For the artist its meaning implies 'a kind of dealing with fate and fatalism'.[204]

Not unlike Graham's work, this painting suggests more than it declares since a single narrative, a simple 'tale', is not given. Rather the symbols and the quasi biblical title evoke something of a 'religious epiphany',[205] a strong feeling of mystery, ritual worship, adoration, yet – due to the grey-black background – almost on the verge of touching on something sinister. It fosters the sense of ambivalence, i.e. the idea of Jewish ritual on the one hand, and, on the other hand, the bleak history of the burning of books, i.e. the violent infringement and 'death' of intellectual freedom through the ages. The book/or rib cage(?), i.e. a living, yet bleeding intellect/or 'body', created from the living intellect/body of the writer, enhances this feeling of ambivalence or even of darkness. Is this the tale that is told? Is it the story of the victims whose thoughts, whose theology even, dies precisely through those who perceive themselves as the ones responsible for the proper handing-on of (religious) truth, be it the Pharisees who would regard Christ as a blasphemer and hence his message as to be 'burned', or those who two thousand years later still silence theologians who pose some challenging, uncomfortable questions?[206] As pointed out in the previous chapter, Hall has emphasised the link between ethics and aesthetics. As he sees it, the artist's values are necessarily incorporated in his or her work.[207] His concern with book censoring in this painting strikingly reveals his conviction.

201. Interview, 1.12.1995.
202. Carl S. Ehrlich, 'Israelite Law', in Metzger, Coogan, op.cit., 422.
203. Interview, 1.12.1995. Why Hall should mention Clement of Alexandria here could only refer to the fact that some of that early theologian's writings were regarded as unorthodox, i.e. Clement was at the receiving end of censorship rather than a censor.
204. Ibid.
205. Cone describes the work as such, which this author would support. Cone, op.cit., 11.
206. In this context Küng's call for a 'truthful', 'critical', 'ecumenical' and 'free' theology' which can fulfill its task 'without administrative measures and sanctions' from church leaders is pertinent. Cf. H. Küng, *Grosse christliche Denker* (München: Piper, 1994), 260.
207. Cf. Chapter Two, section on Hall. Cf. also Hall quoted on this issue in Andrew Brighton,

Yet, apart from this socio-political aspect, there is the other, even more pronounced, dimension of the sense of (Jewish) religious ritual, worship, mystery and adoration. The lit candles at each side of the book and the halo suggest reverence for and worship of the written word. Here the painting assumes not only a Jewish aspect in its reference to Judaism as a religion of the book and the law, as an evocation of the Torah, but also a Protestant Christian one. In pictorial form one is reminded somewhat of the Reformers' insistence on the *sola scriptura,* the primary authority of the sacred biblical Word of God to be preached to the followers of Christ. The tale then might refer not only to the Torah, but also to the Hebrew and Christian Bible.

But one could take this even a step further. Hall does not give any definite indication either in the work itself or in the title, which book or tale is concerned. What is definite is the book's sacred aspect, indicated by the halo and the candles. It could be therefore any holy Scripture, whether Jewish, Christian, Muslim, Hindu, or Buddhist etc. In this way the painting becomes an ecumenical, multi-faith expression of reverence for the fundamental sacredness, mystery and disclosure of truth in all holy Scriptures. Such an interpretation is not only encouraged by the work itself but by Hall's adherence to Buddhism. Thus the tale may speak of and perhaps even advocate the idea of and belief in the universal divine, the holy centre, the divine Spirit revealed in all sacred writing.

Finally, however, the red dabs of blood or fire below the book cannot be ignored. Does this imply then that ultimately even the sacred written word must 'burn' or 'bleed' away before the ever-greater, unfathomable divine, before that ultimate reality or truth that words can never express?[208] Both the work and Hall's love of the apophatic theology of the mystics might support such a conclusion. On the other hand, the fire might lead to a different view. Instead of the 'burning away' of even the most sacred writing in the face of the always greater mystery, of the totally Other, this image could be seen as a symbol of divine epiphany, as the presence and revelation of God in sacred Scripture in the midst of the darkness of the human condition. In this way the meaning implied here would be that of the sacred book as the eternal, indestructible witness of the divine. This then is a powerful example of the sense of ambivalence evidenced in Hall's oeuvre that lends his work its strange, mysterious beauty.

'Introduction', in *Patrick Hall, 'Heart' and other recent paintings,* cat. (London: The Pentonville Gallery, 1987), (no p.).
208. This rather obvious truth and apophatic statement has been stressed by mystics and in the context of inter-faith dialogue by someone like Bede Griffiths, whose writing Hall has read and admired. Cf. B. Griffiths, *The Marriage of East and West* (London: Collins, 1982), 101.

10.2. Mountain (See page 189)

Mountains are depicted in a number of Hall's works, notably in a series of several large canvases painted in the early 1990s. In comparison to his other paintings the compositions are strikingly simplified, the iconography limited. Along a vertical and horizontal axis, forming a kind of cross, two triangular shapes are placed one above the other. The lower one, which confronts the viewer and leads almost like a pathway into the painting, is a mountain-heap of skulls. In the distance a horizontal dark-brown line emerges with some small, almost black, vertical strokes, the meaning of which cannot be clearly ascertained. They may be humans or simply posts in a field. Above, the mountain rises monumentally, its apex close to the top of the canvas. The range of colours is also severely limited to pervading earthen browns, with occasional lighter ochre interspersed and light brown and beige in the skulls.

The reality of death is central in the 'Mountain' series. In the present canvas, with its huge mass of skulls, it probably finds its starkest and strongest expression. The paintings are thus intensely eschatological, dealing, as they do, with the inescapable and only certain fact of the finality of earthly, especially human, life. Suffering and death is a central theme in twentieth-century art, and even from the limited number of painters and works analysed in this book, it is obvious that this also applies to Irish art. This theme, as has been shown, is apparent in several of the painters, i.e. Yeats, Middleton, Dillon, Graham and Hall.

Cone, in her commentary on the 'Mountain' series, notes that it 'is inseparable from the dirge of AIDS'.[209] The painter himself has not mentioned this sickness as having influenced his choice of subject matter in particular. Still, as in the previous work, his ethical concern is evidenced once more when he states in relation to the skulls: 'Everywhere you look – Cambodia, the Balkans, Rwanda – these images are coming at you all the time. Humans create death.'[210] Certainly, in the heap of skulls the bleak reality of death caused by murder, violence and mass suffering confronts the viewer in no uncertain terms. The preoccupation with death has been a constant in Hall's work, yet for him the presence of skulls does not mean something negative. Rather, he stresses that death simply needs to be acknowledged as a fact: 'Most 20th century art is about death. The inclination is to run away from it, but we should turn back and see what it's about. Life comes from death. And to me it's about pulling through, it's about survival.'[211] Strangely this work on the stark fact of the finality of life may ultimately reveal something of Hall's idea of life arising from death.

209. Cone, op.cit., 8.
210. Hall quoted in Aidan Dunne, 'The deaths of a century', (exh. review), *Sunday Tribune*, 25.6.1995.
211. Ibid.

From the mountain heap of skulls, of death, the eye is led upwards to the simple 'archetypal' triangular outline of a mountain. In the religious symbolism in both East and West mountains have played a significant role throughout the ages.[212] Some are held as places of vision and revelation, as dwelling places or geographical manifestations of the divine, some are even revered as being central to the stability, permanence and order of the cosmos, as an *axis mundi* 'linking heaven and earth and anchoring the cardinal directions'.[213] In the Bible several hundred references appear in relation to mountains. Moses encountered Yahweh face to face on Mount Sinai, and there God appeared to the Hebrews like a fire (Ex 24:9-18). In this context one is also reminded of the Psalmist who lifts his 'eyes to the hills' from where 'help will come from the Lord, who made heaven and earth' (Ps 121:1-2). Other mountains like Horeb, Gerizim, Tabor, Moriah and Zion, the dwelling place of God, the firm foundation of Jerusalem, are to be mentioned in this context. Jesus went on mountains to pray and to be alone (Mt 14:23; Mk 6:46; Lk 6:12). He was transfigured on a mountain, possibly Mount Hermon, before Peter, John and James (Mt 17:1-8; Mk 9:2-8; Lk 9:28-36), where Elijah and Moses appeared to them, and God's voice – as on Mount Sinai – came to them from a cloud. The mountains' meaning of and association with the revelation of the sacred is in some way obvious, since not only are they material manifestations of the grandeur of creation but their top and height offer both a 'vision of heaven and a broad perspective on earth', a sense of being closer to the heavenly divine.[214] Particularly relevant for our discussion is the fact that mountains are also seen both as giving life as well as abodes of the dead or as paths to heaven for the dead. In the East they are often regarded as the resting-places of the souls of the dead.

Hall himself has referred to the meaning of mountains as signifying 'energy, negative and positive, volcanic eruptions, loneliness, solitude, freedom. They are all kinds of primary things'.[215] Moreover, he is particularly aware of the sacred and mysterious aspect of mountains.

There are two elements then which merge in the work, the fact of human death and the archetypal, sacred symbol of the mountain as the place, manifestation and revelation of the divine. What may one conclude thus from a theological perspective? Naturally the answer must be a tentative one. One wonders whether Hall had in mind the idea of mountain as *axis mundi* since the mountains in the works are arranged along a horizontal and vertical axis

---

212. Cf. Diana L. Eck, 'Mountains', in Mircea Eliade, (ed.), *The Encyclopedia of Religion*, vol. 10 (New York: Macmillan, 1987), 130.
213. Ibid.
214. Ibid., 132.
215. Interview, 1.12.1995.

which alludes thus to the cosmic dimension of the mountain linking earth and heaven and the cardinal directions. However, the two mountains in the present painting each imply different meanings. While the upper, natural one, links earth and heaven, the lower one, a man-made heap of skulls, points from the 'underworld' of death to the cosmic mountain. There is a clear directional pull in this work, not downwards into death but upwards from death to the mountain peak and hence towards heaven. The final message in Hall's work is not death but the possibility of death overcome, the dead raised into eternal life. The strokes of bright colour, i.e. of light, eternal light, towards the mountaintop, enhance that message.

Hall has noted that when he came across the Buddhist idea of emptiness he realised that death was a 'passing thing', that it is emptiness which replaces death.[216] For him the 'Mountain' series then is a contemplation of emptiness. What from a Buddhist perspective may be viewed as emptiness, bliss, peace, i.e. nirvana, finds a kind of Christian parallel in the idea of salvation and life in the eschaton, even if, of course, the Christian idea of salvation is an emphatically theological, christocentric one of eternal life in God. Interestingly, Hall uses neither specifically Buddhist nor Christian iconography but the universal symbol of a mountain, the mountain of the dead which points to and will be finally taken into the cosmic mountain of emptiness or heavenly eternity. Thus, not unlike the previous work, this painting may speak to people of various faiths. Despite the naked, unequivocal reality of death, the painting, ultimately does not create a vision of unredeemable darkness but exudes rather an awe-inspiring presence of sacred mystery and sublime transcendence. The threatening 'grandeur' and bleak fact of – possibly violent, evil and unnatural – death through war and disease confronts the recipient, yet the towering presence of the cosmic mountain seems to imply that death will lead into the eternal divine. In this way the painting conveys a not-immediately-apparent glimmer of salvific hope.

216. G. Thiessen, Personal notes from a public conversation between John Hutchinson and Hall on the occasion of his exhibition 'Mountain' in the Douglas Hyde Gallery, Dublin, 28.6.1995.

10.3. Burning Mountain III (See page 190)

Another work from the 'Mountain' series is 'Burning Mountain III', painted a year after the previous canvas examined. Here a more emphatic sense of death as a 'passing thing', as Hall puts it, of redemption and mystery becomes apparent. However, if there was in himself a development towards a more salvific vision, it appears to have been an unconscious rather than a conscious process.[217]

The present painting is a good deal brighter in colouring than 'Mountain'. The canvas exudes a bright, meditative feeling. In the foreground, instead of a heap of skulls, a strange candelabra of undulating, black lines is placed with seven black lit candles with white flames. A sense of 'empty' space is created between the candelabra and the mountain rising in the distance, as also in the area above the mountain. The red flame of fire on the mountain top and the smaller flames along the mountain, as also the lit candles in the foreground, enliven the otherwise tranquil work.

Again the viewer is presented with some age-old (quasi) religious symbols, mountain, fire and a candelabra with lit candles. The artist relates that his painting of burning mountains was inspired by a memory of his youth of the burning of fields after the harvest on the hills. Thus, as Cone has observed, the works seen 'in this light connect with myths of regeneration from East and West'.[218] Fire here does not mean merely death but the possibility of new energy and life. The painter himself has mentioned the purifying and religious aspect of fire: 'The Zoroastrians worshipped fire. God was in fire in the burning bush. Fire is cleansing also ... It's a purifier. And it's energy.'[219] Here also Hall's idea of the divine as being essentially energy comes to mind. Indeed, there are a few hundred biblical references to fire, often in the context of sacrificial offerings (e.g. Lev 1:7-9; 6:12-13) as also in theophanies (e.g. Ex 3:2; Ps 50:3; 97:3), in the appearance of the Holy Spirit at Pentecost (Acts 2:3), and as an expression of God's wrath and punishment for the transgressions of God's people (e.g. Am 1:4-2:5).[220] Apart from the meaning of fire and of mountains, which was already explored with regard to the previous painting 'Mountain', one more symbol, the menorah, or lampstand, should be mentioned before drawing some final suggestions on the present work. The menorah, which combined the functions of lampstand and lamp, was used in the wilderness tabernacle and in the Jerusalem temples.[221] Made up of a

217. G. Thiessen, Personal notes ..., 28.6.1995.
218. Cone, op.cit., 8.
219. Interview, 1.12.1995.
220. K. Koch, *Reclams Bibellexikon*, 144.
221. Judith R. Baskin, 'Menorah', in *The Oxford Companion to the Bible*, 512.

central shaft and three branches coming forth on each side, it has seven
receptacles for lamps. Its shape, reminiscent of a tree, the Tree of Life, and
hence associated with life-giving divine powers, it served in Hebrew shrines
and sanctuaries as a symbol of 'God's residence', assuring God's availability to
the people.[222] Except for 2 Kgs 4:10, where the lampstand is described as part
of the furniture in a room, all biblical mentions of the menorah refer to it as
an object made of gold 'used in sacred contexts'.[223] After 70 AD it became an
enduring Jewish religious and national symbol.

Once again Hall thus makes a reference to Jewish religion and tradition,
although obviously interpreted very much in a personal manner, as the
menorah as such is not depicted but rather the seven candles which crown
and allude to it. The symbolic significance of numbers is evidenced throughout the Bible, seven being an auspicious one connoting completeness and
perfection, as it is the sum of three, i.e. God, heaven, and four, i.e. the created
world with its four seasons, four wind directions.[224] Why Hall should replace
the sacred, golden menorah with a black wire-like mesh on which the candles are placed is not clear. Is it the barbed wire of war or a type of snake, i.e.
evil, which is finally overcome or transcended by the life-giving light of the
divine? Is it thus another hint of what has been repeatedly asserted about
Hall's work, namely the sense of ambivalence in much of his painting, in this
case the sacred, life-giving aspect of the lit candles joined to the black, sinister, morbid candelabra? Whatever about its intended meaning, this strange
object greatly contributes to the mysterious atmosphere which the whole
canvas evokes. The unusual menorah seems to give the work the impression
almost of an icon – as icons are often surrounded by candles – or the feeling
of an Early Renaissance altarpiece. Except for the dark, enigmatic candelabra,
death, as in the other work, is no longer imaged. Rather the lit candles seen
in conjunction with the fire on the mountain create an overall sense of quiet
adoration, worship, mysterious contemplation and mediation of the presence
of the sacred. It seems as if the seven candles, which are normally lit inside a
temple and now are transferred from their usual religious setting into the
outside before a mountain, convey to the viewer the worship of the divine

222. Carol Meyers, 'Lampstand', in David Noel Freedman, (ed.), *The Anchor Bible
     Dictionary*, vol. 4 (New York, etc.: Doubleday, 1992), 142.
223. Ibid., 141.
224. David H. van Daalen, 'Number Symbolism', in *The Oxford Companion to the Bible*, 561-
     562. A few examples where the number seven plays an important and always positive,
     role: God completed God's work on the seventh day, the Israelites celebrated their great
     festivals for seven days, a sabbath year was declared every seven years, the seven spirits of
     God represent the seven archangels or the Holy Spirit (Rev 1:4), the seven churches con-
     note the whole church (Rev 1:20).

not only *in* the sanctuary but of the whole of creation through the mountain. The mountain becomes the symbol of the universal temple and of creation; therefore the whole of creation attains sacramental status. Whether the Easter fire or Moses at the burning bush, whether Jewish ritual or the mountain Meru, sacred to many Asians, the work may be 'read' as an affirmation that God reveals Godself both outside in the grandeur of nature and inside the holy temple, i.e. in all creation. Or, to put it slightly differently, it is perhaps from the temple, from the menorah, that light radiates out and thereby signifies God's presence in the world. In this context, it is significant also to note that a visitor to the 'Mountain' exhibition in 1995 at the Douglas Hyde Gallery, Dublin, commented that she felt, while viewing the works, as if she had entered a church.[225]

There is, moreover, much 'empty' space in the painting, and this contributes to the sense of inexpressible transcendence glimpsed in the immanent, or immanence, pointing to and merging with the transcendent. The 'empty' space between the menorah and the mountain furthermore might imply a sense of journey, the distance to be travelled by us from the here into the eschaton of full communion with God.

In this work then, Hall's preoccupation with death has given way to a more redemptive, doxological vision. Fundamentally 'Burning Mountain III' evokes a feeling of silent awe, of wonder and mystery.

225. G. Thiessen, Personal notes ..., 28.6.1995.

SUMMARY

In this chapter three paintings by each artist were examined in detail so as to explore spiritual, religious and/or theological aspects disclosed in the images. I now want to briefly look back at Chapter Two and then summarise the findings on each artist. The final section in this chapter will outline some of the wider theological aspects that emerge from the interpretations of the thirty works of art.

In the second chapter the aim was to ascertain and discuss what the artists themselves have said about their faith, their ideas on the divine, on the church and its relationship with the contemporary artist, how their faith and spirituality has found expression in their work etc. Critics and art-historical literature were taken into account, especially for the artists who are no longer alive. It was possible to show links, often by way of correlation and analogy, between the thought of theologians and the ideas/works of the artists. A remarkable diversity of concurrences appeared, ranging, as they do, from Irenaeus to recent liberation and feminist theologies. The disclosure and articulation of these links, between the artists' religious ideas and a manifestation of those in their art, as also between the artists' ideas/works and theological thought, exemplifies and proves what recent writers on aesthetics argue, namely that an analogy exists between thought and artistic expression.[226] In the conclusion of the previous chapter it was finally possible to show divergences, parallels and aspects common to all ten artists with regard to the spiritual and/or theological dimensions in their lives, thought and work.

Findings on Each Artist
Fundamentally, the theological interpretations of the works of art largely correspond to, and at times expand through more specific details in particular paintings, what was established in the previous chapter on each of the artists. On the whole the religious ideas and spiritual dimensions apparent in the lives and thought of the artists are reflected in their work which is evidenced in their choice of subject matter, painterly styles and handling of colour.

While Jellett's Christian faith, her adherence to communal worship, her absolute 'religious' devotion to her art, her choice of biblical themes and 'Thomist' aesthetics were already ascertained in Chapter Two, the interpretation of the works also showed a definite, perhaps surprising – if not necessarily consciously intended – feminist aspect in the rendering of her subject

---

226. Cf. Günter Rombold, 'Schönheit und Wahrheit im Widerstreit', in Schwebel, Mertin, (eds.), *Bilder und ihre Macht*, 30.

matter, i.e. her androgynous Christ. Balance, harmony and radiance, those qualities which Aquinas deemed necessary for an object to be perceived as beautiful are manifested in all three works. All of them are biblically inspired, revealing, as they do, creation theological ('Man and Woman'), mariological ('Man and Woman', 'Madonna and Child'), christological (all three works, especially 'The Ninth Hour'), eschatological ('The Ninth Hour'), and soteriological (especially 'The Ninth Hour') aspects, which allowed for more complex theological readings than one might anticipate at first glance.

Yeats' humanist and social concern, the deeply eschatological dimension in his late works and his Christian faith were noted in the second chapter, and the works examined sufficiently witness these dimensions. The rather subjective application of biblical titles and subject matter to an Irish context in his paintings which *thereby* assume a more universal dimension is rooted in personal experience intertwined with a romantic outlook and a deep sense of affection for his fellow humans and subjects. Existentialist, visionary, at times melancholic, the works express the horror of war, violence and murder ('Grief', 'Tinkers' Encampment, The Blood of Abel'). Yet Yeats provides glimpses of hope (all three works), and he affirms, even if more indirectly than openly, ultimate salvation through the light of Christ ('There is No Night'). It seems right to argue thus that his art provides hints of the artist's faith, unconventional as it may have been. The strong sense of freedom and the non-dogmatic element (no religious subject matter as such) in 'There is No Night', moreover, might be signs that for Yeats human freedom and Christian faith essentially belong together.

Louis le Brocquy's search for essence, for that which lies 'behind' matter, and his sense of the presence of a profound mystery find expression in the works under discussion, especially in the 'Ecce Homo' with its pronounced aspect of simultaneous concealment and revelation. What comes perhaps as a slight surprise is the fact that the artist, despite his repeatedly stated agnosticism, his doubt about a personal God, has, in fact, painted a few works which deal with decidedly christological-soteriological themes, such as 'Lazarus' and 'Ecce Homo'. The paintings exude, moreover, an eschatological, transcendent atmosphere, a feeling of time and timelessness ('Ecce Homo', 'Procession with Lilies IV'), of actuality and eternity, of what is to come anticipated in the 'here and now'. These paintings by le Brocquy serve as examples that contemporary artists, who for the most part are not involved in church life, produce works which are theologically significant, in fact, often far more significant than much of what is commonly perceived as 'sacred art' made for places of worship.

Gerard Dillon, brought up in a strongly Catholic and nationalist environment, never seems to have 'overcome' his Catholic background, even as an adult who had given up church attendance. I concluded in the previous chapter that it was perhaps only in his art that Dillon could still allude to his faith. The analysis of three of his works seems to support this conclusion. At first glance none of the works examined show any obvious religious, Christian dimensions either in their contents or titles. Yet, the images allow rather complex theological 'readings'. Deeply personal and universal at the same time through their symbolism, a strongly eschatological strain became apparent in 'The Brothers' and in 'Entertaining Friends'. Eucharistic aspects emerged in 'Fish Eaters' and in 'Entertaining Friends', as well as a trinitarian dimension in the latter work. It is the symbolist 'language' which perhaps more than anything else contributes to the religious aspect in all three works.

Colin Middleton's panentheist faith, his humanist convictions, his numerous canvases with biblical themes, his Protestant background which manifested itself in his rejection of hierarchical church organisation, in his independent thinking and in his admiration for the Quakers, were explored in Chapter Two. The paintings considered reflect some of these aspects. All three works are biblically inspired and are painted in an individual, contemporary, even challenging and, at least, partly unorthodox style, especially the theologically rich 'Christ Androgyne'. Of the three paintings two deal with Christ's ministry and his death on the Cross. An emphatically feminist theological dimension, arising, I would argue, from Middleton's deeply humanist convictions, from his use of the female archetype throughout his oeuvre and perhaps also from his perception of the divinity of all humans, is revealed in both 'Give me to Drink' and especially in 'Christ Androgyne'. What strikes the recipient is the profound sense of empathy and compassion felt in all three works. It is this dimension which makes them not only remarkable works of art with religious subjects, but unusual, moving testaments of faith.

Patrick Collins, worldly 'monk' and mystic, believed all art to be essentially transcendental. In this artist a strong belief in the divine being present in all creation mingled with a questioning, yet simple, childlike faith. Collins, not unlike Dillon, kept away from communal worship, yet he never quite transcended his Catholic background, and it seems to be in his art – which included several canvases with biblical subjects – more perhaps than in his words that his faith found expression. The analysed paintings with both their christological ('Stations of the Cross') and panentheist aspects ('Hy Brazil', 'A Place with Stones') very much confirm these concerns. A romantic, poetic imagination with reverence for the Celtic past and the feeling of the sublime and of the transcendent in nature are present in the latter works, while the former is a homily in paint and personal expression of trust in Christ.

Tony O'Malley, inward and contemplative, has much in common with

Collins in his profound sense of vocation, his nature spirituality and mystical vision. The christological aspect in his faith and work, particularly in his 'Good Friday' paintings, were noted in Chapter Two. While the first of the two 'Good Friday' paintings examined conveys something of the solemnity of the event, the other, in brighter, more joyful, colours, without the Cross and tiny details of the instruments of the Passion, evokes not so much the suffering of Christ but rather points, if only indirectly, to the resurrection, to salvation. Eschatological anticipation through visual ecstasy encountered in certain abstract works of art (Schwebel) is transparent in 'Shadowy Carvings of an Ancient Execution, Good Friday' and especially in 'Earth Lyre' and, to a lesser extent, also in 'Good Friday'. There are then striking creation theological and christological-soteriological aspects in O'Malley's oeuvre, which as a whole sings a theology of praise.

Scott, as has been shown, holds an interesting, somewhat curious, place among the ten painters due to the fact that he sees himself as an atheist/ agnostic. Moreover, unlike most of the other artists, he has received several church commissions. His abstract canvases – like Jellett's cubist paintings – reflect something of the Thomist ideals of beauty and are experienced as rather meditative and transcendent works. It became obvious that the three works considered exude not only 'something' spiritual, but that it is possible to interpret them in more specifically theological terms, even if the fact that they are abstract calls in the last instance for silence before, rather than for articulation of, what is rendered in the image. The harmonious, quiet, partly gilded works do not speak of the predicaments of the human in the twentieth century but convey - somewhat like fifteenth century altarpieces – a presence of the sacred, of redemption and serenity.

Graham's religious and sexual subject matter, his admiration for masters like Piero della Francesca, his demythologising in his emphatic search for truth in his art and life, his stress on personal experience as the foundation of art, his continuing interest in theological questions and hard-kept faith through personal suffering, were discussed in the previous chapter. In the analysis of three of his works these dimensions are expressed and intensified. The monumental 'Scenes from the Life of Christ' reveal both his knowledge and, to some extent, his reworking of traditional Christian iconography. In his subjective, expressionist approach, presenting as it does two unusual Christian subjects in (modern) art, the artist intended to stress the radical humanity in the God-Man in 'The Agony in the Garden'. At the same time he affirms the continuity between the suffering and risen Jesus in his choice and depiction of 'The Resurrection'. Graham makes much use of religious and sexual symbolism in both 'The Lark in the Morning' and 'The Blackbird Suite'. This and an excerpt from Psalm 22 allowed for complex interpretations, which revealed his existentialist concern with death and suffering and his celebration of the human body, especially of sexuality, i.e. his essential desire for and sense of wholeness. In particular, it became clear that despite the darkness and seeming hopelessness present in much of Graham's works, his last word is not, as a critic like Kuspit has commented, nihilist, but faith, hope and resurrection arising in the midst of and overcoming death and despair. In the powerful, multifaceted, often symbol-filled paintings of this artist, pronounced christological aspects are thus disclosed, including eucharistic imagery and seemingly 'hidden' soteriological dimensions.

Patrick Hall's profoundly contemplative, inward character, his idea of God as mystery, his preoccupation with death in his art, his stress of aesthetic and moral values being revealed in art, his interest in mysticism and his adherence to Buddhism were ascertained in Chapter Two. The paintings examined witness and deepen most of these aspects. What is perhaps a little surprising are his allusions to Jewish faith and ritual – rather than to Buddhist imagery, as one might expect – which are expressed in 'The Tale is Told that Shall be Told' and, to a lesser extent, in 'Burning Mountain III'. A deeply eschatological strain of the stark reality of death is obvious in 'Mountain', yet the feeling of passage towards and the revelation of the ultimate divine are present in all three works. These paintings body forth an awe-inspiring sense of mystery; the mountain, the book and the candelabra as paths to the eternal other, to the eternal logos. The universal, (quasi) religious symbolism as well as the ambivalence encountered in the paintings evoke not only the possibility of contradictory interpretations but also of an ecumenical multi-faith 'reading'. Without being limited to any particular religion his images are thus in a very real sense spiritual, religious and mystical-apophatic.

CONCLUSION: EMERGING BIBLICAL, THEOLOGICAL
AND RELIGIOUS ASPECTS AND THEMES

Painted over a period of almost sixty years between 1937 and 1995, fifteen of the thirty paintings discussed contain explicit biblical-Christian references in their titles and/or subject matter.[227] Six works display implicit biblical-Christian references in titles and/or subject matter.[228] Nine paintings reveal implicit wider spiritual, religious and/or humanist dimensions without

227. Jellett's 'Madonna and Child', 'The Ninth Hour'; Yeats' 'Tinkers' Encampment, The Blood of Abel'; all three works by both le Brocquy and Middleton; Collins' 'Stations of the Cross'; O'Malley's 'Good Friday', 'Shadowy Carvings of an Ancient Execution, Good Friday'; all three works by Graham.
228. Jellett's 'Man and Woman'; Yeats' 'There is No Night'; Dillon's 'Fish Eaters', 'Entertaining Friends'; Scott's 'Chinese Landscape'; Hall's 'The Tale is Told that Shall be Told'.

Christian iconography.[229] Except for Scott and Hall, Christian subject matter or references are disclosed in the examined works of all the artists. Hall's canvases, however, contain allusions to the Hebrew Bible.

The biblical references and subjects in the works are drawn from the Book of Genesis ('Man and Woman', 'Tinkers' Encampment: The Blood of Abel', 'Jacob Wrestling with the Angel') and especially from the gospels, i.e. Jesus' birth ('Madonna and Child', 'Nativity' from 'Scenes from the Life of Christ'), his ministry ('Give Me to Drink', 'Lazarus'), his death and resurrection ('Ninth Hour', 'Christ Androgyne', 'Stations of the Cross', 'Good Friday', 'Shadowy Carvings ...', 'Agony in the Garden' and 'The Resurrection' from 'Scenes from the Life of Christ'). Here the pictorial allusions to the Eucharist which are present in several paintings ('Fish Eaters', 'Entertaining Friends', 'The Lark in the Morning', 'The Blackbird Suite') are also to be mentioned. Further, an excerpt from the Psalms ('The Blackbird Suite') and a reference to the Book of Revelation ('There is No Night') were found.

The image of Christ, in particular his suffering and redemptive death, is thus the dominant biblical-Christian subject depicted. If one compares the Scripture themes revealed in the present works with those of other twentieth century European painters in Schwebel's *Die Bibel in der Kunst, Das 20. Jahrhundert*,[230] a remarkable concurrence becomes obvious as the choice of works is most similar. In Schwebel's book themes from Genesis form the large part of subjects from the Hebrew Bible, while the image of Christ, especially the Passion, not only dominates with regard to New Testament themes but is the most prevalent subject amongst the 48 works shown. There are further two works which pertain to the Psalms and three which refer to the Apocalypse. Apart from these only two other works are included which refer to other writings (Joel and Daniel). Taking into account the limited number of artists and works of art analysed in our study, one might hence tentatively conclude that in modern Irish works of art with biblical-Christian subject matter the choice of themes very much reflects the wider sphere of modern European art.

The christological dimension in the works is central. Naturally, this does not come as a surprise as the Christ event is, of course, the mystery of our faith, and has concerned theologians and artists – be they writers, musicians, sculptors, painters or film makers – throughout the centuries. Indeed, of all Christian themes treated in modern art, (sometimes rather stark, expressive)

229. Yeats' 'Grief'; Dillon's 'The Brothers'; Collins' 'Hy Brazil', 'A Place with Stones'; O'Malley's 'Earth Lyre'; Scott's 'Gold Painting 48', 'Gold Painting 56'; Hall's 'Mountain', 'Burning Mountain III'.

230. Cf. Schwebel, *Die Bibel in der Kunst, Das 20. Jahrhundert* (Stuttgart: Deutsche Bibel-gesellschaft, 1994).

images of Christ suffering are the most prevalent. As mentioned before, this can be explained by the human predicament in the twentieth century, marked by experience and awareness of universal suffering and death through world wars, starvation, the atom bomb etc.

The christological and other theological aspects in the works will be discussed in more detail in the concluding chapter.

The christological theme leads to two other aspects which were abundantly noted in the analysis, namely the eschatological-soteriological dimensions. Death, suffering, including the death of Christ, are encountered in every artist's work examined, except Scott. However, a sense of hope and salvation, whether in more Christian terms or in a wider, less defined, implied manner, is apparent – sometimes just in small glimpses and allusions – in all the paintings, which deal with the reality of death, suffering and despair (except perhaps for Dillon's 'The Brothers').

The unity of creation and redemption is witnessed in the Hebrew Scriptures, in the gospels and in the history of Christian theology, which itself is based on the triple foundation of creation, covenant and universal salvation. Correspondingly, in the works a pronounced panentheist dimension, a sense of the mystery, goodness and beauty of creation is present. The tension between as well as the merging of the 'here' and the 'not yet', of immanence and transcendence, of creation and salvation, is revealed particularly in the works of O'Malley, Collins and also in Scott and Hall. In the (semi-) abstract paintings of Collins and especially of O'Malley this creation-soteriological dimension climaxes frequently into doxology, affirming, as it does, Schwebel's assertion of the possibility of anticipation of the eschaton in art.

Another aspect that was noted in some of the works is moral concern. Yeats' and Middleton's expression of their rejection of war, Graham's pictorial rendering of a holistic notion of sexuality, and Hall's allusion to censorship and mass death exemplify this ethical dimension.

Finally, many of the works are revelatory of and invite meditation and contemplation. This is particularly felt in the encounter with the more abstract works of Collins and O'Malley, in which the presence of mystery and transcendence of the Creator is ultimately perceived through silence, and in Hall's mysterious, symbolist depictions. It is also felt in the reception of the 'Thomist' beauty of both Jellett's colourful, semi-cubist paintings and Scott's abstract, ordered, hieratic works.

What emerges thus from the interpretation of these thirty paintings – which, of course, represent only a very small number of works from the oeuvre of the painters – is a remarkable richness of spiritual, religious and theological dimensions, some of which are not immediately obvious. The interpretations, some less complicated, especially with regard to the more narrative works (e.g. 'The Stations of the Cross', 'Jacob Wrestling with the Angel'), others rather complex, particularly the more abstract and symbolist images (e.g. 'Christ Androgyne', 'The Lark in the Morning'), reveal a colourful, wide, sometimes challenging theological palette. In this context it is important to remember that none of the thirty works was ever commissioned for nor hung in places of worship, but rather – as modern art on the whole – they were produced solely through individual choice, based in the subjective approach of the artist. Thereby personal experience often plays a significant role; this is sensed particularly in the analysed works of Yeats, Dillon, Middleton, Collins, O'Malley, Graham and Hall.

Not only has it been possible to ascertain a considerable variety of theological aspects, but further, in a few instances, the works may be perceived as moving, at times surprising and/or hidden testaments of faith, particularly with Yeats, Middleton, Collins, O'Malley, Graham and possibly Dillon.

Taking into account what has been established both in this and in the previous chapter, I would finally argue that, except for Scott perhaps, all artists examined have lived with a sense of ultimate reality, of mystery and of the transcendent divine, or, at least, an awareness of a meta-physical 'essence' (le Brocquy). Moreover, it seems that, apart from le Brocquy, Scott and Hall, all painters have had faith in the God incarnate in Jesus Christ, whether openly adhered to or implicitly acknowledged in their lives, words and/or works. However, this is not to imply that the greatness and the theological/Christian significance of their works are dependent on and proportionate to their fervour of faith and piety. Rather, if one desires to explain why these paintings are theologically interesting, challenging and convincing, it is in imagination, creativity, deeply felt experience, vision, personal concern, artistic skill, intellectual openness and freedom, search for truth, and also in spirituality, enquiring faith and theological insight, that one might find some answers.

CHAPTER IV

Conclusion: Towards a Theology of Art

By way of conclusion to this study on the theological dimensions in modern Irish visual art as exemplified by ten painters, I want to discuss several aspects which have arisen and are relevant not only with regard to what has been established during the course of this book but also with regard to the wider field of interdisciplinary research on theology and visual art. In an age of pluralism, which is as evident in theology as in other spheres of life, contemporary theologians, like, for example, Tracy, Jeanrond and McFague, are much concerned with hermeneutical and methodological questions. The role and range of human experience reflected in present theological thought, especially of those on the margins, contributes to the variety of theologies and theological approaches in our epoch. If, as Gilkey observes, theology's task is to understand the totality of contemporary experience in terms of Christian symbols,[1] the issue is not only what to understand but the very process or method of understanding, of interpretation. This is relevant as a search for truth still lies at the heart of theology, even, and one might suggest, despite, the deconstructivist critique of postmodernism, which doubts the concept and possibility of truth itself.[2] An analysis of the method adopted in this book of relating theological and artistic concerns therefore will be a central point of discussion in this final chapter.

Further, the role of the imagination, i.e. religious and aesthetic imagination, will be considered. The creative imagination is essential to both the work of the artist and the theologian in its power to perceive something of the transcendent in new ways, to disclose reality and ultimate reality, the always already and the not yet. It is the creation and re-creation of images,

1. Langdon Gilkey, *Reaping the Whirlwind, A Christian Interpretation of History* (New York: The Seabury Press, 1976), 134.
2. Cf. W. Jeanrond, *Text and Interpretation as Categories of Theological Thinking*, trans. Thomas J. Wilson (Dublin: Gill and Macmillan, 1988), xviii. Cf. Tracy, *The Analogical Imagination*, 67-68. For a brief introduction to hermeneutical theology cf. Francis Schüssler Fiorenza, 'Systematic Theology: Tasks and Methods', in F. Schüssler Fiorenza, John P. Galvin, (eds.), *Systematic Theology, Roman Catholic Perspectives* (Dublin: Gill and Macmillan, 1992), 43-47. Cf. Michael Paul Gallagher, S.J., 'Post-Modernity: Friend or Foe?', in E.G. Cassidy, (ed.), *Faith and Culture in the Irish Context* (Dublin: Veritas, 1996), 74-75.

which forms one of the vital links between theological and artistic existence. Moreover, while the role of the imagination and of images in theology is increasingly recognised, especially by theologians like Tillich, Rahner, McFague, Schwebel, Dillenberger, Lynch, Burch Brown, Mackey and, indeed, notably Daly, O'Hanlon,[3] Lane, McDonagh in the Irish context, its fundamental significance for doing theology still deserves more appreciation and acknowledgement.

Finally, the theological dimensions which became apparent in the works of art examined will be discussed in more detail so as to perceive and properly acknowledge the relevance of the concrete, 'unsystematic' image in the context of systematic theology.

A short appreciation of theology in and through visual art as a holistic theology of the spiritual-sensuous will conclude this chapter.

CONTEXT AND INTERPRETATION

Doing theology through art, the genuine dialogue between and the aim of converging theology and modern art, is not, and cannot be, one in which art serves as the lesser partner, as *ancilla theologiae*. Rather the work of art and the artist as an independent agent and equal discussion partner must be recognised.[4] The issue, for this writer as also for others who have written on twentieth-century visual art and theology in recent years, is not the work of art used as a means to illustrate biblical-Christian truths as, for example, happens in much church art. What is of interest here and what has been my own point of departure is an appreciation of the manifestation of theological-spiritual dimensions in the autonomous, so-called 'profane' work of art and how these aspects stimulate further and concur with theological and Christian concerns.[5] It is only in this way that real dialogue between and integration of contemporary art into theology can take place.

---

3. Cf. Gerard O'Hanlon, S.J., 'An Image of God for Ireland Today', *Milltown Studies,* no. 21 (Spring 1988), 13-27, at 13. O'Hanlon argues that images and symbols express better 'our operative, spontaneous perception of that which is ultimate', i.e. God, than 'more exclusively intellectual terms' such as 'idea' or 'concept'.

4. Cf. Schwebel who argues similarly when he writes: 'Nur wenn beide Seiten [Theologie und Kunst] bereit sind, dem anderen zu bestätigen, dass seine Aufrichtigkeit in der Suche nach Wahrheit um keinen Punkt geringer ist als die eigene, kann es zu einem Gespräch kommen.' Schwebel, 'Wahrheit der Kunst - Wahrheit des Evangeliums, Einer Anregung Eberhard Jüngels folgend und widersprechend', in A. Mertin, H. Schwebel, (eds.), *Kirche und moderne Kunst,* 143-144.

5. This, as demonstrated in Chapter One, is both Schwebel's and Tillich's approach, even if Tillich's actual method was problematic. Theologians such as Günter Rombold, John Dillenberger and Friedhelm Mennekes, amongst others, are also to be mentioned in this context. For an expansive discussion of the hermeneutics for a theology of modern

The Contemporary Context of Pluralism

While an elaborate discussion on post-modernity transcends the scope of my discussion, I consider it necessary to briefly reflect on the pluralist postmodern situation, which provides the context for contemporary theology, hence for a theology of the image. In stating that this theology is to be viewed in the context of the post-modern situation immediately presents one with a problem in that the word 'post-modern' itself is elusive, *en vogue* and used in many different senses. However, since the early 1960s the great claims of modernism, i.e. its faith in growth and progress, its reliance on the power of reason, its belief in meta-narrative, meaning and truth, are increasingly doubted in recognition of the estranged, meaningless, atomised and fragmented make-up of human existence.[6] In post-modern works of art, parody, play and pastiche, in which 'the very distinction between artistic-image and commodity-image has virtually faded', challenge the modernist notions of 'high' culture and of art containing metaphysical depth and being revelatory of the transcendent.[7] While on the one end of the post-modern spectrum, deconstructivist, nihilist doubts of truth and values – reflected in superficial lifestyles with instant gratification and lack of commitments – are to be found, there is a constructive critique of modernity which searches for liberating, holistic forms of life. In theology and in other disciplines this has come to expression in social, feminist, ecological and cosmological concerns. Interestingly the search for faith, a greater openness and deep hunger for the spiritual are also features of the post-modern age. This manifests itself – against the background of a general distrust of institutional religion – in a wide range from new Christian movements and ways of life, such as basic communities, to quite doubtful, esoteric preoccupations and the formation of sects. In this context the prophetic, i.e. the voices from the margins, from the arts, from contextual theologians and the mystical, i.e. negative theology which stresses religious experience and refrains from universalist claims, assume growing importance in theology and in the quest for meaning.

Doing theology through art then is to be considered in contextual terms as it takes the specific situation, the experience, the subjective, prophetic voices and images of the artists as its basis. In our study, moreover, contextuality and particularity are further emphasised through country (Irish painters), limited numbers (ten artists), and the artistic medium (painting).

(abstract) art cf. Reinhard Hoeps, *Bildsinn und religiöse Erfahrung, Hermeneutische Grundlagen für einen Weg der Theologie zum Verständnis gegenstandsloser Malerei* (Frankfurt am Main: Peter Lang, 1984).

6. M.P. Gallagher, S.J., *Clashing Symbols, An Introduction to Faith-and-Culture* (London: Darton, Longman and Todd, 1997), 88-90.

7. Richard Kearney, *The Wake of Imagination, Toward a postmodern culture* (London: Routledge, 1994), 4-6.

Finally, it is obvious that the painters under consideration have neither produced works which delight in pastiche and parody nor do they view the world through nihilist eyes. Some of them strikingly and sincerely reveal concern with the human predicament of suffering, fragmentation and ambiguity in our time; hopelessness and meaninglessness, however, is not their final message. Rather, I suggest that the more hope-inspiring post-modern aspects, such as respect for individuality, particularity, plurality and for the natural environment, a sensibility for wholeness, an interest in liberation, in the spiritual and in an open, critical faith, are apparent or at least glimpsed in the thought and work of the painters.

It is precisely this creative, positive dimension that links the ideas and images of these artists to those of contemporary theologians like Schwebel, McFague, Moltmann, Lane, Gallagher, or Tracy, for example, and, as has been shown, even to much older thinkers like Irenaeus and John Scotus Eriugena. A theology of and through art, such as the present one, is developed in our pluralist situation in an essentially life-affirming spirit. Like other contemporary theologies it cannot and must not deny, but rather grapple with, the reality of doubt, destruction, cynicism, relativism and estrangement. Indeed, it is precisely here that a humble search for truth, meaning, authenticity and for the God who is love arises. Theology is eschatology and eschatology means hope – hope, faith and redemption even in the midst of and despite despair.

The Situation of the Theologian and of the Artist:
Experience, Context and Particularity

The realisation that theology must speak to and arise from people in their situation, that faith and meaning can be contemplated truthfully only in being shaped by experience, including the experience of the transforming love of God and one's interpretative understanding of this experience,[8] are primary criteria for theology. As Tracy, in line with Rahner, affirms, all theology is also anthropology, any perception of God is also perception of oneself and vice versa.[9] It is in and from the concrete situation, often of the oppressed – women, the poor, coloured people, sexual and ethnic minorities – that theologians explore the significance of Jesus, of salvation in Christ, for this age. What has brought about a shift in theological method is this awareness that universal claims – as made from the *particular context* of white, middle class, male and mostly European theologians – are problematic since *all* interpretations of the Christian message are developed from a particular situation and

8. Cf. McFague, *Models of God*, 44.
9. Tracy, *The Analogical Imagination*, 429, 435.

perspective.[10] This is not to say that *any* interpretation 'goes'. Rather, a new, more humble, more pluralist way of talking of and understanding the God of Jesus Christ is being acknowledged, which in turn demands creativity and imagination in theological engagement. Doing theology through art, as in this study, is to be seen then in the context of such an approach regarding theological claims.

What unites the artists considered is their Irish background, the fact that all of them are painters, that they are not 'church artists', and that in some of their works specifically biblical-Christian themes, or at least spiritual or religious dimensions are apparent which are of interest to theological discourse. At the same time each of these has been respected and examined as an individual painter with particular concerns arising from personal experience, vision and faith. Although a number of overlapping religious and theological dimensions in their art and lives could be ascertained, it is probably right to conclude that – due to subjectivity and individual experience which bears on the choice and plurality of themes and styles – in some sense there are as many theologies of art as there are artists and even works of art. It is therefore in recognition of the essential particularity, not just of the Irish context but of the very individuality of each painter and each work of art, that some wider conclusions were and could be tentatively drawn.

TOWARDS A HERMENEUTICS FOR A THEOLOGY OF ART

Having outlined the situation in which theologies of art, including my own, are being developed, we will now attempt – with reference to the method applied in this book and its implications for a theology through and of art – to draw some further ideas for a hermeneutics of the image. The central task has been to explore the theological dimensions in the life, thought and work of ten selected twentieth-century Irish artists. The aim throughout was to achieve as comprehensive and objective a picture as possible on each painter and each work, and from there to attempt some more general conclusions which are not only relevant for this particular study but for doing theology through art on the whole. A variety of sources and aspects were taken into account and considered: interviews, letters, art historical and art critical literature, diverse theological writings, mainly from the wider area of systematics, including theological aesthetics, as well as a few works by practical and moral theologians, philosophers and Scripture references.

In the first chapter the focus was on Tillich's and Schwebel's substantial contributions to the dialogue between theology and modern art in order to

10. Cf. McFague, op.cit., 47.

introduce the wider field of theology and visual art. More especially, thereby a number of central hermeneutical questions and thematic and stylistic aspects that henceforth pertained to our own discussion were disclosed.

The main objective in Chapter Two was to explore the religious thought and concerns of the painters, and how these have been expressed in their life and work. In letting the artists themselves speak – the artist-as-'theologian' – as well as taking into account commentators and critics, it was possible to explore a range of theological and spiritual dimensions that are apparent and important in the lives of the painters. Since this book is an attempt to relate and integrate the two disciplines of art (history) and theology, a second interest, moreover, prevailed. In trying to establish how faith and the spiritual have mattered in the artists' lives and work, several correspondences and analogies between the thought/work of the artists and of theologians were uncovered. The intention here was not to achieve a cosy relationship and agreement, but rather to illumine and expand both artistic and theological perceptions through correlation.

The task of the third chapter then was to engage in detailed theological interpretations of three selected paintings by each artist, many but not all of which contain explicit or implicit Christian references. Essentially, the objective here was to treat and explore each work of art (instead of a text) as a *locus theologicus*. A greater or lesser variety of theological dimensions in each painter's work was discovered and in conclusion it was finally possible to show several theological themes which are recurrent in the paintings as a whole. Also it emerged that the findings of Chapter Two and Three largely correspond to and expand on each other. Moreover, as theological concerns in Irish art (even if limited due to the small number of artists examined) were compared to the wider sphere of theological dimensions in twentieth-century European art, the findings in both chapters confirmed that the aspects are largely similar.

After this brief look back at the method applied in this study, what then are the wider conclusions to be drawn with regard to the hermeneutics for a theology through and of art?

Tracy suggests, in the context of interreligious discussions, that to develop real dialogue one needs to allow 'the truth of the other' to become 'a genuine possibility for oneself'.[11] It could be argued that with regard to the dialogue between theology and art the question is not so much the truth of the other but that it is rather a matter of similar aspects of truths being expressed in different modes. The artist's ideas and the work of art are neither primary

---

11. Tracy, *Dialogue with the Other*, 44.

Christian and doctrinal sources, such as the Scriptures or creeds, nor are they 'professional' university theology. Yet any expression concerning the divine and the spiritual through language, gesture, music, silence and image is talk (song, or image) of God.[12] It is this that theology through art seeks to affirm. Given that both art and theology are in the pursuit of meaning and revelatory of (ultimate) truth, theology, on the one hand, therefore can learn from and is greatly enriched by the (prophetic-mystical) theology expressed in artistic work. On the other hand, (academic) theology can enhance, concur with and further our understanding of art. Moreover, as we have seen, in a few instances it was even possible to suggest that theological ideas may have had some influence on the artist's work and thought.

Provided a wider understanding of theology – as advocated by Rahner, amongst others, who insisted that some artistic expressions *are* theology – is acknowledged, a study such as this one essentially hopes to concretely demonstrate that works of art are, and can be discovered as, rich and relevant sources of theology.[13] What has been more particularly emphasised in this writer's method than in Tillich's, Schwebel's and other theological writings on modern art (e.g. Dillenberger) is the attempt at a correlation, frequently by way of analogy, of the artists' thought and especially their works of art with diverse theological writings. This was done so as to develop and sustain theological interpretations of the images and to throw mutual light on both art and theology. In this context of correlating theological thought and art, Burch Brown's observation is apposite. He writes that whereas theology 'in its most typical classical mode strives to be logically consistent, coherent, comprehensive, conceptually precise, and propositional' art explores 'fictively, metaphorically, and experientially what formal theology cannot itself present or contain'.[14] It is, however, significant to note that classical theological discourse, as he describes it, is, in fact, called into question by contemporary theologians like Metz. Metz points out that modern Catholic theology has been largely characterised by a 'deep schism between theological system and religious experience'; interestingly he thus calls for a 'biographical theology',

---

12. Johann Baptist Metz argues much in the same way when he advocates the need for a more 'biographical theology' which takes into account the mystical religious experience of the subject: 'Theologie ist ... nicht einfach Professorentheologie, ist nicht identisch mit Berufstheologie.' J.B. Metz, *Glaube in Geschichte und Gesellschaft, Studien zu einer praktischen Fundamentaltheologie*, 4th edn, (Mainz: Matthias-Grünewald-Verlag, 1984), 196.

13. In this context see also William M. Shea's article 'Dual Loyalties in Catholic Theology, Finding Truth in Alien Texts' (*Commonweal*, 31.1.1992), 9-14.

14. F. Burch Brown, *Religious Aesthetics*, 166-167.

which integrates both strands. Metz stresses that 'the most important achieve-
ments in theology and church history stem indeed from a scientifically
'impure' theology in which biography, fantasy, accumulated experience, con-
versions, visions, prayers were indissolubly woven into the system'.[15] With
regard to change in theological discourse, McFague's concern with a
metaphorical, imaginative theology and Navone's and Tilley's emphasis on
story-telling, i.e. narrative, in theology,[16] also ought to be mentioned.
Naturally, such expanding views on theological method further encourage
the possibility and necessity of theological engagement with the arts.

A significant task in our study has been to explore and treat the work of
art as a *locus theologicus*. Of course, the classical *loci theologici* – Scriptures,
patristics, early councils etc. – are not being challenged here in their role as
fundamental and primary sources in theology. However, I agree with Alex
Stock's suggestion that the term may be applicable also to modern visual art
if the meaning of *locus theologicus* does not simply imply theological sources
from the Christian tradition which have the consensus of all (e.g. Chalcedon)
for the discussion of problems which have not yet found agreement, but
rather if it is seen in the context of exploration, i.e. when art becomes a place
for theological discovery.[17] It is with such a perception of visual and other
artistic expressions that art can provide exciting and new theological sources,
which enhance our understanding of divine presence and our notion of theology itself. Art as theology thus opens up another approach to doing theology, i.e. to discerning revelation and faith, moral questions and sacramental
reality in our torn world.

As discussed in Chapter One, Tillich's method never included any
detailed readings of works of art. The present approach therefore differs significantly from Tillich's since in-depth examinations of a limited number of
artists and paintings have been central here and no particular preconceived
theology was applied. Schwebel has extensively analysed art works from a
theological point of view. The method used here differs from those used in
Schwebel's two major writings in two respects. Firstly, Schwebel proceeds

15. Metz, op.cit., 196-197. 'Biographisch soll eine solche Theologie heissen, weil die mystische
    Biographie der religiösen Erfahrung, der Lebensgeschichte vor dem verhüllten Antlitz
    Gottes, in die Doxographie des Glaubens eingeschrieben wird.' (196)
16. Cf. John Navone, S.J., 'Towards a Theology of Story', *Milltown Studies*, no. 13 (Spring
    1984), 73-94. Cf. Terrence W. Tilley, 'Narrative Theology', *The New Dictionary of
    Theology*, 702-703.
17. Alex Stock, 'Ist die bildende Kunst ein locus theologicus?', in Stock, (ed.), *Wozu Bilder im
    Christentum?: Beiträge zur theologischen Kunsttheorie* (St. Ottilien: EOS Verlag, 1990), 175-
    181, at 181. 'Wenn man den Begriff des *locus theolo*gicus über den Begründungs-
    zusammenhang hinaus auf den Entdeckungszusammenhang der Theologie ausdehnt,
    dann kann die bildende Kunst ein eigenständiger Ort theologischer Entdeckungen sein.'

with his research under artistic style (abstract images) and subject matter (the image of Christ in modern European art) while our analysis focused on individual artists from the same country who have played an important role in the history of modern Irish art. Secondly, in comparison to Schwebel, the present method of interpreting the paintings makes more extensive use of theological writings to support and expand the theological 'reading' of the works.

In this context of hermeneutical considerations it is important to remember that, as Gadamer observed, interpretation does not imply the elimination of one's own preconceptions in order to find one true reading but rather using 'one's own preconceptions so that the meaning of the text [the work of art] can really be made to speak for us'.[18] Through this process we may be transformed and encouraged to see differently or in new ways.

As with all interpretations, the personal dimension, here as anywhere, implied the danger of subjectivism. However, the aim was to be comprehensive, imaginative, personal *and* objective. Thus – with Lonergan's 'transcendental precepts' ringing in the back of one's mind – it was hoped to present reasonable and responsible interpretations, always *grounded in the work of art itself* as well as in the conviction that, as Lonergan puts it, objectivity requires authentic subjectivity.[19] The interpretations do not claim exclusivity but rather they are intended to make obvious that contemporary artistic images *are* of theological relevance. In this way they therefore may invite and stimulate further theological involvement with art.

The work of art, like a text, then is perceived as a *locus theologicus* to be interpreted and reinterpreted. The work becomes a source for theological interpretation, i.e. for theological understanding and knowledge. Although the media of communication in theology and visual art differ – the written word on the one hand, and, as in this study, painting on the other – there are hermeneutical similarities between the methods of (theological) interpretation of works of visual art and of texts. In the context of the growing recognition of the need of making the visual arts sources for doing theology, it is relevant hence to tease out these similarities a little further.

In *Truth and Method,* Gadamer points out that interpretation is 'the act of understanding itself'.[20] Therefore understanding is interpretation. Gadamer's central notion of the 'fusion of horizons' *(Horizontverschmelzung)* holds that

18. Hans-Georg Gadamer, *Truth and Method* (New York: Crossroad, 1984), 358.
19. Bernard Lonergan, *Method in Theology* (London: Darton, Longman and Todd, 1972), 53, 265. Lonergan in his method which is relevant not only to theology but to all sciences advocates that to be 'attentive', 'intelligent', 'reasonable' and 'responsible' is a basic methodological imperative.
20. Gadamer, op.cit., 359.

authentic interpretation does not happen in the interpreter's attempt to put her or himself in the shoes of the author but rather by a merging of one's own horizon with that of the author. In line with Gadamer, Ebeling emphasises the importance of the interpreter's horizon even further when he asserts that 'the more deeply a person penetrates the interpretation of a subject the more strongly one's own relation to the subject matter makes itself felt'.[21] Thus, he argues, the personal theological concerns of a theologian will always shine through in his or her interpretation, which in turn demands exercising self-discipline in one's interpretative tasks. It is quite apparent at this stage that these basic observations, as expressed by Gadamer and Ebeling, apply as much to (theological) interpretations of texts as to works of art; one's own preconceptions and interests will always influence one's interpretations. Or, from a slightly different angle, in the words of Ricoeur, to interpret is 'not a question of imposing on the text our finite capacity of understanding, but of exposing ourselves to the text and receiving from it an enlarged self ...'.[22] Naturally, the same holds for the confrontation with a work of art, since art, like a text, reveals the world, experience and vision of the artist (writer) and thus can broaden the interpreter's knowledge[23] and transform or intensify her or his vision.

Further, and more specifically with regard to this study and its theological context, the *pre*-interpretation (*pre*-understanding) stage, i.e. the very selection of artists and of works, already confirms the involvement and significance of the interpreter's horizon. Indeed, this stage is already a stage of interpretation or pre-understanding, as here the interpreter discerns and decides, even if somewhat more intuitively and less conceptually developed, which artist and/or work (author/text) will be of theological relevance to his or her discussion.[24]

Moreover, one's own theological formation and interests necessarily will have some bearing on the actual interpretation, even if one needs to be aware that this cannot mean to pre-impose a certain view.

Having engaged in extensive theological discussions of the paintings, I would conclude – with caution as it may not always apply – that the less

---

21. Gerhard Ebeling, *The Study of Theology*, trans. Duane A. Priebe (London: Collins, 1979), 24.
22. Paul Ricoeur, *Hermeneutics and the Human Sciences*, ed. and trans. John B. Thompson (Cambridge: Maison des Sciences de L'Homme and Cambridge University Press, 1981), 143.
23. Cf. Schwebel, who speaks of *Erkenntnisvermehrung*, i.e. an increase in (theological) knowledge, which modern art offers to the recipient. Schwebel, *Das Christusbild in der bildenden Kunst der Gegenwart*, 141.
24. Cf. Jeanrond on the role of prior understanding in his book *Theological Hermeneutics: Development and Significance*, 5-6.

obviously religious the subject matter in the work is, the more open and personal an interpretation may result. Abstraction instead of figuration encourages this more personal response even further. Also, the discussion of the works of art has shown that emphatic use of symbolism invites rather complex interpretations (especially works by Graham, Hall, Dillon). The reason for this lies in the 'multivalent quality' of the symbol itself, i.e. in the fact that it participates in what it symbolises and at the same time points beyond itself, in its mysterious and revelatory power of disclosing and concealing, its stirring the imagination and its transforming effect.[25] However, here one could rightly ask whether such rather open interpretations do not entail the danger of too much subjectivity. As stated above, reasonableness and responsibility must prevail, and what has been already established by the community of interpreters – theologians, art historians and critics – must be sufficiently and properly taken into account.

Jeanrond points out that interpretation does not mean repetition of texts but rather 'the new creation of the truth of these texts in the always different situation of the interpreter and his or her social environment'.[26] The foundational biblical texts to be interpreted, however, are not neutral and propositional. Rather the way God is revealed in these happens through narrative, poetry, doxology, and instruction. Hence in these, as in later theological writings, revelation of the divine is recorded and made transparent from and through the subjective religious experience of the writers and/or of those of whom they write. What is common to these classic writings is their communication through symbols and imagery. Revelation, God's self-communication, therefore happens through and is dependent on stories and images.[27] It is the task of theology to reflect critically on these texts from the contemporary viewpoint of the interpreter. Moreover, the mystic, saint, prophet or academic theologian expresses and interprets religious experience through symbol and imagery in text.

Similarly the modern work of art – also through symbol and imagery –

25. Avery Dulles, S.J., *Models of Revelation* (Dublin: Gill and Macmillan, 1983), 136-138. Cf. also Dulles on theology being fundamentally concerned with communication through symbols, in Dulles, *The Craft of Theology, From Symbol to System* (Dublin: Gill and Macmillan, 1992), 17-39.

26. Jeanrond, *Text and Interpretation,* 151.

27. Heinrich Fries, 'Mythos und Wissenschaft', in Franz Böckle, Franz-Xaver Kaufmann, Karl Rahner, Bernhard Welte, (eds.), *Christlicher Glaube in moderner Gesellschaft,* Enzyklopädische Bibliothek, vol. 2 (Freiburg: Herder, 1981), 36-37. 'Der Mythos ist Rede in Anschaulichkeit, in Bildern und Symbolen. Auch in diesem Betracht besteht eine Zuordnung zur Offenbarung. Ihre Vermittlung kann der Bilder und Gleichnisse nicht entbehren. Denn es gibt kein Wort ohne die es begleitende Vorstellung.' (36) Fries understands myth as 'Rede in der Form der Erzählung'.

can be an expression and interpretation of the artist's religious experience and faith in paint on canvas. Again, Gadamer's and Tracy's insistence that all understanding is interpretation is evidenced in the fact that not only is it the theologian's task to interpret, but rather that the interpreter needs to be aware that the text or work of art for interpretation itself already presents the artist's or writer's interpretation of her or his experience and *Weltanschauung*.

However, in this context one ought to take into account that between the religious classic and other classics from the arts or science, for example, a difference exists, which lies essentially in their claim to truth. As Tracy observes, religious like other classics always 'involve a claim to meaning and truth as one event of disclosure and concealment of the reality of lived experience'.[28] But, he continues, unlike other classics, 'religious classic expressions will involve a claim to truth as the event of a disclosure-concealment of the whole of reality *by the power of the whole* – as, in some sense, a radical and finally gracious mystery'. Hence it is because of the experience of the religious classics as coming from the power of the whole, or, as one might say, from the ultimate, that they are experienced as and attain thereby a sense of and claim to authority and truth not achieved through oneself but received as gracious gift. Here the question of divine revelation, grace and faith are concerned. One may thus conclude that while in the great religious and theological texts, ultimate concern, claims to truth, the sense of worship, and absolute trust in and passionate commitment to the Other are, or at least tend to be, more explicit, more final and more universal than in other classics, there exists, nevertheless, an analogical connection between revelation and truth in religion and in art. It is the revelation of ultimate reality in art – visual art, literature, music etc. – that can point to and can be experienced as moments of divine self-communication.

The painter's 'language', unlike the writer's, is paint on canvas, and the expression of personal faith and religious experience within the painted image and one's reception of it is, one might argue, less direct, in some ways less clear than words. Paradoxically, on the other hand and at the same time, it is more direct because of its sensuous nature, its colour and lines and especially because of its immediacy as the work can be seen in its totality at once. Hence the work of art *possibly* may be a little more open to misinterpretation.[29] Also,

---

28. Tracy, *The Analogical Imagination,* 163.

29. In recognition of the validity of the plurality of interpretations it could be argued that misinterpretations cannot arise. However, it is possible, indeed, that this may occur in the case of subjectivism or mere carelessness on the interpreter's part, if, for example, she or he ignores or does not bother to inform her/himself on certain established facts about the artist/author and/or the work of art/text. In this context see also Anne Sheppard, *Aesthetics, An introduction to the philosophy of art* (Oxford: Oxford University Press, 1987), 112-113.

one's reaction to visual art, in comparison to texts, poetry and literature, occasionally *may* be more emotional due to the expressive, immediate, confrontational, sensuous and frequently highly experiential nature of (contemporary) artistic images. The interpretative, reflective act that follows may be influenced (unconsciously) by this first emotional response. As such, an emphatically emotional reception could be the very part that makes the interpretation an interesting one, but it may also be in danger of being simply too subjective, even arbitrary. This calls once more for a continuous recognition and application of Lonergan's principles of interpretation.

Moreover, the contemporary painter's depiction of specifically biblical and Christian subject matter will be his or her reaction to and interpretation of the story as told in the Scriptures. Being confronted with it, the interpreter may draw connections between the painter's appropriation of the story and the narrative itself, and then draw his or her conclusions. (Such has been my own method with regard to several biblically inspired works.) Hence the interpretation of a work of art with Christian subject matter, which in itself presents an interpretation of the biblical subject, is once removed from the way one encounters and interprets the biblical text as such. It is this that makes the 'reading' of works of art with Christian iconography both enriching, due to the artist's interpretation of it, and limiting, also because of the artist's interpretation, i.e. the individual particularity of his or her rendering of the theme. In the context of text-understanding a similar situation arises when the biblical text is not directly received through one's own reading, but rather through someone's retelling of or sermon on it, i.e. through an interpretation of it.

Further, a central task in our discussion was to show – as others, like Tillich, Schwebel, Rombold and Dillenberger have done in relation to other European and North American art – that modern works of art without Christian subject matter or Christian symbols can be perceived as being revelatory of the divine, of ultimate reality and truth, and, more specifically, of Christian truth. Works like Newman's 'Stations of the Cross' and Rothko's abstract canvases for the Rothko Chapel in Houston, Texas, come to mind, as do O'Malley's, Dillon's or Hall's paintings. However, as mentioned above, the theological interpretation of those works may be even more dependent on the pre-understanding and horizon of the interpreter, i.e. her or his theological interests, than the 'reading' of works with explicitly Christian themes.

Finally, as the process of reading is foundational to word theology, the process of seeing is the basis for doing theology through visual art. It is this act of seeing, of engaging with the material image, which fundamentally expands traditional theological method. Yet, as I have tried to demonstrate, it functions in many ways analogous to reading/hearing. In a theological interpretation of art one becomes open to, experiences and interprets visions of the transcendent, of the divine, of the *deus absconditus* and of the *deus revelatus* in Christ, bodied forth in surprising, gentle, challenging, shockingly immediate, or meditative fashion in the work of art.

THEOLOGY, ART AND THE IMAGINATION

The Power of the Creative Imagination: Perceiving the Possible

In his book *The Wake of Imagination* Richard Kearney traces the understanding and place of the imagination from Hebrew biblical to postmodern times. He points out that what 'most distinguishes the modern philosophies of imagination from their various antecedents is a marked *affirmation* of the creative power of man'.[30] While in biblical and Greek thought and later in medieval times imagination and images were generally perceived in mimetic terms – at best as an imitation or copy of some truth – and as subordinate to reason (Plato, Augustine, Thomas), in modernity the 'mimetic paradigm' has been replaced by the 'productive paradigm'.[31] The imagination now becomes the 'hidden condition of all knowledge',[32] the 'immediate source of its own truth'. The imagination is acknowledged as being capable of inventing worlds, and not simply as a mirror and source of reproduction (Kant, Fichte, Schelling). Hence images and, more particularly, works of art were to be increasingly valued for their originality. The imagination, Kearney observes, would be hailed as the 'divine spark' in the human being, as 'a transcendental product of the human mind'. The possibility of original creation thus was no longer seen as exclusive to the divine creator. In recent post-modernist views, finally, the very idea of originality and of the imagination is challenged or denied by way of deconstruction, which, for example, finds expression in (self-)parody in art. But, as Kearney rightly observes, is it not precisely in a world which now is deprived of all certainties and in which the experience of suffering is encountered and brought to mind daily through television, that imagination is urgently needed? Indeed, the power of the imagination as a creative, rather than as a reproductive, faculty is important so as to go on and perceive anew, to imagine the other, the as yet unrealised, to develop 'the ability to think of what is not' (Sartre).

Essentially thus, imagination has to do with possibility. It is this sense of the possible, of transformation, which, as will be argued in more detail, presents a fundamental link between religious and artistic imagination, and therefore between theology and the arts.

30. R. Kearney, *The Wake of Imagination*, 155.
31. Ibid., 130, 155.
32. Ibid., 167.

Images and Imagination in Theology and in Art:
In Search of Prophetic Vision, Truth and Transformation
While many leading theologians, like Rahner, Tillich, von Balthasar, Moltmann, Francis Schüssler Fiorenza or Tracy acknowledge the importance of the creative imagination in religious experience and in theology, it is, however, true that on the whole the voice, paint or tunes of the artists, i.e. those in whose work imagination plays an especially important role, have been left out of the theological enterprise. Despite the modern affirmation of the importance of creative imagining, and the gradual shift away from aligning the scientific with the rational, and the imaginative with the non-rational,[33] residues of these schisms are still with us. To argue with Metz, theology has been carried out in systematic, scientific fashion often exclusive of religious experience as recorded in biography, mystical-spiritual writings, artistic vision, prophesy, fantasy. It is in a study such as this one that the attempt is made to include some of these diverse elements. The aim here is not to challenge the value of the 'purely' scientific – as much as that applies to a discipline which in itself is founded on *faith* seeking understanding. Rather, the intention has been not only to recognise and state the importance of the creative imagination as revealed through the image in doing theology, but to actively uncover, discover, appreciate and use the image as a source of gaining religious and theological knowledge. McFague, in her advocating of a constructive, metaphorical theology, emphasises the necessity of trying out 'new pictures that will bring the reality of God's love into the imaginations of the women and men of today'.[34] Such a theology 'insists on a continuum ... between image and concept, the language of prayer and liturgy and the language of theory and doctrine'. Since, as she points out, this theology is heuristic and speculative by nature due to its trying out of new models, metaphors and images, it is a theology of risk, namely the risk of ending up with nonsense rather than truth. However, I would wholeheartedly agree with her that theology needs to take such risks. Theology needs to develop and explore new images, it needs to walk new and difficult paths in order to remain relevant to people's lives and to its own life and *raison d'être*. Notably with the advance of contextual theologies, more daring, creative approaches

33. James P. Mackey, (ed.), *Religious Imagination* (Edinburgh: Edinburgh University Press, 1986), 4. In this context cf. also Mackey's article 'Theology, Science and the Imagination: Exploring the Issues', in *The Irish Theological Quarterly*, vol. 52, no. 1 (1986), 1-18. Here Mackey argues that the imagination is not only propaedeutic to analytical intellect but that it is essential to our being in and envisioning the world, including the empirical sciences, as it enables us to really see 'what is and what can be, so that seeing truly we might truly live'. (17)
34. McFague, *Models of God*, xii.

in theological thinking are being explored. In line with McFague, one would suggest that theological interpretation of works of art is to be seen in similar creative and somewhat heuristic terms. It is the religious imagination that is at work in the theological interpretations of works of art (or religious texts) which are themselves born of the imagination, – including the religious imagination – artistic skill and of the experience of the artist.

The selection of metaphors for speaking of God is, at least partly, a subjective one. It is the individual theologian who chooses and makes use of these out of her or his perspective. Likewise, the interpretation of the work of art is a personal attempt, shaped by the horizon of the image, of the artist (to some extent) and of the interpreter. A theology, which risks trying out and interpreting new and challenging images, symbols and metaphors, naturally is less prone to ending up in non-sense, if, as Lonergan puts it, 'authentic subjectivity',[35] i.e. sincerity and responsibility, prevails. It is here that glimpses of truth emerge, that the scientific and the imaginative are united in the search for the God who is mystery.[36] In this way theology becomes relevant and exciting, as it is inclusive, a little tentative, open to transformation, to possibility – the possibility to imagine in new ways, of celebrating and interpreting the past (tradition) and present, and anticipating the future. Or, as McFague writes: 'Because religions, including Christianity, are not incidentally imagistic but centrally and necessarily so, theology must also be an affair of the imagination.'[37]

Acts of the imagination are always bound up with questions of truth and freedom. Although in post-modernity the very ideas of truth and freedom may be doubted and cynically dismissed, they still are aspirations – even if in more nuanced, humble modes – among artists, theologians and in contemporary life. As Noel Dermot O'Donoghue writes, individual freedom is required in 'the order of imagination', yet it is 'inseparable from responsibility'.[38] Truth is not simply a matter of scientifically verifiable propositions and hard facts;[39] it is not a box of static doctrines and concepts. Rather it is dynamic and open *(aletheia)*, particular *and* universal. It is the freedom and responsibility of the artist to render in images or other artistic form her or his vision, and thus his or her truth. It is for the recipient then to interpret freely and responsibly and thus as truthfully as possible meaning(s) and truth(s) in

35. Lonergan, *Method in Theology,* 265.
36. Cf. John Macquarrie, *Thinking about God* (London: SCM, 1975), 82. 'The mystery always stretches beyond the furthest reaches of thought, and an adequate theology requires both a logical structure and the open texture of an imaginative outreach.' (82)
37. McFague, op.cit., 38.
38. Noel D. O'Donoghue, 'The Mystical Imagination', in J.P. Mackey, *Religious Imagination,* 190.
39. Mary Warnock, 'Religious Imagination', in Mackey, op.cit., 151.

the work of art. Whether in a painting, sculpture, installation, symphony, poem, novel, play or film, truth is transmitted through the singular vision and imagination of the artist. The subjective truth of the artist/work of art which in itself is formed by the universal and particular context of his or her horizon *may* make the beholder glimpse not only that particular truth, but *through, in* and *beyond* that truth universal truth. In fact, one would suggest that only if art manages to render more than purely subjectivist preoccupations has it the chance of being appreciated as great. Moreover, the work of art may reveal to the recipient truth that the artist her or himself had not even been conscious of or intended.

Revelation and truth, grace, love, and beauty, happen in the particular, in the sensuous, in the visible world, in the Scriptures. It is in this way that ultimate truth and ultimate reality is experienced and known. The dialectic of particularity and universality, of normativity and plurality, freedom and responsibility thus is not one which ends in unbridgeable schisms, but rather in a dynamic unity in and of diversity, made possible precisely through the use of the imagination. Indeed it is the gift of the imagination to creatively transcend dualisms through its power to connect opposites, to juxtapose and hold in creative unity light and darkness, to bring together what otherwise may be regarded as disjointed or irreconcilable. It is the imagination that makes possible and builds dialogue, including that between theology and the arts. The imagination enables a person to free her/himself from their own confines; it can bring about a unified perspective arising from the depths of the human being, i.e. one's emotion *and* intellect.[40] It is by its power to overcome constrictions of despair and fear that the imagination becomes an ally of hope, a way of coping with, rather than avoiding, reality, an instrument of healing.[41] I will come back to this link between imagination and hope, especially eschatological hope, towards the end of this section.

The work of art then is revelatory of truth and ultimate reality through its prophetic, mystical and aesthetic dimension, in its concrete 'speaking' through and to the senses, soul and mind. This is what Tillich meant when he experienced something of the divine source of all things when he was confronted with and found himself personally transformed by the Botticelli painting in Berlin. Because, as Burch Brown points out, the work of art represents 'things felt to matter ... and amounting to more than what is strictly quantifiable, and measurable, the mind that thinks through the alternate

40. Cf. Gerald J. Bednar, *Faith as Imagination, The Contribution of William F. Lynch, S.J.* (Kansas City: Sheed & Ward, 1996), 168-170. I am also indebted to Dermot Lane for his comments
41. William F. Lynch, *Images of Hope, Imagination as Healer of the Hopeless* (Notre Dame, London: University of Notre Dame Press, 1974), 21-27, 243-256.

worlds of works of art reconsiders even this present world in terms of qualities and values and purposes'.[42] It is in such moments of recognition that our sense of truth and our experience of and faith in ultimate truth, in the divine, may be challenged, affected and enlarged. If God is the totality of all being, it is in the particular beings and things that the sacramental may be encountered. The universality of God, of truth, beauty and goodness, is revealed in works which, by the power of their imaginative, aesthetic and even ethical manifestation, may have a transformative effect on people, hence on their faith and spirituality, their aesthetic sense and morality.[43] It is in this way that the artistic and religious realms can merge. It should be clear, however, that, in acknowledging the revelatory-sacramental aspect of art, Christ as the supreme sacrament and revelation of the divine, as believed by the Christian, is not being called into question here. Rather, the work of art, and for that matter beauty in nature or human loving relationships, are to be seen as pointing us to and uncovering, to a greater or lesser extent, *something* of that God of and in Jesus Christ. In this way they are *loci theologici.*

Both, religion and (visual) art search for truth; both do so in their exploration and use of symbols.[44] Since our knowledge and speaking of God is essentially symbolic, the religious and the artistic imagination are fundamentally not to be seen as unrelated, different spheres. Theology, as Gilkey writes, is taken to be true if its 'symbols are experienced to communicate a real encounter with God'.[45] One would suggest that something similar could be said with regard to the theological relevance of art, even if in more indirect fashion. As demonstrated in the second chapter, the painters consider commitment to and faith and truthfulness in their work to be central to their lives as artists. It is precisely in the free choice and treatment of an explicitly or implicitly religious subject, or even of a non-religious theme in a work of art, that such a 'real encounter' with the divine, with the Spirit, may have

---

42. F. Burch Brown, *Religious Aesthetics,* 110.
43. Cf. George Steiner on the ethical role of art in Steiner, *Real Presences* (London, Boston: Faber and Faber, 1989), 145. 'No serious writer, composer, painter has ever doubted, even in moments of strategic aestheticism, that his work bears on good and evil, on the enhancement or diminution of the sum of humanity in man and the city. To imagine originally, to shape into significant expression, is to test in depth those potentialities of understanding and of conduct ... which are the life-substance of the ethical. A message is being sent; to a purpose.'
44. Even non-figurative art can have symbolic meaning due to its display of particular colours, for example. The significance of colours, especially with regard to modern art, has been repeatedly stressed during the course of this study. In abstract art, for example, it is very bright, light colouring which may be the sole indication of a sense of salvation or resurrection. Dark colours, on the other hand, may intimate hopelessness, suffering and death.
45. Gilkey, *Reaping the Whirlwind,* 148-149.

given rise to the production of the work, and/or is felt by the recipient. In this context it is worth noting that, as Lynch has observed, it is the task of the imagination to cut through any darkness, fantasy and any kind of lies in order to discover reality.[46] To imagine is to imagine the real. And this reality can only emerge if there is reality and authenticity in the artist's (as well as in the theologian's or preacher's) imagination in and love of her or his work. It is in this way that the creative imagination, religious and artistic, is affirmed as being born of love, truth and freedom – hence of God. This is the situation when the Spirit, the source of life, reigns where it wills, provokes, sustains and transforms human beings through the written word or through the glory, sublimity and joyfulness of colour and artistic form. Without freedom, truthfulness, sincere commitment, critical appreciation of tradition and openness to imagine the new, the possible, neither theology nor art is convincing. Profundity, theological and artistic depth, can ultimately only be achieved when these elements are present.

Artistic Imagination, Religious Imagination and Eschatology:
An Intimate Relationship
A final aspect to be considered regarding the imagination is one which, if not stated explicitly so far, nevertheless has become obvious not only during the course of this chapter but at various points in the present study, namely the connection between the creative/artistic imagination and eschatology. While the imagination plays its part in memory and in dealing with immediate reality, it functions in particular in the perception of what may, could and will be – in short, in picturing the possible. In more theological terms, it is the power of the imagination which makes the followers of Christ envision and comprehend something of the meaning of and being in the kingdom of God. It was hardly accidental that Jesus sought to make known, to those who had eyes to see and ears to hear, the presence of God through highly imaginative communication. As Mackey writes, it was 'through the poetry of parable, of prayer and of dramatic action, that he elicited recognition of and encounter with what he called the reign of God; and in this way he made new perceptions possible, marshalled emotion and moved people to action … The truth of this act of imagination is in the transformation of life, of perception, emotion and action.'[47] This sense of the possible, of the future, of the other, of transformation is what unites the creative imagination with and makes it an instrument in eschatological concerns. Without vision, without acts of the imagination, hope for transformation, both in the present and in the ulti-

---

46. Lynch, *Images of Hope*, 244.
47. J.P. Mackey, 'Introduction' in Mackey, (ed.), *Religious Imagination*, 22-23.

mate future, which lies at the heart of contemporary, holistic eschatology, is unthinkable.[48] Transformed being, glimpses of the kingdom of God realised through justice, peace, liberation and the integrity of creation, as well as eternity's ultimate transcendence and fulfilment need to be envisioned, imagined; this is what is central to eschatology.

In this context, Tracy's observation that religious language basically occurs in two forms, the prophetic (proclamation) and the mystical (manifestation), is significant. The importance of the imagination in prophetic and mystical writing, hence its epistemological relevance in religion and theology, has been noted by other theologians and thinkers, like Mackey, Mary Warnock and Noel Dermot O'Donoghue. It is probably in both their mystical-prophetic dimension that artistic and religious imagination are most obviously connected. In the previous chapters, especially in the interpretation of the works of art, these aspects repeatedly emerged. One only needs to recall Yeats' 'There is No Night', Middleton's 'Christ Androgyne', Collins' 'Hy Brazil', or Hall's 'The Tale is Told that Shall be Told' to become aware of the prophetic and mystical expressed in art.

It is interesting to note that even a Marxist like Marcuse would speak of the meaning of art in eschatological fashion. He maintained that truth in art was to be found in the 'estranging language and images which make perceptible, visible, and audible that which is no longer, or not yet, perceived, said, and heard in everyday life'.[49] Significantly, he asserted that art is therefore 'fictitious reality', it is not less but more real than actual reality and therefore contains more truth than present reality. He added that the 'utopia in great art is never the simple negation of the reality principle but its transcending preservation *(Aufhebung)* in which past and present cast their shadow on fulfilment'.[50] Peter Fuller, one of the most remarkable art critics of his time who, for a while, was also much influenced by Marxist ideology, but later distanced himself from it, was to write in similar terms. As a self-professed 'incorrigible atheist' he stated that 'given the ever-present absence of God,

---

48. Cf. Lane, *Keeping Hope Alive,* 123-131.
49. Herbert Marcuse, *The Aesthetic Dimension, Toward a Critique of Marxist Aesthetics,* trans. H. Marcuse, Erica Sherover (London: Macmillan, 1979), 72. 'The world intended in art is never and nowhere merely the given world of everyday reality, but neither is it a world of mere fantasy, illusion, and so on. It contains nothing that does not also exist in the given reality, the actions, thoughts, feelings, and dreams of men and women, their potentialities and those of nature. Nevertheless the world of a work of art is 'unreal' in the ordinary sense of this word: it is a fictitious reality. But it is 'unreal' not because it is less, but because it is more as well as qualitatively 'other' than the established reality. As fictitious world, as illusion (Schein), it contains more truth than does everyday reality.' (54)
50. Ibid., 73.

art, and the gamut of aesthetic experience provides the sole remaining glimmer of transcendence. The best we can hope for is that aesthetic surrogate for salvation: redemption through form'.[51] It certainly is significant, and supports the whole dialogue between theology and art, that the religious dimension in art and therefore in artistic imagination, particularly its transcending, transforming, thus its eschatological aspect, has been acknowledged by thinkers from a non-theological, even atheistic, background. It corresponds, moreover, to one of the central concerns in this study, namely to demonstrate that the spiritual, transcendent, or even specifically Christian dimension in art, felt and experienced by the recipient, is not – or at least is not necessarily – dependent on religious subject matter and/or the artist's personal adherence to faith and (organised) religion (cf. especially Scott, le Brocquy).

If religion and theology 'by nature' have to do with ultimate reality, revelation and salvation, a similar eschatological aspect thus is apparent also in art. As has been shown, this dimension, which is central to the meaning and truth in art, has been recognised – even if not in explicit theological terminology – by diverse thinkers, all of whom agree that great art can be perceived as a 'provisional manifestation and reflection of a future consummation'.[52] It goes without saying that those theologians who have dealt with aesthetics and the arts as such, especially visual art, like Tillich, Dillenberger, Schwebel, Pattison or von Balthasar, are also to be counted among these writers.

It is through the gift of the imagination that we may conceive of the possible, of an ultimate wholeness in ever-new ways and in all the different realms of life. It is the unifying power of the imagination that allows and enables us to envision that nature and grace, immanence and transcendence, the sacred and the secular are distinct, yet interdependent, ultimately striving towards a dynamic whole. In the context of theology and art then, it is in their prophetic, mystical and eschatological dimension that the artistic and religious imagination travel an often remarkably intertwined route towards the transcendent other.

51. Peter Fuller, *Images of God, The Consolations of Lost Illusions* (London: The Hogarth Press, 1990), xiv.
52. Hans Küng, *Art and the Question of Meaning*, trans. Edward Quinn (London: SCM, 1981), 51.

THEOLOGY IN ART — ART IN THEOLOGY

The appreciation of the work of art as a *locus theologicus* has been funda-mental to our study. In the interpretation of the thirty images in the third chapter, some recurrent theological dimensions became apparent and were already briefly discussed at the end of the chapter. In this section I hope to consider and synthesise these theological aspects a little further. In order to do so, I will first reflect in more detail on the work of art as a relevant source in the theological discipline and then make some final observations on the theological dimensions in the paintings and how these compare with the the-ological aspects in other European and North American art.

An 'Unsystematic Systematic' Theology
The underlying issue, not only in this study but in the whole dialogue between theology and art, is to what extent and in which ways the work of art, especially modern, autonomous visual art, truly is relevant to doing theo-logy. I have tried to demonstrate throughout and concluded, in particular in this chapter, that although art has not been traditionally regarded a *locus the-ologicus* as such, it ought to be and is increasingly valued as a source of and for theology.[53] Principally the reason for this is art's revelatory power, its con-cern with (ultimate) truth and with meaning that can make one's encounter with art a religious experience and hence gives rise to theological reflection. Further, the aesthetic as well as the ethical-social dimensions of art should also be mentioned in this context.

The theologian explores and interprets the content of faith in ever-new ways in and for her or his age. Theology's focus is God's self-disclosure to humankind and the human search for the transcendent; it is 'the attempt of faith giving an account of itself',[54] of Christians trying to formulate what they understand by faith and Christian life in their situation. With 'histori-cal exactitude, conceptual rigour, systematic consistency, and interpretative clarity' theology does so in a scientific, scholarly, manner[55] However, as Francis Schüssler Fiorenza rightly observes, theology, in 'its relation to faith, shares the fragility of faith itself. It is much more a hope than a science'.

53. It is, for example, interesting and significant to note that the second enlarged edition of *The Modern Theologians* (ed. David Ford), which is an introduction to major contempo-rary theological thinkers and theological concerns, includes a section on theology and visual art. Cf. Graham Howes, 'Theology and the Visual Arts', in D.F. Ford, (ed.), *The Modern Theologians* (Oxford: Blackwell, 1997), 669-684.
54. W. Joest, *Dogmatik, Die Wirklichkeit Gottes*, vol. 1 (Göttingen: Vandenhoeck & Ruprecht, 1995), 14-15.
55. F. Schüssler Fiorenza, 'Systematic Theology: Task and Methods', in F. Schüssler Fiorenza, J.P. Galvin, (eds.), *Systematic Theology, Roman Catholic Perspectives*, 5.

Theology is based on hope, i.e. the hope of faith. It is a hope not only nourished by the orthodox places of revelation, the Scriptures, tradition and theological classics, but also by human experience in everyday life.

It is because humans have attested to the *experience* of revelation of ultimate concern and truth in art that gives the unsystematic, non-scientific artistic image and the artistic imagination their rightful and essential place in the work of theology. In this way one might speak of an 'unsystematic-systematic' theology. Precisely because theology asks questions about meaning, love, truth, justice, beauty, Christ, transcendence, it can and ought to integrate the arts in which similar concerns feature. There is neither one language nor one method for attaining knowledge of the divine, and the first to recognise, respect and cherish this fact obviously should be those who make it their life's profession to talk of God.[56] As Rahner put it succinctly, if theology 'is not identified a priori with verbal theology, but is understood as man's total self-expression insofar as this is borne by God's self-communication, then religious phenomena in the arts are themselves a moment within theology taken in its totality'.[57] It is with such a concept of theology that the arts occupy a place in religious life and make their way into, challenge, sustain and widen the work of the theologian. Although this writer's method and concerns have been from an angle which is broadly located in systematic theology, there are, of course, a huge range of aspects in art which are of interest to the various spheres of the whole discipline of theology. For example, social, political and ethical issues, which play a considerable role in modern art, might be of particular interest to and provide sources for the moral theologian. In turn theological ethicists might be dialogue partners for artists who are especially concerned with ethical questions. Artistic images, sculpture, architecture, literature and music from past epochs may be of special relevance and provide an enriching angle to the work of church historians and the history of theology. Biblical scholars may be particularly interested in the representation of biblical subject matter in art. Theologians whose work focuses on feminist issues might become conversation partners for those who are engaged with these issues in their artistic work.

However, these are only a few possibilities for doing theology through art, and for artists to become interested in theological questions. And the most important point to be made here is not one of limitation but one of taking open, unusual, imaginative approaches in which theologians who deal with art will apply writings from the various theological and other (art historical,

---

56. Cf. John Dillenberger who argues similarly. Dillenberger, *A Theology of Artistic Sensibilities*, 215-228.
57. Rahner, 'Theology and the Arts', in *Thought, A Review of Culture and Idea*, vol. 57, no. 224 (March 1982), 25.

philosophical) disciplines. Obviously, the interdisciplinary nature of theology in art and of art in theology itself implies essentially a broad, inclusive approach.

Theological Dimensions in the Works Examined: Some Final Observations
With the conclusion of the third chapter, it was possible to ascertain several recurrent theological dimensions in the paintings. These we will now explore a little further. On the whole it is the eschatological element that appears most pervasive. In a way, this is not surprising since what we understand as being eschatological extends from the reality of the present to the memory of the past, especially to the Christ event, and emphatically to hope for the future, to the kingdom of God. Eschatology is therefore almost synonymous with the term theology itself and can be applied in a somewhat broad manner. As Moltmann writes, the eschatological dimension is not merely one of several in Christianity, but 'the medium of Christian faith as such'.[58]

Another central aspect is the christological one; a third of the works directly or indirectly refer to Christ. It is the dominant biblical subject depicted and, of course, it is essentially linked with the eschatological dimension. Ethical concern regarding the individual, politics and society is evidenced implicitly or explicitly in various works. Several paintings contain a special creation theological strain in which the fundamental unity of matter and spirit, creation and salvation, and the beauty of nature are conveyed. A few of these images exude an atmosphere of celebration and praise. Again, these elements link in with the ultimate eschatological aspect in the works.

This rich palette thus pertains to a number of central subjects in theology. However, it is interesting also to note for a moment what is absent in terms of specific Christian content. One aspect, in particular, namely the trinitarian image of God, comes to mind. Apart from Dillon's 'Entertaining Friends' with its possible hints of the Trinity, there are no other such references in the paintings. Although it is the task of this study to deal with the theological dimensions which are in the paintings rather than with those which are not, a brief speculation on why the Trinity does not feature is, I suggest, important in the context of Christian faith and its expression in art. Despite the fact that the followers of Christ confess God as the triune Father, Son and Holy Spirit, the concept of a God who is three and yet one is tremendously difficult, even paradoxical. Throughout the centuries it has captured a few minds of professional theologians and mystics, but has otherwise remained

58. J. Moltmann, *Theology of Hope, On the Grounds and the Implications of a Christian Eschatology,* trans. James W. Leitch (New York: Harper & Row, 1967), 16.

somewhat remote and enigmatic to the believer.[59] As Rahner and Moltmann observe, *de facto* Christians have worshipped in quite monotheistic fashion, rather than with a conscious sense of a triune God. This then is reflected also in visual art. Although the Trinity is present and symbolised in some great works from the past, like the Ghent altarpiece or Rublev's famous icon, for example, visual images with explicit references to the Trinity are not too numerous. It therefore does not come as a surprise – especially in an age in which Christian faith at any rate is marginalised – that the trinitarian aspect basically plays no role in contemporary Irish art. In other modern art the situation is no different.

Christological Aspects
From the total number of works examined, the theme of Christ is captured in over a third of the paintings. It is obvious that – as with other European artists (see Schwebel) – the Crucified still occupies a place in the imagination of twentieth century Irish painters. Even by taking into account that this study has only examined a rather limited number of painters and images, it is to be concluded and to be pointed out once more, that whatever critical reservations artists may have towards organised religion, the history, reality and mystery of Jesus Christ continues to inspire the artistic mind. In retrospect I would suggest that – apart from le Brocquy perhaps – the choice and treatment of this subject among the examined painters is, at least to some degree, ultimately grounded in the painter's personal relationship with or faith in Christ. In our age when religious themes take up about four percent of the range of subjects rendered in art,[60] it seems almost inconceivable that an artist, who purely out of her or his desire engages with the one who Christians believe to be the redeemer, would do so without any kind of faith, however critical, non-conformist or hidden it may be.

Christology is no more and no less than the effort to elucidate the confession that Jesus is the Christ.[61] It explores the life, words and message of Jesus, his death and resurrection, his role in the economy of salvation, his mystery as the Son of God, his mediation between God and humans, his stance for and solidarity with the marginalised. The question thus arises whether a theological term such as Christology – or doxology, eschatology or creation for that matter – can be rightfully applied to spheres which expand traditional theology. I have done so throughout as it appeared and emerged as being appropriate and beneficial to use terms like these in exploring the

59. Cf. J. Moltmann, *Trinität und Reich Gottes*, 17.
60. Cf. Keith Walker, *Images or Idols? The place of sacred art in churches today* (Norwich: The Canterbury Press, 1996), 131.
61. Cf. W. Kasper, *Jesus the Christ,* trans. V. Green (London: Burns & Oates/New York: Paulist Press, 1976), 15.

work of art as a *locus theologicus.* Indeed, the interpretation of the works themselves has clearly shown that such terminology is in order when the work of art is to be discussed with regard to its theological content.

The fundamental norm for Christology and for dogmatics on the whole is the words, life and praxis of Jesus as witnessed in the Scriptures. However, dogmatic statements are always bound by the situation and time in which they are made, by the state of research and knowledge already acquired. If dogmatic discourse on the whole is critically concerned with human and divine truth, Christology specifically reflects on the truth of the Christ-event and its implications and meaning for human reality and Christian life. What is conveyed in the present paintings significantly expresses and concurs with some central christological aspects. Christ is shown explicitly or referred to implicitly as the one who identifies with the suffering through and in his own suffering ('Christ Androgyne'). He is portrayed as the one who undergoes his journey of suffering ('Ninth Hour', 'Stations of the Cross', 'Ecce Homo', 'Christ Androgyne', 'Scenes from the Life of Christ', 'Good Friday') and as the risen Christ and/or as the eternal redeemer (indirectly in 'There is No Night' and in 'Lazarus', 'Give me to Drink', 'Scenes from the Life of Christ', indirectly in 'Shadowy Carvings of an Ancient Execution'). He is conveyed as the prophet of the kingdom, teacher and minister ('Give me to Drink'), as the immanent-transcendent God ('Ecce Homo', 'Scenes ...'), and as the God who transcends gender ('The Ninth Hour', 'Christ Androgyne').[62] Further, several references are made to the Eucharist, the sacrament of communion, *anamnesis,* sacrifice and hope ('Fish Eaters', 'Entertaining Friends', 'The Lark in the Morning', 'The Blackbird Suite').

Thus, it is interesting to note that what is captured in these images is not just 'something' of Christ, e.g. a special, yet 'merely' human being who once walked the earth. These are not purely humanist or subjectivist responses in which Christ might be used to fit a purely personal agenda. What is, in fact, witnessed, whether in glimpses or in more open fashion, is nothing less than the God-man, the historical Jesus, the Word made flesh, the Crucified, the distorted human being, the 'androgynous' God, the lover of and co-sufferer with humans, the Christ of faith, the divine image and revelation in whom the eschaton is realised and fulfilled. Here then we find evidenced what a theologian like Aidan Nichols asserts, namely that 'the theology of the image provides one of the richest veins of ore in exploring what Christians mean by "revelation".'[63] Indeed, if Christology is engaged with an elucidation of God's

---

62. The paintings listed in brackets are given as examples where the respective dimensions are particularly emphasised. Naturally, in many of the works various christological aspects merge.

63. A. Nichols, *The Art of God Incarnate,* 105.

self-revelation and communication in Christ, and with what this means in a contemporary context, the analysis of the images has abundantly demonstrated their significant contribution and relevance in this respect.

Ethical Concerns

A number of works make apparent something of the moral consciousness of the artist, both with regard to the individual and to society and politics. What is addressed in these works is the taking of innocent life through murder ('Tinkers' Encampment: The Blood of Abel'), the evils of war, especially the Second World War, its destruction, horror, senselessness, suffering, the Holocaust ('Grief', 'Christ Androgyne' and 'Mountain' from a more recent, global perspective). Another theme is human sexuality, the beauty, pain and 'death' involved in erotic love, and a holistic view of the goodness of sexual loving ('The Lark in the Morning', 'The Blackbird Suite'). Obviously such issues and their pictorial manifestations often arise out of deeply felt experience, convictions, or moral outrage, as Yeats, Middleton, Hall and Graham, at times rather strikingly, demonstrate in their paintings.

Issues of war, peace, social justice, the fate of the Jews, gender and sexuality have been and are central in both art and theology, especially theological ethics. Fundamentally, what lies at the heart of both moral theology and images like the ones examined, especially when they contain Christian references, is the question of how the human is meant to live responsibly with fellow humans and the rest of creation. It is thus the commandment and the social implications of love, as God is love and wills us to love, both individually and in community, that matters here.[64] It is the failure of love, the failure of living in God, or, as Boff terms it, the 'brute fact' of the 'dis-grace' of total absurdity (e.g. war),[65] the ever-present reality and mystery of evil as the turning-away from God, i.e. from love, communion and oneness, which is captured in some of the paintings. It is a work like 'Christ Androgyne' that reveals that the Cross is ultimate distortion, yet the ultimate ground of hope in the out-pouring of divine love, that hope, however faint, may be born in the midst of estrangement and alienation. Precisely through witnessing what is opposite to love and goodness, these are implied as that which the human should strive for in her or his existence as a social being and as a believer. Here again the eschatological dimension comes to the fore in the tension between the reality of sin and the possibility of individual and social conversion, between what is and what we hope. If God's kingdom is one of justice,

---

64. Cf. E. McDonagh who draws attention to the social dimension of love in E. McDonagh, *The Gracing of Society* (Dublin: Gill and Macmillan, 1989), 44-45.
65. L. Boff, *Liberating Grace,* trans. John Drury (Maryknoll, New York: Orbis Books, 1979), 4-5.

liberation, love, relationship and solidarity, Christians are called to anticipate something of that kingdom.[66] Glimpses of this reality – often through stark reminders of the *aberration* from that reality – are revealed in the images. Dashes of light colour, moreover, may also indicate such tiny rays of hope. Works like these therefore raise questions of theodicy, of God's omnipotence and the possibility of faith in the face of evil and suffering, of free will, of justification and of love in its various dimensions. The paintings make us aware that there are no easy consolations for those who suffer. Often hope happens against hope in and from the situation of brokenness.

Creation, Salvation, Praise
From the christological and ethical aspects, the path leads to those images in which transcendent hope and redemption are not merely – sometimes barely – glimpsed, but more emphatically felt and revealed. In the course of our study and particularly in the conclusion to the third chapter, it was suggested that the religious and biblical themes in the Irish works of art examined largely concur with those in other modern European painting.[67] The strong christological strain, existential, ethical, creation theological, doxological and eschatological dimensions are found in works by Kandinsky, Nolde, Corinth, Rouault, Chagall, Jawlensky, Bacon, Rainer and Beuys, among others.

However, as has been shown, one aspect that appears to be more pronounced in Irish art is the holistic, panentheistic dimension. It ultimately finds its basis in the Celtic past, in which pre-Christian and Christian beliefs easily merged, in a romantic vision and respect and love of primordial nature, in the beauty of Irish landscape and ancient culture. The creation theological aspect in this context – as artists like Collins and O'Malley, and, to a lesser extent and with different emphases, Middleton, Scott, and Hall[68] manifest in their ideas and/or in their oeuvre – concerns epiphanies in nature. The beauty and mystery of landscape becomes a revelation and sign of the beauty and mystery of the Other ('Hy Brazil', 'Field of Stones', 'Earth Lyre', 'Chinese Landscape', 'Goldpainting 48', 'Goldpainting 56', 'Burning Mountain'). What is conveyed is transcendence in nature and the 'quasi-sacramentality of nature'.[69] This is an aspect which has some strong affinities with the Romantic painters and thinkers like Caspar David Friedrich,

---

66. Cf. Denis Carroll, *A Pilgrim God for a Pilgrim People* (Dublin: Gill and Macmillan, 1988), 169. 'The law of divine life is to love.'
67. Cf. Schwebel's study on the image of Christ and Günter Rombold's *Der Streit um das Bild, Zum Verhältnis von moderner Kunst und Religion* (1988).
68. Hall demonstrates this not in the context of the Celtic past and culture, but from a more mystical, universal perspective.
69. D. Carroll, *Towards a Story of the Earth, Essays in the Theology of Creation* (Dublin: Dominican Publications, 1987), 169.

Philipp Otto Runge, William Turner and Schleiermacher, whose works and writings disclose something of the religious desire for the infinite, of the sublime in nature, of the *mysterium tremendum et fascinans.*

The aforementioned works are meditative, hieratic and mystical *without* any specific Christian subject matter. Some of these, through their joyful, magical colours, become a special means of doxology, praising the splendour of creation and thus the one through whom everything exists. In so doing they anticipate in their own modest way the heavenly eschaton and manifest the fundamental unity of creation and salvation. If one keeps in mind that biblical and theological statements on God are by nature analogical (indirect) and doxological,[70] paintings like O'Malley's 'Earth Lyre' or Scott's 'Gold-painting 48', for example, become such 'statements'. Through their exuberant (O'Malley) and hieratic (Scott) colours, the presence of the unfathomable, incomprehensible divine, of supreme beauty, is felt and anticipated. This frequently happens with little or no specific Christian references in the works or their titles.

Paul writes that 'the earth and its fullness are the Lord's' (1 Cor 10:26, cf. also Psalm 24:1). Not only is this a clear call to wise stewardship of the earth, but it affirms that *all* creation, non-human and human, belongs to God and is therefore sacred. Those then who believe Christ to be the Son and the incarnate image of God, the ultimate revelation of the divine, cannot but have reverence for creation. Creation, incarnation and salvation are bound up as an intimate whole. In this context it is significant to remember that both O'Malley and Collins have not only witnessed nature spirituality but also their faith in Christ on canvas and in thought. This shows, therefore, their truly panentheist spirit and a connection with both biblical and contemporary (ecological) creation theological ideas, such as Carroll's, Moltmann's, or McFague's, for example.

Although the creation theological dimension in the works largely refers to the natural environment, Jellett's 'Man and Woman' finally should also be mentioned as a work which specifically belongs in this discussion due to its evocation of the creation of the first humans, Adam and Eve, and of the 'new Adam' and 'new Eve', i.e. Christ and Mary. It is the human being created in the divine image and the fullness of that image in Christ, which are revealed.

What is affirmed thus in these paintings is the goodness and sacredness of

---

70. Cf. Wolfhart Pannenberg, 'Analogy and Doxology', in Pannenberg, *Basic Questions in Theology,* vol. 1, trans. George H. Kehm (London: SCM, 1970), 211-238. 'For the appearance of the *doxa,* the glory of God, at the end of all history is nothing else than his definitive revelation. The expression 'doxology' thus contains a reference to the fact that all worshipful speech about God anticipates his ultimate revelation.' (237)

all creation in its ecological and anthropological dimension.[71] The aesthetic process, i.e. the appreciation of the wondrous beauty of creation, is 'the result of our participation in the created order'.[72] Adoration happens through a deep love of, reverence for, and faith in what is praised. It also arises from a sense of wonder, fascination and mystery that the object of adoration instils in the adorer. The artist and the theologian witness their participation in creation through their praise of creation by and in their own creativity and journey of discovery.

Eschatological Presence: Hope Abides

In the introduction to this section I pointed out that the theological element which is most apparent in the thirty works of art examined is the eschatological one. One might suggest, of course, that due to the expansive meaning of eschatology[73] such a conclusion is not all that surprising. After all, Barth, or, more recently, with less christocentric emphasis, theologians like Moltmann and Lane, have emphasised that the whole of Christian existence is essentially eschatological in our living in hope for and by the promise of the kingdom.[74] However, such eschatological existence can and must not be understood as an opium which leads to passivity and irresponsibility but, rather, to critical awareness, to action towards justice, peace and liberation, towards respect for and healing of the earth. The absolute future in Christ, the promise of ultimate communion in the eschaton, demands not cosy, self-satisfied faith, but real human effort and courage, i.e. taking to heart one's charisms received through grace. It is Christ himself who through his own life and death calls for nothing less than utter courage and commitment. Resignation, despair, cynicism and hate are antipathetic to the life of faith, hope and love (1 Cor 13:13) which Christ's followers are asked to witness.

Not all of the images examined in this study contain references to Christ, thus one might infer that strictly speaking the term 'eschatological', which is so much bound up with Christ's announcement of and reign in the kingdom, is not applicable to those works. On the other hand, we recall Schwebel who

71. In a broader perspective, images like 'Madonna and Child', 'Procession with Lilies IV', 'Fish Eaters', 'Give Me to Drink', 'The Lark in the Morning' also may be mentioned in the creation theological context.
72. D. Sölle, with Shirley A. Cloyes, *To Work and to Love, a theology of creation* (Philadelphia: Fortress Press, 1984), 1.
73. Lane, op.cit, 2-5. 'Within theology, eschatology serves as a powerful reminder that all theological claims are subject to the qualifications and reservations that come from the promise of an open eschatological future.'(2)
74. John Macken, S.J., *The Autonomy Theme in the Church Dogmatics: Karl Barth and His Critics* (Cambridge: Cambridge University Press, 1990), 150. Lane, op.cit., 17-20, 38-41. Moltmann, *Theology of Hope*, 39-41.

uses precisely 'eschatological anticipation' in relation to what he sees conveyed in abstract art, hence in a work which, more likely than not, contains no Christian references. Eschatology, as Lane notes, then may be applied in a more specific christological sense or in a wider context connoting essentially the presence of and search for hope as a fundamental necessity to human living. The believer might argue that even in its 'merely' ontological and anthropological dimension, hope pertains to and is born of divine grace. Hope, life, action, love and relationship are as intimately connected as despair, cynicism, apathy, loneliness and death. The one who still hopes still believes in the possibility of life, however faint or vulnerable such faith may be. Indeed hope is essential to believe in a tomorrow, to trust in a future.

In the light of contemporary eschatology – with its balanced perception of hope as this- and other-worldly, with its emphasis on the tension between and convergence of the here and the not yet, with its perception of ultimate redemption being anticipated through individual and social justice, liberation and love – it is to be asserted in conclusion that the eschatological element is the one which is most persistently encountered in the paintings. In all of these works, even in a painting like 'Grief' or 'Christ Androgyne' with their overwhelming sense of darkness and death, a glimmer of hope, a ray of light, a hint that death is not the ultimate end are manifest. Whether in Jellett's 'Ninth Hour', Graham's 'Scenes from the Life of Christ', Hall's 'The Tale is Told that Shall be Told', Scott's meditative Gold Paintings, Collins' and O'Malley's contemplative, panentheist visions, Middleton's 'Give Me to Drink', le Brocquy's 'Ecce Homo', Yeats' 'There is No Night', or even Dillon's 'The Brothers', a tiny hint or a bright atmosphere of salvific hope – at times through the light of Christ, at times simply as a fact of human existence – are apparent. It is hope in the midst of despairing reality, immanence and transcendence, the mystery and beauty of creation, the ultimate triumph of (eternal) life over death, redemption in Christ, and (ultimate) truth which the works reveal in open, or imply in hidden, fashion. I suggest, moreover, that this sense of hope in the paintings accords with and reflects the basic outlook and faith of the artists, several of whom struggled with deep trauma, illness and suffering, but none of whom retreated into permanent despair. On the contrary, it is in the experience of suffering that, at least for some of them, painting itself came to be a truly redemptive, cathartic force (e.g. O'Malley, Graham, Hall).

A final and significant observation is to be made at this point and brings this section to its conclusion. The fundamental connection between eschatology and the imagination was discussed earlier. I argued that it is the imagination which enables both the artist and the theologian to show through symbol, metaphor, story, image or scholarly text, the world as they experience it, and at the same time as transformed, as other, as possibility, as ultimate reality. In short, without imagination, without memory and anticipation, there can be no eschatology. In my reflection on the theological dimensions in the works of art in this section, I then pointed out that it is the eschatological aspect which is most prominent in the paintings. What I argued from a somewhat different angle and from a more theoretical perspective on the imagination before is thus concretely evidenced and supported by the examination of actual images. Therefore the present discussion does not only confirm and correspond to what was previously established, but it shows once more, both through the particular work of art and from the wider reflection on imagination and eschatology, that images can be relevant and challenging sources in and of theology. Both the contemporary theologian and the artist can speak of and image hope to fellow humans. It may be hope in the midst of darkness and, more specifically, eschatological-Christian hope. Such hope is genuine, when – as with the present paintings and with the mentioned theologians – it is not born of or reverts to cheap consolations, illusions or false optimism, but when it acknowledges, arises from and survives in and despite the concrete reality of human existence.

Theology in and through Art:
The Power of the Image, the Spirit in Matter, the Feast of the Senses
In this final chapter, relevant questions of a hermeneutic for theological engagement with art, the role and importance of and the convergences between the artistic and the religious imagination, and a deepened reflection on the emerging theological aspects in the works of art, were principal concerns. In this way some conclusions were drawn and issues were considered which pertain to the topic of art in theology and theology in art.

What is fundamental to a theology of and through art, as to other current theological approaches, is the conviction that theology must be radically based in and draw its inspiration from life, from the experience of people. It cherishes the central place and makes use of the classical *loci theologici* and asserts at the same time that the theologian, in order to be credible and relevant to contemporary life, especially Christian life, and to the task of theology, must firmly place herself or himself in and operate from the reality of our existence in which surprising new *loci* can be found.

During the course of our study, painted images were not only discovered and discussed as such sources of theology, but it was possible, moreover, to uncover sometimes remarkable parallels, convergences and mutual illumination between the painted image and the written theological word. However, it was also pointed out that theology conveyed in art, unlike in traditional theological writing, tends to be less defined, unsystematic, more visionary, imaginative and metaphorical in character. Yet, the image can be intensely direct, shocking, even confrontational, due to its visual immediacy, the freedom of the artist's imagination and expression. It is precisely here that the artistic image can make its relevant contribution to theological endeavour. Indeed, as significant correspondences between the content of theology and of art have been revealed, some final remarks on the specific nature of a theology of and through art are appropriate.

Theology based on the visual image is an embodied theology; it is located in particularity and matter, i.e. in a concrete painting, sculpture, installation etc. To make the image the source of one's theological engagement implies a radical 'yes' to creation, to creativity, and to the capacity of the imagination. It is a positive affirmation of our life-giving senses, of the sensuous and sensual, of the aesthetic, of eros, of the fact that spirit, even the divine Spirit, can be perceived in and through the material. It is the seemingly paradoxical assertion that ultimate reality or, more especially, the invisible face of the always-greater God, is glimpsed and known in the bits and pieces of earthly existence, which is at the centre of this theology. It acknowledges eros in the profoundest sense, God's deepest desire, love and yearning for us as created beings and our desire for the divine and for union with one another. This is what pictorial images, poetry, music or the writings of mystics can powerfully reveal. Doing theology through art affirms and takes as its basis the very fact that the human being experiences and learns through the senses. Body, soul, mind and spirit, all that makes up our being, is intimately related, connected and sacred.

Everything is in God and God is revealed in everything the panentheist would suggest, or, in other words, it is the belief that, as McFague notes, the world is the body of God[75] which pertains to a theology of art. Thus it shares a central concern with what has been stressed in recent years, especially in feminist thinking, namely that life is, and theology therefore needs to be, embodied or, as one might put it, 'enmattered'. As we trust in an incarnate God, our theology and Christian living must be concerned with the earth, with both the physical and spiritual wellbeing and healing of people and of creation. Such faith in the Word-made-flesh allows us to delight in visual images of the divine, to celebrate the wonder and beauty of the sensuous, even if and because we perfectly know that the face of God will never be fully revealed in our earthly life. In fact, it is essentially the incarnation that allows for a theology through the material visual image. Since the belief that we are made in the image of God is at least as old as the first chapter of Genesis, there is nothing new in this basic assertion of the goodness and sacredness of

75. Cf. McFague, *The Body of God, An Ecological Theology* (London: SCM, 1993), 207-212.

creation. But it is the radical insistence on and contemplation of an embodied theology – mainly from an eco-feminist perspective – against the history of a dualistic outlook on matter and spirit, body and soul, natural and supernatural, which places it in the forefront of contemporary theological thinking. A theology focused on the image supports and is situated therefore in close proximity to such current theological concerns. Of course, while ecological theology deals mainly with organic, living matter, with good stewardship of and care for the earth, the embodied or 'en-mattered' theology of art looks at a cultural product, something created by a person. Nevertheless, both eco-feminist and theology through art are related as they both challenge and strive to replace a dualistic perception of the world with a more holistic one, each from its own angle. Moreover, both have a contextual dimension. As a theology of art is centrally inspired by individual works of art, by the life experience of the artists and the context in which their works are produced, it thus takes seriously particularity and abstains from absolute claims. Or, in other words, *if* more universal claims are made, they arise from and through the particular. In this manner and through its dialogical nature, a theology like this one enjoys a certain freedom and humility and knows itself as being *one* way of discovering glimpses of ultimate reality.

In the examined paintings, feelings and expressions ranging from deepest pain and suffering to exuberant, ecstatic joy are encountered. Prophetic and visionary, the work of art 'speaks' of life in all its aspects, including death. In this way it may also 'speak' of the divine, whether directly through Christian iconography or in less obvious fashion. Naturally, the written word does the same. However, there is a difference. While a text *describes* the beauty or ugliness, happiness or suffering of a human being, for example, which the reader has to image in her or his mind, the painting *visually shows* that figure which can be glanced in one moment. It is this – at times confrontational and shocking – immediacy which provokes instant reactions of repulsion or attraction, disgust or delight, wonder and awe. This is its beauty and danger. Real engagement with visual art demands more than a glance, it demands to go beyond one's immediate reactions. What is required, precisely because of the sensuous, seductive nature of art, is a discipline of seeing.[76] Disciplined, intensive seeing is essential in order to appreciate the work of art not merely in terms of its sensuous quality on the one hand or its moral dimension, for example, on the other, but rather to be illumined by what it conveys as a whole, i.e. its intertwined aesthetic, spiritual, intellectual and ethical dimensions. Moreover, ultimately true seeing and genuine understanding happens through affection and love, a love free of naïvety or sentimentality. The old

---

76. John Dillenberger, *A Theology of Artistic Sensibilities*, 244.

notion that one must love a person or something to really know him, her or it, is pertinent. In this way seeing becomes profound, creative and a possibility for healing or transformation.

Visual images, positive and often negative, confront the human being daily and have become and are becoming increasingly more powerful through the media of television, advertisement and computers. It is high time then for the theological world and the churches to treat and value the artistic image – paintings, sculptures, installations, films – as a relevant source of and in theology. It is both paradoxically and obviously in the concrete materiality of the work of art that human beings may continue to glimpse the incomprehensible, unimaginable Other, the God of creation, 'the glory of Christ who is the image of God' (2 Cor 4:4), the God of freedom and love. In this way, art, especially contemporary art, will not only play an increasingly important role in theology, but hopefully it will gain and regain its place and importance in church life, i.e. in places of worship. In opposition to the many destructive images that surround us, art, like theology, may yet offer something different, something life-giving and life-affirming, a critical view of our existence, a call to change, a glimmer of hope, an anticipation of what may be and could be.

Nevertheless, in all our efforts to truly see and to treat and acknowledge the work of art as a *locus theologicus,* it is vital to be aware of the tension that exists between the artistic image and the written word. The tension lies in the very fact that, as Rahner rightly observed, the arts cannot be translated entirely into other modalities. It is precisely this tension that provides the ground for and gives life to doing theology through art. But tension in this context is not negative, and distinction does not mean separation. As long as the written word and the visual work of art can be distinguished, and as long as they *both* express reality and ultimate reality, intimate relations and infinite bridges between the two can be discovered, built and enlarged. The river of life from which each draws its inspiration is nothing less than our reality embraced by the wonderful mystery of God. It is in this way that a theology based on images takes its place in the colourful palette of our polyphonic and symphonic reflection on the divine, in our search for meaning, in our faith seeking understanding.

Bibliography

Very short articles and reviews annotated in detail in the footnotes in the book are not again mentioned in this bibliography.

I. PRIMARY SOURCES

Oral evidence, letters, MSS, articles. (Unless otherwise stated the interviews were conducted by and the letters were addressed to the author.)

ARMSTRONG, Arthur, Letter, (undated), October, 1995

ARNOLD, Bruce, Interview, 30.9.1995

COLLINS, Patricia and Penelope, Interview, 29.8.1995

___, Patrick, 'George Campbell, A Profile of the Artist', *Envoy,* vol. 1, no. 2 (1950), 44-50

DILLON, Gerard, 'The Artist Speaks', *Envoy,* vol. 4, no. 15 (1950), 39-40

___, 'Connemara is Ireland to Me', *Ireland of the Welcomes,* vol. 13, no. 2 (1964), 8-11

FALLON, Brian, Interview, 20.10.1995

GRAHAM, Patrick, CARSON, John, 'Two Points of View', *Circa,* no. 14 (1984), 30-33

___, 'On Irish Expressionist Painting', *The Irish Review,* no. 3 (1988), 31-34

___, 'A Letter from the Artist', in *Patrick Graham,* cat., Los Angeles, Jack Rutberg Fine Arts, Inc., 1989, 5

___, 'Patrick Graham on Patrick Graham', in *Works 5 – Patrick Graham,* Dublin, Gandon Editions, 1992, 17-26

___, Interviews, 28.9.1995 and 10.10.1995

HALL, Patrick, 'On Irish Expressionist Painting', *The Irish Review,* no. 3 (1988), 27-31

___, 'Presentation to the 8th General Assembly of Aosdána', unpubl. Paper, delivered in Dublin, Royal Hospital Kilmainham, 25.5.1988

___, Letter, (undated), Sept., 1993

___, Letter, 12.12.1993

___, 'Patrick Hall in conversation with John Hutchinson', in *Works 12 – Patrick Hall,* Dublin, Gandon Editions, 1993, 9-24

___, Letter, 30.8.1994

___, Interview, 1.12.1995

___, Communication, 22.9.1996

HIGGINS, Aidan, Letter, 4.9.1995

JELLETT, Mainie, 'My Voyage of Discovery' (first publ. as 'Definition of My Art', *Dublin Art Handbook,* 1943),

___, 'What is called Abstract Art',

___, 'The Dual Ideal of Form in Art' (first publ. in *Motley,* Dublin, 1932),

___, 'Art as a Spiritual Force' (first publ. in *Commentary,* 1941),

___, 'The Importance of Rhythm in Modern Painting', all in *Mainie Jellett, The Artist's Vision,* ed. Eileen MacCarvill, Dundalk, Dundalgan Press, 1958, 47-51, 57-59, 64-67, 68-69, 91-102 respectively

KENNEDY, Samuel B., Interview, 2.11.1995

LE BROCQUY, Louis, 'The Artist Speaks', *Envoy,* vol. 4, no. 15 (1950), 38-39

___, 'Notes on painting and awareness', in *Louis le Brocquy,* Dorothy Walker, Dublin, Ward River Press, 1981, 135-152

___, Interview, 20.9.1995

___, Communication, 6.9.1996

LONGLEY, Michael, Interview, 2.11.1995

O'MALLEY, Tony, Interview, 30.10.1995

PHILLIPS, Rosamund, Interview, 22.9.1995

SCOTT, Patrick, Interview, 17.10.1995

THIESSEN, Gesa, Personal notes from a public conversation between John Hutchinson and Patrick Hall in Dublin at the Douglas Hyde Gallery, 28.6.1995

VAN STOCKUM, Hilda, Letter, 16.11.1995

WHITE, James, Interview, 14.9.1995

YEATS, Anne, Interview, 13.10.1995

2. BOOKS AND ARTICLES

ADAMS, Doug, APOSTOLOS-CAPPADONA, Diane, eds., *Art as Religious Studies,* New York, Crossroad, 1987

AGNEW, Una, 'Religious Themes in the Work of Patrick Kavanagh: Hints of a Celtic Tradition', *Studies,* vol. 82, no. 327 (1993), 257-264

ALLEN, Máirín, 'Contemporary Irish Artists VII. Jack B. Yeats, R.H.A.', *Father Mathew Record,* vol. 35, no. 12 (1941), 3-4

___, 'Contemporary Irish Artists XI. Miss M.H. Jellett', *Father Mathew Record,* vol. 36, no. 4 (1942), 3-4

___, 'Jack Yeats: An Impression', *The Capuchin Annual,* 1942, 579-587

ANSELM of Canterbury, *Cur Deus Homo,* in *Basic Writings, St Anselm,* 2nd edn, trans. S.N. Deane, Peru, Illinois, Open Court Publishing Company, 1962

APOSTOLOS-CAPPADONA, Diane, ed., *Art, Creativity, and the Sacred,* New York, Crossroad, 1984

St Thomas Aquinas Summa Theologiae, Existence and Nature of God (Ia. 2-11), vol. 2, ed. Timothy McDermott, O.P., London, Blackfriars, 1964

St Thomas Aquinas Summa Theologiae, Father, Son and Holy Ghost (Ia. 33-43), vol. 7, ed. T.C. O'Brien, London, Blackfriars, 1976

St Thomas Aquinas Summa Theologiae, The Emotions (Ia2ae. 22-30), vol. 19, London, Blackfriars, 1967

ARNOLD, Bruce, 'Noble Deeds: Jack Yeats', *Éire-Ireland,* vol. 6, no. 2 (1971), 39-42

___, *Irish Art, A Concise History,* 2nd edn, London, Thames and Hudson, 1977

___, *Mainie Jellett and the Modern Movement in Ireland,* New Haven, London, Yale University Press, 1991

___, 'The Turning Point for Irish Modernism', in *Art is My Life: A Tribute to James White,* ed. Brian P. Kennedy, Dublin, National Gallery of Ireland, 1991, 3-13

___, 'Mainie Jellett (1897-1944) and the Modern Movement in Irish Art', in *Mainie Jellett 1897-1944,* cat., Dublin, Irish Museum of Modern Art, 1992, 15-24

BALLINGER, Philip, 'Ruskin: Hopkins' "Silent Don"', *Studies,* vol. 85, no. 338 (1996), 116-124

VON BALTHASAR, Hans Urs, *The Glory of the Lord, A Theological Aesthetics,* vol. 1: *Seeing the Form,* trans. Erasmo Leiva-Merikakis, ed. Joseph Fessio, S.J. and John Riches, Edinburgh, T. & T. Clark, 1982

___, *Love Alone: the Way of Revelation,* London, Sheed & Ward, 1968

BARRETT, Cyril, S.J., 'The Painter's World, An Introduction', *Capuchin Annual,* 1961, 286-322

BARTH, Karl, *Dogmatik im Grundriss,* Zürich, Theologischer Verlag, 1947

___, *Einführung in die evangelische Theologie*, 3rd edn, Gütersloh, Mohn, 1980

BAUCKHAM, Richard, 'God Who Raises the Dead: The Resurrection of Jesus and Early Christian Faith in God', in *The Resurrection of Jesus Christ*, ed. Paul Avis, London, Darton, Longman and Todd, 1993, 136-154

BECKETT, Samuel, 'Homage to Jack Yeats', in *Jack B. Yeats: Drawings and Paintings*, James White, London, Secker and Warburg, 1971, 10

BECKETT, Wendy, *Art and the Sacred*, London, Rider, 1992

BEDNAR, Gerald B., *Faith as Imagination, The Contribution of William F. Lynch*, S.J., Kansas City, Sheed & Ward, 1996

BEGG, Christopher T., 'Sacrifice', in *The Oxford Companion to the Bible*, eds. B.M. Metzger, M.D. Coogan, New York, Oxford, Oxford University Press, 666-667

BERGER, John, 'Jack Yeats', in *Selected Essays and Articles, The Look of Things*, J. Berger, Harmondsworth, Pelican/Penguin, 1971, 54-60

BERRYMAN, Phillip, *The Religious Roots of Rebellion, Christians in Central American Revolutions*, London, SCM, 1984

BINGEMER, Maria Clara, Gebara, Ivone, *Mother of God, Mother of the Poor*, trans. Phillip Berryman, Liberation and Theology Series, 7, Tunbridge Wells, Burns & Oates, 1989

BOFF, Leonardo, *Liberating Grace*, trans. John Drury, Maryknoll, New York, Orbis Books, 1979

___, *Jesus Christ Liberator, A Critical Christology for Our Time*, trans. Patrick Hughes, London, SPCK, 1980

___, *Ave Maria, Das Weibliche und der Heilige Geist*, trans. Horst Goldstein, 2nd edn, Düsseldorf, Patmos Verlag, 1985

___, *Church: Charism & Power, Liberation Theology and the Institutional Church*, trans. John W. Diercksmeier, London, SCM, 1985

BONHOEFFER, Dietrich, *Bonhoeffer Auswahl, Anfänge 1927-1933*, vol. 1, 3rd edn, Gütersloh, Mohn, 1982

BOWE, Nicola G., 'Wilhelmina Geddes', *Irish Arts Review*, vol. 4, no. 3 (1987), 53-59

BOWEN, Elizabeth, 'Mainie Jellett', *The Bell*, vol. 9, no. 3 (1944), 250-256

BOWIE, Andrew, *Schelling and Modern European Philosophy, An Introduction*, London, Routledge, 1993

BOYDELL, Brian, 'The Virgin Mary in Music', *Milltown Studies*, no. 22 (1988), 87-91

BOYLAN, Harry, *A Dictionary of Irish Biography*, Dublin, Gill and Macmillan, 1988

BRENNAN, Kathleen, 'Mainie Jellett', *The Leader*, 26.2.1944, 9-10

BRETT, David, 'The Land and the Landscape', *Circa*, no. 43 (1989), 14-18

BRIGHTON, Andrew, 'Introduction', in *Patrick Hall, "Heart" and other recent paintings*, cat., London, Pentonville Gallery, 1987, no p.

BROOKE, Peter, 'Introduction' to an article 'Modern Art and the New Society' by Albert Gleizes, *Cubism*, Belfast, (1983-84), 1-7(-23)

___, 'Albert Gleizes – Another Way of Cubism', in *Mainie Jellett 1897-1944*, cat., Dublin, Irish Museum of Modern Art, 1992, 25-32

BROWN, Raymond E., Fitzmyer, Joseph A., Murphy, Roland E., eds., *The New Jerome Biblical Commentary*, pbk edn, London, Geoffrey Chapman, 1993

BULTMANN, Rudolf, *Jesus Christ and Mythology*, New York, Charles Scribner's Sons, 1958

___, 'New Testament and Mythology', in *Kerygma and Myth, A Theological Debate*, R. Bultmann, E. Lohmeyer, J. Schniewind, H. Thielicke, A. Farer, F. Schumann, vol. 1, 2nd edn, ed. Hans Werner Bartsch, trans. Reginald H. Fuller, London, SPCK, 1964, 1-44

___, *Jesus*, Tübingen, J.C.B. Mohr (Paul Siebeck), 1983 (1926)

BURCH BROWN, Frank, *Religious Aesthetics, A Theological Study of Making and Meaning*, Princeton, N.J., Princeton University Press, 1989

BUTLER, Anthony, 'The Irish Art Scene', *Éire-Ireland*, vol. 6, no. 1 (1971), 100-104

CAMPBELL, George, 'A Simple Complex Man', *The Irish Times*, 8.7.1971

CAMPBELL, Julian, 'Patrick Collins and "The Sense of Place"', *Irish Arts Review*, vol. 4, no. 3 (1987), 48-52

CARROLL, Denis, *Towards a Story of the Earth, Essays in the Theology of Creation*, Dublin, Dominican Publications, 1987

___, *A Pilgrim God for a Pilgrim People*, Dublin, Gill and Macmillan, 1988

CATTO, Mike, *Art in Ulster 1957-1977*, Belfast, Blackstaff Press/The Arts Council of Northern Ireland, 1977

CHAKRABARTI, Arindam, 'Buddhist philosophy', in *The Oxford Companion to Philosophy*, ed. Ted Honderich, Oxford, Oxford University Press, 1995, 107-108

DE CHARDIN, Pierre Teilhard, *Le Milieu Divin, An Essay on the Interior Life*, London, Collins, 1960

___, *Hymn of the Universe*, trans. Gerald Vann, O.P., London, Collins, 1961

___, *Christianity and Evolution*, trans. René Hague, London, Collins 1971

___, *The Heart of Matter*, trans. René Hague, London, Collins, 1978

CHIPP, Hershel B., ed., *Theories of Modern Art, A Source Book by Artists and Critics*, Berkeley, Los Angeles, London, University of California Press, 1968

CHRYSSIDES, George, *The Path of Buddhism*, Edinburgh, The Saint Andrew Press, 1988

CLIFFORD, Richard J., S.J., MURPHY, Roland E., O.Carm., 'Genesis', in *The New Jerome Biblical Commentary*, eds. R.E. Brown, J.A. Fitzmyer, R.E. Murphy, pbk edn, London, Chapman, 1993, 9-43

COLLINS, Adela Yarbro, 'The Apocalypse (Revelation)', in *The New Jerome Biblical Commentary*, eds. R.E. Brown, J.A. Fitzmyer, R.E. Murphy, pbk edn, London, Chapman, 1993, 996-1016

CONE, Michele C., 'Patrick Hall', in *Patrick Hall, Mountain*, cat., Dublin, Douglas Hyde Gallery, 1995, 8-12

CONGAR, Yves, KERN, Walter, 'Geist und Heiliger Geist', in *Christlicher Glaube in moderner Gesellschaft*, vol. 22, eds. Franz Böckle, Franz-Xaver Kaufmann, Karl Rahner, Bernhard Welte, in assoc. with Robert Scherer, Freiburg, Herder, 1982, 59-116

CONGAR, Yves, *I Believe in the Holy Spirit*, vol. 1, trans. David Smith, New York, The Seabury Press and London, Geoffrey Chapman, 1983

___, *The Word and the Spirit*, trans. David Smith, London, Geoffrey Chapman, 1986

COOKE, Harriet, 'Harriet Cooke talks to the quiet man of Irish Painting', *The Irish Times*, 26.7.1972

___, 'Louis le Brocquy', *The Irish Times*, 25.5.1973

___, 'Harriet Cooke talks to Tony O'Malley', *The Irish Times*, 7.12.1973

CRAGHAN, John F. 'Kerygma', in *The New Dictionary of Theology*, eds. J.A. Komonchak, M. Collins, D.A. Lane, Dublin, Gill and Macmillan, 1987, 556-57

CURRAN, Constantine P., 'The Yeats Exhibition', *The Capuchin Annual*, 1945-1946, 102-109

VAN DAALEN, David H., 'Number Symbolism', in *The Oxford Companion to the Bible*, eds. B.M. Metzger, M.D. Coogan, New York, Oxford, Oxford University Press, 1993, 561-563

DALY, Gabriel, O.S.A., 'Faith and Imagination', *Doctrine and Life*, vol. 32, no. 2 (1982), 72-80

___, *Creation and Redemption*, Dublin, Gill and Macmillan, 1988

___, 'Conscience, Guilt and Sin', in *Ethics and the Christian*, ed. Seán Freyne, Dublin, Columba Press, 1991, 57-74

___, 'Art and Religion', *Doctrine and Life*, vol. 46, no. 10 (1996), 586-591

DEVLIN, Brendan P., 'The Christian and the Arts', *The Furrow*, vol. 13, no. 6 (1962), 337-347

DEVONSHIRE JONES, Tom, ed., *Images of Christ, Religious Iconography in Twentieth Century British Art*, Northampton, St Matthew's Church Centenary Art Committee, 1993

DILLENBERGER, Jane, 'Reflections on the Field of Religion and Visual Arts', in *Art as Religious Studies,* eds. D. Adams, D. Apostolos-Cappadona, New York, Crossroad, 1987, 12-25

DILLENBERGER, John, *A Theology of Artistic Sensibilities, The Visual Arts and the Church,* London, SCM, 1986

Gerard Dillon, cat., London, Mercury Gallery, 5.4.-29.4.1967

Gerard Dillon A Retrospective Exhibition, cat., Belfast, The Arts Council of Northern Ireland and Dublin, An Chomhairle Ealaíon, 1972

DOMINIAN, Jack, *Proposals for a New Sexual Ethic,* London, Darton, Longman and Todd, 1977

DRUMM, Michael, 'Irish Catholics: A People Formed by Ritual', in *Faith and Culture in the Irish Context,* Dublin, Veritas, 1996, 83-99

DUBE, Wolf-Dieter, *The Expressionists,* London, Thames and Hudson, 1972

DULLES, Avery, S.J., *Models of Revelation,* Dublin, Gill and Macmillan, 1983

___, *The Craft of Theology, From Symbol to System,* Dublin, Gill and Macmillan, 1992

DUNNE, Aidan, 'Life Lines: The paintings of Patrick Hall', in *Patrick Hall, Heart and other recent paintings,* cat., London, The Pentonville Gallery, 1987, no p.

___, 'The Later Work', in *Tony O'Malley,* ed. Brian Lynch, Aldershot, Hants, Scolar Press and Kilkenny, Butler Gallery, 1996

DYCH, William V., 'Theology and Imagination', in *Thought,* vol. 57, no. 224, New York (1982), 116-127

EBELING, Gerhard, *Wort und Glaube,* Tübingen, Mohr, 1960

___, *The Study of Theology,* trans. Duane A. Priebe, London, Collins, 1979

ECK, Diana L., 'Mountains', in *The Encyclopedia of Religion,* vol.10, ed. Mircea Eliade, New York, Macmillan, 1987, 130-134

EGENTER, Richard, *The Desecration of Christ,* London, Burns & Oates, 1967

EHRLICH, Carl S., 'Israelite Law', in *The Oxford Companion to the Bible,* eds. B.M. Metzger, M.D. Coogan, New York, Oxford, Oxford University Press, 1993, 421-422

ELIADE, Mircea, 'The Sacred and the Modern Artist', in *Art, Creativity, and the Sacred,* ed. D. Apostolos-Cappadona, New York, Crossroad, 1984, 179-183

ELLIS, Ian, *Vision and Reality, A Survey of Twentieth Century Irish Interchurch Relations,* Belfast, The Institute of Irish Studies, The Queens University of Belfast, Belfast, 1992

FALCONER, Alan D., ed., *Reconciling Memories,* Dublin, Columba Press, 1988

FALLON, Brian, *Tony O'Malley, Painter in Exile,* cat., Dublin, An Chomhairle Ealaíon and Belfast, The Arts Council of Northern Ireland, 1984

___, 'Appreciation, Interview with Tony O'Malley', *Éire-Ireland,* vol. 25, no. 3 (1990), 107-113

___, *Irish Art 1830-1990,* Belfast, Appletree Press, 1994

___, 'Forty Years a-growing', *The Irish Times,* 2.8.1994

FARMER, David Hugh, *The Oxford Dictionary of Saints,* Oxford, New York, Oxford University Press, 1987

FENTON, John, 'The Four Gospels: Four Perspectives on the Resurrection', in *The Resurrection of Jesus Christ,* ed. Paul Avis, London, Darton, Longman and Todd, 1993, 39-49

FITZGERALD, Marion, 'The Artist Talks', *The Irish Times,* 23.9.1964

___, 'Patrick Collins, The Artist Talks to Marion Fitzgerald', *The Irish Times,* 27.2.1965

FORSYTH TORRANCE, Thomas, *The Ground and Grammar of Theology,* Belfast, Christian Journals Ltd., 1980

FRIES, Heinrich, (GADAMER, H.-G.), 'Mythos und Wissenschaft', in *Christlicher Glaube in moderner Gesellschaft, Enzyklopedische Bibliothek,* vol. 2, eds. Franz Böckle, Franz-Xaver Kaufmann, Karl Rahner, Bernhard Welte, Freiburg, Herder, 1981, 5-42

FUCHS, Eric, 'The Mutual Questioning of Ethics and Aesthetics', *Crosscurrents, The Journal of the Association for Religious and Intellectual Life,* vol. 43, no. 1 (1993), 26-37

FULLER, Peter, *Images of God, The Consolations of Lost Illusions,* London, The Hogarth Press, 1990

GADAMER, Hans-Georg, *Truth and Method,* New York, Crossroad, 1984

___, *The Relevance of the Beautiful and Other Essays,* trans. Nicholas Walker, ed. Robert Bernasconi, Cambridge, Cambridge University Press, 1986

GALLAGHER, Djinn, 'Still Shocking after all Those Years', *Dublin Opinion,* vol. 2, no. 2 (1988), 45-47

GALLAGHER, Michael Paul, S.J., 'Post-Modernity: Friend or Foe?', in *Faith and Culture in the Irish Context,* ed. Eoin G. Cassidy, Dublin, Veritas, 1996, 71-82

GILKEY, Langdon B., *Reaping the Whirlwind, A Christian Interpretation of History,* New York, The Seabury Press, 1976

___, 'Can Art Fill the Vacuum?', in *Art, Creativity, and the Sacred,* ed. D. Apostolos-Cappadona, New York, 1984,187-192

GILLESPIE, Elgy, 'What's the point of painting?', *The Irish Times,* 11.5.1972

GLEIZES, Albert, 'Hommage a Mainie Jellett' (Engl. trans.), in *Mainie Jellett, The Artist's Vision,* ed. E. MacCarvill, Dundalk, Dundalgan Press, 1958, 35-46

___, 'Modern Art and the New Society' (Engl. trans.), in *Cubism,* Belfast (1984), (first publ. in French, Moscow 1923), 9-23

GOLLWITZER, Gerhard, *Die Kunst als Zeichen,* 2nd edn, Munich, Chr. Kaiser, 1958

GOODMAN, Theodore, 'Jack Yeats', *Commentary,* vol. 2, no. 7 (1943), 3-4

GRIFFITHS, Bede, *Return to the Centre,* London, Collins, 1978

___, *The Marriage of East and West,* London, Collins, 1982

GUNKEL, Hermann, *Genesis,* Göttingen, Vandenhoeck und Ruprecht, 1902

HAIGHT, Roger, S.J., 'Jesus and World Religions', *Modern Theology,* vol. 12, no. 3 (1996), 321-344

HALKES, Catharina J.M., *Gott hat nicht nur starke Söhne, Grundzüge einer feministischen Theologie,* trans. Ursula Krattiger-van Grinsven, 4th edn, Gütersloh, Mohn, 1985

HALL, James, *Dictionary of Subjects and Symbols in Art,* London, James Murray, 1974

Patrick Hall, cat., Belfast, Fenderesky Gallery, 1990

HÄRING, Bernhard, *Free and Faithful in Christ,* vol. 2: *The Truth Will Set You Free,* Middlegreen, St Paul Publication, 1979

HARRIES, Richard, *Art and the Beauty of God,* London, Mowbray, 1993

HAUGHT, John F., *What Is God, How to Think about the Divine,* Dublin, Gill and Macmillan, 1986

HAUSKELLER, Michael, ed., *Was das Schöne sei, Klassische Texte von Platon bis Adorno,* München, dtv, 1994

HEIDEGGER, Martin, 'The Origin of the Work of Art', in *Basic Writings, M. Heidegger,* ed. David Farell Krell, London, Henley, Routledge & Kegan Paul, 1978, 143-188

HEWITT, John, 'Under Forty, Some Ulster Artists', in *Now in Ulster,* ed. Arthur Campbell, George Campbell, Belfast, 1944, 13-35

___, *Art in Ulster 1557-1957,* Belfast, Blackstaff Press/Arts Council of Northern Ireland, 1977

___, *Colin Middleton,* Belfast, Arts Council of Northern Ireland and Dublin, An Chomhairle Ealaíon, 1979

HIGGINS, Aidan, '"Paddy" – An Appreciation', in *Patrick Collins,* Frances Ruane, Dublin, Belfast, An Chomhairle Ealaíon, 1982, 9-13

HOEPS, Reinhard, *Bildsinn und religiöse Erfahrung, Hermeneutische Grundlagen für einen Weg der Theologie zum Verständnis gegenstandsloser Malerei,* Frankfurt/Main, Peter Lang, 1984

HÖFER, Joseph, RAHNER, Karl, eds., *Lexikon für Theologie und Kirche,* vol. 8, 2nd edn, Freiburg, Herder, 1963

HUTCHINSON, John, 'Interview with Patrick Graham', *Irish Arts Review,* vol. 4, no. 4 (1987), 16-20

___, 'Myth and Mystification', in *A New Tradition, Irish Art in the Eighties,* Dublin, Douglas Hyde Gallery, 1990, 77-87

IRENAEUS, Paragraph from *Adversus Haereses,* V.i.1, in *Sources Chrétiennes,* vol. 153, ed. A Rousseau, L. Doutreleau, C. Mercier, Paris, Cerf, 1979, repr. in *The Christian Theology Reader,* ed. Alister E. McGrath, Oxford, Blackwell, 1995, 176

The Irish Imagination 1959-1971, cat., Dublin, Hugh Lane Municipal Gallery of Modern Art, 1971

IRSIGLER, Hubert, RUPPERT, Godehard, eds., *Ein Gott, der Leiden schafft?,* Bamberger Theologische Studien, vol. 1, Frankfurt/Main, Peter Lang, 1995

JEANROND, Werner G., 'Hermeneutics', in *The New Dictionary of Theology,* eds. J. A. Komonchak, M. Collins, D. A. Lane, Dublin, Gill and Macmillan, 1987, 462-464

___, *Text and Interpretation as Categories of Theological Thinking,* trans. Thomas J. Wilson, Dublin, Gill and Macmillan, 1988

___, *Theological Hermeneutics: Development and Significance,* London, Macmillan, 1991

JOEST, Wilfried, *Dogmatik, Die Wirklichkeit Gottes,* vol. 1, 4th edn, Göttingen, UTB, Vandenhoeck & Ruprecht, 1995

JOHN OF THE CROSS, 'Stanzas Concerning an Ecstasy Experienced in High Contemplation', in *The Collected Works of St. John of the Cross,* trans. Kieran Kavanagh, O.C.D., Otilio Rodriguez, O.C.D., Washington, D.C., Institute of Carmelite Studies, 1979, 718-719

JOHNSTON, William, *The Inner Eye of Love,* London, Collins/Fount Paperbacks, 1978

JUNG, Carl Gustaf, *The Collected Works of C.G. Jung,* trans. R.F.C. Hull, vol. 9, part 1, 2nd edn, London, Routledge and Kegan Paul, 1969

JÜNGEL, Eberhard, *Tod,* Gütersloh, Mohn, 1983

KANDINSKY, *Concerning the Spiritual in Art,* trans. M.T.H. Sadler, New York, Dover Publications, 1977 (first publ. 1914)

KASPER, Walter, *Jesus the Christ,* trans. V. Green, London, Burns & Oates and New York, Paulist Press, 1976

KEARNEY, Richard, 'Le Brocquy and Post-Modernism', *The Irish Review,* no. 3 (1988), 61-66

___, *Transitions, Narratives in Modern Irish Culture,* Dublin, Wolfhound Press, 1988

___, *The Wake of Imagination, Toward a postmodern culture,* London, Routledge, 1994

KEE, Alistair, *From Bad Faith to Good News,* London, SCM, 1991

KENNEDY, Brian P., *Jack B. Yeats 1871-1957,* Dublin, Townhouse/The National Gallery, 1991

___, 'Jack B. Yeats, An Irish Romantic Expressionist', *Apollo* (March 1991), 193-195

KENNEDY, Samuel B., *Irish Art and Modernism 1880-1950,* Belfast, The Institute of Irish Studies, 1991

KING, Thomas M., S.J., WOOD GILBERT, Mary, *The Letters of Teilhard de Chardin and Lucile Swan,* Washington D.C., Georgetown University Press, 1993

KNITTER, Paul F., *No Other Name? A Critical Survey of Christian Attitudes Toward the World Religions,* London, SCM, 1985

KOCH, Klaus, OTTO, Eckhart, ROLOFF, Jürgen, SCHMOLDT, Hans, eds., *Reclams Bibellexikon,* Stuttgart, Reclam, 1978

KOMONCHAK, Joseph A., COLLINS, Mary, LANE, Dermot A., eds., *The New Dictionary of Theology,* Dublin, Gill and Macmillan, 1987

KSELMAN, John S., S.S., BARRÉ, Michael L., S.S., 'Psalms', in *The New Jerome Biblical Commentary,* eds. R.E. Brown, J.A. Fitzmyer, R.E. Murphy, London, Geoffrey Chapman, 1993, 523-552

KÜNG, Hans, *Art and the Question of Meaning,* trans. Edward Quinn, London, SCM, 1981

___, *Eternal Life?,* trans. Edward Quinn, London, Collins, 1984

___, *Grosse christliche Denker,* München, Piper, 1994

___, *Theology for the Third Millennium, An Ecumenical View,* trans. Peter Heinegg, London, HarperCollins, 1991

KUSPIT, Donald, 'Patrick Graham: Painting as Dirge', in *The Lark in the Morning, Patrick Graham,* cat., Dublin, Douglas Hyde Gallery and Cork, Crawford Gallery, 1994, 7-11

LANE, Dermot, *The Experience of God,* Dublin, Veritas, 1981

___, 'Eschatology', in *The New Dictionary of Theology,* eds. J. A. Komonchak, M. Collins, D. A. Lane, Dublin, Gill and Macmillan, 1987, 329-342

___, *Keeping Hope Alive, Stirrings in Christian Theology,* Dublin, Gill and Macmillan, 1996

LE BROCQUY, Louis, *Images 1975-1987,* cat., Dublin, Arts Council, 1987

___, *Procession,* Kinsale, Cork, Gandon Editions and Louis le Brocquy, 1994

LIECHTY, Joseph, *Roots of Sectarianism in Ireland,* Belfast, J. Liechty, 1993

LIVINGSTONE, Elizabeth A., *The Concise Oxford Dictionary of the Christian Church,* Oxford, New York, Oxford University Press, 1977

LONERGAN, Bernard, *Method in Theology,* London, Darton, Longman and Todd, 1972

LONGLEY, Michael, 'Talking to Colin Middleton', *The Irish Times,* 7.4.1967

___, 'Colin Middleton', *The Dublin Magazine,* vol. 6, no. 3 and 4 (1967), 40-43

___, *The Arts in Ulster,* Belfast, Arts Council of Northern Ireland in connection with Gill and Macmillan, 1971

___, 'Colin Middleton', *Introspect,* no. 1 (1975), 21-22

LOSSKY, Vladimir, *In the Image and Likeness of God,* London, Oxford, Mowbray, 1974

Lutheran Book of Worship, Minneapolis, Augsburg Publishing House and Philadelphia, Board of Publication, Lutheran Church in America, 1978

LYNCH, Brian, 'Irish Painting? There is No Such Thing', *Hibernia,* 28.6.1970

___, 'Introduction' and 'The Concept of Shibui', in *Tony O'Malley,* ed. Brian Lynch, Aldershot, Hants, Scolar Press and Kilkenny, Butler Gallery, 1996, 7-13 and 315-316 respectively

LYNCH, William F., S.J., *Images of Hope, Imagination as Healer of the Hopeless,* Notre Dame, London, University of Notre Dame Press, 1974

MacCARVILL, Eileen, ed., *Mainie Jellett, The Artist's Vision,* Dundalk, Dundalgan Press, 1958

MacGREEVY, Thomas, 'Three Historical Paintings by Jack B. Yeats', *The Capuchin Annual,* 1942, 238-251

___, 'Introduction', in *An Exhibition of Paintings by Jack Yeats,* cat., London, The Arts Council of Great Britain, Tate Gallery, 1949, 5-7

MACKEN, John, S.J., *The Autonomy Theme in the Church Dogmatics: Karl Barth and His Critics,* Cambridge, Cambridge University Press, 1990

MACKEY, James P., ed., *Religious Imagination,* Edinburgh, Edinburgh University Press, 1986

___, 'Theology, Science and the Imagination: Exploring the Issues', in *The Irish Theological Quarterly,* vol. 52, no. 1 (1986), 1-18

MACQUARRIE, John, *Thinking about God,* London, SCM, 1975

MADDEN LE BROCQUY, Anne, *Louis le Brocquy, A Painter, Seeing His Way,* Dublin, Gill and Macmillan, 1994

MARCUSE, Herbert, *The Aesthetic Dimension, Toward a Critique of Marxist Aesthetics,* trans. H. Marcuse, Erica Sherover, London, Macmillan, 1979

MARITAIN, Jacques, *Art and Scholasticism and the Frontiers of Poetry,* trans. Joseph Evans, New York, Charles Scribener's Sons, 1962

MARTIN, James A., Jr., *Beauty and Holiness, The Dialogue between Aesthetics and Religion,* Princeton, Princeton University Press, 1990

MAYES, Elizabeth, MURPHY, Paula, eds., *Images and Insights,* cat., Dublin, Hugh Lane Municipal Gallery of Modern Art, 1993

Maynooth College Bicentenary Art Exhibitions, Ecclesiastical Art of the Penal Era & Art and Transcendence, cat., Maynooth, St. Patrick's College, 1995

McAVERA, Brian, *Art, Politics and Ireland,* Dublin, Open Air, year not given

McCRUM, Seán, 'God, Freud & Crossed Wires', *Circa,* no. 26 (1986), 27-31

McDONAGH, Enda, *Between Chaos and New Creation,* Dublin, Gill and Macmillan, 1986

___, *The Gracing of Society,* Dublin, Gill and Macmillan, 1989

___, *Survival or Salvation, A Second Mayo Book of Theology,* Dublin, Columba Press, 1994

McDONAGH, Seán, *The Greening of the Church,* London, Geoffrey Chapman, 1990

McFAGUE, Sallie, *Models of God, Theology for an Ecological Age,* Philadelphia, Fortress Press and London, SCM, 1987

___, *The Body of God, An Ecological Theology,* London, SCM, 1993

MENNEKES, Friedhelm, RÖHRIG, Johannes, *Crucifixus, Das Kreuz in der Kunst unserer Zeit,* Freiburg, Herder, 1994

METZ, Johann Baptist, *Glaube in Geschichte und Gesellschaft, Studien zu einer praktischen Fundamentaltheologie,* 4th edn, Mainz, Matthias-Grünewald-Verlag, 1984

METZGER, Bruce M., COOGAN, Michael D., eds., *The Oxford Companion to the Bible,* New York, Oxford, Oxford University Press, 1993

MEYERS, Carol, 'Lampstand', in *The Anchor Bible Dictionary,* vol. 4, ed. David Noel Freedman, New York, London, Toronto, Sydney, Auckland, Doubleday, 1992, 141-143

Colin Middleton, cat., Dublin, An Chomhairle Ealaíon and Belfast, Arts Council of Northern Ireland, 1976

Paintings, Drawings and Watercolours from the Studio of the Late Colin Middleton, M.B.E., R.H.A., cat., London, Christie, Manson & Woods Ltd., 1985

MODRAS, Ronald, 'Catholic Substance and the Catholic Church Today', in *Paul Tillich: A New Catholic Assessment,* eds. Raymond F. Bulman, Frederick J. Parella, Collegeville, Minnesota, Michael Glazier, The Liturgical Press, 1994, 33-47

MOFFETT, Margot, 'Young Irish Painters', *Horizon,* vol. 11, no. 64 (1945), 261-67

MOLTMANN, Jürgen, *Der gekreuzigte Gott,* 4th edn, Munich, Chr. Kaiser, 1972

___, *Theology of Hope, On the Ground and the Implications of a Christian Eschatology,* trans. James W. Leitch, New York, Harper & Row, 1975 (first publ. in Engl. 1967)

___, *The Church in the Power of the Spirit,* New York, Harper and Row, 1977

___, *Trinität und Reich Gottes,* Zur Gotteslehre, Munich, Chr. Kaiser, 1980

___, *God in Creation, An Ecological Doctrine of Creation,* London, SCM, 1985

MONTAGUE, John, 'Primal Scream, The Later Le Brocquy', *The Arts in Ireland,* vol. 2, no. 1 (1973), 4-14

MOORE, Albert C., 'Religion und Landschaft, Die spirituellen Landschaften von Caspar David Friedrich und Colin McCahon', in *Bilder und ihre Macht,* eds. H. Schwebel, Andreas Mertin, Stuttgart, Verlag Katholisches Bibelwerk, 1989, 80-95

MOORE, Des, 'Collins paints "dramatic Ireland" from Normandy', *The Sunday Independent,* 13.7.1975

MORAN, Dermot, *The philosophy of John Scottus Eriugena, A Study of Idealism in the Middle Ages,* Cambridge, Cambridge University Press, 1989

MÜLLER, Helmut A., 'Das Schöne im Gotteshaus, Zum Verhältnis von Kirche und Gegenwartskunst', *Evangelische Kommentare,* vol. 1, Stuttgart (1990), 44-47

MURPHY, Paula, 'Re-reading Mainie Jellett', in *Mainie Jellett 1897-1944,* cat., Dublin, Irish Museum of Modern Art, 1992, 33-44

MURRAY, Peter and Linda, *Dictionary of Art and Artists,* 6th edn, London, Penguin, 1989

NAVONE, John, S.J., 'Towards a Theology of Story', *Milltown Studies,* no. 13 (1984), 73-94

NELSON, James B., *Embodiment, An Approach to Sexuality and Christian Theology,* Minneapolis, Minnesota, Augsburg Publishing House, 1978

NICHOLS, Aidan, O.P., *The Art of God Incarnate, Theology and Image in Christian Tradition,* London, Darton, Longman and Todd, 1980

O'BRIEN, Michael, 'A Talk with the Painter Patrick Hall', *The Beau, An Annual Publication of Art and Enquiry,* no. 3 (1983-1984), 32-41

O'BRIEN, Patrick, 'Cassandra Island in Mayo', in *Faith and the Hungry Grass*, ed. Enda McDonagh, Dublin, Columba Press, 1990, 146-156

O'DOHERTY, Brian, 'Irish Painter, Jack B. Yeats', *The Irish Monthly*, vol. 80, no. 947 (1952), 201-203

___, 'Humanism in Art: A Study of Jack B. Yeats', *University Review*, vol. 1, no. 5 (1955), 21-26

___, 'A Farther Shore – The Yeats Exhibition', *The Irish Ecclesiastical Record*, vol. 84 (1955), 185-192

___, 'Obituary Jack Butler Yeats, 1871-1957', *Dublin Magazine*, vol. 32, no. 3 (1957), 55-57

___, 'Ambiguities: The Art of Patrick Collins', *Studies*, Spring (1961), 51-56

O'DONOGHUE, Noel D., 'The Mystical Imagination', in *Religious Imagination*, ed. J.P. Mackey, Edinburgh, Edinburgh University Press, 1986, 186-202

O'HANLON, Gerard, S.J., 'An Image of God for Ireland Today', *Milltown Studies*, no. 21 (1988), 13-27

___, 'Religious and National Influences on Our Vision of Humanity in Ireland', *Milltown Studies*, no. 37 (1996), 31-55

Ó MÓRCHÁIN, Leon, 'A Lost Tradition?', in *Faith and the Hungry Grass, A Mayo Book of Theology*, ed. Enda McDonagh, Dublin, The Columba Press, 1990, 54-63

OTTEN, Willemien, *The Anthropology of Johannes Scottus Eriugena*, Brill's Studies in Intellectual History, vol. 20, Leiden, New York, E.J. Brill, 1991

OTTO, Rudolf, *The Idea of the Holy*, trans. John W. Harvey, 2nd edn, London, Oxford University Press, 1950

OVID, *Metamorphoses*, trans. Mary M. Innes, London, Penguin, 1955

PALMER, Michael, 'Paul Tillich's Theology of Culture', in *Main Works/Hauptwerke*, Paul Tillich, vol. 2, Berlin, New York, De Gruyter, Evangelisches Verlagswerk, 1990, 1-31

PANIKKAR, Raimundo, *The Intrareligious Dialogue*, New York, Mahwah, Paulist Press, 1978

PANNENBERG, Wolfhart, *Basic Questions in Theology*, vol. 1, trans. George H. Kehm, London, SCM, 1970

PATTISON, George, *Art, Modernity and Faith, Towards a Theology of Art*, London, Macmillan, 1991

PAWLIKOWSKI, John T., O.S.M., *Christ in the Light of the Jewish Christian Dialogue*, New York, Paulist Press, 1982

PERKINS, Pheme, 'The Gospel According to John', in *The New Jerome Biblical Commentary*, eds. R.E. Brown, J.A. Fitzmyer, R.E. Murphy, pbk edn, London, Chapman, 1993, 942-985

PHILLIPS, Catherine, ed., *Gerard Manley Hopkins*, The Oxford Authors, Oxford, Oxford University Press, 1986

PIEPER, Joseph, *Only the Lover Sings: Art and Contemplation*, trans. Lothar Krauth, San Francisco, Ignatius Press, 1988

PLOTKIN, Cary H., 'Toward a Poetics of Transcendence after Darwin: The Aspect of Nature', *Studies*, vol. 85, no. 338 (1996), 136-143

POLKINGHORNE, John, *One World, The Interaction of Science and Theology*, London, SPCK, 1986

___, *Science and Creation, The Search for Understanding*, London, SPCK, 1988

PURSER, John, *The Literary Works of Jack B. Yeats*, Gerrard's Cross, Colin Smythe, 1991

PYLE, Hilary, 'Modern Art in Ireland: An Introduction', *Éire-Ireland*, vol. 4, no. 4 (1969), 35-41

___, *A Biography Jack B. Yeats*, revised edn, London, André Deutsch, 1989 (first publ. 1970)

___, 'About to Write a Letter', *Irish Arts Review*, vol. 2, no. 1 (1985), 43-47

___, 'There is No Night', *Irish Arts Review*, vol. 3, no. 2 (1986), 36-40

___, *Jack B. Yeats in the National Gallery of Ireland*, Dublin, National Gallery of Ireland, 1986

___, *Jack B. Yeats A Catalogue Raisonne of the Oil Paintings*, vol. 1, London, André Deutsch, 1992

___, *Jack B. Yeats, His Watercolours, Drawings and Pastels*, Dublin, Irish Academic Press, 1993

RADFORD RUETHER, Rosemary, 'Catholicism, Women, Body and Sexuality', in *Women, Religion and Sexuality, Studies on the Impact of Religious Teachings of Women,* ed. Jeanne Becher, Geneva, WCC, 1990

RAHNER, Karl, *Theological Investigations,* vol. 7, trans. David Bourke, Darton, Longman and Todd, 1971

___, *Theological Investigations,* vol. 13, trans. David Bourke, London, Darton, Longman and Todd, 1975

___, *Grundkurs des Glaubens, Einführung in den Begriff des Christentums,* 12th edn, Freiburg, Herder, 1979

___, 'Theology and the Arts', in *Thought,* vol. 57, no. 224, New York, Fordham University Press (1982), 17-29

___, *Theological Investigations,* vol. 23, trans. Joseph Donceel S.J. and Hugh M. Riley, London, Darton, Longman and Todd, 1992

RÉGAMEY, Pie-Raymond, *Religious Art in the Twentieth Century,* New York, Herder and Herder, 1963 (first publ. in French 1952)

REID, Herbert, *A Concise History of Modern Painting,* London, Thames and Hudson, 1974

RICHARDSON, Alan, BOWDEN, John, eds., *A New Dictionary of Christian Theology,* London, SCM, 1983

RICOEUR, Paul, *Hermeneutics and the human sciences, Essays on language, action and interpretation,* ed. and trans. John B. Thompson, Cambridge, Paris, Maison des Sciences de L'Homme and Cambridge University Press, 1981

RIEDER, Joachim, 'Kunst und Religion in der Frühromantik', in *Bilder und ihre Macht, Zum Verhältnis von Kunst und moderner christlicher Religion,* eds. H. Schwebel, A. Mertin, Stuttgart, Verlag Katholisches Bibelwerk, 68-79

RIVERS, Elizabeth, 'Modern Painting in Ireland', *Studies,* vol. 50, no. 198 (1961), 175-183

RÖHRIG, Johannes, DANCH, Kurt, *Bacon, Triptych '71,* Cologne, Kunst-Station St. Peter, 1993

ROMBOLD, Günter, *Der Streit um das Bild, Zum Verhältnis von moderner Kunst und Religion,* Stuttgart, Katholisches Bibelwerk, 1988

___, 'Schönheit und Wahrheit im Widerstreit', in *Bilder und ihre Macht, Zum Verhältnis von Kunst und christlicher Religion,* eds. H. Schwebel, A. Mertin, Stuttgart, Verlag Katholisches Bibelwerk, 1989, 14-31

ROUSSEAU, Jean Jacques, *The Social Contract and Discourses,* trans. G.D.H. Cole, London, Dent: Everyman's Library, 1973

RUANE, Frances, *Patrick Collins,* Dublin, An Chomhairle Ealaíon and Belfast, The Arts Council of Northern Ireland, 1982

___, 'Patrick Collins', in *Six Artists from Ireland, An Aspect of Irish Painting,* cat., Dublin, An Chomhairle Ealaíon and the Cultural Relations Committee Department of Foreign Affairs, 1983, 23-27

___, 'Personal Inscapes', in *Tony O'Malley,* ed. B. Lynch, Aldershot, Hants, Scolar Press and Kilkenny, Butler Gallery, 1996, 239-246

RUSSELL, John, 'Introduction', in *Louis le Brocquy,* Dorothy Walker, Dublin, Ward River Press, 1981, 9-18

RYAN, Vera, 'Transition Years', in *Tony O'Malley,* ed. Brian Lynch, Aldershot, Hants, Scolar Press and Kilkenny, Butler Gallery, 1996, 37-68

SACHS, John R., S.J., *The Christian Vision of Humanity,* Minnesota, Michael Glazier The Liturgical Press, 1991

SCHELLING, Friedrich Wilhelm J., 'Über das Verhältnis der bildenden Künste zu der Natur' (1807), in *Schellings Werke,* ed. Manfred Schröter, 3. Ergänzungsband, Munich, C.H. Beck'sche Verlagsbuchhandlung, 1959, 388-429

___, Paragraphs 16, 21, 33 from 'Philosophie der Kunst', in *Was das Schöne sei, Klassische Texte von Platon bis Adorno,* ed. Michael Hauskeller, Munich, dtv, 1994, 296-302

SCHILLEBEECKX, Edward, *The Schillebeeckx Reader,* Edinburgh, T. & T. Clark, 1984
___, *Church, The Human Story of God,* London, SCM, 1990
SCHLEIERMACHER, Friedrich E.D., 'Über die Religion. Reden an die Gebildeten unter ihren Verächtern.' (1799), 'Monologen. 1800', both in *Schleiermacher-Auswahl,* ed. Heinz Bolli, Gütersloh, Mohn, 1983, 6-11 and 78-85 respectively
SCHNEIDERS, Sandra M., *The Revelatory Text: Interpreting the New Testament as Sacred Scripture,* San Francisco, Harper and Row, 1991
SCHRÖDINGER, Erwin, *Mind and Matter,* Cambridge, Cambridge University Press, 1958
SCHÜSSLER FIORENZA, Elisabeth, *In Memory of Her, A Feminist Theological Reconstruction of Christian Origins,* London, SCM, 1983
SCHÜSSLER FIORENZA, Francis, 'Systematic Theology: Tasks and Methods', in *Systematic Theology, Roman Catholic Perspectives,* eds. F. Schüssler Fiorenza, J.P. Galvin, Dublin, Gill and Macmillan, 1992, 1-87
SCHWEBEL, Horst, *Autonome Kunst im Raum der Kirche,* Hamburg, Furche Verlag, 1968
___, *Das Christusbild in der bildenden Kunst der Gegenwart,* Textband, Schriftenreihe Bild und Raum des Instituts für Kirchenbau und kirchliche Kunst, Giessen, Wilhelm Schmitz Verlag, 1980
___, 'Bildverweigerung im Bild, Mystik – eine vergessene Kategorie in der Kunst der Gegenwart',
___, 'Wahrheit der Kunst – Wahrheit des Evangeliums, Einer Anregung Eberhard Jüngels folgend und widersprechend', both in *Kirche und moderne Kunst, Eine aktuelle Dokumentation,* eds. H. Schwebel, Andreas Mertin, Frankfurt, Athenäum, 1988, 113-123 and 135-145 respectively
___, MERTIN, A., eds., *Bilder und ihre Macht, Zum Verhältnis von Kunst und christlicher Religion,* Stuttgart, Verlag Katholisches Bibelwerk, 1989
___, *Die Bibel in der Kunst des 20. Jahrhundert,* Stuttgart, Deutsche Bibelgesellschaft, 1994
SCHWÖBEL, Christoph, 'Tillich, Paul', in *The Blackwell Encyclopedia of Modern Christian Thought,* ed. Alister E. McGrath, Oxford, Blackwell, 1993, 638-642
SHARP, Henry J., 'Patrick Graham', in *Patrick Graham, Brian Maguire, Paintings 1984,* cat., Belfast, Octagon Gallery, 1984, no p.
SHEA, William M., 'Dual Loyalties in Catholic Theology, Finding Truth in Alien Texts', *Commonweal,* 31.1.1992, 9-14
SHEEHY, Edward, 'Jack B. Yeats', *The Dublin Magazine,* vol. 20 (July-Sept. 1945), 38-41
___, 'Recent Irish Painting, The Irish Exhibition of Living Art 1950' *Envoy,* vol. 3, no. 10 (1950), 45-52
___, 'Art Notes', *The Dublin Magazine,* vol. 26 (Jan.-March 1951), 51-54
___, 'Art Notes', *The Dublin Magazine,* vol. 28 (July-Sept. 1953), 35-38
SHELDON-WILLIAMS, I.P., ed., *Johannis Scotti Eriugenae Periphyseon,* Book III, Dublin, Institute of Advanced Studies, 1981
SHEPPARD, Anne, *Aesthetics, An introduction to the philosophy of art,* Oxford, Oxford University Press, 1987
SHERRY, Patrick, *Spirit and Beauty, An Introduction to Theological Aesthetics,* Oxford, Clarendon Press, 1992
SHIELDS, Daniel, S.J., 'Memories of Some Recent Art Exhibitions in Dublin', *The Irish Monthly,* vol. 76 (Jan. 1948), 37-39
SIMEON THE NEW THEOLOGIAN, *Hymns of Divine Love,* 7, in *Supplementa Byzantina: Texte und Untersuchungen,* eds. H.G. Beck, A. Kambylis, R. Keydell, Berlin, New York, 1976, 71.29-42 repr. in *The Christian Theology Reader,* ed. A.E. McGrath, Oxford, Blackwell, 1995, 181
SKELTON, Robin, ed., *The Selected Writings of Jack B. Yeats,* London, André Deutsch, 1991

SMITH, Alistair, 'Louis le Brocquy: On the Spiritual in Art', in *Louis Le Brocquy Paintings 1939-1996,* Dublin, Irish Museum of Modern Art, 1996, 12-52

SÖLLE, Dorothee, *The Truth Is Concrete,* trans. Dinah Livingstone, London, Burns & Oates, " 1969

___, *Stellvertretung, Ein Kapitel Theologie nach dem 'Tode Gottes',* Stuttgart, Kreuz Verlag, 1982

___, with Shirley A. CLOYES, *To Work and to Love, a theology of creation,* Philadelpia, Fortress Press, 1984

STEINER, George, *Real Presences, Is there anything in what we say?,* London, Boston, Faber and Faber, 1989

STOCK, Alex, 'Ist die bildende Kunst ein locus theologicus?' in *Wozu Bilder im Christentum?: Beiträge zur theologischen Kunsttheorie,* ed. A. Stock, St. Ottilien, EOS Verlag, 1990, 175-181

___, *Zwischen Tempel und Museum; theologische Kunstkritik; Positionen der Moderne,* Paderborn, München, Zürich, Wien, Ferdinand Schöningh, 1991

SUZUKI, Daisetz T., *Zen and Japanese Culture,* 2nd edn, London, Routledge and Kegan Paul, 1973

TAVARD, George H., *The Church, Community of Salvation, An Ecumenical Ecclesiology,* New Theology Studies, vol. 1, Collegeville, Minnesota, Michael Glazier The Liturgical Press, 1992

THEISSEN, Gerd, *On Having a Critical Faith,* trans. John Bowden, London, SCM, 1979

THIESSEN, Gesa, 'Religious Art is Expressionistic, A Critical Appreciation of Paul Tillich's Theology of Art', *The Irish Theological Quarterly,* vol. 59, no. 4 (1993), 302-311

___, 'Faith into Art: Religion and Vincent van Gogh', *Doctrine and Life,* vol. 43, no. 5 (1993), 267-273

___, 'Imaging God: Spiritual Dimensions in Modern Art', in *Neglected Wells: Spirituality and the Arts,* eds. Anne M. Murphy, Eoin G. Cassidy, Dublin, Four Courts Press, 1997, 97-113

TILLICH, Paul, *The Religious Situation,* trans. H.R. Niebuhr, Ohio, The World Publishing Company, 1956, (first publ. in German 1926)

___, *Morality and Beyond,* London, Glasgow, Fontana, 1963

___, *On the Boundary,* London, Collins, 1967

___, *Main Works/Hauptwerke,* Writings in the Philosophy of Culture/Kulturphilosophische Schriften, ed. Michael Palmer, vol. 2, Berlin, New York, De Gruyter, Evangelisches Verlagswerk, 1990. This volume includes the following articles used in the book:

___, 'Über die Idee einer Theologie der Kultur' (1919), 69-85

___, 'Religiöser Stil und Stoff in der bildenden Kunst' (1921), 87-99

___, 'Theology and Architecture' (1955), 263-268

___, 'Existentialist Aspects of Modern Art' (1956), 269-280

___, 'Art and Ultimate Reality' (1960), 317-332

___, 'Zur Theologie der bildenden Kunst und Architektur' (1961), 333-343

___, 'Contemporary Protestant Architecture' (1962), 353-363

___, 'Honesty and Consecration in Religious Art and Architecture' (1965), 365-371

___, *On Art and Architecture,* eds. John and Jane Dillenberger, New York, Crossroad, 1987 This volume includes the following articles used in the book:

___, 'Excerpts from Mass and Personality' (first publ. in German 1922), 58-66

___, 'Art and Society' (1952), 11-41

___, 'One Moment of Beauty' (1955), 234-235

___, 'Protestantism and Artistic Style' (1957), 119-125

___, *Systematic Theology, Reason and Revelation, Being and God,* vol. 1, Chicago, Chicago University Press, 1951

___, *Systematic Theology, Life and the Spirit, History and the Kingdom of God,* vol. 3, London, SCM, 1978 (first publ. 1963)

TINSLEY, John, 'Art and the Bible', in *The Oxford Companion to the Bible,* eds. B.M. Metzger, M.D. Coogan, New York, Oxford, Oxford University Press, 1993, 56-60

TRACY, David, *Blessed Rage for Order, The New Pluralism in Theology,* New York, The Seabury Press, 1975

___, *The Analogical Imagination, Christian Theology and the Culture of Pluralism,* London, SCM, 1981

___, 'The Religious Classic and the Classic of Art', in *Art, Creativity, and the Sacred,* ed. Diane Apostolos-Cappadona, New York, Crossroad, 1984, 236-249

___, *Dialogue with the Other: The Inter-Religious Dialogue,* Louvain Theological & Pastoral Monographs, 1, Louvain, Peters Press and Grands Rapids, Michigan, Eerdmans, 1990

TURPIN, John, 'Irish Painting in a European Context', *Éirigh* (Jan. 1968), 20-23

URECH, Edouard, *Lexikon christlicher Symbole,* Bibel, Kirche, Gemeinde, 9, 7th edn, Konstanz, Christliche Verlagsanstalt, 1992

WALKER, Dorothy, *Louis le Brocquy,* Dublin, Ward River Press, 1981

___, 'Patrick Scott', in *Patrick Scott,* cat., Dublin, Douglas Hyde Gallery, 1981, 15-34

___, 'Indigenous Culture and Irish Art', in *The Crane Bag Book of Irish Studies* (1977-1981), eds. Mark Patrick Hederman, Richard Kearney, Dublin, Blackwater Press, 1982, 131-135

___, '"Images, Single and Multiple" 1957-1990', *Irish Arts Review* (1991-1992), 87-94

WALKER, Keith, *Images or Idols? The place of sacred art in churches today,* Norwich, The Canterbury Press, 1996

WALLACE, Martin, 'Moving Artist', *The Belfast Telegraph,* 4.1.1957

WARNOCK, Mary, 'Religious Imagination', in *Religious Imagination,* ed. J.P. Mackey, Edinburgh, Edinburgh University Press, 1986, 142-157

WESTERMANN, Claus, *Der Segen in der Bibel und im Handeln der Kirche,* Gütersloh, Mohn, 1981

WHITE, James, 'Contemporary Irish Artists (VI), Louis le Brocquy', *Envoy,* vol. 2, no. 6 (1950), 52-65

___, *Gerard Dillon, Early Paintings of the West,* cat., Dublin, Dawson Gallery, 1971

___, 'Mainie Jellett, A Personal Memoir', in *Mainie Jellett 1897-1944,* cat., Dublin, Irish Museum of Modern Art, 1992, 9-12

___, *Gerard Dillon An Illustrated Biography,* Dublin, Wolfhound Press, 1994

WOLTERSTORFF, Nicholas, *Art in Action, Toward a Christian Aesthetic,* Grands Rapids, Michigan, Eerdmans, 1980

WOODS, Richard, O.P., *Eckhart's Way,* London, Darton, Longman and Todd, 1986

Works 5 – Patrick Graham, Dublin, Gandon Editions, 1992

Works 12 – Patrick Hall, Dublin, Gandon Editions, 1993

Works 14 – Tony O'Malley, Dublin, Gandon Editions, 1994

ZIMMERLI, Walther, *Grundriss der alttestamentlichen Theologie,* 4th edn, Theologische Wissenschaft, 3, eds. Carl Andresen, Werner Jetter, Wilfried Joest, Otto Kaiser, Eduard Lohse, Stuttgart, Berlin, Cologne, Mainz, Kohlhammer, 1982

Index of Names and Subjects